Strategies for Resolving Individual and Family Problems

Strategies for Resolving Individual and Family Problems

Fred W. Vondracek
Pennsylvania State University

Sherry Corneal
Pennsylvania State University

BROOKS/COLE PUBLISHING COMPANY

I(T)P™ An International Thomson Publishing Company

Pacific Grove • Albany • Bonn • Boston • Cincinnati • Detroit • London • Madrid • Melbourne
Mexico City • New York • Paris • San Francisco • Singapore • Tokyo • Toronto • Washington

A CLAIREMONT BOOK

Sponsoring Editor: *Claire Verduin*
Marketing Team: *Connie Jirovsky and*
 Roxane Buck Ezcurra
Editorial Associate: *Gay C. Bond*
Production Editor: *Laurel Jackson*
Production Assistant: *Tessa A. McGlasson*
Manuscript Editor: *Catherine Cambron*

Permissions Editor: *Marie DuBois*
Interior and Cover Design: *Susan H. Horovitz*
Typesetting: *Weimer Graphics, Inc.*
Cover Printing: *Phoenix Color Corporation,*
 Inc.
Printing and Binding: *Quebecor Printing*
 Fairfield

I(T)P ™ The ITP logo is a trademark under license.

For more information, contact:

BROOKS/COLE PUBLISHING COMPANY
511 Forest Lodge Road
Pacific Grove, CA 93950
USA

International Thomson Publishing Europe
Berkshire House 168-173
High Holborn
London WC1V 7AA
England

Thomas Nelson Australia
102 Dodds Street
South Melbourne, 3205
Victoria, Australia

Nelson Canada
1120 Birchmount Road
Scarborough, Ontario
Canada M1K 5G4

International Thomson Editores
Campos Eliseos 385, Piso 7
Col. Polanco
11560 México D. F. México

International Thomson Publishing Gmbh
Königswinterer Strasse 418
53227 Bonn
Germany

International Thomson Publishing Asia
221 Henderson Road
#05-10 Henderson Building
Singapore 0315

International Thomson Publishing Japan
Hirakawacho Kyowa Building, 3F
2-2-1 Hirakawacho
Chiyoda-ku, Tokyo 102
Japan

Printed in the United States of America
10 9 8 7 6 5 4 3 2 1

Library of Congress Cataloging-in-Publication Data

Vondracek, Fred W.
 Strategies for resolving individual and family problems / Fred W.
Vondracek and Sherry Corneal.
  p.   cm.
 Includes bibliographical references and index.
 ISBN 0-534-25470-5
 1. Counseling. 2. Psychotherapy. I. Corneal, Sherry, [date].
 II. Title.
 BF637.C6V64 1994   94-21195
 158′.3—dc20   CIP

Credits continued on p. 479.

To my wife, Kathie A. Vondracek;
and my children, Elizabeth Spielvogel and Jon Hooven

To my daughters, Kelly Bates and Molly Countermine

CONTENTS

CHAPTER 2

The Analytical Psychology of Carl G. Jung

31

CHAPTER 3

The Individual Psychology of Alfred Adler

48

P A R T I I
Behaviorist Approaches
65

C H A P T E R 4
Systematic Desensitization
67

C H A P T E R 5
The Token Economy
81

C H A P T E R 6
Aversion Therapy and Punishment
96

PART III
Cognitive Approaches
115

CHAPTER 7
Rational-Emotive Therapy
117

CHAPTER 8
Reality Therapy
135

CHAPTER 9

Cognitive-Behavioral Therapy
149

PART IV

Humanistic Approaches
161

CHAPTER 10

The Person-Centered Therapy of Carl Rogers
163

CHAPTER 11

Child-Centered or Nondirective Play Therapy
178

C H A P T E R   1 2
Existential Psychotherapy
194

P A R T   V
Family Therapy Approaches
207

C H A P T E R   1 3
Structural Family Therapy
209

CHAPTER 14

Strategic Family Therapy
226

CHAPTER 15

Family Sculpting
238

CHAPTER 16

Relationship Enhancement
248

P A R T V I
Expressive Approaches
263

C H A P T E R 1 7

Gestalt Therapy
265

C H A P T E R 1 8

Psychodrama
282

C H A P T E R 1 9

Art Therapy
293

CHAPTER 20

Music Therapy
302

CHAPTER 21

Dance Therapy
313

P A R T   V I I
Relaxation-Based Approaches
321

C H A P T E R   2 2
Biofeedback
323

C H A P T E R   2 3
Clinical Applications of Hypnosis
343

PART VIII
Psychopharmacologic Approaches
363

CHAPTER 24
Antipsychotic Drug Therapy
365

CHAPTER 25
Antidepressant Drug Therapy
382

CHAPTER 26
Antianxiety Drug Therapy
397

PART IX
Career Counseling
411

CHAPTER 27
Counseling for Effective Career Choices
413

CHAPTER 28
Counseling Adults to Cope with Life and Career Transitions
429

■
PREFACE

"I'm so depressed that I can't get out of bed and go to work." "It seems that all we do is fight and scream at each other." "I don't know what is happening to me. It seems like I'm losing my mind." These are the statements heard by social workers, nurses, counseling psychologists, psychiatrists, clinical psychologists, and various other professionals in the helping professions—made by individuals who seek help for individual and family problems. Clients, customers, consumers, patients—whatever the preferred designation—are unlikely to be concerned about the specific professional orientation of the person offering help. Individuals are, however, entitled to receive competent help, and if the professional person who is initially consulted cannot provide it, they are entitled to an appropriate referral.

What is the appropriate level of knowledge required to offer competent help? There can be little question that properly supervised, practical training, usually associated with lengthy, advanced academic work, is required to achieve a satisfactory level of competence in implementing any of the strategies discussed in this text. Many individual practitioners eventually achieve competence in several techniques; many others specialize in just one. No one, however, is qualified or competent to practice all of them. Yet, more than superficial acquaintance is necessary to make informed referral decisions and judgments about the appropriateness or desirability of any of the intervention techniques available today.

This text is designed to help students and professionals expand their understanding and knowledge of intervention strategies over a broad range of theory and application. The common practice of separating theory and application (sometimes called theory and practice), although convenient for pedagogical purposes, is not followed here. In our judgment, when genuine understanding is the goal, application must be informed by theory. Practice can be described properly only with reference to the underlying theoretical formulations, which themselves tend to emerge from the theorists' fundamental assumptions about human nature. Consequently, sections on theory and application are integral components of each chapter.

The decision to offer extensive treatment of both theory and application in a single text was relatively easy, compared with the decision of what to include and what to exclude. From the start, we decided to avoid the common error of either discussing a few carefully selected approaches in depth or discussing a great number superficially. Nevertheless, it was clear that no two "experts" would agree on the content of a text such as this one. Indeed, every reviewer had suggestions about chapters to delete and others to add.

Ultimately, our judgments about the book's contents were based on many years of experience in teaching and professional practice. We decided to write a text that would offer some historical perspective on the field, include serious discussion of the theoretical underpinnings of major contemporary strategies, afford lively insight into some more fanciful approaches of particular interest to undergraduates, and inform readers about the "nitty-gritty" and "how-to" of various approaches. Most of all, we endeavored to write a substantive, informative, and serious text without being tedious or boring—a text that could excite and stimulate, document the fantastic diversity of the subject, and serve as a valuable reference for professionals in the field. Perhaps most of all, though, we sought to help students reach a level of understanding that will effectively deter them from making premature and uninformed commitments to one or another approach or orientation.

The 28 chapters that resulted from our efforts are grouped into nine parts, each of which endeavors to incorporate a significant and representative, though not necessarily exhaustive, presentation of intervention strategies within its domain. The part domains do not uniformly correspond to readily recognized theoretical frameworks; the diversity of the interventions covered made that kind of uniformity impossible. The guiding principles at work in the part designations are rational and practical. Some parts follow a theoretical framework (for example, psychoanalytic approaches); others are designed to focus on targets of intervention (such as family approaches); still others, on a particular mode of intervention (for example, psychopharmacologic approaches). Each chapter, however, is organized according to a common descriptive and analytical framework, which is presented in the Introduction and is designed to enhance the comparability of the strategies presented. Extensive documentation is provided, and in most cases original sources, as well as current references, are listed to encourage further reading.

In each chapter, we tried to capture the flavor of the intervention strategy discussed. We preferred this strategy to homogenizing the book by forcing a common language and terminology on each approach. Thus, when we discuss psychopharmacologic approaches, we write about "patients," and when we discuss cognitive-behavioral approaches, we write about "clients." We kept an open mind in discussing less widely accepted approaches, such as art and dance therapy, that are often perceived as less rigorous than others. We hope our readers will do the same. Judgments about the relative merits of any approach to intervention must be made judiciously and knowledgeably rather than on the basis of prejudice and hearsay. We hope our work will contribute to helping others do good work in the field of individual and family intervention.

Acknowledgments

First of all, we wish to acknowledge those who reviewed earlier drafts of this manuscript for their valuable insights and suggestions. These reviewers include Anne S. Hatcher, Metropolitan State College of Denver; Mary Maples, University of Nevada, Reno; William Lynn McKinney, University of Rhode Island; Nancy Murdock, University of Missouri, Kansas City; and Ronald L. Partin, Bowling Green State University.

We sincerely thank Kathie A. Vondracek for typing the entire manuscript and preparing the indices. Her help was truly invaluable. We would also like to thank Tina Meyers for her assistance in producing this manuscript. Finally, we want to express our appreciation for the supportive environment offered by Pennsylvania State University's Department of Human Development and Family Studies under the guidance of Dr. Leann Birch.

Fred W. Vondracek
Sherry Corneal

■
INTRODUCTION

Watching the evening news on the local television station or opening the pages of the hometown newspaper has become an increasingly discouraging activity. The news is filled with reports of human misery, much of it caused by distraught individuals who have apparently run out of rational options for reducing their misery or resolving their conflicts with others. The resulting tragedies affect individuals, families, communities, and in many cases whole regions of the world—witness the long-term conflicts in the Middle East and in Northern Ireland. What may be most disturbing about all these circumstances is that they persist, despite the attempts during the past century of thoughtful individuals from many different backgrounds to design strategies that will be effective in resolving problems among individuals and the various groups to which they belong. Although many of these strategies are still relatively new and have not yet been subjected to extensive, rigorous scientific examination, most have been shown capable of making a significant difference if applied competently and appropriately. Competent and appropriate application, however, presupposes a sound understanding of an ever-increasing variety of intervention methods—something that has been beyond the reach of most practitioners. A brief review of the reasons for this deficiency is instructive.

Rationale for This Text

In their introductory chapter to Bergin and Garfield's (1971) *Handbook of Psychotherapy and Behavior Change*, Urban and Ford made the case for an updated and current handbook by observing that the field of psychotherapy and behavior change had undergone a significant expansion in (1) the range of behavioral difficulties to which psychotherapy and other methods of behavior change were applied; (2) the methods used to conduct psychotherapy and to achieve behavior change; and (3) the types of individuals professionally engaged in psychotherapy and behavior change activities. Today, more than two decades after those observations were published, lateral expansion in all three areas continues unabated. Clearly, it is socially acceptable to consult specialists in behavioral change with regard to an ever-increasing range of behavioral and emotional difficulties. Individuals seek assistance with a wide range of difficulties ranging from problems of everyday living to severe mental illness; families seek assistance in resolving conflicts, in dealing with intergenerational issues, and in remaining viable units in the face of economic hardship. Organizations and institutions in both the private and public sectors have come to recognize the value of specialized assistance designed to improve and enhance the functioning of individuals in organizations, as well as the functioning of the organizations themselves.

The methods used to produce desired changes have expanded dramatically, ever since such methods' legitimacy and importance in enhancing individuals' health and overall functioning were first recognized. Although it was hoped at one time that a single breakthrough could offer the key to the human mind, and therefore to changing human behavior, thoughtful observers eventually recognized that different problems very likely necessitated different solutions. Just as no single drug has proved effective in treating all diseases, no single approach to behavior change is likely to be effective in dealing with all the problems of different individuals in widely differing circumstances. Some methods of behavior change are particularly effective in addressing some specific problems; others are especially useful for dealing with certain special populations; and yet others are ideally suited to certain situational circumstances or settings. Because no one method is likely itself to be the key to resolving human problems, professionals who deal with human problems must have more than a passing acquaintance with the major representative types of behavior change methods currently used.

The ever-increasing complexity and variety of today's methods of interventions has made it more difficult for counselors and other human intervention professionals to stay abreast of new developments and to maintain a sound understanding of the basic concepts and practices in their own field.

This difficulty has remained even though major recent works have addressed the scientific foundations of human change processes (Mahoney, 1991), and the scientific and professional basis of counseling psychology (Brown & Lent, 1992). Moreover, established textbooks (for example, George & Cristiani, 1990; Hansen, Rossberg, & Cramer, 1994) in the field almost invariably address theory and process separately. Although this separation may conform to the prevailing structure of many academic courses, we view it as a compromise that may prevent students from effectively integrating these two equally important aspects of intervention. Moreover, most texts further compromise their coverage of intervention strategies and methods by also including sections on professional issues. There can be no argument about the importance of having students become well acquainted with these issues. Nevertheless, that degree of inclusiveness has, by necessity, abridged the value of such textbooks for students and professionals who seek to both broaden and deepen their understanding of the great variety of intervention strategies.

Both breadth and depth of understanding are particularly important in view of the significant change in the level of specialized training expected of individuals who are professionally engaged in applying various intervention methods. The professions involved in the practice of psychotherapy and other behavior change methods 25 years ago were psychology, psychiatry, and social work, to the virtual exclusion of all others. Today, in the aftermath of staggering budget deficits and a significant shift in the funding of human services from the federal government to state and local governments, human service workers with baccalaureate degrees are employed as gatekeepers and referral agents to more specialized behavior change services. Moreover, those individuals, who have relatively little specialized training, are called upon today to provide a major portion of direct behavior change services in both public and private agencies.

Regardless of the ultimate level of training achieved by the human service professional, basic knowledge regarding a wide range of strategies, techniques, or approaches must be considered a necessary component of that training. All too often, ignorance of alternative interventions leads students to commit themselves prematurely to a single intervention approach that precludes consideration of alternatives, which may in many cases be preferable for any number of different reasons. Although specialization may be desirable and necessary in the field of behavior change, such specialization, and preference for a specific set of interventions over all others, is inappropriate in individuals who do not have the requisite specialized training. Specialization is also inappropriate if accompanied by relative ignorance of alternatives, when to consider those alternatives might be in the interest of those seeking help.

The present volume addresses some of these issues, offering discussion of a very broad range of intervention methods. Covering such a range is fraught with difficulties. The panoply of behavior change methods currently used creates the danger of being overinclusive and superficial. If one chooses to be selective, however, one risks missing the core objective of increasing students' understanding of the diversity of behavior change methods available today. Moreover, each method of intervention has unique theoretical constructs and unique conceptualizations of problems, and each often uses unique and sometimes idiosyncratic language to represent what it aims to accomplish and how—posing an additional problem for a text such as this one. In light of these potential pitfalls, considerable care was taken in selecting the methods to be included in the current volume. Because including every major method would be impracticable, if not impossible, we did the next best thing by covering a representative selection of major methods in each of nine distinct approaches to change. The 28 chapters of this text represent the diversity and vitality of the most influential and widely used methods available to various types of professionals whose principal objective is to help people change.

A Framework for Analyzing Methods

After selecting the methods to be covered in this text, it became immediately clear that a common expositional framework was needed to enhance the various methods' relative comparability. To this end, each chapter contains six major sections devoted to important considerations common to all behavior change methods. These are presented in the following, along with a rationale for their inclusion. Because of the great diversity of the methods discussed in this volume, some chapters are organized somewhat differently, and many contain numerous subsections in order to optimize the presentation.

Introduction

The first, introductory section is designed to establish the defining parameters of each behavior change method and to identify and trace its historical roots. Although all the methods discussed in this volume share the objective of producing some form of behavior change, the nature of the sought-after change varies from one method to another and reflects important and fundamental differences in their respective underlying assumptions. Consequently, the general purpose of each method is stated up front and as succinctly as possible. An additional defining parameter of each method, however, is its scope or range of applicability. Often, this scope includes applications well beyond those originally envisioned by the originators of particular behavior change methods.

Theoretical Foundations

The second major section analyzes the theoretical foundations of each behavior change method. The relative importance assigned to theory varies considerably from one behavior change method to another. Some methods rely more on the professional's intuition than on explicit theoretical formulations. Reliance on theory is preferable for a number of reasons. Most important, theory guides our assumptions about what constitutes functional or dysfunctional, "normal" or "abnormal" behavior—that is, behaviors that should or should not be changed (for a more extensive discussion of these issues see Ford & Urban, 1963; Urban & Vondracek, 1977). Theory also guides our understanding of how humans develop and how their course of development may be altered in the desired direction. Theory is a way of making explicit the assumptions that govern the conduct of a given intervention. The bottom line is the rather straightforward notion that if one understands how problems developed in the first place, one can arrive at some pretty good ideas about how those problems can be resolved or eliminated.

Some professionals in the area of behavior change may be skeptical about the value of theory in their work. Closer examination, however, will reveal that virtually every professional behavior change specialist has notions about how human behavior works and how it may be changed. The problem is that these important belief systems are often implicit rather than explicit (Osipow, 1983). Making explicit theoretical assumptions about how specific behavior change methods work makes communication about such methods easier and more meaningful. Being explicit about theory facilitates the evaluation and integration of research findings and may lead to new hypotheses and insights, both in developing and refining intervention methods and in working with individuals or groups of individuals.

Implementing the Behavior Change Technique

The third major section of each chapter is designed to provide a detailed description of the step-by-step procedures employed in a particular behavior change technique. All too often such descriptions in the professional and scientific literature suffer from idiosyncratic language (jargon) and sweeping descriptions that obscure what really happens when a technique is applied in a real-life situation. Only through clear and detailed descriptions of what the application of a technique actually entails can the reader begin to fully appreciate the intricacies and subtleties of work in this area. The text also uses case examples to bring to life the real challenge of intervening in individuals' and families' lives in an effort to help them function more adequately and experience greater success and satisfaction.

Means and Conditions for Implementing the Technique

The means and conditions for implementing each technique are discussed in the fourth major section of each chapter. Most important are the educational, experiential, and legal qualifications that behavior change specialists must meet. These qualifications often depend on the specific method that is employed. For example, psychopharmacologic methods of behavior change may be applied only by duly qualified and licensed medical practitioners. Many other forms of behavior change methodology require specialized training, experience, and certification. Aspiring practitioners obviously must be well informed about the specific qualifications required to offer services to others legitimately. Less obviously, those who serve as referral agents and, often by default, as gatekeepers must also be in a position to judge the legitimacy of various types of practitioners. Charlatans, con artists, and quacks show up in every field; the field of behavior change is no exception. Moreover, because those likely to seek assistance from behavior change specialists may be particularly vulnerable to fraud, it is incumbent upon individuals in responsible positions to be well informed about the necessary qualifications for the practice of each major behavior change methodology.

Proper implementation of most behavior change methods has few requirements other than administration by fully qualified personnel. Some methods, however, require sophisticated biomedical instrumentation (for example, biofeedback) or special supplies and facilities (for instance, aversive conditioning and psychopharmacologic procedures). Each chapter details the requisite conditions, facilities, and equipment needed to implement the particular behavior change method.

Limitations

The specific limitations of each behavior change method are the subject of the fifth major section of each chapter. Claims of having discovered the cure for human problems have probably been made as long as humankind has existed. Such claims have issued from self-promoters seeking to enrich themselves by exploiting others' misery, but also from serious scientists who really believed they had found the keys to human happiness. The scientists and practitioners most closely associated with the methods of behavior change described in this volume have generally taken a more modest position. They have acknowledged not only specific limitations of their methods but also outright contraindications—circumstances in which the application of a specific behavior change method is considered unwarranted, unwise, and potentially or actually dangerous. Moreover, responsible practitioners advise their clients or patients against use of a contraindicated method and refuse to apply such a method, even if specifically requested to do so.

When a behavior change method is not contraindicated, and even when it is specifically recommended, identifiable hazards may be involved in its application. These hazards must be called to the attention of potential consumers and must certainly be known by the professionals who implement behavior change methods or recommend their implementation. In each case a judgment must be made regarding the proper relationship between the benefits obtained from implementation of the method on the one hand and the hazards associated with its implementation on the other. Although side effects from the use of prescription medication are the most commonly recognized hazards in the use of behavior change methods, many other hazards exist that may be more subtle and therefore more difficult to recognize. These include the potential for misconduct on the part of the behavior change specialist. Even when high standards of ethical conduct and rigorous guidelines for competence are observed, some methods may still represent hazards to some individuals under some circumstances. Awareness of this potential must be fostered in everyone associated with the difficult task of helping people change. Consequently, each chapter contains a section not only on contraindications, but also on hazards associated with each technique discussed.

Research

The development and application of behavior change methods require an explicit theoretical base and an identifiable and specific set of procedures or operations. In addition, however, empirical research is needed to evaluate the effectiveness of the method under a variety of circumstances. Ultimately, only sound research evidence can elevate an experimental or unproven method to the status of a proven and reliable mainstay of behavior change specialists. Research evidence regarding a method's effectiveness is much more difficult to obtain with some techniques than with others. For example, techniques relying on complex constructs that can be inferred, but never directly observed—such as the unconscious—are more difficult to evaluate than techniques that deal predominantly with observable behaviors. Even as to observable behaviors, observers may disagree about whether the desired change has actually taken place, how significant a change is, whether it is lasting or only temporary, and so on. These difficulties explain why more than 100 years after Freud began his groundbreaking work on psychoanalysis, some serious scientists claim that psychoanalysis has been shown to be highly effective, whereas other, equally serious scientists claim that it is completely worthless. Similar disagreements exist about most of the other techniques covered in this volume.

A detailed review of all the available research on a given intervention method is impossible in the framework of the current volume. What has been provided is a summary assessment of the current state of knowledge regarding each technique. The reader is also given references to further readings regarding the latest research findings in each area. The vitality and importance of the behavior change field is reflected in the literally thousands of research reports and scientific papers dealing with some aspect of this methodology that are published every year. Serious students of the field have a responsibility to augment their understanding of the basic concepts and procedures of any given technique with knowledge of the latest research findings.

References

Brown, S. D., & Lent, R. W. (Eds.). (1992). *Handbook of counseling psychology* (2nd ed.). New York: Wiley.

Ford, D. H., & Urban, H. B. (1963). *Systems of psychotherapy: A comparative study*. New York: Wiley.

George, R. L., & Cristiani, T. S. (1990). *Counseling: Theory and Practice* (3rd ed.). Englewood Cliffs, NJ: Prentice-Hall.

Hansen, J. C., Rossberg, R. H., & Cramer, S. H. (1994). *Counseling: Theory and process*. Boston, MA: Allyn & Bacon.

Mahoney, M. J. (1991). *Human change processes: The scientific foundations of psychotherapy*. New York: Basic Books.

Osipow, S. H. (1983). *Theories of career development* (3rd ed.). Englewood Cliffs, NJ: Prentice-Hall.

Urban, H. B., & Ford, D. F. (1971). Some historical and conceptual perspectives on psychotherapy and behavior change. In A. E. Bergin & S. L. Garfield (Eds.), *Handbook of psychotherapy and behavior change: An empirical analysis* (pp. 32–35). New York: Wiley.

Urban, H. B., & Vondracek, F. W. (1977). Dysfunctions in development: What can we expect? In S. Goldberg & F. Deutsch (Eds.), *Life-span individual and family development* (pp. 391–408). Pacific Grove, CA: Brooks/Cole.

P A R T   I

Psychoanalytic Approaches

CHAPTER 1
The Psychoanalysis of Sigmund Freud

CHAPTER 2
The Analytical Psychology of Carl G. Jung

CHAPTER 3
The Individual Psychology of Alfred Adler

CHAPTER 1

The Psychoanalysis
of Sigmund Freud

In his introductory lectures on psychoanalysis, Freud stated that "psycho-analysis is a method of medical treatment for those suffering from nervous disorders" (1935, p. 17). This meaning of psychoanalysis is the focus of this chapter. The legion of writers who have addressed the topic ever since Freud published his original findings have given quite different meanings to the concept of psychoanalysis. Among other things, psychoanalysis has been regarded as a philosophy of life, a key to happiness and success, and the starting point for various schools of psychoanalytic thought. Freud himself went beyond the relatively narrow definition of psychoanalysis as a treatment, since he considered himself the founder of the new science of psychoanalysis, which he maintained was a branch of psychology (Fine, 1973).

History of Psychoanalysis

No approach to understanding and changing human behavior has been as influential as the psychoanalytic approach introduced by Sigmund Freud. Freud's own writings on psychoanalysis span more than half a century before his death in 1939. A review of current publications reveals that the stream of writings on psychoanalysis and psychoanalytic thought has continued unabated to the present time. Psychoanalysis has become almost a religion to some, while others deride it as totally irrelevant, leading Fine to conclude that

"Freud has become a totem figure, to be deified or reviled, not a human being with a profound message that has to be understood" (1973, p. vii).

Freud was born in 1856 in Moravia, then part of the Austro-Hungarian empire. His father Jacob was a merchant, and the family was part of the Jewish minority of Moravia. In 1860, the family moved to Vienna. Although the family was not well off, Freud's childhood was relatively unremarkable. Always an outstanding student, first at the gymnasium in which he was at the top of his class, and starting in 1873 at the University of Vienna, Freud achieved his Doctor of Medicine degree in 1881 and started to work as a clinical assistant at a general hospital. He soon transferred to the department of psychiatry, where he was described as an extremely good neurologist who was particularly interested in the neuroanatomy of the brain as a means of understanding psychiatric disorders. By 1885 he had an opportunity to visit Paris for five months and to become a student of the famed neurologist Charcot at the Salpétrière, the most famous psychiatric hospital of its day. In 1886 he set up his first private practice. At the same time he maintained his scientific interests, publishing a controversial paper in which he promoted cocaine use, lecturing on the subject of hypnotism, and translating Bernheim's book on hypnotism from the French (Isbister, 1985).

Psychoanalysis eventually grew out of these early experiences, as well as Freud's growing dissatisfaction with hypnosis as a method of treatment. Also critical was Freud's association with Josef Breuer, a well-respected physician in Vienna, who used what he called "the talking cure" to treat hysteria. The busy Breuer referred "difficult" patients to Freud, offering the young Freud an opportunity both to improve his poor financial condition and to explore and develop his "analytic treatment" for neuroses. Breuer and Freud's collaboration culminated in the publication of *Studies on Hysteria* (Freud & Breuer, 1895). The publication of this book may be seen as marking Freud's transition from neurology to psychoanalysis. Freud first used the term *psychoanalysis* in 1896 (Isbister, 1985, p. 66).

Freud's life and work are inseparable from the history of psychoanalysis. Ernest Jones is considered the definitive biographer of Freud's life and work as a consequence of his writing the three-volume masterpiece *The Life and Work of Sigmund Freud*, published in 1955. Many others have attempted to capture the legacy of Freud and to capture the development of psychoanalysis from its beginnings to the present day. Fine, for example, divided the legacy of Freud into four periods: the exploration of neurosis (1886–1895); self-analysis (1895–1899); id psychology (1900–1914); and ego psychology (1914–1939) (1979, pp. 19–71). Bergman proposed that the history of psychoanalytic technique should be divided into five stages. During the first stage, from 1893 to 1898, Freud applied the cathartic procedure first developed by Breuer. The second stage, from 1898 to 1910, is described as a period of basic discoveries; the third, from 1910 to 1919, as a period of consolidation. The fourth period, from 1919 to 1926, Freud devoted to reformulating the instinct theory and developing the structural theory. The final and fifth stage, covering the period from 1926 to 1939, is defined by the development of psychoanalytic ego psychology (Bergman, 1990, p. 18).

Another perspective on psychoanalysis would examine both the mainstream of psychoanalysis and the schools founded by disciples who disagreed with various aspects of Freud's theory, or who chose to emphasize aspects different from those Freud considered central. Fine (1973) proposed that the division of psychoanalysis into different schools represents a historical error, because closer inspection reveals that they are all variations on themes proposed by Freud.

Ultimately, Freud himself maintained that, as analysts practice their science, they would uncover new truths and have new insights. He did not insist on dogmatically adhering to the original tenets of psychoanalysis, and he made a number of noteworthy revisions in his own thinking and writing. Current emphases in psychoanalysis are varied; it is probably fair to say that post–World War II analysts have focused on the role of the ego. Most prominent among them are Hartman (1950) and Erikson (1950). More recently, psychoanalysts have introduced new emphases within psychoanalysis, including the object relations model (for example, Winnicott, 1953, 1975) and the self psychological model (for instance, Kohut, 1971, 1977). The continuing development of new ideas and approaches within the field of psychoanalysis is clear evidence of the vitality and importance of the revolution in the science of the mind that Freud initiated more than 100 years ago.

Range of Applicability

Freud's original psychoanalytic formulations were clearly intended to illuminate and treat neuroses. Indeed, psychoanalytic practice has continued to focus on the treatment of neuroses, but, especially in recent years, increasing attention has been given to applying psychoanalysis to so-called borderline patients and even to psychotics (for example, Dince, 1981; Fine, 1979).

It is clear from Freud's earliest writings, however, that he considered the psychoanalysis of neurotic patients to be a key to understanding people's normal, nonmedical, everyday psychological functioning. This view is demonstrated in what he considered his most important work, *The Interpretation of Dreams* (1900), and in *The Psychopathology of Everyday Life* (1904). In the latter volume, Freud developed the theme that unconscious processes can interfere with conscious functioning; he wrote about the significance of "forgetting," "unintentional" slips, and "accidental" acts and behaviors. He attempted to show that everyday functioning in nonneurotic individuals could also be explained by many of his discoveries, which are now basic features of the psychoanalytic approach.

Although Freud, as a physician, focused the majority of his work on treating patients, he also considered himself a scientist, and he proclaimed psychoanalysis to be an important new method of scientific investigation. Moreover, he eventually proposed that psychoanalysis could be part of a "depth-psychology," which could become "indispensable to all the sciences which are concerned with the evolution of human civilization and its major institutions" (Freud, 1926, p. 248). He also suggested that historians, psychologists of religion, and researchers in many other disciplines could make significant contributions using psychoanalysis as a method of investigation.

Theoretical Foundations

In examining the theoretical foundations of psychoanalysis, two cautions must be observed. The first has to do with the many formulations and reformulations that psychoanalytic thought and theory have undergone over the last 100 years, at the hands of both Freud and others. Even when exclusively considering the principles and constructs Freud formulated, thoughtful scholars may disagree about the proper interpretation and whether a given formulation was, indeed, Freud's final word on the matter. Consequently, a summary of the theoretical foundations of psychoanalysis within the context of a single chapter must of necessity be selective and even somewhat arbitrary. The second consideration in any exposition of the theoretical foundations of psychoanalysis has to do with the social, cultural, and scientific context—in other words, the historical period—in which Freud and the early followers of psychoanalysis lived.

Assumptions About Human Nature

Freud was very much impressed by the work of Charles Darwin, which offered Freud a scientific justification for viewing humankind as not apart from, but a part of, the rest of nature. Freud saw human nature as a product of natural forces. He considered human characteristics to be merely transformed animal desires, and human rationality, morality, and self-consciousness to be only superficially removed from their ultimate sources—namely, irrationality, biological necessity, and the unconscious (Isbister, 1985, p. 3). Interestingly, however, Freud did not attempt to account for the specific biological roots of the psychic phenomena he sought to explain. He simply assumed that the biological science of his day was completely inadequate to the task. Because individuals are seen as ultimately controlled by their biologically rooted instincts, Freud's view of human nature must be characterized as highly deterministic.

One striking and persistent feature of Freud's ideas regarding human nature was his focus on humanity's dark side. He was insistent in proclaiming the imperfect condition of human beings, viewing them as driven by powerful and usually poorly understood impulses and drives. Freud felt that those who succeeded in converting these impulses into adaptive or creative behaviors were the great scientists, artists, and leaders, whereas those who were unsuccessful were doomed to perpetuate the cycle of selfishness and destruction that has been a hallmark of human existence. Freud's ultimate appraisal of the nature of humanity was pessimistic. Thoughtful students of psychoanalysis have argued that Freud overemphasized the dark, destructive, and irrational elements as a source of human behavior, and that human behavior is far more complex than Freud's formulations would have one believe (Isbister, 1985).

The Basic Theory of Psychoanalysis

Freud made several efforts to present the complex theoretical underpinnings of psychoanalysis in ways that would make them understandable to the uninitiated. For example, Freud delivered three series of lectures at the University of Vienna from 1915 to 1917, which were published in English translation in 1920 under the title *A General Introduction to Psycho-analysis: A Course of 28 Lectures Delivered at the University of Vienna*. Another effort to present a concise summary of psychoanalysis was Freud's last book, first published in 1940 in German under the title *Abriss der Psychoanalyse*. An English-language version, entitled *An Outline of Psycho-analysis*, was published in 1949. These writings of Sigmund Freud form the basis of the following discussion. On some topics Calvin Hall's classic *A Primer of Freudian Psychology*, first published in 1954, has also been consulted.

In his Vienna lectures, Freud noted that psychoanalysis has two basic tenets, one of which clashes with well-established intellectual prejudices, and the other with moral and aesthetic prejudices. Freud noted that his struggle against these prejudices had been a hard one. The first of these basic propositions of psychoanalysis is that "mental processes are essentially unconscious"; the second is that "impulses, which can only be described as sexual in both the narrower and the wider sense, play a peculiarly large part, never before sufficiently appreciated, in the causation of nervous and mental disorders"

(1935, pp. 22–23). Although these propositions are of central importance, they were probably singled out by Freud early in his lectures as a means of shocking his audiences so as to ensure their attention. Freud wrote extensively about many other basic tenets of psychoanalysis, which collectively represent a comprehensive theory of both normal and abnormal development. A basic understanding of his comprehensive psychoanalytic theory is essential for understanding his psychoanalytic therapy.

The organization of personality.   Perhaps the most widely known aspect of psychoanalytic theory is Freud's description of what he called the psychical apparatus. Freud acknowledged that he arrived at his understanding of this psychical apparatus through studying individual human development. The oldest structure developmentally in this psychical apparatus he called the id; this structure, he thought, contains the genetic and constitutional inheritance of the person, including the basic instincts. Freud proposed that as a consequence of interacting with the environment, one portion of the id becomes specialized to act as an intermediary between the id and the external world. Freud called this structure the ego. He proposed that first and foremost, the ego has the task of self-preservation, which it accomplishes through dealing not only with external stimuli, but also with internal events. In the latter case the ego serves as a means of control over the demands of the instincts, usually in such a way as to generate pleasure and avoid its opposite.

Humans have a particularly long childhood period during which they are completely dependent on their parents. Freud proposed that during this period a specialized formation called the superego develops within the ego, which continues this parental influence. The superego contains two subsystems, the ego-ideal and the conscience; the former represents the developing person's internalization of what his or her parents consider to be good, whereas the latter contains the internalization of what the parents consider to be morally bad (Hall, 1954). Freud noted that the superego may be opposed to the ego (at least some of the time), thereby leaving the ego to cope with three forces: the demands of the id, of the superego, and of reality. When the ego is able to deal with these forces successfully, the individual is likely to be functioning well. It is noteworthy that Freud's conceptualizations of the functioning of this psychic apparatus account for the influences of heredity (through the id); of the individual's own experience (through the ego); and of parents and significant others, as well as of cultural traditions and the "immediate social milieu" represented by them (through the superego) (Freud, 1949, pp. 1–4).

The theory of instincts.   According to Freud, the id is the primary source of psychic (or instinctual) energy, and its function is to discharge that energy in order to reduce tension, thus producing pleasure. The id thus operates by what Freud called the pleasure principle. The ego, as mediator between the forces of the id and the realities of the world, operates not by the pleasure principle but by the reality principle. In effect, the reality principle enables a person to postpone satisfaction of the pleasure principle. The ego recognizes that such postponement is required because the conditions necessary for satisfying a need—which is the basis of all instinctual or psychic energy—may not be present in reality.

Freud's theory of instincts originally proposed that the single most important instinct is represented by libido, or sexual energies. While maintaining his conviction that libido is of central importance, Freud later decided that there are two basic instincts: Eros, also called the love or life instinct; and thanatos, the death or destructive instinct. The life instincts, which include the sexual instincts, have been referred to as "somatic demands upon the mind" (Freud, 1949, p. 5)—in other words, the mental representation of all of a person's bodily needs. The most important derivative of the life instinct is love. The death instincts are seen, ultimately, as the desire of the organic to return to an inorganic state. The most important derivatives of the death instinct are aggressiveness and destructiveness.

Freud described several important attributes of instincts. He maintained that they represent quantities of energy that vary in terms of their intensity. Because they are ever-present, they must be regularly discharged to avoid excessive accumulation. The ultimate aim of the instincts is to produce behavior—in other words, to find an object or event through which the quantity and intensity of the accumulated instinctual (psychic) energy can be reduced. If one object is not available for the discharge (cathexis), the energy can be rechanneled to another object, in a process called displacement. Displacement is extremely important in the development of personality; both the ego and the superego develop through the displacement of energy from the id. Freud believed that sexual energy, for example, can be distributed through displacement among such diverse activities as gardening, daydreaming, attending a ball game, or writing (Hall, 1954, p. 84).

Psychosexual stages of development.   One of Freud's most important contributions was his focus on early childhood experiences as critical in the formation of personality. Freud was convinced that such early experiences often bore the seeds of future neurotic functioning. Consequently, the practice of psychoanalysis as a method of treatment views as one of its central tasks the recall and interpretation of early and often "forgotten" experiences from early childhood. These experiences include the passage through phases of psychosexual development that are focused around the three principal erotogenic or erogenous zones: the mouth, the anus, and the genital organs. In this connection it must be noted that Freud was emphatic about these observations:

1. Sexual life starts soon after birth.
2. The term *sexual* refers to much broader processes and behaviors than the term *genital*.
3. As part of sexual life individuals obtain pleasure from various zones (the erogenous zones) of the body. (Freud, 1949, p. 9)

The first phase of psychosexual development is the oral phase. During this phase the developing infant obtains primary satisfaction through sucking and eating—through satisfaction of the oral need. Freud wrote:

> The baby's obstinate persistence in sucking gives evidence at an early stage of a need for satisfaction which, though it originates from and is instigated by the taking of nourishment, nevertheless strives to obtain pleasure independently of nourishment and for that reason may and should be termed *sexual*. (1949, p. 11)

How a mother (or other caretaker) attends to oral needs will usually influence infants' relationships and may eventually be reflected in adult personality traits. Behaviors during the oral phase represent prototypes for personality traits that may or may not develop depending on the amount of frustration and anxiety an infant experiences (Hall, 1954). For example, development of the traits of dependence and independence has been related to processes occurring during the oral stage.

During the second phase, the anal phase—or what Freud called the sadistic-anal phase—the toddler seeks satisfaction in the excretory function, which Freud considered symbolically related to aggression. Parental toilet training represents the child's initial experience with external control of an impulse. Consequently, toilet training is viewed as of critical importance in the development of personality. Successful passage through this phase may result in creativity and productivity, whereas difficulties in its passage may produce so-called anal-retentive personalities, often characterized by cruelty and sometimes aggressive or sadistic traits.

The third phase of psychosexual development, the phallic phase, Freud viewed as "a forerunner of the final form taken by sexual life" (1949, p. 11). For both boys and girls, the genital area represents the focus of development during this phase, although their specific experiences differ because the reproductive organs are structurally different. Freud suggested that during this phase, boys enter the Oedipal period, when they begin to manipulate their penis and have fantasies of doing something with it in relation to their mothers. When parents attempt to interfere with masturbatory activities, and especially when boys discover that girls do not have a penis, boys experience castration anxiety, representing the fear that their father will cut it off.

Henceforth, sexual interest declines, because the Oedipus complex is repressed by fear of castration. From ages 5 to 12 is a latency phase, which ends when physiological changes occur with the onset of puberty that revive latent sexual impulses. For girls, the equivalent of boys' castration anxiety is penis envy. Girls also experience a period of latency that is brought to an end by puberty.

The three phases of psychosexual development—the oral, anal, and phallic—have been referred to collectively as the pregenital period (Hall, 1954). Some writers have seen the latency period as a separate phase. The final phase of psychosexual development, which Freud called the fourth phase, is that of genital sexuality. During this phase, the individual moves from self-love (narcissism) to love of others and the ability to form intimate relationships. When this process is inhibited or flawed in some way, various disturbances in sexual life may occur, including fixations on earlier stages of psychosexual development and a variety of sexual perversions.

Defense mechanisms.   In the course of development, a major task of the ego is to deal with dangers that threaten its integrity and arouse anxiety in the individual. A well-functioning ego will typically deal with danger using effective and realistic coping methods. The ego may, however, resort to alleviating anxiety through methods that distort and deny reality, thus impeding the development of healthy personality. Freud called these methods the ego's defense mechanisms. Hall (1954, pp. 85–97) summarized the most important of these defense mechanisms as follows.

1. *Repression* basically involves the removal of painful or threatening thoughts or experiences from consciousness. In each case, whatever is repressed, the purpose is to abolish the associated anxiety by denying the existence of the threat. Although repression may serve useful purposes in personality development, it can also produce a variety of psychological and physical symptoms. Whenever the ego gains or regains sufficient strength to cope with danger by rational methods, repression is no longer necessary.

2. *Projection* involves a person's attempt to relieve anxiety by attributing the cause of anxiety to the external world rather than to his or her own id or superego. For example, a person who experiences anxiety as a consequence of sexual impulses may attribute those impulses to someone else, thereby obtaining some relief from anxiety.

3. *Reaction formations* may be used against either external or internal threats. When one instinctual impulse produces anxiety, the ego may try to defeat this anxiety by concentrating on the opposite impulse. An example of reaction formations would occur if feelings of anger toward a person created

anxiety, resulting in the anxious person bending over backward to show kindness toward the other instead of anger.

4. *Fixation* represents another defense against anxiety. Basically it consists of a person getting stuck, or becoming fixated at a certain stage of psychological development. Separation anxiety is a form of fixation, namely fixation on the old and familiar and associated fear of the new and unfamiliar.

5. *Regression* occurs when a person retreats from a prior level of psychological development because of fear. Freud believed that various neurotic habits such as eating too much, biting fingernails, and getting drunk all represented regressions designed to reduce anxiety.

Assumptions About Conducting Psychoanalysis

According to psychoanalytic theory, psychopathological states are produced by a weakening of the ego that makes it impossible for the ego to keep down the demands of the id, to deal with the sometimes relentless demands of the superego, and to cling to reality. Psychoanalysis involves a pact between the analyst and the patient, who form an alliance in order to strengthen the ego in its struggle against its enemies: the instinctual demands of the id and the conscientious demands of the superego. The basic content of the alliance is a collaboration, in which the patient agrees to disclose, with complete candor, any and all material that is available, and the analyst uses his or her knowledge and experience in interpreting material that has been influenced by the unconscious. Thus, the patient, through strengthening and healing a sick ego, is returned to "mastery" (Freud, 1949, pp. 29–30).

Implementing Psychoanalysis

Freud struggled for many years with the task of developing his psychoanalytic method. Frequently, he made important contributions to psychoanalytic technique by publishing case studies that illustrated the insights he was gaining as he was practicing psychoanalysis. He never published a comprehensive review on how to conduct psychoanalysis, although he reportedly planned to prepare such a summary (Jones, 1955). Apparently, his failure to do so was based in part on concerns that if patients read such a summary, the conduct of psychoanalysis might become more difficult, if not impossible. In addition, he felt that, although aspiring psychoanalysts could learn some things from reading about psychoanalysis, only after undergoing analysis themselves and accumulating years of experience would they become fully competent psychoanalysts.

Preliminary Considerations

Although Freud was initially optimistic about the prospects for applying psychoanalysis to all patients suffering from intrapsychic conflict, he soon discovered that psychotic patients were unable to meaningfully enter into the alliance required to conduct psychoanalysis. He therefore suggested that psychoanalysts confine themselves to working with neurotic patients. Freud also felt that only patients able to pay for the psychoanalyst's services should be accepted into analysis. He justified this stricture by noting the significant amount of time required by each patient and by suggesting that the guilt feelings and sense of obligation of patients treated free of charge might interfere with the process of analysis. In addition, Freud required that patients should have a minimum of intellectual capacity (Ford & Urban, 1963, p. 166). Finally, Freud stated that he preferred to take on only patients who were comparatively free of well-meaning or self-protective relatives who were likely to interfere in the patient's efforts to get well (Freud, 1935, pp. 399–400).

Initial Evaluation and Initial Session

Freud likened the beginning of treatment to the beginning of a chess match. Wrong moves could have dire consequences, especially for the analyst. He accepted new patients initially for only a two-week period, which would offer him the opportunity to observe the patient's ability to cope with the requirements of analysis and to determine whether the problem was neurosis or whether there was an underlying psychotic process. Apparently, Freud felt that involving patients in the initial stages of psychoanalytic treatment (without, however, making interpretations) offered a better chance to determine the treatment's suitability for them than did conducting the more common series of diagnostic interviews (Jones, 1955, Vol. 2).

During the initial phase of psychoanalysis, patients are introduced to the couch. Freud customarily required patients to lie down on a couch throughout the session, a carryover from his early interest in the practice of hypnosis. Freud would then sit in a chair slightly behind and to the side of the patient. Although some have (erroneously) interpreted this positioning as an attempt to establish dominance, Freud saw the main advantages of this procedure as first, relieving the analyst of the burden of having his or her facial expression scrutinized for many hours each day, and second, preventing the patient from being distracted by the analyst. Patients were never told what they should talk about, but they were always advised of the importance of adhering to the rule of never withholding any information for any reason

whatsoever. If a patient was found able to abide by these fundamental procedures, the process of psychoanalysis was set to begin in earnest.

The Conduct of Psychoanalysis

Free association.   The rule against withholding information from the analyst
Freud called the fundamental rule of analysis. It represents the essence of the
process of free association, which is considered the basic principle guiding
patient behavior during psychoanalytic sessions. Specifically, Freud insisted
that patients tell everything that came to mind, even if it was disagreeable or
seemed unimportant or even nonsensical (Freud, 1949, p. 31).

Transference.   A second source of information in psychoanalysis is one
whose discovery surprised even Freud—namely, the process of transference.
Freud discovered that patients did not simply regard the analyst as a helper
and adviser.

> On the contrary, the patient sees in him the return, the reincarnation, of
> some important figure out of his childhood or past, and consequently trans-
> fers on to him feelings and reactions which undoubtedly applied to this
> prototype. (Freud, 1949, p. 31)

Because this important figure is usually a parent figure, the transference, just
like the original feelings and attitudes toward parents, tends to be ambivalent,
comprising both positive and negative attitudes. As long as it is positive, it
changes the analytic situation to one in which the patient will now actively
strive to please the analyst. Transference can thus be a powerful force that
gives the patient strength to make even difficult changes. Moreover, because
the patient's parents were also the origin of the patient's superego, the analyst
now has superego power over the patient's ego.

In order to abolish and dissolve neurotic symptoms, Freud insisted, it
was necessary to return to the point of their origin—namely, early childhood
conflicts with one's parents. The transference relationship makes possible the
creation of new editions of those early conflicts, in which patients tend to
behave in their original and dysfunctional way while the analyst strives
mightily to motivate the patient to reach a better decision this time around.
Not surprisingly, Freud called transference the "battlefield" of psychoanalysis
(1935, p. 395). Before the end of psychoanalysis, the transference relationship between patient and analyst must be resolved successfully, an important
task that requires careful attention and experience on the part of the analyst.

The transference relationship between the patient and the analyst repro-
duces, in effect, the patient's relation with his or her parents. Just as early

erotic desires in relation to one's parents meet with frustration and ultimately result in a more mature relationship with them, the desire for sexual intimacy with the analyst meets with rebuff and may result in negative transference— feelings of hatred for the analyst. The analyst can prevent this outcome by showing the patient again and again that the feelings of positive transference are a reflection of the past, and not present, real life. If the analyst succeeds in this task, mostly by recognizing the first signs of either extreme love or extreme hostility, the patient can be prepared to use the experiences obtained during transference to enhance the self-knowledge ultimately needed to over-come neurosis (Freud, 1949, p. 34).

Dream interpretation.   A third source of information analysts use is the inter-pretation of dreams. Freud wrote extensively on this subject and considered it one of his greatest discoveries. He assumed that during dreams, the contents of the unconscious id force their way into the ego and into consciousness. Dreams thus offer a wonderful opportunity to learn about processes generally not accessible to conscious thought or recollection. Freud proposed that what one remembers upon waking up is the manifest content of a dream, but that the true dream process consists of latent dream-thoughts. The process that converts latent dream-thoughts into manifest dream content is dream-work. The analyst's interpretation of dreams and the processes involved in dream-work can uncover material that the dreamer has forgotten and that is com-pletely inaccessible in a waking state. Perhaps most important in the process of psychoanalysis is that dreams often produce impressions from the dreamer's early childhood that had become unconscious due to repression. In view of the importance of early childhood experiences in the formation of neuroses, it is readily apparent that dream analysis and interpretation repre-sent an important source of information for the analyst (Freud, 1935).

Slips and parapraxes.   A final source of information is gathered from the patient's slips or parapraxes. These mental errors include slips of the tongue and of the pen, misreading, miswriting, mishearing, misplacing, and forget-ting. Freud explained these phenomena in considerable detail in a number of works, including three of his University of Vienna lectures (1935). Character-istically, Freud first acknowledged that slips or errors certainly seemed too trivial to occupy the mind of a scientist or physician. He then systematically demonstrated that errors have meaning and that they are mental acts arising from the mutual interference of two intentions. Moreover, he emphasized that as meaningful mental acts, slips and parapraxes should be viewed as having "significance, intention, tendency and a position in a sequence of mental con-catenations" (p.55). The process of analysis can discover the meaning of errors, producing additional information about the patient's intrapsychic functioning.

Interpretation.   The analyst uses all the information gathered through the methods just described to make constructions about what has happened to the patient that has been forgotten. In effect, the analyst discovers the meaning of the patient's neurotic symptoms. Freud believed that ultimately the analyst should prefer to lead the patient to discover such constructions, or at least nearly to discover them. He felt that the analyst should not overwhelm the patient with information about these constructions, or interpretations, until the patient was prepared for them (Freud, 1949, pp. 34–35). Once the patient has been prepared, however, interpretation returns unconscious, repressed material to the ego—in other words, to conscious awareness— thereby strengthening the ego in ways that were previously impossible. Freud considered analysis to be completed when "all obscurities in the case are explained, the gaps in memory filled out, and the original occasions of the repressions discovered" (1935, p. 394).

Resistance.   If patients were eagerly willing to accept the analyst's interpretation of what has been happening to them, the process of analysis would be relatively simple. Freud reported, however, that to his own great surprise, patients always put up a vigorous and tenacious resistance throughout the entire course of treatment. This resistance, Freud observed, could take many different forms, and the analyst always needed to be on guard against it. As particular examples of resistance, Freud mentioned the many barriers to free association that patients erect. In addition to such intellectual resistances, Freud noted that the transference relationship offers means of resisting, first through what he called transference love, and when that is rejected by the analyst, through rejection of the analyst. Another kind of resistance Freud discussed occurs when patients question the basic premises of psychoanalysis itself. Although sensitive to the perception that defining such questioning as resistance could be seen as self-serving, Freud nevertheless insisted that all of these examples are resistances, that some of them are bound to appear in every analysis, and that "the overcoming of these resistances is the essential work of the analysis, that part of the work which alone assures us that we achieved something for the patient" (1935, p. 257).

Means and Conditions for Implementing Psychoanalysis

Freud typically referred to the analyst as a physician, but he eventually decided that being a physician was not essential (Freud, 1926). Freud generally thought of psychoanalysts as male, probably as a result of the virtual absence of women from the ranks of physicians and scientists especially during the years when Freud wrote most prolifically about psychoanalysis. He did not feel, however, that women were incapable of being psychoanalysts, and indeed, his daughter Anna Freud became a psychoanalyst of great prominence.

The Analyst's Qualifications

The most important component of psychoanalytic training is the personal analysis of the psychoanalyst-to-be. Freud insisted that aspiring psychoanalysts needed to have a thorough theoretical understanding of psychoanalytic theory, including the organization and functioning of what he called mental life. He suggested that some of this knowledge can be acquired through reading about psychoanalytic theory, but that the process of undergoing analysis is essential for gaining the kind of self-knowledge required to ensure that the future analyst's observations and understanding of patients would not be distorted by his or her own deficiencies. In addition to undergoing analysis, Freud observed that several years' experience practicing psychoanalysis (under supervision) was likely to be a necessary precondition for realizing the full potential of psychoanalytic therapy.

Psychoanalysts have had disagreements ever since Freud's work became known—about psychoanalytic theory, the practice of psychoanalysis, and the training requirements for aspiring analysts. Various psychoanalytic organizations have dealt with these issues, beginning in 1910 when Freud founded the International Psychoanalytical Association and appointed Carl Jung as its first president. The New York Psychoanalytic Society was founded in 1911, as was the American Psychoanalytic Association (Fine, 1979). To this day, competing societies disagree about who should have the authoritative voice regarding the training of analysts.

Conditions for Conducting Psychoanalysis

In the early years of psychoanalysis, Freud took a rather informal approach, often inviting his patients to have dinner with his family. Gradually, however, he developed a more formal methodology and recommended that the analyst's personality and personal life be excluded as much as possible from patients' psychoanalysis. He proposed that the analyst adopt a passive, receptive, observational posture, and abstain from note-taking (which could be distracting to both analyst and patient). Patients were asked to lie on a couch in the analyst's quiet consultation room, with the analyst sitting slightly behind the couch and to the patient's side. Freud explained that this position would allow the analyst to concentrate on observing and listening to the patient, without having to worry about whether the analyst's facial expressions would distract the patient or interfere in the formation of transference (Jones, 1955). Many psychoanalysts continue today to follow the procedures originally outlined by Freud.

Limitations of Psychoanalysis

Psychoanalysis had its detractors from the very beginning. Not surprisingly, Freud's emphasis on sexual instincts was shocking to the Victorian mentality of his time. Moreover, the idea of being treated by simply talking about one's problems ran counter to the contemporary excitement regarding the amazing progress that had been achieved in the physical and biological sciences of that period. Added to those difficulties was the fact that Freud, like most of the early psychoanalysts, was Jewish, a characteristic sufficient to produce a certain amount of prejudice among some segments of Freud's society. In any case, the various preconceptions and prejudices that Freud and his followers encountered were unable to stop the growth of psychoanalysis. Freud recognized that little could be done about prejudice beyond persevering until it faded.

Apart from various forms of prejudice, psychoanalysis has also suffered from a variety of more or less self-inflicted limitations. The divisiveness and argumentativeness that have characterized psychoanalysts from the very beginning of Freud's Vienna circle have often resulted in one group of psychoanalysts discrediting another, often in public forums (Fine, 1979). As a consequence, psychoanalysts have become a favorite subject of cartoonists and professional humorists—a development that surely would have appalled Freud. The difficulties involved in subjecting psychoanalytic theory, as well as clinical work, to rigorous scientific investigation have only added to the public perception of psychoanalysis as highly suspect.

Contraindications

Freud was explicit that psychoanalysis requires the patient to be able to engage in free association without withholding any information for any reason. A patient's inability to do so for any reason whatsoever he considered to contraindicate the use of psychoanalysis. Freud also believed that the patient needs to be intellectually capable of participating in the analytic process. Psychoanalysis would therefore be contraindicated for developmentally disabled individuals. Freud suggested, too, that individuals who are enmeshed in their families may not be appropriate candidates for psychoanalysis, because he found family members could interfere in the process of psychoanalysis to an intolerable degree. Freud realized, of course, that this last contraindication was not an absolute one. Practical considerations were likely to make it impossible for all psychoanalysts to be as restrictive in their criteria for accepting patients as he had come to be.

When Freud originally developed psychoanalysis, he felt that it might be a reasonable approach for all patients with mental disorders. He soon discovered, however, that the ego functioning of psychotic patients was so disturbed and weak that they were unable to participate fully in the process of psychoanalysis. Freud felt that, as more knowledge accumulated from the psychoanalytic investigation of mental disorders, psychosis might eventually also be treatable through psychoanalysis. During his lifetime, however, he continued to believe that psychoanalysis as a treatment was effective primarily in the treatment of neurotic disorders. Although some analysts have broadened the range of disorders they are willing to treat, the majority of psychoanalysts continue to view psychotic functioning as contraindicating psychoanalysis.

Hazards

We have seen that Freud viewed the intervention of patients' relatives as a distraction and a danger. He acknowledged that he did not know how to deal with it, and consequently he selected patients who were not particularly subject to pressure from their relatives. The most serious hazard in the course of psychoanalysis is undoubtedly transference, which, as Freud acknowledged, can be misused by unscrupulous analysts. Freud was adamant, therefore, in insisting that any kind of sexual relationship between analyst and patient is out of the question, because the transference relationship places the patient in a position of great vulnerability. It should be noted in passing that Freud's concept of countertransference showed that the analyst may also be vulnerable to influences that may distort his or her transactions with the patient.

Freud was sensitive to the criticisms of the medical establishment and to occasional reports that application of his psychoanalysis had produced harmful consequences for some patients. At the end of his Vienna lectures he suggested that the harmful effects reported were confined, for the most part, to "transitory manifestations of an exacerbation of the conflict" (1935, pp. 402–403). He added that these effects may occur when the analyst is clumsy or when the patient breaks off analysis suddenly. In general, he maintained that psychoanalysis, when used properly by competent analysts with appropriate patients, was unlikely to be harmful.

The Effectiveness of Psychoanalysis

Freud viewed psychoanalysis as treatment and at the same time as a method of scientific investigation. He developed his theory and his method of treatment primarily on the basis of careful and patient observation and study of his patients. His voluminous writings are replete with literally hundreds of examples from actual patients, as well as many case studies. As might be expected, most of the case studies Freud reported illustrated various aspects of successful psychoanalysis, although he occasionally reported failures (for example, 1935, pp. 400–401). Freud resisted the idea of developing a statistical profile of his successes and failures, primarily because he believed that each case was unique and could not sensibly be compared to all others. Moreover, he indicated that long-term longitudinal data would be needed to arrive at any meaningful judgment of the permanence of changes achieved by the patient.

In spite of Freud's reluctance to accept experimental science or statistical treatment of data as applicable to his formulations of psychoanalysis, his theories have nevertheless been subjected to a significant amount of research, much of it using those very methods. This may come as something of a surprise to those critics of psychoanalysis who have generally maintained that psychoanalytic concepts are so far removed from observable data that they would require too much artificial simplification to be studied experimentally. Fisher and Greenberg (1977) conducted a major review of the evidence pertaining to the scientific credibility of Freud's theories and therapy. Their 75-page bibliography contains approximately 2,000 references—a testament to the scope of their task, as well as the productivity of research in this area. Although the stream of research on psychoanalysis and psychoanalytic concepts continues unabated, a brief summary of the conclusions Fisher and Greenberg reached on the basis of their review is instructive.

First of all, Fisher and Greenberg concluded that significant evidence has been accumulating regarding the psychoanalytic personality theory developed by Freud. In particular, they pointed to numerous studies that confirmed the existence of oral and anal personality typologies. At the same time they concluded that evidence regarding the relationship between oral and anal phases of development on the one hand, and the emergence of oral or anal personality constellations on the other, was mostly absent, possibly because such evidence would have to come from expensive and difficult longitudinal studies. The reviewers also found that several aspects of Freud's Oedipal theory were at least partly confirmed. They noted, however, that Freud's formulations about male development tended to be more on target than his ideas about female development.

On the issue of scientific evidence regarding the effectiveness of psychoanalytic treatment, Fisher and Greenberg concluded that such evidence is largely lacking. Psychoanalytic treatment certainly has not been shown to be superior to other treatments, which tend to be shorter in duration and, therefore, less expensive. Fisher and Greenberg attributed these disappointing findings to the fact that "the field is filled with vagueness, appeals to authority rather than evidence, lack of specificity in the definitions used, and unreliability in the application of techniques and dynamic conceptualizations" (p. 411). They also noted that although Freud implied that patient changes would occur as a consequence of making the unconscious conscious, many psychoanalysts deliberately deemphasize behavioral change in patients as a necessary outcome of therapy. They concluded:

> If we are to have both better therapy and better therapy research, we will need fewer meaningless labels and a greater respect for clarity and precision in defining what we are doing. (p. 414)

That admonition is likely to be as true today as it was in 1977.

References

Bergman, M. S. (1990). Notes on the history of psychoanalytic technique. In M. S. Bergman & F. R. Hartman (Eds.), *The evolution of psychoanalytic technique* (pp. 17–40). New York: Columbia University Press.

Dince, P. R. (1981). Implications of the treatment of borderline patients for psychoanalytic technique. In S. Klebanow (Ed.), *Changing concepts in psychoanalysis* (pp. 33–45). New York: Gardner Press.

Erikson, E. H. (1950). *Childhood and society.* New York: Norton.

Fine, R. (1973). *The development of Freud's thought: From the beginnings (1886–1900) through id psychology (1900–1914) to ego psychology (1914–1939).* New York: Aronson.

Fine, R. (1979). *A history of psychoanalysis.* New York: Columbia University Press.

Fisher, S., & Greenberg, R. P. (1977). *The scientific credibility of Freud's theories and therapy.* New York: Basic Books.

Ford, D. H., & Urban, H. B. (1963). *Systems of psychotherapy: A comparative study.* New York: Wiley.

Freud, S. (1900). Interpretation of dreams. In J. Strachey (Ed.), *The standard edition of the complete psychological works of Sigmund Freud*, Vols. 4 & 5. London: Hogarth Press.

Freud, S. (1926). The question of lay analysis. In J. Strachey (Ed.), *The standard edition of the complete psychological works of Sigmund Freud*, Vol. 20 (pp. 183–258). London: Hogarth Press.

Freud, S. (1935). *A general introduction to psycho-analysis: A course of 28 lectures delivered at the University of Vienna* (rev. ed). New York: Liveright.

Freud, S. (1938). The psychopathology of everyday life. In A. A. Brill (Ed.), *The basic writings of Sigmund Freud* (pp. 35–178). New York: Random House. (Original work published 1904.)

Freud, S. (1949). *An outline of psycho-analysis*. New York: Norton. (Original work published 1940.)

Freud, S., & Breuer, J. (1957). *Studies in hysteria*. New York: Basic Books. (Original work published 1895.)

Hall, C. S. (1954). *A primer of Freudian psychology*. New York: New American Library.

Hartman, H. (1950). Comments on the psychoanalytic theory of the ego. *The Psychoanalytic Study of the Child*, Vol. 5 (pp. 74–96). New York: International Universities Press.

Isbister, J. N. (1985). *Freud: An introduction to his life and work*. Cambridge, England: Polity Press.

Jones, E. (1955). *The life and work of Sigmund Freud*, Vols. 1, 2, & 3. New York: Basic Books.

Kohut, H. (1971). *The analysis of the self*. New York: International Universities Press.

Kohut, H. (1977). *The restoration of the self*. New York: International Universities Press.

Winnicott, D. W. (1953). Transitional objects and transitional phenomena. *International Journal of Psychiatry*, 34, 89–97.

Winnicott, D. W. (1975). *Through pediatrics to psychoanalysis*. New York: Basic Books.

....

CHAPTER 2

The Analytical Psychology
of Carl G. Jung

....

■

The analytical psychology of C. G. Jung has been controversial from its very beginning. Some claim that Jung is remembered today only as a result of his association and correspondence with Sigmund Freud. Others see in Jung an original thinker, a philosopher, a scientist, and a psychiatrist who dared to pursue ideas and directions that were believed to be unapproachable, especially from the perspective of modern-day science. Jung was prolific in his writings on subjects ranging from alchemy to Eastern religion, from archetypes to the collective unconscious. Because of the diversity of his interests, most summaries of his work cannot possibly do justice to it. In that respect, this chapter will be no different. Nevertheless, Jung was neither the lunatic nor the mystic he has been portrayed as, nor was he some kind of ultimate genius offering definitive answers about the nature of humankind or of God. As a practicing therapist for many decades, Jung acquired important insights into the nature and treatment of neuroses. He did not, however, leave a specific set of techniques or procedures for doing therapy.

What is being practiced as Jungian analysis or individual psychotherapy represents a collection of approaches that is extremely varied but loosely connected to the essential features of Jung's analytical psychology. Although perhaps short on technique, the analytical psychology of Jung is rich in important concepts that have increasingly found their way into the language of psychology and of everyday life. Moreover, Jungian analysis represents an alternative and addresses human issues that other therapies typically neglect, justifying its inclusion here.

Purpose of Jungian Analysis

Jung was relatively vague in describing the aims of psychotherapy.

> In any concrete case I am at pains to avoid all theoretical presuppositions about the structure of the neurosis and about what the patient can and ought to do. As far as possible I let pure experience decide the therapeutic aim. This may perhaps seem strange, because it is commonly supposed that the therapist has an aim. But in psychotherapy it seems to me positively advisable for the doctor not to have too fixed an aim. (Jung, 1966b, Vol. 16, pp. 40–41)

Because Jung felt that other approaches, most notably Freudian psychoanalysis, overemphasized rationality, his therapeutic approach focused on bringing unconscious parts of the self into closer relationship with extant ego-consciousness. Rather than focusing on treating neuroses, Jungian analysis may be viewed as a journey, taken together by analyst and analysand (as Jungians call their patients), with the ultimate aim of furthering self-knowledge and thereby enhancing the "whole psychic human being" (Jung, 1966b, Vol. 16, p. 89).

History of Jungian Analysis

Carl Gustav Jung, a Swiss psychiatrist, was Sigmund Freud's junior by almost two decades. Yet their close personal and professional association, which lasted from 1906 to 1913, was significant for both men and for the development of their respective professional formulations. The eventual break in their relationship has been described ad nauseam, with the fault attributed to one or the other, depending on the author's particular bias. In fact, the extensive correspondence between Freud and Jung has been preserved and published (McGuire & Sauerlander, 1974). That correspondence suggests that the two men had substantive differences. They disagreed in their views on the content and origin of the unconscious; they disagreed regarding the nature of psychic energy, with Jung objecting to Freud's emphasis on sexuality; they held differing views on the interpretability and meaning of manifest dream content; they held opposing views on religion; and they differed in their approach to analysis. Personal differences also probably contributed to their break. Freud was known as being relatively dogmatic and not permitting open dissension among his followers, something that Jung must have experienced as a difficult constraint. Jung was interested in the occult, alchemy, the supernatural—and, eventually, even in UFOs. Both men went their separate ways after 1913, and both continued to make major independent contributions for many years thereafter. Jung's work has survived in spite of attempts by some Freudian scholars (for example, Fine, 1979) to discredit him personally as an anti-Semite and professionally as an "obscurantist mystic." In fact, Jung's work has been increasingly appreciated, not just in the fields of psychology and psychiatry, but also in anthropology, the humanities, and the arts (Mattoon, 1981).

Jung's version of psychotherapy—which he originally referred to as psychoanalysis and later as analytical psychology, as a way to set it apart from Freudian psychoanalysis—is now most often called Jungian analysis. Jung personally analyzed (in other words, trained) many leaders in Jungian analysis who, especially following World War II, went on to develop Jungian training institutes in the United States and in other countries around the world (Henderson, 1982). Henderson reported the interesting observation that the large majority of early Jungian analysts in the United States were women, who perhaps found the Jungian view of women more appealing than the Freudian view. Today institutes and centers for training Jungian analysts can be found throughout the United States.

Range of Applicability

Because the goals of Jungian analysis are very broadly defined, Jungian analysis has been used with numerous different types of individuals in a range of settings. For example, whereas Freud generally confined the practice of psychoanalysis to neurotic individuals, Jung imposed no such restriction. One precaution that Jung recommended that analysts take in treating psychotic individuals was to refrain from intensively dealing with unconscious material and instead to provide the analysand with as much psychological knowledge as possible (Mattoon, 1981). Jung's position on the treatment of children was that, since most of their problems reflected parental conflicts, the children should be treated through treatment of their parents. Today, however, some Jungian analysts work directly with children. Moreover, virtually all of the leading Jung Institutes (training centers for Jungian analysts) have special training programs for analysts who intend to work with children (Sullwood, 1982).

Jung was doubtful about the value of group therapy, and most Jungian analysts apparently share this view. Nevertheless, some attempts have been made to adapt Jungian analysis for use in groups (for example, Brookes, 1974). Overall, however, Jungian analysis continues to occur mainly within the context of an interactive one-to-one relationship between analyst and analysand. It should be noted that Jungian analysis has never been nearly as dogmatic as Freudian psychoanalysis, and as a consequence Jungian analysts continue to extend the boundaries of their therapeutic approach, in terms of both methods and range of applicability. Mattoon (1981) reported that "Jungians sometimes say that Jung incorporated such a broad range of treatment modalities that the Jungian approach can be adapted to virtually any client" (p. 243).

Theoretical Foundations

To understand the theoretical foundations of Jungian analysis, one must realize that by 1951, Jung felt that both the science of psychology and everyday psychological experience were too limited in scope to permit the formulation of general theories. Above all, Jung, as a philosopher and psychologist, was committed to diversity of thought as well as of theoretical formulations. For example, he stated: "We must observe the rule that a psychological proposition can only lay claim to significance if the obverse of its meaning can also be accepted as true" (1966b, Vol. 16, p. 115). For example, he stated that the divergent viewpoints of Freud and Adler could be viewed as both partly wrong or instead as mutually complementary. He called particular attention to the fact that the observer's subjective experience—the individual's own philosophy of life (Weltanschauung)—must be taken into account when examining his or her theoretical propositions.

Assumptions About Human Nature

Jung believed that the individual can be understood only when both conscious and unconscious aspects of the human personality are taken into consideration. He often complained about the common assumption that "consciousness is the whole of the psychological individual." Instead, he proposed that "unconscious processes . . . must surely belong to the totality of the individual, even though they are not components of the conscious ego." The process of individuation represents the means by which a person becomes an "in-dividual" who is a separate, indivisible unity or "whole" (1968, Vol. 9, Part I, p. 275). The process itself involves interaction between the person's conscious and unconscious, which is ultimately driven by a striving for fulfillment that Jung believed to be inherent in every person. Individuation thus represents a process of integrating the world of consciousness and the inner world of the unconscious, resulting in "the assimilation of the ego to a wider personality" (1966a, Vol. 8, p. 292).

Assumptions About Conducting Jungian Analysis

No two Jungian analysts are likely to conduct Jungian analysis in exactly the same manner. Jungian analysis is a highly individual process. It is dialectical and consists of constant give-and-take between analyst and analysand. In the process, both analyst and analysand change. Jung was neither dogmatic nor highly systematic in his writings. At times he contradicted himself, although regarding his major concepts he was remarkably consistent (Singer, 1972). Because of the highly individual nature of Jungian analysis and because Jung, explicitly and by example, gave his followers permission to experiment and to develop new avenues of conducting analysis, the use of basic theoretical formulations in Jungian analysis varies considerably. Nevertheless, a brief overview of the most important theoretical concepts used in Jungian analysis is essential.

The structure of the psyche.   According to Jung, the psyche or personality has four basic components: ego, persona, shadow, and animus/anima. The ego in Jung's formulation is similar to the ego in Freudian psychoanalysis. As the center of consciousness, it perceives reality and differentiates the outer world from inner experiences, and it directs the flow of conscious behavior. The persona and the shadow represent two complementary parts of the personality. The persona represents the part of the personality that is presented to the outside world, usually in an effort to gain social approval. The persona may vary from one occasion to another, as one presents oneself differently according to specific circumstances and environments. The totality of a person's public representations makes up his or her persona. The shadow, on the other hand, represents aspects of the personality that the person chooses not to share with others because those aspects are seen as socially unacceptable, unpresentable, or even evil. Jung believed that joint consideration of persona and shadow is necessary to understand the full person. Moreover, he felt that, although the shadow is often a negative force, it also may have positive attributes (Mattoon, 1981).

The animus and anima are the respective contrasexual contents of the male and female. Jung proposed that women have a predominantly feminine consciousness and a predominantly masculine unconscious. He postulated that the reverse is true for men, who have a primarily masculine consciousness and a primarily feminine unconscious. Consequently, Jung is often credited as a pioneer in recognizing the existence of a masculine side in women and a corresponding feminine side in men. He proposed that the content of the animus for women is determined, in part, by women's experiences with men, particularly their fathers, whereas the content of the anima for men is determined by men's experiences with women, particularly their mothers. At another time, however, Jung proposed that the anima may be a psychic representation of the minority of female genes in a man's body, with the reverse being true for the animus (Bennet, 1967, p. 127). In addition, Jung acknowledged that archetypal images and cultural influences also determine the anima and animus.

Archetypes and the collective unconscious.   Defining and explicating the concept of the collective unconscious is often considered one of Jung's greatest contributions. Jung differentiated the personal unconscious, which is "made up essentially of contents which have at one time been conscious but which have disappeared from consciousness through having been forgotten or repressed," from the collective unconscious, whose contents "have never been in consciousness, and therefore have never been individually acquired, but owe their existence exclusively to heredity." Jung referred to the contents of the collective unconscious as archetypes, which he defined as "definite forms . . . which seem to be present always and everywhere" (Jung, 1968, Vol. 9, Part I, p. 42).

To Jung, archetypes represented patterns of perception, apprehension, and understanding common to all human beings. Through his extensive knowledge of ancient mythology and his deep interest in archaeology and anthropology, Jung became convinced that symbols and figures that appeared across the ages in different cultures around the world share identical content. This phenomenon, he believed, could be explained only by the concept of archetypes and the collective unconscious of humankind. Jung believed that the instincts (inborn, unlearned tendencies) originated in the collective unconscious and that they "form very close analogies to the archetypes, so close, in fact, that there is good reason for supposing that the archetypes are the unconscious images of the instincts themselves, in other words, that they are *patterns of instinctual behaviour*" (Jung, 1968, Vol. 9, Part I, pp. 43–44).

Hopcke (1989) suggested that a common misunderstanding is based on confusing the content of the archetype with the archetype itself. He proposed:

> The archetype itself is neither an inherited idea nor a common image. A
> better description is that the archetype is like a psychic mold into which
> individual and collective experiences are poured and where they take shape,
> yet it is distinct from the symbols and images themselves. (1989, p. 15)

The confusion between the content of the archetype and the archetype itself probably comes about because some archetypes are referred to by their symbolic or imaginal manifestations. For example, Jung introduced the archetypes of the Great Mother, the Father, the Hero, the Maiden, and many others, "whose personalization is necessary in order to bring the psychological power of the pattern into consciousness for greater awareness and individual growth" (Hopcke, 1989, p. 15).

Complexes and the personal unconscious.   Jung believed that the personal unconscious was made up largely of forgotten or repressed material from the person's past. He accepted Freud's explanation that repression occurs when a conscious experience is painful or unacceptable to the person. Moreover, Jung accepted Freud's idea that this repressed material is understandable only through the interpretation of dreams, or the discovery of the meaning of symptoms. To facilitate the discovery of this meaning, Jung introduced the concept of the complex to account for what he considered to be a set of unconscious impulses characterized by a peculiar and perhaps painful quality of feeling (Bennet, 1967, p. 27). Everybody has complexes, and they have entered into everyday discourse very much as Jung originally conceptualized them. Consequently, for example, a person may be said to have a complex about sex when sexually suggestive material produces emotional upset or when the person reads sexual innuendos into other people's perfectly inno-cent statements. When the emotionality associated with a complex becomes overwhelming, it produces psychopathology, which may include hallucina-tions and delusions (Mattoon, 1981, p. 116).

Attitude and function types.   One outgrowth of Jung's disagreements and eventual break with Freud was Jung's keen interest in understanding how the same empirical data can yield contrasting viewpoints on the meaning of those data. Using the occasion of Freud's earlier disagreements with Adler as a case study, Jung concluded that Freud and Adler possessed different character-ological attitudes or psychological types, with Freud being an extrovert and Adler an introvert. Jung believed that extroversion and introversion represent normal personality characteristics, which, by virtue of their constitutional nature, predispose individuals to see life differently. Thus, people described as introverts "are aware that *they* are moved by their reflection upon an external object, while others, the extraverts, attribute the change in themselves to the object, something outside themselves affecting them" (Bennet, 1967, pp. 51–52). Jung believed that every individual has characteristics of both extrover-sion and introversion and that one's basic psychological type is determined by the relative predominance of one attitude or the other.

Jung realized that a typology based on only two types was far too simple to capture meaningfully the great diversity of human individuality. His empir-ical and clinical studies eventually led him to propose a subdivision of each type according to the functions of thinking, feeling, sensation, and intuition. Jung did not view this classification as complete or comprehensive, but he considered it a valuable means of analyzing individual character and understanding individual differences, including psychopathology.

Implementing Jungian Analysis

Jung, unlike Freud, did not believe that his way of doing analysis was the only right way. Speaking before a convention of Swiss physicians in 1945, he stated:

> Psychotherapy can be practiced in a great variety of ways, from psychoanalysis, or something of that kind, to hypnotism, and so on right down to cataplasms of honey and possets of bat's dung. Success can be obtained with them all. (1966b, Vol. 16, p. 88)

Jung went on to state that any seemingly absurd remedy could, under the proper circumstances, be exactly the right treatment—if not for a particular neurosis, them for a particular patient. He stressed over and over the need to view each patient as unique and to treat the total human being, not some fictional abstraction called a neurosis. He also stressed the importance of the analyst's individuality in this process: as he wrote, "every psychotherapist not only has his own method—he himself is that method" (1966b, Vol. 16, p. 88). Although Jung was reluctant to commit himself to any specific set of methods in the conduct of analysis, he wrote extensively about the process, permitting the delineation of the major features of Jungian analysis.

The Stages of Analysis

When pressed to summarize and explain the process of what he preferred to call "analytical psychology," Jung reluctantly proposed that the process of analysis has four stages: confession, elucidation, education, and transformation (Jung, 1966b, Vol. 16, p. 55). He emphasized, however, that these stages did not represent any kind of universal, lockstep procedure to be followed in every case.

Confession.   Jung believed that having secrets and holding back emotions represented psychic misdemeanors, the consequence of which was neurosis. The beginning of all analysis should therefore be a full confession, including "not merely the intellectual recognition of the facts with the head, but their confirmation by the heart and the actual release of suppressed emotion" (Jung, 1966b, Vol. 16, p. 59). Noting that catharsis by itself had proved to be no panacea, however, Jung explained that confession needed to be followed by elucidation.

Elucidation.   Essentially, elucidation represents what Freud called "interpretation." Jung felt that elucidation was necessary to resolve the attachment (transference in Freud's theory) that developed in many cases between therapist and patient, especially after catharsis had occurred. He credited Freud with discovering these phenomena and with elucidating "man's shadow-side," opening the way to better self-understanding and the abandonment of "sentimentality and illusion" (Jung, 1966b, Vol. 16, pp. 64–65).

Education.   Just as Jung had found that confession and catharsis might be therapeutically adequate for a few patients with relatively minor problems, he determined that mere insight, occurring as a consequence of elucidation, might also be sufficient for "morally sensitive natures," but that it, too, would be inadequate for most. He observed that no amount of insight could really eliminate bad neurotic habits and replace them with other, better habits. He stated that new "habits are won only by exercise, and appropriate education is the sole means to this end. The patient must be *drawn out* of himself into other paths, which is the true meaning of 'education' " (Jung, 1966b, Vol. 16, p. 68). During the stage of education, substantive focus is on adaptation to social needs and demands.

Transformation.   In introducing his fourth stage of analysis, Jung again warned against assuming that it necessarily represents the final and only valid truth, although he acknowledged that it was intended to fill a gap left by the earlier stages. To Jung, the essence of the fourth stage is the mutual transformation that occurs as a consequence of the dialectical interaction between doctor and patient (or analyst and analysand in the terminology of modern Jungian analysis). In the process, the analysand discovers and develops a fulfilling individual life pattern based on a far more comprehensive self-understanding than would have been possible without analysis. Further, Jung claimed that the fourth stage also involved "the counter-application to the doctor himself of whatever system is believed in—and moreover with the same relentlessness, consistency, and perseverance with which the doctor applies it to the patient" (Jung, 1966b, Vol. 16, p. 73). The implication is that analysis is not just a method for treating patients, but also a means to the analyst's self-education and self-perfection.

Diagnosis

Jung did not place much faith in the utility of diagnosis, which he saw as an inappropriate extension of the medical model into the realm of psychology. At one point he reported that about one-third of his clients could not be shown to suffer from "any clinically definable neurosis," but simply could not find any direction or meaning in their lives (Jung, 1966b, Vol. 16, p. 41). Although modern Jungian analysts have generally continued Jung's rejection of standard psychiatric diagnosis, some consider certain types of assessment acceptable. For example, some Jungian analysts believe that at the start of analysis the patient's consciousness and character should be appraised. Central to this task is the assessment of type, which permits, among other things, the determination of the patient's typical response to his or her inner and outer world, as well as "the locus of the patient's failures at adaptation" (Quenk & Quenk, 1982, p. 161). Interviews or more structured tests, such as the Myers-Briggs Type Indicator (Myers, 1962), may be used for this purpose.

Dream Interpretation in Analysis

Jung considered dreams to be the key to the unconscious, and consequently the study of dreams and dream interpretation are central in Jungian analysis. Although Freud had called attention to the importance of dreams in tapping into the patient's unconscious, Jung departed in some important respects from Freud's notions about dreams and their interpretation. Most important, Jung felt that the dreams patients remember do not consist simply of manifest content that disguises latent meaning, as Freud claimed, but instead that dreams can be understood more directly if placed within the patient's own psychic context. As a consequence, Jung usually asked patients to produce "personal associations"—experiences and facts related to their own dream images—as a means of gaining insight into the meaning of dreams (Mattoon, 1981). Another important feature of Jungian dream interpretation is that, following the collection of dream material and the dreamer's personal associations, "archetypal parallels for understanding the deeper levels of the dream symbols" are examined in order to discover their similarity to motifs in myths, legends, and folktales, which in turn are important in identifying the archetypal basis of a dream (Hopcke, 1989, pp. 25–26).

Both Jung and Freud extensively reported many of the dream analyses they performed in their clinical work. These reports demonstrate, among other things, that the interpretation of dreams requires extensive clinical experience as well as a broad understanding of the dreamer's social and cultural context. Jung placed particular emphasis on the first dream a client reported, which he felt sometimes had special prognostic significance (Jung,

1966b, Vol. 16, p. 140). Jungian dream interpretation involves many other subtleties. For example, Jung felt that most dreams are compensatory in the sense that they counter the position of the conscious ego. Thus, a person who is sexually very inhibited may have dreams involving sexual promiscuity. In effect, then, through compensation the dream presents an alternative vision of the ego. Interpretation of the dream thus brings to consciousness aspects of the patient's circumstances that have been unknown or insufficiently emphasized by the waking ego (Hall, 1982, pp. 136–137).

In view of the central importance of dreams in Jungian analysis, one important concern during the initial stages of analysis is to obtain accurate dream reports. Although some people readily remember and report their dreams, others have trouble remembering any of their dreams. It is known, of course, that everyone dreams. Consequently, Jungian analysts sometimes instruct their patients on how they can maximize the remembering of dreams and thus produce accurate and detailed dream reports, which then facilitate analysis. For example, some analysts instruct the analysand to lie awake with eyes closed for a few minutes each morning after waking up, thus allowing time for the remembering and recording of dreams. Recording dreams is most important because dream memories fade very quickly. Analysands are urged to report as much detail as possible to reflect their actual dream memory (Hall, 1982).

Other Methods

Jung believed that analyzing dream material was a critically important method of gaining access to a person's unconscious. In addition, however, he felt that unconscious material could be reflected in fantasies, daydreams, play activity, art, and dance. Moreover, he agreed with Freud that a person's various accidents and errors may reflect the contents of the person's unconscious. In Jungian analysis, engaging the unconscious in interaction with consciousness (the ego) is of central importance. Modern Jungian analysts have therefore developed a number of methods that complement dream interpretation as a means of tapping the unconscious.

Active imagination. In the process of active imagination, the analysand, under the guidance of an analyst, produces a dialogue between the ego (the conscious mind) and the archetypes of the collective unconscious. Von Franz (1980, p. 88; quoted by Dallett, 1982, p. 177) suggested that active imagination involves four steps:

1. The analysand sets aside thoughts of ego-consciousness in order to give the unconscious a chance to enter.

2. As the unconscious begins to come in, usually in the form of fantasies, images, or emotions, these thoughts are written down or recorded in some other way.
3. As the ego reacts, a confrontation takes place with the unconscious material that has come up.
4. Conclusions are then drawn and put to work in the analysand's life.

Nonverbal methods of active imagination.   The use of drawing, painting, sculpting, dancing, and sand play have also been promoted by various Jungian analysts as means of revealing the unconscious. In his voluminous writings, Jung often made reference to the importance of painting, gestures, and movement, pointing out that what we call the psychic includes both the physical and spiritual dimensions (for example, Jung, 1966b, Vol. 16, p. 47). Some proponents of dance therapy, for example, have relied on a Jungian framework in exploring the utility of movement in contacting the unconscious or symbolic world of the individual (Chodorow, 1982). Because Jungian analysis is considered a dynamic, evolving process, a great deal of experimentation with new methods is generally promoted; Jung would have approved.

Means and Conditions for Implementing Jungian Analysis

Jung believed that analysis could not be anything but

> the product of mutual influence, in which the whole being of the doctor as well as that of his patient plays its part. . . . Hence the personalities of doctor and patient are often infinitely more important for the outcome of the treatment than what the doctor says and thinks. (Jung, 1966b, Vol. 16, p. 71)

Those who call themselves Jungian analysts and who are responsible for training new members of their profession appear to have taken to heart Jung's statements on training analysts.

The Analyst's Qualifications

Singer (1972, pp. 369–372) summarized the personal qualities of prime importance in candidates for training as Jungian analysts:

1. The candidate needs to have a sense of vocation—a fascination with the mysteries of the human soul.

2. A "sense of the symbolic dimension of life" is important in an applicant for training.
3. The candidate needs to be committed to a process of personal growth.
4. Personal integrity, the ability to take personal responsibility for one's behavior, and a willingness to be self-critical are considered important.
5. Flexible self-presentation is deemed desirable.
6. A real liking for people as individuals will help the candidate genuinely to accept others.
7. The capacity to reflect upon experience is a necessary core capacity.
8. A candidate for training as an analyst should have the psychic energy helpful in fulfilling the many requirements of the training process.
9. The applicant should have sufficient life experience to be considered seasoned, but also to be wise and compassionate.

The actual training in Jungian analysis is carried out by Jung Institutes, which exist in major cities in the United States and in many countries throughout the world. They are fashioned after the C. G. Jung Institute in Zurich, the original Jungian training center. Prior to the establishment of institutes in the United States, virtually the only way to become a Jungian analyst was to be analyzed by Jung or one of his close associates. Today, the International Association for Analytical Psychology sets training standards and accredits new Jung Institutes. Applicants who are accepted into Jungian training programs may have very diverse backgrounds, including medicine, psychiatry, and psychology, but also pastoral counseling, nursing, social work, art, literature, education, anthropology, mental health counseling, and human development. Candidates with insufficient background in psychotherapy and related areas may be asked to obtain additional training in those areas. It is important to note that the training offered by Jung Institutes does not qualify its graduates for professional state licensure or certification. Typically, individuals obtain an educational and experiential background that already qualifies them for such credentials prior to entering what may be considered postprofessional Jungian analysis training (Singer, 1972).

As a young doctor, Jung suggested to Freud "that every doctor should submit to a training analysis before interesting himself in the unconscious of his patients for therapeutic purposes" (Jung, 1966b, Vol. 16, p. 115). Thus, the concept of a training analysis was accepted by Freudian psychoanalysts even before it became an integral part of Jungian training. Jung took the position that a training analysis—that is, an analysis of the aspiring Jungian analyst—would eliminate the most serious obstacles in the way of psychological judgment: namely, individuals' personal and theoretical prejudices. He stated:

What the doctor fails to see in himself he will either not see at all, or will see grossly exaggerated, in his patient; further, he encourages those things to which he himself unconsciously inclines and condemns everything that he abhors in himself. (Jung, 1966b, Vol. 16, p. 115)

Modern Jung Institutes offer trainees a personal analysis as a means of furthering their self-understanding, but they also provide a rich background in Jungian theory and empirical research. Supervised clinical practice includes practice in the analysis of dreams and learning to deal with problems of transference and countertransference. Individual supervision of cases—or what is called control work—involves a supervising analyst reviewing the candidate's work with actual patients. It goes without saying, of course, that the collected works of Jung are required reading. In addition, however, students acquire specialized knowledge in the history of analytical psychology and in their understanding of archetypal images and symbols, as found in mythology, folklore, and religion.

Conditions for Conducting Jungian Analysis

As a predominantly verbal method, Jungian analysis does not necessitate any particular facilities above and beyond the quiet consulting room atmosphere required by most verbal psychotherapies. In contrast to Freudian psychoanalysis, Jungians eschew the couch and prefer face-to-face interactions with the analysand. Moreover, because Jungian analysis is assumed to be a dialectical procedure that changes both the analyst and the analysand, an atmosphere of equality is fostered. Clearly, the analyst-analysand relationship is unlike the doctor-patient relationship fostered in many other kinds of intervention.

Limitations of Jungian Analysis

Most methods of behavior change have their critics. Regarding Jungian analysis, however, the criticism has been particularly harsh, from psychoanalysts who have never forgiven Jung for breaking with their "father," Sigmund Freud, who at one time regarded Jung as the crown prince of psychoanalysis. For example, Fine (1979) in his history of psychoanalysis, reached the conclusion that Jung had "little merit" and accused him of more or less going off the deep end by pursuing astrology, occultism, alchemy, religion, and the lore of the East. Fine concluded by claiming that "had it not been for Freud, Jung would long since have been relegated to the limbo of history, like many of the mystics and alchemists for whom he had so much admiration" (p. 87). Like most criticisms, Fine's has some truth, but his overall position is absurd. Jung made lasting contributions to our understanding of the human psyche. Included in his contributions is a sensible perspective on the role of Jungian analysis within the context of other methods of behavior change. Freudian psychoanalysts would do well to give up their indefensible notion that their theories and methods represent the only truth.

Contraindications

Jung felt that some potential patients should not be analyzed. He reported one such case in some detail. Following his practice of paying a good deal of attention to his patient's initial dream, he analyzed the dream of a physician who wanted to enter analysis in order to become an analyst himself. After listening to the patient's dream, Jung concluded that essential features of the dream images represented a latent psychosis and that analysis might activate it. Consequently, he talked the patient out of taking up analysis (Jung, 1961, pp. 134–136). Jung generally was concerned about the possibility that analysis and the probing of a person's unconscious could produce psychosis. Consequently, Jung generally felt that latent psychosis was a firm contraindication for the use of analysis.

Hazards

Jung considered analysis an adventure. He marveled at the complexity of the human imagination and the fascinating symbolism often found in dreams. He emphasized, however, that in interpreting a dream or fantasy he made it a rule never to go beyond the meaning that could be apprehended and utilized by the patient. He was aware that if patients accept an interpretation that is beyond their grasp—that does not feel right to them—it may limit them in their development (1966b, p. 46).

Various practices of present-day Jungian analysts, particularly active imagination, produce circumstances that may be hazardous to some patients' well-being. Dallett (1982) suggested that the dialogue of active imagination involves "talking to the gods." In pursuing this process in analysis, she pointed out how important it is for the analysand to be rooted in external reality. Clearly, however, probing the depths of psychic experience through Jungian analysis is hazardous only to those who already have a tenuous hold on reality. The majority of others are likely to be enlightened and enriched by the experience.

The Effectiveness of Jungian Analysis

Wehr (1987), in his definitive biography of Jung, reported that shortly before his death, Jung stated: "I stand isolated between the faculties and must depend on someone else to seriously concern himself with this line of research, which up until now has happened only in a very few cases" (p. 486). If scientific research is defined by hypothesis testing and experimental control, Jung's lament has gone unanswered. If, however, research is defined by careful empirical observation, then a great deal of research has indeed been done in Jungian analytic psychology. This research consists primarily of the thousands of case studies that Jungian analysts have reported.

As his life was coming to a close, Jung was dismayed by the lack of attention his work had received. Interestingly, he had started his career by producing a good deal of highly regarded and influential research related to his studies in word association and his development of the word association test. Jung was quite familiar with the experimental methods of science, but he felt that many of his concepts, such as archetypes, simply were not subject to research using standard experimental methodology.

To his critics, though, Jung will always remain a mystic who strayed too far from the basic scientific disciplines to be taken seriously. In spite of these limitations, many parts of Jung's theories, such as his introversion/extroversion typology, have been examined scientifically and found to be valid. Mattoon (1981) concluded that Jung was a pioneer in bringing new areas of research to the attention of scientists and thereby opening up for scientific investigation phenomena that had been shunned by researchers. She also concluded that his formulations have proved fertile ground for generating hypotheses.

References

Bennet, E. A. (1967). *What Jung really said.* New York: Schocken Books.

Brookes, C. E. (1974). The group as corrective for failure in analysis. In G. Adler (Ed.), *Success and failure in analysis* (pp. 144–152). New York: Putnam.

Chodorow, J. (1982). Dance/movement and body experience in analysis. In M. Stein (Ed.), *Jungian analysis* (pp. 192–203). La Salle, IL: Open Court.

Dallett, J. (1982). Active imagination in practice. In M. Stein (Ed.), *Jungian analysis* (pp. 173–191). La Salle, IL: Open Court.

Fine, R. (1979). *A history of psychoanalysis.* New York: Columbia University Press.

Hall, J. A. (1982). The use of dreams and dream interpretation in analysis. In M. Stein (Ed.), *Jungian analysis* (pp. 123–156). La Salle, IL: Open Court.

Henderson, J. L. (1982). History and practice of Jungian analysis. In M. Stein (Ed.), *Jungian analysis* (pp. 5–26). La Salle, IL: Open Court.

Hopcke, R. H. (1989). *A guided tour of the collected works of C. G. Jung.* Boston: Shambhala.

Jung, C. G. (1961). *Memories, dreams, reflections.* New York: Pantheon.

Jung, C. G. (1966a). *Collected works, Vol. 8: The structure and dynamics of the psyche* (2nd rev. ed.). Princeton, NJ: Princeton University Press.

Jung, C. G. (1966b). *Collected works, Vol. 16: The practice of psychotherapy* (2nd rev. ed.). Princeton, NJ: Princeton University Press.

Jung, C. G. (1968). *Collected works, Vol. 9, Part I: The archetypes and the collective unconscious* (2nd rev. ed.). Princeton, NJ: Princeton University Press.

McGuire, W., & Sauerlander, W. (Eds.). (1974). *Briefwechsel: Sigmund Freud und C. G. Jung.* Frankfurt am Main: S. Fischer.

Mattoon, M. A. (1981). *Jungian psychology in perspective.* New York: Free Press.

Myers, I. B. (1962). *Manual: The Myers-Briggs Type Indicator.* Princeton: Educational Testing Service.

Quenk, A. T., & Quenk, N. L. (1982). The use of psychological typology in analysis. In M. Stein (Ed.), *Jungian analysis* (pp. 157–172). La Salle, IL: Open Court.

Singer, J. (1972). *Boundaries of the soul: The practice of Jung's psychology.* Garden City, NY: Doubleday.

Sullwood, E. (1982). Treatment of children in analytical psychology. In M. Stein (Ed.), *Jungian analysis* (pp. 235–255). La Salle, IL: Open Court.

Wehr, G. (1987). *Jung: A biography.* Boston: Shambhala.

CHAPTER 3

The Individual Psychology of Alfred Adler

■

Adler wrote that individual psychology's "foremost task is to establish among the broad masses of the people a firm basis for a sound, optimistic view and conduct of life, promoting the welfare of all" (cf. Ansbacher, 1992). Adler thus was concerned not only with treating his patients, but also with gaining a more profound understanding of human nature and improving the human condition through fostering "social interest." He proposed that these ends could be accomplished through education, as well as through treatment such as psychotherapy. In psychotherapy Adler tried to understand both the client's current behavior and his or her whole life situation. Adler's therapeutic approach focused particularly on the individual's subjective opinions, perceptions, and interpretations as the most valid basic data to use in therapy. Adler assumed that his patients' basic problems stemmed from feelings of personal inferiority, underdeveloped social interest, and a misguided striving for personal superiority. Accordingly, his therapeutic approach focused on examining carefully the client's basic approach to life (or life-style) and helping the client, through interpretation and explanation, to modify that life-style so that the client ultimately is able to demonstrate social interest through cooperative behaviors and activities directed toward others' welfare. Along the way, Adler felt the client would develop a more positive self-image, leave behind unwanted symptoms, and deal effectively with other people.

History of Individual Psychology

Like Freud, Adler was born the son of a Jewish merchant. Both lived in Vienna for many of their formative years; and both studied medicine at the Vienna Medical School, apparently attending some of the same lectures and being influenced by some of the same professors. Unlike Freud, however, Adler practiced general medicine for a number of years, serving mostly a lower middle-class population (Furtmueller, 1964). He was known for his down-to-earth manner with patients and students, but his keen scientific mind led him to study his patients and to begin formulating his later theory. Because Freud and Adler were contemporaries in the same city (Adler was 14 years younger than Freud), they knew of each other before they actually met. As a matter of fact, early on Adler came to Freud's defense in medical circles where Freud's ideas had not been at all well received (Orgler, 1963).

In 1902 Freud invited Adler and a few others to his home to discuss Freud's work, in the initial meeting of what was later to become the Vienna Psychoanalytical Society (Jones, 1955). Adler participated in the meetings of the society and later became a member of the editorial staff of *Zentralblatt fuer Psychoanalyse*, the main scientific journal of psychoanalysis, edited by Freud. All of Adler's biographers agree that Adler owed much to Freud and his groundbreaking work. At the same time, they have documented that Adler always was his own person, whose mind was as powerful as Freud's and who gradually developed formulations that conflicted with Freud's ideas, especially concerning the preeminence Freud assigned to his sexual theory. Apparently, however, not just scientific ideas separated the two men; their personalities were so different that they might be considered diametrically opposed. Adler easily communicated with common people, deeply cared about social issues, and earnestly desired to change the world for the better. Moreover, Adler believed that such change is possible. Freud, on the other hand, was passionate about his science, but could not bring himself to devote time to social causes. He was basically pessimistic about people and their prospects for betterment (Orgler, 1963).

Adler's formal break with Freud occurred in 1911 as a consequence of his refusing to accept Freud's doctrines unconditionally. Freud blamed Adler's ambition for the break. Characteristically, followers of Freud and Adler, respectively, continue to argue about who was at fault (for example, Fine, 1979; Orgler, 1963). By 1912 Adler published in German his important book, *The Neurotic Constitution*, and wrote to his friend Hertha Orgler, "With this book I have founded the school of Individual Psychology" (Orgler, 1963, p. 13). Adler devoted the remainder of his life to developing individual psychology. Much of his work took place in countries outside Austria where he had many followers virtually from the very beginning. Starting in 1926, he made several lecture tours to the United States, and in 1934, after Hitler had come to power in Austria, Adler left Vienna for good and made New York his home until his death in 1937 (Furtmueller, 1964).

Adler was convinced that faulty child-rearing—especially pampering the child—was the source of many problems in adulthood. This conviction led him to concern himself extensively with educating parents about proper child-rearing practices. The result was the establishment of many educational counseling centers, usually referred to as child guidance clinics in English translations, in association with the Vienna school system (Ansbacher, 1992). The success of these guidance clinics was so significant that by 1931, a school was developed, organized entirely around the principles of individual psychology. In later years, similar educational counseling centers and individual psychology schools were developed in many other countries around the world (Bottome, 1939).

Range of Applicability

Individual psychology is more than a therapy. Adler was extremely productive, both as a writer and lecturer, and he covered a great many subjects. As a physician, he was, of course, interested in treating his patients. Firmly committed to a holistic approach, he believed that treating the whole person—body and soul—was essential. He wrote extensively about problems of juvenile delinquency, prostitution, and homosexuality, as well as sexual deviance. Adler believed that his individual psychology could be useful in helping individuals to overcome these and many other kinds of problems, a belief he often demonstrated in public advice sessions (Orgler, 1963). He also believed that his individual psychology could be useful to ordinary people experiencing ordinary problems of life.

Adler's work as a pioneer in the field of prevention was recently summarized for the first time (Ansbacher, 1992). Adler was deeply concerned about the need to identify and properly treat various children at risk, including physically handicapped children, pampered or spoiled children, and neglected or hated children. He was tireless in conducting and promoting adult education and teacher training. All these emphases continue to this day in the broadly defined realm of Adlerian practice, undoubtedly due in part to the visionary nature of Adler's ideas, which anticipated many of today's social problems and issues.

Adler was not particularly systematic about prescribing specific steps in the course of therapy. Consequently, many different kinds of therapeutic approaches have been derived from his individual psychology. For example, a single book devoted entirely to "applications of Adlerian theory" (Nikelly, 1971) includes chapters on various types of individual interventions as well as on group psychotherapy, family counseling, and marital therapy, among other applications. Chapters are also devoted to "special syndrome techniques" (techniques for dealing with specific disorders) and to implementing Adlerian educational techniques. A survey of contemporary practices of Adlerian therapists (Kern, Yeakle, & Sperry, 1989) indicated that they conducted individual, group, family, couples, and extended family therapy; cotherapy and multiple therapist techniques; and multiple therapies. They also assumed therapeutic roles that varied from educator to role model, dynamic interpreter, facilitator, significant other, provider of support, and surrogate parent.

As Adler's stature grew in the scientific world and especially in Vienna, he devoted less time to treating patients and more time to education, especially of children. As an educator he became a social reformer, extending his pedagogical work to the education of teachers, whom he instructed in how to handle children's mistaken self-evaluations and how to help children to strive toward useful activity and to adopt "community feeling" or Gemeinschaftsgefuehl (Stepansky, 1983). Adler's individual psychology has also been influential in the field of women's psychology. Adler often wrote and lectured about his view that women had unfairly and unnecessarily been placed in a disadvantaged position. Among other things, he wrote eloquently against prostitution, which he interpreted as a consequence of viewing women as objects (Adler, 1927). It is not surprising that Adler's writings have been gaining increasing attention in the present age of feminism.

Theoretical Foundations
Basic Assumptions

Adler was one of the first psychologists to stress the unity of the person. By this concept, he meant that the individual is truly indivisible—that no aspect of the person can be viewed in isolation but instead must always be viewed in relation to the total person. Interestingly, Adler acknowledged his debt to South Africa's prime minister, General Jan Smuts (1961), whom many regard as the father of holistic psychology thanks to his book *Holism and Evolution*, originally published in 1926. Apparently, Adler was impressed by the integration and unity apparent in all human behavior. As a consequence, he developed the notion that individuals organize their behavior around a single unifying guiding theme, which he came to call the person's life-style.

Adler was deeply influenced by Hans Vaihinger's (1925) philosophy of the "As If." Consequently, he took the position that objective factors do not directly determine a person's behaviors, but rather that the individual's perceptions, thoughts, and interpretations concerning these events create internal causation of human behavior. Adler's position was thus largely phenomenological or subjective. Some writers have suggested that Adler's individual psychology is appropriately identified as subjective depth psychology, and that, whereas Freud should be identified as an objective psychologist, Adler should be identified as a subjective psychologist (Ansbacher & Ansbacher, 1956).

Assumptions About Human Nature

Adler's conception of human nature was more optimistic and more charitable than that of Freud, who saw humans as constantly struggling to tame their libidinal impulses. Adler's views were precursors of what today are considered existential and humanistic viewpoints. He saw humans as in a process of becoming—as creatures who strive tirelessly to give meaning to themselves and to life in general (Mosak, 1973). Adler asserted that because of the redeeming influence of social interest, individuals' drives can be guided in constructive directions, toward the common good (Adler, 1964a, p. 211). He (1964b) was eloquent in asserting the uniqueness of the individual:

> He does not relate himself to the outside world in a predetermined manner, as is often assumed. He relates himself always according to his own interpretation of himself and of his present problem. His limits are not only the common human limits, but also the limits which he has set himself. It is neither heredity nor environment which determines his relationship to the outside world. Heredity only endows him with certain abilities. Environment only gives him certain impressions. These abilities and impressions, and the manner in which he "experiences" them—that is to say, the interpretation he makes of these experiences—are the bricks which he uses in his own "creative" way in building up his attitude toward life. It is his individual way of using these bricks—or in other words, it is his attitude toward life—which determines his relationship to the outside world. (p. 67)

Ultimately, Adler felt that social interest was the key not only to individual mental health, but to human progress.

Key Concepts

Inferiority feelings and the striving for superiority.   Adler viewed life as a neverending effort directed toward overcoming, perfection, and success. He conceptualized the underlying psychological processes as running parallel to physical growth and as being an "intrinsic necessity of life itself." Adler liked to describe this as a movement "from minus to plus," or "from below to above" (Adler, 1956a, p. 103). Adler subsumed in his notion of striving for superiority all human activities designed to enhance security or to ensure self-preservation. He proposed that such striving is simply part of life, and that life without it would be unthinkable. In his later writings Adler acknowledged that this striving for superiority can take the form of a neurotic striving for self-enhancement and personal power. In the normal person, Adler felt that a striving for self-enhancement as part of the person's striving for superiority may well be quite functional because the normal person is not interested in self-aggrandizement, but in self-enhancement that is focused on reality, interest in others, and interest in cooperation (Ansbacher & Ansbacher, 1956, p. 112).

The individual's striving toward superiority may be rooted in inferiority feelings that represent part of the human condition. Adler originally traced this universal feeling of inferiority to the child's smallness and dependence in a world of adults. The child's feelings of inferiority and inadequacy ultimately emerge as the driving force in the child's efforts to overcome and to improve this inferior position. Adler proposed that the power of the urge to conquer weakness is directly related to the depth of the person's feeling of inferiority—the deeper the feeling of inferiority, the more powerful the urge to conquer it.

In addition to this conceptualization of "normal" inferiority feelings, Adler proposed that children born with inferior organs (a weakness or defect in any organ or organ system of the body) were thus suffering an organ inferiority, which invariably would lead to very severe or "abnormal" inferiority feelings and very probably to neurotic or deviant adjustment. Adler felt that neglected children, or those growing up in unfavorable environments, were likely to develop similar abnormal inferiority feelings and share the fate of children with organ inferiorities (Adler, 1956a, pp. 118–119). Another group of children likely to develop abnormal inferiority feelings Adler described as pampered children. Robbed of the opportunity to become competent in their own right and to stand on their own two feet, these children, when grown up, constitute "the most dangerous class in our community," according to Adler. Neither parents nor the community want to continue the pampering process indefinitely; therefore the successor of the pampered child is an adult who is no longer being humored and who believes that everyone is against him or her and acts accordingly (Adler, 1956b, p. 370). On balance, however, Adler viewed inherent feelings of inferiority as the underlying condition upon which striving for perfection and superiority are based, thus eventually leading to all human progress.

Social interest.   Adler placed great importance on the notion of social interest.

> We conceive the idea of social interest, social feeling, as the ultimate form of mankind, a condition in which we imagine all questions of life, all relationship to the external world as solved. It is a normative ideal, a direction-giving goal. This goal of perfection must contain the goal of an ideal community, because everything we find valuable in life, what exists and what will remain, is forever a product of this social feeling. (Adler, 1964d, p. 35)

Not surprisingly, Adler felt very strongly that enhancement of social interest in individuals was perhaps the most important goal for any educator or therapist. Conversely, Adler wrote at length about the association of lack of social interest (that is, an underdeveloped repertoire of positive social patterns) with neurotic behavior. Developmentally, Adler felt that social interest grew out of the love and affection a mother gives her child. Moreover, he felt that most humans can express love toward others, especially close family members, but that well-developed social interest facilitates the expression of this sentiment toward humankind as a whole. People who can so broaden their social interest can thereby in the most constructive manner overcome their own feelings of inferiority. Thus, the higher the degree of social interest in the person's striving toward perfection and superiority, the better the person's adaptation to life.

The style of life.   One of Adler's unique contributions was his conceptualization of the individual's style of life or life-style. Adler formulated a number of different ways of describing this life-style. Relating it to his holistic emphasis, he proposed that the totality of each individual (including thinking, feeling, acting, perception, conscious and unconscious mind, and personality) represents the person's life-style. Adler developed his concept of life-style as a dynamic one, which includes the individual's self-evaluations as well as the individual's unique ways of striving for the goal (of overcoming the complex of inferiority and moving toward perfection, superiority, and success) (Ansbacher & Ansbacher, 1956, p. 172).

The individual's life-style is created by the child, typically by the time the child is five years old, and it changes little after that point. Ultimately, it is the life-style that dictates everything a person does and everything the person feels. The unity of the personality springs from the manner in which the life-style guides and organizes a person's behavior. Interestingly, Adler felt that individuals may not be completely aware of their particular life-styles. He identified a number of different life-styles, pointing out that he did so for teaching purposes only because, in principle, each individual's life-style is unique to that individual and not duplicated exactly by anyone else. Among the different life-styles he identified, some lack social interest and therefore lead to neurotic or criminal behavior. A life-style that incorporates social interest, however, represents a socially useful type and is characterized by activity that benefits others (Adler, 1964b).

Implementing Individual Psychology
Preliminary Considerations

The impact of Adler's individual psychology reaches far beyond the conduct of psychotherapy. Although Adler was recognized during his lifetime, Freudians continued to dominate the psychiatric profession for several decades after Adler's death. In fact, the hostility of Freud and of his followers toward Adler, based on what they perceived as his disloyalty and ambition, surely delayed the wide acceptance of Adlerian thought into the world of professional practice. Interestingly, Adler's ideas on many subjects struck such responsive chords in so many who became acquainted with his ideas (in part through the child guidance clinics) that concepts such as birth order, inferiority complex, and life-style were accepted into everyday language even before they were accorded their rightful standing in the world of science and professional practice.

Although it is impossible to address all the various interventions that have been developed on the basis of Adler's individual psychology, it should be noted that his establishment of numerous child guidance clinics represented the first systematic effort to practice mental health prophylaxis (Brodsky, 1971). Adler was concerned with the prevention of psychopathology in children; hence, he spent much energy in promoting the education of parents and guidance in raising children in a way that would enhance their social interest and promote their well-being. The open manner in which Adler conducted his consultations in child guidance clinics is often considered a precursor of modern-day group psychotherapy (Ansbacher & Ansbacher, 1956, pp. 392–394). Adler extended his efforts to reach as many children as possible through the establishment of individual psychology schools, first in Vienna and later in other cities around the world. These schools were organized around the principles of individual psychology, devoted to fostering social interest and preventing neurotic behavior in children. In these applications of individual psychology, Adler anticipated the development of widely accessible community mental health centers as well as the growing importance of educational psychology.

Understanding the Patient

Adler believed that successful psychotherapy involved three processes (Ansbacher & Ansbacher, 1956, pp. 326–327):

1. Understanding the patient's life-style and the specific significance of the patient's symptoms, as well as the patient's specific problem situation.
2. Explaining the patient to herself or himself.
3. Strengthening the patient's social interest.

Although these three components can be distinguished from one another conceptually, it should be noted that to Adler these processes were closely related, and in practice they often merged.

The initial interviews.   Adler took the position that the therapist should conduct a careful and unhurried exploration during the initial psychotherapy session. He urged therapists to "suffer" through the patient's complaints and, if necessary, through the patient's incessant talking. Therapists should be tactful and inquisitive, asking for the history of symptoms and complaints. At the same time, however, Adler insisted that therapists should "strive to debase the great significance which the neurotic attributes to his symptoms" (Adler, 1964e, p. 192). Specifically, Adler felt that patients use their neurotic symptoms as "oversized safeguards" in protecting themselves against the dangers that they expect and incessantly seek to avoid, because of their feelings of inferiority. Moreover, Adler felt that patients have a tendency to use symptoms as excuses to rely on others to solve their problems and to permit them to cite "extenuating circumstances" for their failures (Adler, 1956c, pp. 263–266).

Early on in the treatment process, the patient must be helped to understand the importance of cooperation with the therapist and the fact that the patient ultimately must assume responsibility for himself or herself. Once the patient has had a chance to ventilate, to complain, and to detail symptoms, the therapist can direct the patient's attention away from the symptoms. The therapist subsequently attends to three areas of exploration, which Adler called the "three entrance gates to mental life" (Orgler, 1963, p. 21): first childhood memories, dreams, and the position of the child within the family constellation.

First memories and dreams.   Adler believed that people's earliest recollections have great significance for understanding the patient because they reflect the person's entire life-style. He felt that the more a patient is preoccupied with early childhood memories, the more important the earliest recollections are. In a way, early recollections represent a window into the person's inner life. Adler was quick to add, however, that the therapist's clinical skill and intu-ition are important tools in eliciting and understanding the significance of these earliest childhood recollections.

Adler acknowledged his indebtedness to Freud's groundbreaking work on the interpretation and significance of dreams, but he pointed out that others long before Freud had suggested that dreams represented a significant source of meaningful information about the person (Adler, 1956d, p. 357). He disagreed with Freud, moreover, about dreams representing fulfillments of infantile sexual wishes. Rather, Adler proposed that dreams represent important information that reveals the individual's life-style. In addition, he felt that, without being prophetic, dreams could serve a forward-looking and problem-solving function, because dreams in some ways can prepare the dreamer for the attainment of his or her goal or the solution of a problem (Adler, 1956d, pp. 357–359).

Family constellation and birth order.   Adler was the first theorist to call atten-tion to the ways the family environment differs for different children in a family. His concept of birth order has gained wide acceptance in the psycho-logical and psychiatric community. He made specific predictions about the position of children in the family based on the order of their birth. Specifically, he proposed that the entire family environment is different for the oldest and first born child, the second child, the youngest child, and the only child (Adler, 1956b, pp. 376–383). For example, he suggested that the first-born child may be first spoiled, then dethroned when the second child arrives. The second child, according to Adler, is always trying to catch up with the older child. The youngest child is never dethroned and, as the baby of the family, may be the most pampered but also the most stimulated, and thus may excel over his or her siblings. Finally, the only child has no sibling rivals and directs competition against the father. Only children are likely to be pampered by their parents, who are afraid of losing their child. Empirical evidence regarding these patterns of behavior related to ordinal position is not consistently supportive. Moreover, it should be understood that ordinal posi-tion was not viewed by Adler as the cause of certain behaviors, but rather as a circumstance of the child's existence to which the child has to respond (Shulman & Nikelly, 1971).

Adler realized, of course, that many things must be taken into consider-ation in applying these generalizations to the issue of birth order. Moreover, he wrote extensively about parental behaviors, which he felt could either have a great positive impact on the child or be very negative. He wrote at length and lectured about parental overindulgence and overprotectiveness, which he thought result in a pampered child, and on the other hand, about acts of rejection, which result in a neglected or hated child. Adler felt that the ideal parent is loving, supporting, and encouraging, and minimizes punishment and bribery. Adler did, however, acknowledge that some forms of punishment or discipline, used judiciously, can be helpful in certain situations (Adler, 1956b).

Although the concept of birth order is perhaps best known, it would be a mistake to assume that Adler focused on birth order to the exclusion of other family factors. Using Adler's concepts as their guide, Shulman and Nikelly (1971) have proposed:

> Family constellation is a term used to describe the socio-psychological configuration of a family group. The personality characteristics and the emotional distance of each person, age differences, order of birth, the dominance or submission of each member, the sex of the siblings, and the size of the family are all factors in the family constellation and effect the development of the personality. (p. 35)

In the process of getting to understand the client, the therapist elicits the client's family constellation and gets the client to express specific feelings and attitudes toward other members of the family. Ultimately, understanding a client's family constellation and birth order in the family illuminates the client's pattern of behavior. Through the process of reporting these features of family functioning and interrelatedness, the client also has a valuable opportunity to examine self-perceptions and important features of his or her social relatedness (Shulman & Nikelly, 1971, pp. 39–40).

Explaining Patients to Themselves

Adler proposed that patients develop an apperception schema, which represents a network of perceptions and thoughts that make up the person's picture of the world (Ford & Urban, 1963). Adler felt that psychiatric patients tend to have apperceptive schemas that dichotomize everything in a rather primitive way. He felt that as part of explaining the patient to him- or herself, it is necessary to identify this neurotic apperception schema as immature and untenable. In addition, Adler felt that, step by step, the unattainable goal of personal superiority needs to be uncovered and its purposive concealment unmasked. In the process, he felt that the patient's error of confusing a fictional world with the real, objective world needs to be made clear. After that, no longer needing to be superior to others, the patient's courage will increase, and connectedness with others will increase at the expense of giving up the previously dominant neurotic "private sense" (Adler, 1956e, p. 333).

In facilitating the patient's achievement of insight, Adler stressed that, on the one hand, it is useful to use a straightforward and direct method but that, on the other hand, simply telling patients the information about which they need insight is counterproductive. He offered as an explanation that "every neurotic is partly right" (Adler, 1956e, p. 334)—meaning that every neurotic life-style has a certain purpose and goal directedness, and even the skillful therapist can bring the patient around only gradually. In this connection, Adler specifically warned that the therapist should not be moralistic or unkind, and that patients should under no circumstances be offended.

Strengthening Social Interest

Adler felt that only through the development of social interest can patients overcome their selfish striving for personal superiority and adopt a healthy life-style. Behaviorally, to help a patient develop social interest is "to get the patient to interact and co-operate with other people, to implement his objectives in social contexts, and to behave in ways nonantagonistic to the interests and purposes of other people" (Ford & Urban, 1963, p. 357). Adler felt that awakening social interest in the patient requires cooperation and the therapist's genuine interest in the patient. The relationship between therapist and patient he saw as absolutely critical. Adler stressed that the key to this relationship is nonjudgmental acceptance, gentle explanation, and empathy. Moreover, he felt that the therapist's intuition and educated guesses can be important in moving the patient toward improvement and thus greater expression of social interest.

Means and Conditions for Implementing Individual Psychology
The Therapist's Qualifications

In some of his early writings, Adler referred to therapists as physicians. Moreover, he suggested, consistent with his holistic view of the person, that a thorough medical examination is appropriate at the beginning of therapy, although he indicated that it should be carried out in the presence of the family physician. One must keep in mind, however, the context of Adler's practice and his early background in family medicine. Clearly, the modern practice of Adlerian psychotherapy and counseling has grown beyond anything Adler could have envisioned in his days. Training in Adlerian practice has been kept vital over the years by a variety of institutions, in this country and abroad, devoted to the dissemination of Adlerian thought and training. Among the best-known have been the Alfred Adler Institutes in Chicago and New York. In addition, Alexandra Adler and Kurt Adler, both psychiatrists and children of the founder, served for many years in various leadership positions in the American Society of Adlerian Psychology and the International Society for Individual Psychology. Today, the North American Society of Adlerian Psychology conducts a major annual conference as well as numerous regional meetings that serve as a means for communication among diverse professionals who share Adlerian ideals and techniques in their work.

Evidence suggests that Adlerian therapists are becoming ever more diverse in terms of their preparation, as well as in terms of the issues and problems they frequently encounter in their professional practice. A 1972 survey by Kal found that 90% of those who identified themselves as being involved in Adlerian practice had doctorate-level education, with most of them having Ph.D.s and a smaller number having M.D.s. A more recent survey (Kern, Yeakle, & Sperry, 1989) found that only 48 percent of Adlerian clinicians had doctorate-level preparation. One reason for the lower percentage of doctorate-level professionals in Adlerian practice may be their emphasis on education, as well as their likely involvement in couples therapy, family therapy, and group therapy. Those types of interventions are frequently conducted as part of professional practices that emphasize marriage and family therapy, and are not explicitly devoted to severe psychopathology. Consequently, doctorate-level preparation is often not required in those settings.

Conditions for Conducting Individual Psychology

Adlerian psychotherapy does not require any facilities other than those necessary for verbal intervention methods in general—namely, a consultation room or office that affords relative quiet and privacy. Adler saw most of his individual psychotherapy patients in his physician's office. Special facilities are necessary, however, for group sessions—generally, a room that comfortably seats at least a dozen. Also, implementing the principles of individual psychology other than through some form of therapy requires considerably more in the way of facilities. For example, Adler attributed his ability to institute his principles in various types of school settings to the cooperation and support of the Vienna school superintendent, who was one of his friends. The broader the application of Adlerian principles, the more special facilities and supportive conditions are needed.

Limitations of Individual Psychology
Contraindications and Hazards

Adler believed that the application of his principles could result in real progress for humankind. He felt that strengthening the social interest could ultimately result in a reduction in prejudice and hatred, the elimination of wars, and the creation of a sense of universal community (Adler, 1964c). Adler considered application of the principles of individual psychology appropriate to all circumstances. He insisted, of course, on a thorough evaluation of the patient's overall condition to ensure that no obvious medical or physical needs were left unattended. Once satisfied, however, that such conditions were attended to, Adler insisted resolutely that no person should be given up as incurable or beyond help. Consequently, no firm contraindications to Adlerian therapy exist.

Adler identified many hazards that could keep people from developing the social interest they needed in order to be strong, adaptive, and satisfied with themselves and their life circumstances. These hazards, however, were not seen as part of therapy. Rather, Adler felt that inappropriate and dysfunctional behaviors on the part of parents, teachers, and other authority figures were most often to blame for the development of disordered behavior. He saw parental overprotection and overindulgence as a significant hazard, along with hatred and neglect of children. In school situations, he saw the teacher's behavior as potentially demotivating students. From Adler's perspective, counseling and psychotherapy were designed to reverse the effects of those mistakes. He admonished therapists never to upbraid or scold patients, never to put them down, and always to respect their uniqueness and their innate ability to develop social interest. He took the position that therapy or counseling can be hazardous only if applied insensitively or incompetently.

The Effectiveness of Individual Psychology

Individual psychology is distinguished by having its own journal, *Individual Psychology* (created in 1981 as the result of the merger of *Individual Psychologist* and the *Journal of Individual Psychology*). The journal is devoted to examining issues of Adlerian theory and to publishing research and commentary on the practice of individual psychology. Watkins (1983) conducted a review of research studies published from 1970 to 1981 in the *Journal of Individual Psychology*. He then compared the findings from that survey with a new survey of research studies published between 1982 and 1992 in its successor journal, *Individual Psychology* (Watkins, 1992). He found that research in the area of individual psychology had flourished during both survey periods, with an increase apparent in recent years.

Watkins found that major topics of research included birth order, social interest, early recollections, and life-style, as well as a wide variety of miscellaneous studies. Research on birth order was most popular (probably in part because the variable involved is easily quantifiable), whereas research on life-style was most limited (probably because it is a construct that is very difficult to assess) (Watkins, 1992). It is beyond the scope of the present chapter to report on specific research findings regarding Adlerian psychotherapy itself or individual psychology in general. Therapy outcome studies on Adlerian psychotherapy share many difficulties and complications in common with therapy outcome studies on other approaches—especially when those other approaches are comprehensive and complex, like Alderian psychotherapy. Nevertheless, the vigor of research in the area, and the continued enthusiasm of those who pursue Adlerian psychotherapy and other applications, attest to the considerable empirical support that has been generated for this approach, which gives every indication of ascending in popularity.

References

Adler, A. (1912). *Ueber den nervoesen Charakter: Grundzuege einer vergleichenden Individual Psychologie und Psychotherapie (The nervous character: Outline of comparative individual psychology and psychotherapy)*. Wiesbaden: Bergmann.

Adler, A. (1927). *The practice and theory of Individual Psychology*. New York: Harcourt Brace Jovanovich.

Adler, A. (1956a). Striving for superiority. In H. L. Ansbacher & R. R. Ansbacher (Eds.), *The individual psychology of Alfred Adler: A systematic presentation in selections from his writings* (pp. 101–125). New York: Basic Books.

Adler, A. (1956b). The origin of the neurotic disposition. In H. L. Ansbacher & R. R. Ansbacher (Eds.), *The individual psychology of Alfred Adler: A systematic presentation in selections from his writings* (pp. 366–383). New York: Basic Books.

Adler, A. (1956c). Neurotic safeguarding behavior. In H. L. Ansbacher & R. R. Ansbacher (Eds.), *The individual psychology of Alfred Adler: A systematic presentation in selections from his writings* (pp. 261–280). New York: Basic Books.

Adler, A. (1956d). Early recollections and dreams. In H. L. Ansbacher & R. R. Ansbacher (Eds.), *The individual psychology of Alfred Adler: A system-*

atic presentation in selections from his writings (pp. 351–365). New York: Basic Books.

Adler, A. (1956e). Understanding and treating the patient. In H. L. Ansbacher & R. R. Ansbacher (Eds.), *The individual psychology of Alfred Adler: A systematic presentation in selections from his writings* (pp. 326–349). New York: Basic Books.

Adler, A. (1964a). The differences between individual psychology and psychoanalysis. In H. L. Ansbacher & R. R. Ansbacher (Eds.), *Alfred Adler: Superiority and social interest* (pp. 205–218). Evanston, IL: Northwestern University Press. (Originally published in 1931.)

Adler, A. (1964b). Typology of meeting life problems. In H. L. Ansbacher & R. R. Ansbacher (Eds.), *Alfred Adler: Superiority and social interest* (pp. 66–70). Evanston, IL: Northwestern University Press. (Originally published in 1935.)

Adler, A. (1964c). *Social interest: A challenge to mankind.* New York: Capricorn Books. (Originally published in 1933.)

Adler, A. (1964d). On the origin of the striving for superiority and of social interest. In H. L. Ansbacher & R. R. Ansbacher (Eds.), *Alfred Adler: Superiority and social interest* (pp. 29–40). Evanston, IL: Northwestern University Press. (Originally published in 1933.)

Adler, A. (1964e). Technique of treatment. In H. L. Ansbacher & R. R. Ansbacher (Eds.), *Alfred Adler: Superiority and social interest* (pp. 191–201). Evanston, IL: Northwestern University Press. (Originally published in 1932.)

Ansbacher, H. L. (1992). Alfred Adler, pioneer in prevention of mental disorders. *Individual Psychology, 48,* 3–34.

Ansbacher, H. L., & Ansbacher, R. R. (1956). Individual psychology in its larger setting. In H. L. Ansbacher & R. R. Ansbacher (Eds.), *The individual psychology of Alfred Adler: A systematic presentation in selections from his writings* (pp. 1–18). New York: Basic Books.

Bottome, P. (1939). *Alfred Adler: A biography.* New York: Putnam.

Brodsky, P. (1971). Mental health prophylaxis. In A. G. Nikelly (Ed.), *Applications of Adlerian theory: Techniques for behavior change* (pp. 211–216). Springfield, IL: Charles C Thomas.

Fine, R. (1979). *A history of psychoanalysis.* New York: Columbia University Press.

Ford, D. H., & Urban, H. B. (1963). *Systems of psychotherapy: A comparative study.* New York: Wiley.

Furtmueller, C. (1964). Alfred Adler: A biographical essay. In H. L. Ansbacher & R. R. Ansbacher (Eds.), *Alfred Adler: Superiority and social interest* (pp. 311–393). Evanston, IL: Northwestern University Press.

Jones, E. (1955). *The life and work of Sigmund Freud,* Vols. 1, 2, 3. New York: Basic Books.

Kal, E. F. (1972). Survey of contemporary Adlerian practice. *Journal of Individual Psychology, 28,* 261–266.

Kern, R. M., Yeakle, R., & Sperry, L. (1989). Survey of contemporary Adlerian clinical practices and therapy issues. *Individual Psychology, 43,* 38–47.

Mosak, H. H. (1973). Preface. In H. H. Mosak (Ed.), *Alfred Adler: His influence on psychology today* (pp. v–vi). Park Ridge, NJ: Noyes Press.

Nikelly, A. G. (Ed.). (1971). *Applications of Adlerian theory: Techniques for behavior change.* Springfield, IL: Charles C Thomas.

Orgler, H. (1963). *Alfred Adler, the man and his work: Triumph over the inferiority complex.* New York: Liveright.

Shulman, B. H., & Nikelly, A. G. (1971). Family constellation. In A. G. Nikelly (Ed.), *Applications of Adlerian theory: Techniques for behavior change* (pp. 35–40). Springfield, IL: Charles C Thomas.

Smuts, J. C. (1961). *Holism and evolution.* New York: Viking Press. (Originally published in 1926.)

Stepansky, T. E. (1983). *In Freud's shadow: Adler in context.* Hillsdale, NJ: Analytic Press.

Vaihinger, H. (1925). *The philosophy of "as if": A system of the theoretical, practical and religious fictions of mankind.* New York: Harcourt Brace Jovanovich. (Originally published in 1911.)

Watkins, C. E., Jr. (1983). Some characteristics of research on Adlerian psychological theory, 1970–1981. *Individual Psychology, 39,* 99–110.

Watkins, C. E., Jr. (1992). Research activity with Adler's theory. *Individual Psychology, 48,* 107–108.

PART II

Behaviorist Approaches

CHAPTER 4

....

Systematic
Desensitization

....

■

S ystematic desensitization is a method to treat neurotic anxiety and fear (phobias). Wolpe described it as "one of a variety of methods for breaking down neurotic anxiety-response habits" (Wolpe, 1973, p. 95). Systematic desensitization has been used most commonly in the "treatment of fears evoked by situations that do not lend themselves to 'being handled,' " such as classical phobias and many social fears (Wolpe, 1990, p. 156).

History of Systematic Desensitization

The history of systematic desensitization is best understood as part of the history of behavior therapy in general. That history is embedded in the development of psychology as a science. Krasner (1990) argued that the behavioral movement, which provides the scientific basis for behavior therapy, should be viewed as a scientific and social movement that evolved in the context of the social, political, cultural, educational, and economic forces of the early 20th century. These forces were in turn deeply affected by positivistic philosophy, which rejected metaphysics and focused on the discovery of facts. Although the earliest publications on behavior therapy are from the 1920s (for example, Jones, 1924; Watson & Rayner, 1920), Krasner (1971) argued that no fewer than 15 streams of development in the field of psychology converged during the 1950s and 1960s to produce what is now called behavior therapy.

Systematic desensitization represents one widely used method within behavior therapy. It is based primarily on the work of Joseph Wolpe, who recently recounted how he came to discover the therapeutic potential of combining reciprocal inhibition and progressive relaxation into a method now called systematic desensitization (1990, pp. 150–152). Specifically, he emphasized that the technique had its roots in his early experimental work (Wolpe, 1948, 1952, 1958). On the basis of his laboratory work with animals, he began to work with patients to help them overcome anxiety by performing acts antagonistic to the experience of anxiety. Originally, these antagonistic actions were assertion responses, but Wolpe discovered that they often did not work very well. Eventually, he learned about Jacobson's work on progressive relaxation (Jacobson, 1938), which he eventually adapted to serve as an anxiety-inhibiting procedure.

In his efforts to expand the applicability of this new method, he experimented with getting patients to use imaginary situations to produce anxiety, because the application of any therapeutic technique to severely anxious patients in real life (in vivo) situations is very difficult. Wolpe discovered that anxiety produced in this manner could be diminished progressively when patients were asked to repeatedly imagine mildly anxiety-producing situations while in a state of deep muscle relaxation. He then found that increasingly threatening imagined situations could "be divested of their anxiety-evoking potential" in this manner (1990, p. 152). Wolpe maintained that this positive change (the extinction of the anxiety response) can be transferred rather routinely from imagined situations to corresponding real-life ones. Some studies, however, have compared the effectiveness of systematic desensitization in real life (in vivo) and in imagination, and have found the former to be more effective (Dyckman & Cowan, 1978; Sherman, 1972).

Range of Applicability

The decision to use systematic desensitization can be made only after careful behavioral analysis. This analysis typically involves obtaining from the patient a great deal of personal data, as well as information about the circumstances surrounding the anxiety or fear responses to be eliminated. The nature of the presenting complaints is a critical variable in determining whether systematic desensitization is a proper method of treatment. Generally, the method is indicated when the presenting complaints have as their central feature an anxiety or fear response to situations or stimuli that are not dangerous to the patient and when the undesirable responses are not based on cognitive misconceptions, such as beliefs about the phobic stimulus that are incorrect (Foa, Steketee, & Ascher, 1980).

Specific phobias are probably the most likely candidates for treatment by systematic desensitization. Such phobias are generally treated most effectively when the fear is of a specific situation or object. If the fear is relatively non-specific, such as free-floating anxiety, systematic desensitization may not be effective. Systematic desensitization may also be applied in the treatment of social anxieties, especially when assertiveness training alone has been unsuccessful. Systematic desensitization has also been used in the treatment of sexual dysfunctions, including erectile failure and orgasmic dysfunction (Foa, Steketee, & Ascher, 1980).

Theoretical Foundations
Assumptions About Human Nature

Wolpe has little to say about normal development, having defined psychiatry as the study of maladaptive human habitual behavior. In this context, Wolpe has taken the position that adaptive behavior satisfies needs; offers relief from pain, discomfort, and danger; and avoids unnecessary expenditure of energy (1990, p. 8). Wolpe believes that not all unsuccessful behavior is maladaptive and that individuals generally discontinue unsuccessful behaviors as soon as they discover that they do not work to achieve their objectives. Only when unsuccessful behaviors persist do they become burdensome and require treatment. Wolpe's conception of normal behavior appears to be based on the view that behavior occurs by means of stimulus and response sequences. In this view, any response is the consequence of the situational and response events preceding it; by the same token, every response is an antecedent or stimulus to every other response following it. It is readily apparent that the basic paradigm Wolpe uses to account for normal behavior is taken from learning theory, specifically Hull's (1943, 1952) reinforcement theory. Hull's work, in turn, was based primarily on the work of Pavlov, the famous Russian physiologist and psychologist, who is credited with the discovery of the classical or respondent model of conditioning.

Wolpe has acknowledged that some behaviors are organically based, and others based on learning. He has focused exclusively on learned behaviors, since behavior therapy in his view is applicable only to those behaviors. Moreover, Wolpe's focus has been mostly on how learning occurs, rather than on what is learned. The sequence of learning is assumed to be identical for all individuals and for all kinds of responses. Basically, responses are evoked by what he calls sensory stimuli, and if responses are followed by a reduction in the intensity of neuroexcitation (drive reduction), learning takes place. The amount, strength, and speed of the learning that takes place depends on a number of factors, such as the number of times the sequence is repeated, the intensity of the underlying drive, and the timing of reinforcements. In any case, the result of learning is the formation of habits, which to Wolpe represent recurring ways of responding to a particular stimulus.

Assumptions About Maladaptive Behavior

When the habits acquired in this manner are maladaptive, behavior therapy is the proper treatment. Wolpe classified such maladaptive behaviors into five syndrome categories:

1. Neuroses, which "are persistent maladaptive habits that have been acquired in anxiety-generating situations and in which anxiety responses are almost invariably central."
2. Maladaptive learned habits not associated with anxiety, which include nail-biting, enuresis, chronic tardiness, and some others.
3. Psychopathic personality (notwithstanding a possibility of biological predisposition, which Wolpe acknowledged, he maintained that the particular patterns of antisocial behavior are learned).
4. Drug addictions (different, in Wolpe's view, from the other maladaptive habits because many types of addiction create biological changes along with the learned maladaptive behaviors, complicating the unlearning process).
5. Learned behavior of schizophrenics (again, Wolpe acknowledged a likely biological basis for schizophrenia but maintained that some characteristic maladaptive habits of schizophrenic patients are learned). (Adapted from Wolpe, 1990, pp. 8–10)

Systematic desensitization is not, of course, the treatment of choice for all these maladaptive habits. As a matter of fact, only neuroses—maladaptive habits learned in an anxiety-generating situation—are appropriately treated through systematic desensitization. Anxiety occupies an important central role in Wolpe's ideas about the acquisition of maladaptive behaviors. Anxiety—to use another word, fear—Wolpe has defined operationally as "the individual organism's characteristic pattern of autonomic responses to noxious stimulation" (Wolpe, 1990, p. 23). Both normal fear and neurotic fear develop on the basis of classical conditioning and, in some cases, on the basis of cognitive learning. Wolpe has been very insistent, however, on the point that his definition of fear is based on an *unconditioned* response.

Assumptions About Conducting Systematic Desensitization

Since neurotic habits are learned through the establishment of a link between an initially neutral stimulus and an anxiety response, the obvious treatment goal is to dissociate the stimulus from the anxiety response, thereby undoing the previous maladaptive learning (Foa, Steketee, & Ascher, 1980). Wolpe has demonstrated that the mechanism of reciprocal inhibition is effective in unlearning neurotic anxiety, and that deep muscle relaxation can be used as the response that should occur in antagonism to the response of anxiety.

Reciprocal Inhibition.   According to Wolpe (1976), Sherrington (1906) first noted the phenomenon of reciprocal inhibition. Originally, reciprocal inhibition was noted in relation to reflex activity, but it was later also demonstrated for autonomous responses and other physiological systems. Since emotionality has definite physiological correlates, reciprocal inhibition of emotions, such as anxiety, can also be demonstrated. Wolpe capitalized on the phenomenon of reciprocal inhibition by realizing that "when a stimulus is conditioned to a response, it is simultaneously conditioned to inhibitions of the antagonist of that response" (p. 13). In order to demonstrate how this phenomenon applied in treating neuroses, Wolpe conducted a number of now classic experiments in which he experimentally produced neurotic behavior in cats. He demonstrated that the experimental environment itself could become conditioned to be an elicitor of intense anxiety. This anxiety in turn caused the animal to refuse available food, because eating and the experience of anxiety are reciprocally inhibitory. Wolpe then desensitized the animal by offering food to the animal in a very dissimilar environment initially, then gradually making the environment more similar to that in which the conditioned anxiety occurred. Eventually the animal was able to eat in the environment that had previously elicited intense anxiety (Wolpe, 1952, 1958). Wolpe derived from these experiments his reciprocal inhibition principle of psychotherapy, which stated that "an anxiety response habit can be weakened by evoking a response incompatible with anxiety in the presence of the anxiety evoking stimulus" (1976, p. 17).

Muscle Relaxation.   Since feeding as a reciprocal inhibitor of anxiety had been shown to be effective only with animals and in children, Wolpe proceeded to search for another response that would reciprocally inhibit anxiety-produced maladaptive habits in adults. He adapted the muscle relaxation procedures developed by Jacobson (1938), who had demonstrated that deep muscle relaxation produced physiological responses diametrically opposed to those produced by anxiety. Wolpe was attracted to Jacobson's method in part because Wolpe determined that when counterposed to anxiety-evoking stimuli, relaxation responses diminished the anxiety responses evoked by those stimuli. For example, Wolpe reported a study by Van Egeren, Feather, and Hein (1971), who found that with repetitions of a phobic stimulus, the magnitude of effects decreased progressively in those subjects in whom relaxation had been induced, but remained the same in unrelaxed subjects.

Implementing Systematic Desensitization

In the practice of systematic desensitization, the therapist serves as the behavioral expert who determines how the patient's troublesome behaviors are conceptualized and how they should be remedied. The overall goal is to eliminate troublesome behaviors related to anxiety and to permit patients to go through life without the frequent and disruptive occurrence of anxiety or fear in their lives. In order to accomplish these objectives, the therapist must gather a significant amount of information prior to reaching a decision about whether systematic desensitization is appropriate. Moreover, once the decision is made that systematic desensitization is, indeed, the treatment of choice, further information needs to be collected prior to its implementation.

Behavior Analysis

Wolpe defines behavior analysis as "the process of gathering and sifting information for use in the conduct of behavior therapy" (1990, p. 59). He stressed that the behavior therapist must be objective as well as empathic and sensitive to suffering. One of the first determinations that the therapist must make is whether the patient's complaints are attributable to learning, and hence subject to treatment through behavior therapy, or whether they have an organic basis requiring some form of biological treatment. Once the therapist is satisfied that the patient's complaints are based on maladaptive anxiety, the therapist must identify the stimuli that trigger such anxiety. Wolpe stressed that therapists can be trained to obtain the necessary information by interviewing patients and getting them to complete various data-gathering instruments.

Wolpe has often emphasized the importance of thoroughness in the behavior analysis procedure. He suggested that after obtaining information about the patient's presenting complaints, the therapist should take a careful background history—including basic facts about the patient's early family life, the patient's education, the patient's sexual history and current sex life, and the patient's present social relationships. In addition, Wolpe (1990) recommended the administration of two specific data-gathering instruments: (1) the Willoughby Personality Schedule (Willoughby, 1932), a 25-item questionnaire dealing with neurotic problems; and (2) the Fear Survey Schedule (Wolpe & Lange, 1969), which asks patients to indicate on a 5-point scale how disturbed they become in a number of stimulus situations to which fear is unadaptive. A third instrument, the Bernreuter Self-Sufficiency Inventory (Bernreuter, 1990), is also recommended for occasional use because it may be helpful in identifying overdependence associated with agoraphobia and low self-sufficiency, which makes it difficult to follow instructions in self-assertion training.

Once behavior therapy has been established as appropriate for an individual, and the therapist has gathered initial background information, the therapist can usually determine whether systematic desensitization is the appropriate treatment. At that point, it becomes critical to identify the specific phobia, as well as the various dimensions of the maladaptive anxiety or fear behaviors that are the focus of concern. Particularly important is the process of gathering information about the degree of anxiety experienced in a large variety of situations. For this purpose, Wolpe (1973, p. 120) developed the concept of Subjective Units of Discomfort, or SUDs, which allows patients to quantify the magnitude of anxiety experienced in any given situation. Wolpe suggested that this procedure be introduced as follows:

> Think of the worst anxiety you can imagine and assign to it the number 100. Then think of being absolutely calm—that is, no anxiety at all—and call this zero. Now you have a scale of anxiety. At every moment of your waking life you must be somewhere between 0 and 100. How do you rate yourself at this moment? (Wolpe, 1990, p. 91).

The SUDs subjective anxiety scale is used throughout the systematic desensitization procedure, as will be discussed in the following sections. The main benefit of using the SUDs scale is the opportunity it affords the therapist to obtain a quick assessment of the patient's present state of anxiety (or its opposite, relaxation), or the patient's assessment of the anxiety-producing potential of any particular stimulus.

Hierarchy Construction

Once the therapist and client have established a good working relationship and the therapist has determined that the patient's maladaptive habits are anxiety-related, the therapist is in a position to explain to the client how his or her neurotic anxiety was learned and how behavior therapy works. When systematic desensitization has been identified as the appropriate form of treatment, the therapist can then introduce the task of constructing an anxiety hierarchy. An anxiety hierarchy is a rank-ordered list of anxiety-producing stimuli that have a common theme. At the top of the list is the stimulus that evokes the greatest fear or anxiety; that which evokes the smallest amount of anxiety is at the bottom. Wolpe pointed out that the theme of a patient's anxiety hierarchy usually concerns something extrinsic to the patient; examples are the common phobias of spiders, furry animals, snakes, or rejection from others. Some themes may, however, be internal, such as a feeling of losing control.

The construction of hierarchies is a collaborative task that must be completed by client and therapist. Various kinds of information may be used in completing this task, including the patient's history and information from the data-gathering instruments introduced earlier. When more than one theme is identified in examining the reported sources of neurotic disturbance, the therapist classifies them. Hierarchies may then be constructed for each thematically related group of anxiety-producing stimuli. The hierarchy's essential feature must always progressively increase in intensity or salience as one works up the hierarchy. For example, in constructing a hierarchy of claustrophobic anxiety, the essential feature—amount of confinement—must progressively increase as one moves up the hierarchy (Wolpe, 1990, p. 63).

Relaxation Training

As discussed earlier, deep muscle relaxation is used most frequently as the counter-anxiety response in systematic desensitization. Wolpe has acknowledged, however, that in some circumstances, alternative ways of producing calmness (such as introducing a counter-anxiety response) may be appropriate. These alternative ways include autogenic training, transcendental meditation, yoga, and biofeedback (1990, pp. 195–196). When relaxation is used, the preferred method is that developed by Jacobson (1938), although Wolpe adapted the training procedure to be much shorter than the procedure Jacobson originally recommended. Wolpe has reported that instruction in relaxation is completed in about six lessons, each of which takes about one-third of a session (1990, p. 6). The construction of anxiety hierarchies is accomplished, in most cases, concurrently with training in relaxation.

Training in deep muscle relaxation can be conducted in a number of different ways. Several common elements, however, should be noted. First, the therapist explains to the patient how relaxation works in countering anxiety and why it is important to learn deep muscle relaxation. Second, the patient is informed about the use of relaxation as part of the desensitization procedure and the necessity for participating in a sequence of training activities. Third, the therapist explains and demonstrates the basic relaxation training procedure. The procedure involves the patient's repeatedly tensing and then relaxing specific muscles while the therapist instructs the patient to pay careful attention to how the sensations differ from a tensed muscle to a relaxed one. Fourth, in successive sessions the patient is instructed in relaxing different muscle groups. Wolpe has reported that he prefers to start by helping the patient to relax the muscles of both arms during the initial session, in part because the arms are convenient for demonstrating the practice of muscle relaxation. In the second lesson, Wolpe proceeds to the muscles of the head and neck, except for the masseters and temporales, which are involved in biting down on one's teeth. Also included in the third lesson is relaxation of the muscles of the tongue. The fourth lesson involves relaxation of the neck and shoulders, and the fifth lesson deals with learning to relax the muscles of the back, abdomen, and thorax. Finally, the sixth lesson involves the muscles of the legs and feet (Wolpe, 1990, pp. 156–160).

Virtually all patients can be taught to achieve some degree of muscle relaxation. Most report a feeling of calmness and relaxation—some to such an extent that they have to be reassured about falling asleep. Some patients, however, report feeling little difference when they are in a relaxed state, and in those instances using an objective measure of relaxation such as an electromyogram may be helpful. Usually, however, such a measure is unnecessary.

The Desensitization Procedure

The actual desensitization procedure can commence once the patient has mastered the relaxation procedure and a satisfactory hierarchy of anxiety-producing stimuli has been constructed. The procedure is quite straightforward. Basically, it involves presenting to the patient the lowest item on the anxiety hierarchy while he or she is relaxed. The patient is then asked to raise a finger when the image is clear. The therapist then lets the scene remain for 5 to 7 seconds, after which the therapist instructs the patient to stop the scene and to indicate in SUDs how much anxiety the scene produced. If the patient indicates that the scene produced some anxiety (measured in SUDs), the patient is told to relax again, and the procedure is repeated until the scene can be imagined without evoking any anxiety (zero SUDs). At that point, the next item on the anxiety hierarchy is presented. The underlying assumption is that in a properly constructed hierarchy, generalization will occur so that, as relaxation can be maintained while imagining one scene from the hierarchy, the succeeding scene, while still evoking some anxiety, will evoke less than previously.

The duration of desensitization varies greatly depending on how many hierarchies are used in treating a given patient and how many presentations of a scene are needed to eliminate the anxiety associated with it. Some patients with multiple phobias may undergo desensitization to as many as four hierarchies in a single therapy session. Wolpe has reported that three or four presentations of a given scene are often sufficient to bring the anxiety down to zero, but sometimes 10 or more sessions may be needed. Moreover, while some patients may recover in 6 sessions, others may require 100 or more sessions to remove a phobia (Wolpe, 1990, pp. 175–176).

Means and Conditions for Implementing Systematic Desensitization
The Behavior Therapist's Qualifications

Individuals who use systematic desensitization as part of their therapeutic repertoire are, by definition, behavior therapists. Eysenck (1959) popularized use of the term *behavior therapy* to describe therapeutic methods that applied both classical and operant conditioning principles. In a recent review of training in behavior therapy, Alberts and Edelstein (1990) noted, however, that great diversity of opinion exists about the knowledge and skills essential for behavior therapists. For example, they note that Wolpe and Boynton (1978) described behavior therapists as creative, empirically based, behavioral problem solvers. Although there is considerable diversity in the training of behavior therapists, most training takes place in graduate programs with psychology as their core discipline. Moreover, most training programs rely on both academic training and clinical, or hands-on, learning experiences to convey a basic knowledge of behavior therapy. Alberts and Edelstein recommended that students of behavior therapy become "scientist-practitioners whose domain of study includes the behavior of both the client *and the student*" (1990, p. 224). Perhaps most important, they urged that training programs demonstrate their efficacy by demonstrating the competence of trainees.

Although competence in the technology of behavior change is essential in a successful behavior therapist, no less an authority than Wolpe (1990) has noted that nonspecific therapy effects, due to the therapist's emotional impact on the patient, play a significant role in ultimately determining the success of any intervention. In addition to noting that behavior therapists should be sensitive to the patient's suffering, he proposed that the therapist must be trusted and viewed as a wise and competent person. In the language of behavior therapy, Wolpe noted that nonspecific therapy effects are "due to the inhibition of maladaptive anxiety by positive emotions that the therapist engenders in the patient" (1990, p. 334). Thus, in addition to technical competency, behavior therapists must have certain personal attributes in order to be effective. In addition, if behavior therapists are psychologists or physicians, they must also be properly licensed by the appropriate licensing authority.

Conditions for Conducting Systematic Desensitization

No specific requirements for the conduct of systematic desensitization exist beyond those common to other types of verbal psychotherapy. Obviously, an office that offers sufficient comfort and quiet to permit relaxation training is necessary. Most practitioners also would want to have either a couch or comfortable chair to facilitate this procedure. If the desensitization procedure is carried out by a licensed physician, Wolpe suggested that when relaxation training is inadequate, drugs such as diazepam or codeine may facilitate relaxation. In cases of pervasive anxiety, Wolpe recommended the use of carbon dioxide-oxygen mixtures in order to decrease anxiety (Wolpe, 1990). These procedures require additional equipment and facilities but are generally not considered essential for the large majority of cases. Some practitioners also like to use instrumentation for psychophysiological monitoring in order to have an objective measure of relaxation.

Limitations of Systematic Desensitization
Contraindications

Wolpe apparently does not exclude any type of patient from treatment by reciprocal inhibition beyond specifying that the disorder to be treated should be anxiety-related and learned. By implication, people whose disordered behavior is caused organically (for example by a brain lesion) should not be treated using systematic desensitization. People who, for one reason or another, are unable to participate in the relaxation training or to provide sufficient information for the construction of anxiety hierarchies are clearly also unsuitable for systematic desensitization. Such people would include severely developmentally disabled individuals and some individuals whose physical conditions preclude deep muscle relaxation—although for the latter, use of alternative methods such as hypnosis may help the patient achieve a state of calm.

Hazards

No hazards are specifically associated with the procedure of systematic desensitization. Indirect hazards include inappropriate application of systematic desensitization with individuals who, for reasons just noted, cannot benefit from it. Incompetent use of systematic desensitization could also be a hazard—for example, if desensitization is attempted using misleading or irrelevant hierarchies. When these problems are not discovered and corrected, patients may, in fact, become persuaded that systematic desensitization, which is possibly their only realistic chance of overcoming a serious phobia, will not work for them.

Ascertaining Success

Systematic desensitization is considered successful if the most anxiety- or fear-producing item of the anxiety hierarchy can be presented while the patient's SUDs level remains at zero. In other words, when the patient experiences no anxiety at all when presented with a vivid description of the previously anxiety-producing stimulus, systematic desensitization is successful. As noted previously, the number of presentations and the number of sessions required varies significantly with the nature of the problem and the patient's characteristics. Wolpe has reported that the median number of sessions per patient was 10, and the mean number of sessions per fear was 11.2 (Wolpe, 1990, p. 186). Frequently, therapists insist on follow-up evaluation in order to verify generalization from the therapy situation to real-life situations. Moreover, some therapists do follow-up sessions in order to ascertain the permanence of the obtained change.

The Effectiveness of Systematic Desensitization

One key early review of the effectiveness of systematic desensitization was conducted by Paul (1969). It consisted of a summary of 75 "overwhelmingly positive" studies regarding the effectiveness of systematic desensitization. Unfortunately, however, of these, only eight were studies controlled for a common problem of outcome studies—namely, that therapist characteristics and treatment techniques can become hopelessly confounded. Nevertheless, those ten studies were all found to provide solid evidence for the effectiveness of systematic desensitization.

Wolpe (1990) reported many empirical studies, as well as numerous case studies, demonstrating the effectiveness of systematic desensitization in treating a great variety of phobias. Wolpe also addressed some factors that may cause systematic desensitization to fail. Generally, these factors have consisted of some form of difficulty in achieving relaxation, misleading or irrelevant hierarchies, or some difficulty in imagery. Overall, however, systematic desensitization has generally been shown to be a remarkably effective treatment. Kazdin and Wilcoxin (1976) have summarized this view by observing that systematic desensitization is so well established that the evidence of its efficacy is virtually overwhelming.

References

Alberts, G. M., & Edelstein, B. A. (1990). Training in behavior therapy. In A. S. Bellack, M. Hersen, & A. E. Kazdin (Eds.), *International handbook of behavior modification and therapy* (2nd ed., pp. 213–226). New York: Plenum.

Bernreuter, R. G. (1990). Appendix D: Bernreuter Self-Sufficiency Inventory and Scoring Key. In J. Wolpe (Ed.), *The practice of behavior therapy* (pp. 360–363). New York: Pergamon Press.

Dyckman, J. M., & Cowan, P. A. (1978). Imagining vividness and the outcome of in vivo and imagined scene desensitization. *Journal of Consulting and Clinical Psychology, 48,* 1155–1156.

Eysenck, H. (1959). Learning theory and behaviour therapy. *Journal of Mental Science, 105,* 61–75.

Foa, E. B., Steketee, G. S., & Ascher, L. M. (1980). Systematic desensitization. In A. Goldstein & E. B. Foa (Eds.), *Handbook of behavioral interventions: A clinical guide* (pp. 38–91). New York: Wiley.

Goldstein, A., & Foa, E. B. (Eds.). (1980). *Handbook of behavioral interventions: A clinical guide.* New York: Wiley.

Hadley, N. H. (1985). *Foundations of aversion therapy.* New York: Spectrum.

Hull, C. L. (1943). *Principles of behavior.* New York: Appleton-Century-Crofts.

Hull, C. L. (1952). *A behavior system: An introduction to behavior therapy concerning the individual organism.* New Haven, CT: Yale University Press.

Jacobson, E. (1938). *Progressive relaxation.* Chicago: University of Chicago Press.

Jones, M. C. (1924). The elimination of children's fears. *Journal of Experimental Psychology, 7,* 383–390.

Kaplan, S. J. (1986). *The private practice of behavior therapy: A guide for behavioral practitioners.* New York: Plenum.

Kazdin, A. E., & Wilcoxin, L. A. (1976). Systematic desensitization and nonspecific treatment effects: A methodological evaluation. *Psychological Bulletin, 83,* 729–758.

Krasner, L. (1971). Behavior therapy. In P. H. Mussen (Ed.), *Annual review of psychology,* Vol. 22 (pp. 483–532). Palo Alto, CA: Annual Reviews.

Krasner, L. (1990). History of behavior modification. In A. S. Bellack, M. Hersen, & A. E. Kazdin (Eds.), *International handbook of behavior modification and therapy* (2nd ed., pp. 3–25). New York: Plenum.

Matson, J. L., & DiLorenzo, T. M. (1984). *Punishment and its alternatives: A new perspective for behavior modification.* New York: Springer.

Paul, G. L. (1969). Outcome of systematic desensitization II: Controlled investigations of individual treatment, technique variations, and current status. In C. M. Franks (Ed.), *Behavior therapy: Appraisal and status* (pp. 105–159). New York: McGraw-Hill.

Sherman, A. R. (1972). Real-life exposure as a primary therapeutic factor in the desensitization treatment of fear. *Journal of Abnormal Psychology, 79,* 19–28.

Sherrington, C. S. (1906). *Integrative action of the nervous system.* New Haven, CT: Yale University Press.

Van Egeren, L. F., Feather, B. W., & Hein, P. L. (1971). Desensitization of phobias: Some psychophysiological propositions. *Psychophysiology, 8,* 213.

Watson, J. B., & Rayner, R. (1920). Conditioned emotional reaction. *Journal of Experimental Psychology, 3,* 1–4.

Willoughby, R. R. (1932). Some properties of the Thurstone Personality Schedule and a suggested revision. *Journal of Social Psychology, 3,* 401.

Wolpe, J. (1948). An approach to the problem of neurosis based on the conditioned response. M.D. thesis, University of the Witwatersrand.

Wolpe, J. (1952). Experimental neurosis as learned behavior. *British Journal of Psychology, 43,* 243–268.

Wolpe, J. (1958). *Psychotherapy by reciprocal inhibition.* Stanford, CA: Stanford University Press.

Wolpe, J. (1973). *The practice of behavior therapy* (2nd ed.). Elmsford, NY: Pergamon Press.

Wolpe, J. (1976). *Theme and variation: A behavior therapy casebook.* New York: Pergamon Press.

Wolpe, J. (1990). *The practice of behavior therapy* (4th ed.). New York: Pergamon Press.

Wolpe, J., & Boynton, P. (1978). The training programs of the Behavior Therapy Unit at Temple University. *Journal of Behavior Therapy and Experimental Psychiatry, 9,* 295–300.

Wolpe, J., & Lange, P. J. (1969). *Fear survey schedule.* San Diego, CA: Educational and Industrial Testing Service.

CHAPTER 5

....

The Token
Economy

....

■

The basic idea behind the token economy approach to behavioral change is to create an effective way to increase and strengthen socially desirable and adaptive behaviors primarily within institutional settings. Moreover, token economy programs are based on the notion that an individual's learning such behaviors will eventually lead to social reinforcement from others—a process that will teach individuals that they can control important aspects of their own environment and obtain the good things in life. Among other things, token economy programs can be used to empower individuals who lack a sense of self-efficacy.

History of Token Economy Programs

The economic systems that have evolved in most civilizations may be thought of as large and complex versions of token economy systems, the token being money. Developing the use of token reinforcement into token economy programs as they are known today is generally credited to Ayllon and Azrin (1968). Kazdin (1977) noted, however, that token economy programs resembling their modern counterparts were already used, in the United States and several other countries, as long as 150 years ago. Modern token economy programs, however, have not been based on these early pioneering efforts, implemented in educational and penal institutions; instead they were based on a new understanding of the laws of reinforcement and extinction, developed in the laboratories of Guthrie (1935), Skinner (1953), and Thorndike (1935). All these giants of learning theory contributed to the emerging understanding of operant conditioning and the effects of reinforcement, punishment, and extinction on behavior. Although most of this early work took place with laboratory animals, concern with the systematic extension of operant principles to humans dates back at least to the publication of B. F. Skinner's *Walden Two* in 1948.

Research with people was pioneered by Bijou and Baer and their colleagues at the University of Washington in the early 1960s (cf. Kazdin, 1977, p. 28), in work dealing primarily with the operant conditioning of children. Other investigators (for example, Ayllon & Haughton, 1962) experimented with using token reinforcement to change the behavior of psychiatric patients. The first full-fledged design and application of a comprehensive token economy system is generally credited to Ayllon and Azrin, who reported that they first conceived of the token economy in 1961 when they submitted a proposal to determine its feasibility and effectiveness to the Illinois Psychiatric Training and Research Fund. The first experimental program was initiated at Anna State Hospital in 1961 and continued at the time they published their important book *The Token Economy: A Motivational System for Therapy and Rehabilitation*, in 1968. In it they described the extensive theoretical and practical considerations necessary for developing a workable token economy program in a real-life setting. Their groundbreaking work will be cited extensively throughout this chapter.

The work of Ayllon and Azrin was soon extended to other psychiatric populations. For example, Atthowe and Krasner (1968) applied a token economy program in a Veteran's Administration Hospital with long-term patients. Soon after the initial pioneering efforts with chronic psychiatric patients were published, other investigators applied token economy programs to control the classroom behavior of emotionally disturbed children (O'Leary & Becker, 1967). Still others used token reinforcement programs outside of institutional settings to enhance couples' marital functioning (Stuart, 1969). Since these early beginnings, the use of token economy programs has been extended into almost every conceivable setting, although judging from the number of studies published on this topic, the popularity of using token reinforcement programs appears to have declined during the 1980s.

Range of Applicability

Token economy programs were initially developed to enhance the institutional and self-care behaviors of chronic hospitalized psychiatric patients (for example, Ayllon & Azrin, 1968). Subsequently, these programs were used to enhance the work skills and performance, social interaction skills, and personal hygiene of such patients. Since then, token economy programs have been used in many different settings and applied to a variety of different target behaviors.

Kazdin (1977) classified token economy programs according to their focus on (1) target behaviors, (2) settings, and (3) populations. Target behaviors strengthened through token economy programs have included routine self-care activities such as properly using toilets, cleaning rooms, making beds, eating, and so on. In addition, these programs have targeted behaviors necessary for social interaction and successful interpersonal relations. Whatever the specific nature of the behavior to be increased and strengthened, it generally has been designated as desirable and therefore reinforceable. Because it is well established that operant procedures such as reinforcement serve to increase and strengthen any designated behaviors, there are practically no limits on the range of applicability of any method that, like the token economy, uses operant procedures as its principal means of changing behaviors. In addition, token economies have been used extensively to decrease undesired behaviors while at the same time increasing desired ones (for example, Kazdin, 1990). Some ethical and practical limitations, however, are specific to token economy programs; these will be discussed later.

Different settings may, of course, predispose the behavior therapist or the institutional staff to designate different behaviors as desirable. Application of token economy procedures in psychiatric hospitals is thus more likely to focus on enhancing self-care skills and social behaviors; in institutions for delinquents or criminals, the focus may be on enhancing behaviors that increase control and manageability of the institutional population. In school settings, the token economy program may focus on developing discipline related to learning tasks, as well as prosocial behaviors such as cooperation. Different populations have also been the focus of token economy programs. For example, various populations of students with special needs have commonly been the focus of token economy programs (for instance, Patterson, 1976). Kazdin (1977) has pointed out that focusing instead on an alternate population—namely, teachers—may be more effective and produce longer-lasting results.

A variety of researchers have investigated applications of token economy programs extending beyond the psychiatric hospital, the detention center or prison, and the classroom (cf. Krasner, 1990). For example, Miller and Miller (1970) used a token economy approach to enhance self-help skills among low-income families. Baltes (1973); Burgess, Clark, and Hendee (1971); and Chapman and Risley (1974) reported successful use of positive reinforcement techniques in the control of littering. Everett, Hayward, and Meyers (1974) used token reinforcement to increase the use of mass transit. These specialized applications simply illustrate the wide-ranging potential applications for token economy procedures to change the behaviors of diverse individuals in various unique settings. Ultimately, token economy programs' range of applicability is limited only by the behavior therapist's imagination.

Theoretical Foundations

The basic theoretical foundation for token economy programs is provided by learning theory. More specifically, the principles of operant conditioning form the basis of virtually all procedures used in connection with token economy programs. Skinner discussed these principles (1938, 1953) and offered an extensive example of their application in his novel *Walden Two* (1948). The work of Skinner and other early learning theorists has been credited with developing the major principles that form the basis of operant conditioning and thus of the token economy. A basic ingredient of the operant conditioning methodology Skinner advocated was his empty organism concept, which proposed that individuals' overt behavior should be studied without concern for the organism's inner states. Skinner called this type of study the "experimental analysis of behavior." Consistent with this approach, Skinner urged psychiatrists and clinical psychologists, who were concerned with treating abnormal behavior in psychiatric patients, to shift from their traditional focus on internal mental events to focus instead on contingencies of reinforcement as the principal means for controlling behavior. This shift in focus eventually preceded the first implementation of operant procedures in a token economy program.

Although token economy programs rely primarily on positive reinforcement to strengthen desirable behaviors, they use other procedures as well. Other concepts of operant conditioning must therefore be included in a discussion of the theoretical underpinnings of token economy programs. Before discussing these other concepts, it may be useful to review the basic assumptions about human behavior that are generally endorsed by behavior therapists. First of all, those likely to apply operant conditioning principles in a token economy program generally stress the importance of learning in determining human behavior. They assume that such learning is based on the consequences individuals experience in their environments as a result of various behaviors. Thus, although acknowledging that certain biological predispositions may exist for certain behaviors and that internal mental events may be important in some ways, those conducting token economy programs clearly focus on observable behaviors that can be influenced through contingent environmental manipulation.

Operant Conditioning Principles

The concepts of positive and negative reinforcement are most central to the operant conditioning paradigm. Specifically, "positive reinforcement refers to an increase in the frequency of a response, which is followed by a favorable event (positive reinforcer)" (Kazdin, 1977, p. 2), whereas "negative reinforcement refers to an increase in the probability of a response by removing an aversive event immediately after the response is performed" (Kazdin, 1977, p. 5). Both positive and negative reinforcement may be used in a token economy program to increase the occurrence of desirable behaviors. Token economy programs may also use two additional principles—namely, punishment and extinction. These are procedures that decrease the probability of unwanted or undesirable behaviors. Kazdin defined punishment as "the presentation of an aversive event or the removal of a positive event following a behavior which decreases the probability of that behavior" (1977, p. 6). He noted that "extinction refers to no longer reinforcing a response that has been previously reinforced" (1977, p. 8).

The effectiveness of behavior change methods based on operant procedures depends on a number of other features of the behavior change situation. For example, it is well-established that to maximize the effectiveness of positive reinforcement (the main feature of token economy programs), the reinforcement must immediately follow the desired response. Moreover, a large reinforcement usually works better than a small one, and reinforcers of one type may work better than reinforcers of another, depending on the individual's preferences and reinforcement history. Still another important consideration has to do with schedules of reinforcement—a complex topic in its own right that cannot be discussed in detail here. Suffice it to note that schedules of reinforcement determine the manner, type, frequency, and timing of the consequences following specified behaviors. Kazdin (1977) reviewed several basic features of schedules of reinforcement that need to be considered in the design of token economy programs.

Implementing a Token Economy Program
Main Components

Krasner (1976) succinctly defined the basic elements necessary for the design and implementation of token economy programs. He suggested that the first task in planning a token economy program consists of systematically observing the behavior of the individuals for whom the program is being designed. Krasner was particularly careful to stress that basic observation must include not only a given individual's specific behaviors, but also the responses those behaviors elicit from the environment—that is, their consequences in the specific situations in which they are occurring. Systematic observation is particularly important because the design of the token economy program must ultimately incorporate a clear specification of the behaviors to be reinforced, as well as the environmental circumstances that may serve as reinforcers.

The second necessary element of token economy programs is designation of certain specific behaviors as desirable and therefore reinforceable. Implicit in this decision is the assumption that target behaviors identified in this way are occurring relatively infrequently and that the manipulation of behavioral consequents designed to increase their frequency will benefit the client. For example, in a psychiatric hospital the treatment team may determine that "processing" behaviors—that is, patient behaviors that focus on sharing concerns with staff in order to attain improved understanding of those behaviors—are particularly desirable. Teachers in a classroom for retarded children may designate attending behaviors to be desirable. Detention center staff may identify compliant and cooperative behaviors as particularly desirable. In each case, the determination of what constitutes behaviors to be reinforced within the token economy program is made by someone who, usually by virtue of training, is in a position to make these decisions. Since these decisions always represent value judgments, favoring certain behaviors over others, adherence to the highest ethical standards of the appropriate professional community is a necessity for those who design any kind of operant conditioning program, including token economy programs.

The third element Krasner identified is determination of the environmental consequents that will serve as the reinforcers for individuals whose behavior is being modified. Although Krasner collectively referred to them as "the good things in life," they may be as mundane as a particularly well-liked food, a cassette tape of music, a special privilege, or some form of social recognition. Essentially, in a token economy program, these constitute the backup reinforcers that can be obtained with tokens.

The tokens themselves make up the fourth essential element of the token economy. Krasner noted:

> Despite the label of *token* economy, the tokens themselves are merely a gimmick, a training device to help teachers and others included in the classroom (or hospital ward) to learn how to observe behavior and its consequences, how to use their own behavior in a reinforcing manner, how to respond contingently, and how to arrange the environment to maximize the possibility of the individual child (or patient) receiving reinforcing stimuli at the appropriate time. (1976, p. 147)

In spite of Krasner's somewhat flip assertion that tokens are only gimmicks, some serious questions can be raised about why tokens should be used in the first place, rather than administering the actual reinforcing events (or objects) directly. This question has several answers (Kazdin, 1977, pp. 44–45). First, if one thinks about a sizable institutional program, it becomes immediately clear that the contingent (in other words, immediate) dispensation of reinforcers to numerous different individuals is a logistical impossibility. Consequently, use of token reinforcement allows for operant principles to be applied on a much larger and more systematic scale than is ordinarily possible. Tokens can be given immediately for use later to purchase a backup reinforcer that cannot, as a practical matter, be given immediately following a target behavior. In addition, use of tokens allows for administration of an identical reinforcer to different clients who may have quite different reinforcer preferences (which they can later exercise when "cashing in" their accumulated tokens). Kazdin summarized research concerning the use of tokens that has pointed to additional advantages of token reinforcement. For example, research has established that tokens are often able to maintain behavior more successfully than other conditioned reinforcers, including verbal feedback and praise. In addition, tokens appear less likely to lose their potency through a client's satiation, since tokens can be backed up by a large variety of reinforcers.

The fifth and final element of token economy programs Krasner identified is exchange rules. These rules specify the basic economic relationship between tokens and the backup reinforcers, including how many tokens are needed to obtain a given reinforcer. Very specific economic rules are necessary in a token economy program, in order to determine such things as the total number of tokens an individual may earn in a given period of time and the total value (in tokens) of backup reinforcers that an individual may reasonably seek to obtain. Since a token economy program is a motivational system, the values placed on backup reinforcers, and the number of tokens that can be earned for certain behaviors, must be designed so as to maintain the individual's incentive to earn tokens.

Kazdin described three types of exchange rules, which he called "contingencies," that may govern the acquisition of tokens and their exchange for reinforcing consequences (1977, pp. 60–64). Some token economy programs may use only one of these sets of rules or contingencies, and others may use all of them. The first type consists of individualized contingencies—rules regarding the acquisition and use of tokens that are specific to an individual. Unique target behaviors may thus be identified for a particular client, who earns a specific number of tokens for exhibiting the target behavior, and who may use accumulated tokens to purchase unique backup reinforcers. Although individualized contingencies offer obvious advantages in individualizing treatment, they are naturally more difficult to administer, since staff who hand out tokens contingently must treat each client in accordance with the client's set of individualized contingencies. The second type, standardized contingencies, are designed to apply across the various clients in a group (such as a hospital ward or a classroom). Standardized contingencies are more easily administered than individualized contingencies, but they assume a certain homogeneity in the behavior change objectives of everyone in the group. The third type, group contingencies, may be used when the rules of the token economy program are applied to the behavior of the group collectively, rather than to individuals within the group. This latter method is also easily administered and may be particularly effective in changing certain types of group behaviors.

Practical Considerations

Although use of tokens has many clear advantages, some practical considerations have to be addressed in any token economy program. Particularly important is that individual clients obtain tokens only in the manner specified in the program rules. Program rules have to be extremely detailed and easy to understand, specifying unambiguously what the target or reinforceable behaviors are. In addition, they must specify the number of tokens associated with each target behavior, as well as the number of tokens needed to purchase any of the available backup reinforcers. Frequently, ways have to be found to prevent the trading of tokens for illicit backup reinforcers, such as sexual or other favors from other patients, or their use in gambling. This effort sometimes requires the development of a recordkeeping system, or a means of individualizing tokens so that each participant has his or her own.

Although most token economy programs emphasize positive reinforcement that consists of giving tokens for specified target behaviors, many programs also include a procedure called response cost. Typically, this procedure involves specifying contingencies when participants may lose tokens, so that they are "fined" for undesirable behaviors. Kazdin (1977) summarized findings from a number of studies suggesting that token economy programs that combined the use of positive reinforcement with response cost procedures were more effective than those using positive reinforcement alone. Such findings should serve as a reminder that behavior change programs in real-life settings often are less concerned with pure applications of specific behavior change principles and methods than might be the case in laboratory studies. Behavior therapists who have pioneered the use of tokens in operant behavior change programs have often innovatively combined procedures in order to achieve maximum benefit for their clients, whether students, psychiatric patients, or delinquents.

Means and Conditions for Implementing
Token Economy Programs
Personnel Qualifications

By their very nature, token economy programs require the participation of all personnel who have regular contact with the individuals in the program. The involvement of all personnel is necessary to ensure that contingent reinforcement in the form of tokens is provided according to the predetermined schedule of reinforcement when the target behaviors occur. Thus, in hospitals, attendants, aides, nurses, orderlies, and psychologists need to administer the contingencies of a token economy program consistently. In schools, teachers and teacher's aides may administer a token program, and in other settings parents, peers, spouses, and others may be involved. To be effective, a token economy program requires whoever administers the contingencies to do so in an entirely consistent and systematic manner.

In training staff to properly administer a token economy program, it is important not only to acquaint staff with the specific contingencies to administer, but also to help them understand the rationale for the program's rules. Kazdin (1977) noted that traditional staff training procedures that rely primarily on instruction are not as successful as training methods that rely on modeling, role playing, and giving feedback. In many cases, those who administer the token economy program may go through training procedures that result in fundamental shifts in attitude—such as changing from a crisis orientation to one in which consistent attending to positive behaviors was seen as the rule rather than an exception. Various researchers have specifically commented on the beneficial impact of involvement in token economy programs on staff morale and attitudes (for example, McReynolds & Coleman, 1972; Milby, Pendergrass, & Clarke, 1975).

Although virtually anyone can be trained to participate effectively in the operation of a token economy program, not everyone can design these programs. Krasner (1976) discussed the potential dangers of implementing what superficially might seem to be operant conditioning procedures by individuals not properly trained as behavior therapists. Implicit in his discussion was the notion that operant procedures, including token economies, are perhaps deceptively simple and therefore easily misused or misunderstood. He suggested that designers of token economy programs must not only be competent in the technical aspects of operant conditioning, but also demonstrate "respect for the integrity of the individual" and adhere to the ethical standards of legitimate behavior therapists. Moreover, findings from diverse behavior change methods continue to show that so-called nonspecific therapy effects with a salutary influence on intervention outcome are often attributable to therapist characteristics and attitudes, such as friendliness and warmth. There is every reason to believe that they are also operative in operant conditioning methods in general, and in token economy programs, specifically.

Conditions for Conducting a Token Economy

Token economy programs have been used in many different institutional settings and in community settings, and they have been applied to small groups, couples, and individuals. Their application does not require any specific physical facilities. It does, however, require the use of tokens. Many different types of tokens have been used, including readily available poker chips, gold stars, and tickets. Sometimes a problem has arisen because clients were able to obtain tokens outside the program. Consequently, other token economy programs have used tokens specially devised for the program, including coins and credit card–like devices. In still other programs, points on a tally sheet or check marks were used in place of tokens. Whatever the nature of the tokens, they need to be easily administered and monitored by the program staff.

Apart from tokens the only physical requirement of token economy programs is the availability of backup reinforcers. Obviously, if backup reinforcers are not readily available, the tokens cannot serve their intended purpose. In some institutional settings, backup events, such as food, money, and various privileges, are typically readily available. Frequently, backup reinforcers may be listed in the form of a menu, which allows clients to identify readily what they can exchange for tokens (Kazdin, 1977). In some programs, provision of some backup reinforcers may require special administrative clearance. For example, in some programs patients or detainees may graduate to a halfway house or other follow-up program if they accumulate a specified number of tokens and meet certain administrative requirements.

Limitations of Token Economy Programs
Contraindications

Strictly speaking, there are no absolute contraindications to the use of token economy programs. Well-conceived, properly designed, and competently administered token economy programs have shown their value in so many different settings that their a priori exclusion from consideration is typically not warranted. In some circumstances, however, institutional mandates may conflict with the types of objectives legitimately pursued by token economy programs. For example, Kennedy (1976) noted that the priority mission of a prison may be viewed as control, whereas the primary objective of a token economy program should be oriented toward rehabilitation, including the facilitation of release for those prisoners who perform well in a properly designed token economy program. Clearly, when such conflicting objectives are apparent, institution of a token economy program would be contraindicated. It is also contraindicated if institutional leadership or significant segments of institutional staff are antagonistic to the basic concepts underlying token economy programs. In those instances, a token economy program's likelihood of success would be seriously diminished from the start and end up undermining subsequent efforts to change behavior through other legitimate means.

Hazards

One hazard involved in the use of token economy programs is the possibility that behavioral change is not maintained after the token economy program has terminated. The question of maintaining gains from therapeutic intervention is of concern in a variety of different settings and applies to most types of intervention. The concern may be highlighted in token economy programs, however, because tangible evidence of the program (namely, the tokens) is no longer available as a reinforcer when the program ceases. Fortunately, this issue has received a good deal of attention in the literature. Kazdin (1977) suggested that specific steps must be taken to maximize the chances that behavior change is maintained not only when the token economy program is ended, but also across situations, such as from the psychiatric hospital to the family or community environment. Specifically, Kazdin suggested that transferring a token economy program from the training setting to a naturalistic setting before proceeding with the withdrawal of contingencies may ensure the maintenance of behavioral gains. In addition, he suggested that reinforcement contingencies may be faded so that the reinforcement contingencies gradually play a lesser role in maintaining performance. Kazdin also suggested that clients be trained in self-reinforcement so as to ensure behavior change maintenance and transfer. Finally, Kazdin noted that these and other methods may be used independently in promoting the maintenance and transfer of behavioral changes accomplished through a token economy program (1977, p. 196).

Another hazard that is certainly not unique to token economy programs has to do with faulty program design and administration. Most token economy programs are relatively complex and require competent participation by a number of different staff who in some cases operate at significantly different levels in the professional hierarchy. Hence, the potential for errors and problems is significantly greater than in intervention methods that require only the dedication and competence of a single therapist. A related potential hazard arises because an entire institution may be involved in the design and implementation of a token economy program. The possibility of misperception, misattribution, and misunderstanding of the token economy program may lead to outside intervention by people concerned about issues of behavioral control and individual rights.

The Effectiveness of Token Economy Programs

As do most behaviorally oriented treatment methods, token economy programs typically incorporate a means for assessing their effectiveness. In most cases, such evaluation procedures are built into the program from the very beginning. At the most elementary level, such evaluation consists of keeping track of the frequency of the desirable (target) behaviors and judging the success of the program by how much the target behavior has increased. Concurrently, tallies may be kept on the relative decrease in the frequency of undesirable behaviors, whether specifically altered through reinforcement contingencies or instead expected to decrease because they are being progressively replaced by target behaviors.

To ascertain more conclusively the relative efficacy of token economy programs, it is necessary to compare them with alternative treatment modalities and evaluate their long-term effects. This type of evaluation research is difficult and expensive, however, and it has not received as much attention as is desirable. Nevertheless, Kazdin's (1977) comprehensive review of token economies resulted in his concluding that the outcome research on token economy was so vast as to be "somewhat overwhelming." Although the pace of research on token economy programs appears to have diminished somewhat since Kazdin made that comment, it is still beyond the scope of this chapter to comprehensively review the research on token economy programs.

Kazdin concluded that research on "token economies with psychiatric patients, the mentally retarded, and individuals in classroom settings . . . has firmly established the efficacy of token reinforcement in altering a wide range of responses" (1977, p. 110). In discussing token economy programs with "delinquents, adult offenders, drug addicts, problem drinkers, children and adults in outpatient treatment, geriatric residents, stutterers, and aphasics" (p. 139), he concluded that "the token economy appears to be readily adaptive to diverse treatment populations and settings" (p. 140) and that many of these programs have demonstrated impressive accomplishments. Kazdin noted, however, that despite the impressive gains documented due to use of token economy programs with diverse populations and in diverse settings, many outstanding issues and limitations require further development and research.

In a more recent review of token economy programs for psychiatric clients, Fuoco and Tyson (1986) reported that the use of token reinforcement had been reported in treating delusional behavior and hallucinations and in improving self-care skills and interpersonal skills. Curran, Monti, and Corriveau (1982) reported the use of token economy programs in decreasing apathy and withdrawal in psychiatric patients; Paul and Lentz (1977) reported the decrease of disruptive behavior in psychiatric clients using procedures such as token fines.

In summary, the use of token economy procedures has been demonstrated effective when carefully planned, designed, and implemented. The apparent decline in popularity of token economy programs probably relates to a confluence of factors including reduced funding for residential treatment programs, greater emphasis on custodial care and punishment (in the generic sense), and development of alternative methods. Nevertheless, there is every reason to believe that token economy programs will continue to have a place in multifaceted, comprehensive behavioral treatment programs.

References

Atthowe, Jr., J. M., & Krasner, L. (1968). A preliminary report on the application of contingent reinforcement procedures (token economy) on a chronic psychiatric ward. *Journal of Abnormal and Social Psychology, 73,* 37–43.

Ayllon, T., & Azrin, N. (1968). *The token economy: A motivational system for therapy and rehabilitation.* New York: Appleton-Century-Crofts.

Ayllon, T., & Haughton, E. (1962). Control of the behavior of schizophrenic patients by food. *Journal of Experimental Analysis of Behavior, 5,* 343–352.

Baltes, M. M. (1973). Operant principles applied to acquisition and generalization of nonlittering behavior in children. *Proceedings, 81st Annual Convention, American Psychological Association, 8,* 889–890.

Burgess, R. L., Clark, R. N., & Hendee, J. C. (1971). An experimental analysis of anti-litter procedures. *Journal of Applied Behavior Analysis, 4,* 71–75.

Chapman, C. C., & Risley, T. R. (1974). Anti-litter procedures in an urban high-density area. *Journal of Applied Behavior Analysis, 7,* 377–384.

Curran, J. P., Monti, P. M., & Corriveau, D. P. (1982). Treatment of schizophrenia. In A. S. Bellack, M. Hersen, & A. E. Kazdin (Eds.), *International handbook of behavior modification and therapy* (pp. 433–466). New York: Plenum.

Everett, P. B., Hayward, S. C., & Meyers, A. W. (1974). The effects of a token reinforcement procedure on bus ridership. *Journal of Applied Behavior Analysis, 7,* 1–9.

Fuoco, F. J., & Tyson, W. M. (1986). Behavior therapy in residential programs for psychiatric clients. In F. J. Fuoco & W. P. Christian (Eds.), *Behavior analysis and therapy in residential programs* (pp. 231–259). New York: Van Nostrand Reinhold.

Guthrie, E. R. (1935). *The psychology of learning.* New York: Harper & Row.

Kazdin, A. E. (1977). *The token economy: A review and evaluation.* New York: Plenum.

Kazdin, A. E. (1990). Conduct disorders. In A. S. Bellack, M. Hersen, & A. E. Kazdin (Eds.), *International handbook of behavior modification and therapy* (2nd ed., pp. 669–706). New York: Plenum.

Kennedy, R. E. (1976). Behavior modification in prisons. In W. E. Craighead, A. E. Kazdin, & M. J. Mahoney (Eds.), *Behavior modification: Principles, issues, and applications* (pp. 321–340). Boston: Houghton Mifflin.

Krasner, L. (1976). The operant approach in behavior modification. In J. T. Spence, R. C. Carson, & J. W. Thibaut (Eds.), *Behavioral approaches to therapy* (pp. 127–167). Morristown, NJ: General Learning Press.

Krasner, L. (1990). History of behavior modification. In A. S. Bellack, M. Hersen, & A. E. Kazdin (Eds.), *International handbook of behavior modification and therapy* (2nd ed., pp. 3–25). New York: Plenum.

McReynolds, W. T., & Coleman, J. (1972). Token economy: Patient and staff changes. *Behaviour Research and Therapy, 10,* 29–34.

Milby, J. B., Pendergrass, P. E., & Clarke, C. J. (1975). Token economy versus control ward: A comparison of staff and patient attitudes toward ward environment. *Behavior Therapy, 6,* 22–29.

Miller, L. K., & Miller, O. L. (1970). Reinforcing self-help group activities of welfare recipients. *Journal of Applied Behavior Analysis, 3,* 57–64.

O'Leary, K. D., & Becker, W. C. (1967). Behavior modification of an adjustment class: A token reinforcement program. *Exceptional Children, 33,* 637–642.

Patterson, R. L. (1976). (Ed.). *Maintaining effective token economies.* Springfield, IL: Charles C Thomas.

Paul, G. L., & Lentz, R. J. (1977). *Psychosocial treatment of chronic mental patients: Milieu vs. social learning programs.* Cambridge, MA: Harvard University Press.

Skinner, B. F. (1938). *The behavior of organisms: An experimental analysis.* New York: Appleton-Century-Crofts.

Skinner, B. F. (1948). *Walden Two.* Macmillan.

Skinner, B. F. (1953). *Science and human behavior*. Macmillan.

Stuart, R. B. (1969). Operant-interpersonal treatment for marital discord. *Journal of Counseling and Clinical Psychology, 33*, 675–682.

Thorndike, E. L. (1935). *The psychology of wants, interests, and attitudes*. New York: Appleton-Century-Crofts.

■

CHAPTER 6

....

Aversion Therapy
and Punishment

....

■

The basic purpose of aversion therapy and punishment procedures is to reduce the likelihood that undesirable responses will occur, or to eliminate them entirely. Because the term *punishment* carries many negative connotations in everyday language, behavior therapists have been reluctant to use punishment procedures, even though the common notion of punishment differs from the definition of therapeutic punishment. Matson and DiLorenzo (1984) proposed that therapeutic punishment should be defined as the systematic application of "punishing stimuli to decelerate certain aberrant behaviors" (p. 2). The major difference between punishment techniques and aversion therapy is the timing of the aversive stimulus. In punishment, in accordance with operant conditioning principles, the aversive stimulus immediately follows the response that is to be diminished or eliminated; in aversion therapy, in accordance with classical conditioning procedures, the aversive stimulus coincides with the response of concern. Clearly, the two procedures have very similar objectives. In practice, however, punishment techniques are typically employed to weaken or eliminate certain motor responses, and aversion therapy is more commonly used to weaken autonomic responses (Wolpe, 1990).

History of Aversion Therapy and Punishment

Aversion therapy and punishment are discussed as distinctly different approaches because some confusion exists in the literature regarding the proper label for the two. Many researchers (such as Wolpe, 1990) have insisted that aversion therapy should be clearly distinguished from punishment, whereas others (for example, Rachman & Teasdale, 1969) have included both classical and operant conditioning procedures in their definition of aversion therapy. To avoid such confusion, we shall maintain the distinction by referring to aversion therapy when we discuss classical conditioning procedures and to punishment procedures when we discuss operant procedures.

Aversion therapy, defined as a classical conditioning approach, clearly has its roots in the work of Pavlov (1927). It appears, however, that although Pavlov reported a number of animal studies that used classical conditioning procedures to weaken undesirable responses, he did not use these procedures in human experiments or in any kind of psychiatric treatment. Nevertheless, Pavlov's direct influence is quite obvious in the work of Kantorovich (1930), who published the first known attempt to use aversion procedures as therapy. Moreover, as Rachman and Teasdale (1969) reported, Kantorovich indicated that aversion therapy was already being used in the Leningrad Psychiatric Hospital at the time. In the United States, one of the first reported uses of aversion therapy was Max's (1935) *Psychological Bulletin* article, in which he published the results of his treatment of a "homosexual fixation." During the 1930s and 1940s aversion therapy was practiced both in Europe and in the United States, although apparently, and in contrast to subsequent years, chemical aversive stimuli (to produce nausea) were used almost exclusively (Rachman & Teasdale, 1969). Concurrent with the emergence of behavior therapy as a widely practiced alternative to more traditional psychotherapy, aversion therapy experienced a significant revival of interest in the 1960s, prompted in part by the work of Eysenck and Rachman (1965), Franks (1963, 1966), Rachman (1961, 1965), and Wolpe (1958).

The history of punishment procedures in clinical treatment can also be traced ultimately to Pavlov's work on conditioning. Rachman and Teasdale (1969) noted that operant training methods (punishment procedures, according to our definition) represent the application of the work not only of Pavlov, but also of Bechterev and Skinner. Rachman and Teasdale also noted that learning theory has provided the methods of operation or technology of operant training, as well as paradigms on which to base treatment techniques and a framework for making deductions and predictions about abnormal behavior and the effects of therapeutic interventions. Finally, learning theory provided an experimental basis for designing and assessing treatment procedures (Rachman & Teasdale, 1969, pp. 5–6).

Over the history of aversion therapy and punishment, a major contribution toward understanding of these procedures is the chapter on punishment published by Azrin and Holz in 1966 as part of Honig's volume on operant behavior. The chapter continues to be widely quoted as the definitive review of punishment, both for its summary of the historical origins of punishment in experimental psychology and for its thorough conceptual analysis. Further progress has also been made since then in applying these procedures in clinical settings and understanding the nature of aversively motivated behavior. A definite renewal of interest during the last decade is evident in important publications such as the books by Archer and Nilsson (1989), Hadley (1985), and Matson and DiLorenzo (1984).

Range of Applicability

Aversion therapy and punishment procedures have been used extensively to treat alcoholism and sexual deviations. These procedures have also been applied, however, to a wide variety of other undesired impulses, behaviors, and addictions. Wolpe (1990) reported that aversion therapy has been used to treat fetishism, transvestism, food craving, alcoholism, drug addiction, and smoking. Wolpe noted that the application of aversion therapy to such problems is based on the fact that they all involve "pleasurable experience with inappropriate objects, and that the approach behavior is motivated by this" (p. 240). Matson and DiLorenzo have reported that punishment procedures employing noxious substances have been used to control aggressive behavior, tantrums, postural abnormalities, self-stimulation, and chronic vomiting. They also indicated that contingent electric shock has been used to treat self-injurious behavior, tantrum behavior, stereotyped screaming, chronic ruminative vomiting, whining and inattention, soiling, destruction of property, self-induced seizures, window breaking, spasms, alcoholism, and smoking.

Although aversion therapy and punishment procedures have been used successfully to alter problematic behaviors of many different kinds, most practitioners who use these procedures have consistently argued that alternative, more socially desirable methods should be employed when possible. Most have also argued that reinforcement programs should be used concomitantly and that elaborate safeguards (which will be discussed later) should be employed to protect patients from harm and abuse. If these cautions are observed carefully, there is reason to believe that the range of applicability of aversion therapy and punishment procedures will continue to expand in the future, because their effectiveness can be demonstrated and documented and also because the course of treatment is usually much shorter than for most other behavior change procedures.

Theoretical Foundations

Assumptions About Normal and Deviant Behavior

Ullman and Krasner (1975, p. 32) wrote that "abnormal behavior is no different from normal behavior in its development, its maintenance, or the manner in which it may be changed. The difference between normal and abnormal behavior is not intrinsic; rather it lies in a societal reaction." This statement represents a prototype for the conceptualization of human behavioral development generally endorsed by behavior therapists. Clearly, normal or average behavior is considered learned, just like deviant behavior. The emphasis on society's impact reflects a commitment to the notion that behaviors develop in accordance with the consequences provided for them in an individual's physical, social, cultural, familial, and general personal environment. It is also assumed that behaviors are learned through associative experiences as manifested in the classical conditioning paradigm.

The impact of culture and society are considered particularly important when considering the treatment of deviant behavior, which tends to be the focus of punishment and aversive procedures. Of course, what represents deviant behavior in one culture may not be so considered in another, and many different frameworks exist for deciding what is deviant and what is not. Urban and Vondracek (1977), for example, suggested that such diverse concepts as atypicality, nonconformity, maladaptation, maladjustment, illegality, and departure from the ideal can be used in deciding whether behaviors are functional or dysfunctional. Attempts to arrive at universally acceptable definitions of deviancy have failed. What is considered deviant behavior, and therefore treatable through punishment and aversive techniques, is thus a function of the sociocultural context.

Because both normal and deviant behaviors are acquired through learning (that is, the individual's accumulated experience), in clinical settings the two types of behavior are differentiated primarily because deviant behaviors are socially undesirable, or at least against the patient's own long-term interests. Such behaviors include sexually deviant behaviors such as fetishism, transvestism, and pedophilia, as well as antisocial behaviors, alcoholism, and drug addiction. Some exceptions to this argument are acknowledged, including enuresis and homosexuality (Eysenck & Beech, 1971). It has been suggested that to qualify for aversion therapy, deviant behaviors must be somehow reinforcing to the individual, and that deviant behaviors occur in the first place as a result of some failure to condition appropriate behavior patterns. Any definition of deviancy will clearly be met with some controversy. Consequently, some authors (such as O'Leary and Wilson, 1975) have argued that behavior therapy should focus on providing a technology to assist individuals who desire behavior change without making a judgment as to whether the behavior is deviant or normal.

Assumptions About Conducting Aversion Therapy and Punishment

In aversion therapy the basic idea is to pair a stimulus that is typically followed by the maladaptive (pleasurable) behavior with an aversive stimulus. As a consequence, after repeated pairings, the once pleasurable stimulus will produce anxiety or fear. Wolpe's definition of aversion therapy states the same principle in a somewhat different way:

> Its essence is the administration of an aversive (unpleasant) stimulus simultaneously with an unwanted emotional response, with the object of inhibiting the latter and consequently diminishing its habit strength. For example, a painful stimulus may be employed to inhibit sexual arousal by a fetishistic object in order to weaken that arousal. (1990, p. 238)

As mentioned previously, the basic paradigm of aversion therapy is classical conditioning, which is thought to produce an involuntary response and to change the stimulus value of the neutral stimulus.

Punishment procedures, in contrast, are based on operant conditioning, which is thought to involve higher-order behaviors, such as a client's making choices in how to respond. Operant procedures thus generally target changes in the client's response pattern. Church (1963) detailed four different operant procedures that use aversive stimuli to control behavior:

1. Escape training, in which the patient can terminate the aversive stimulus by performing a predefined adaptive behavior.
2. Avoidance training, in which the patient can delay or avoid the onset of the aversive stimulus.
3. Preservation, in which the patient prolongs the presence of an aversive stimulus by engaging in a predefined behavior.
4. Passive avoidance or punishment, in which the aversive stimulus is applied immediately after the patient exhibits a specified maladaptive behavior in order to reduce its probability of future occurrence.

Wolpe stated the difference between aversion therapy and punishment as follows:

> Whereas punishment is intended to discourage a response—that is, to make it less probable by reason of aversive consequences—the intent of aversion therapy is to diminish the habit strength of a response through inhibiting it by the competition of the aversive agent. (1990, p. 238)

Although these conceptual and technical differences between aversion therapy and punishment procedures are commonly accepted, it should be noted that a number of different theoretical models have been proposed to account for aversive control of behavior (Hadley, 1985). Several of these models blur the distinction between aversion therapy and punishment procedures, because they are viewed as combining both classical and operant explanatory concepts.

Implementing Aversion Therapy and Punishment Techniques

Before discussing the concrete steps involved in implementing aversion therapy and punishment techniques, it is important to note that many specific procedures and techniques are subsumed within these topics. Moreover, a great many highly technical aspects regarding these techniques are well beyond the scope of this chapter; they have been discussed extensively by Hadley (1985) and Matson and DiLorenzo (1984). Matson and DiLorenzo stated that the pragmatic issues in applying punishment techniques are complex at best and at worst overwhelming. Although practitioners need to be aware of what is important and what must be attended to, Matson and DiLorenzo maintained that the complexity of these techniques makes their reduction to a simple summary of basic principles unlikely. Eysenck and Beech stated these concerns slightly differently:

> A clear theoretical understanding of the dynamics of each particular situation is essential if the proper therapeutic course is to be followed; rule-of-thumb application of principles not geared to the particular case in question may be worse than no treatment at all. (1971; p. 582)

Consequently, the following sections will selectively describe the application of aversion therapy and punishment procedures, without attempting to be comprehensive or complete.

Selection of Aversive Stimulus

Electric shock has been the aversive stimulus of choice in both aversion therapy and punishment procedures. The use of electric shock in these procedures must not be confused with the use of electroconvulsive shock (ECS), used in psychiatry primarily to treat intractable depression. Whereas electroconvulsive shock produces convulsions and often loss of consciousness, the use of electric shock in aversion and punishment procedures produces neither. It is important also to understand that the pain from the electric shock terminates immediately when the shock is terminated, that it is highly localized and does not radiate, and that it produces no tissue damage.

Noxious substances are also occasionally used as an aversive or punishing stimulus. "Typical noxious substances used in the past include, but are not limited to, 100 percent lemon juice, Lysterine^R, ammonia capsules, and noise" (Matson & DiLorenzo, 1984, p. 39). The use of such noxious stimuli is considered less objectionable than the use of electric shock. Of course, the applicability and appropriateness of various stimuli depends on the specific nature of the behavior to be decelerated and on the overall circumstances of the intervention procedure.

Drugs have been used as punishing or aversive stimuli, although drugs typically are not sufficiently fast-acting to serve as contingent punishment stimuli. Drugs have been used occasionally in special cases. One case, reported by Blanchard, Libet, and Young (1973), involved the treatment of a young man who had a history of inhaling paint vapor in order to get high. The drug Anectine was used in four sessions conducted by an anesthesiologist. Basically, the patient was told to bring a bag containing paint fumes to his face and to inhale. At that precise moment, the anesthesiologist would add Anectine to an intravenous saline drip, which was started previously. Within 20 seconds the Anectine produced paralysis and apnea, which were allowed to continue for 30 seconds before the patient was artificially respirated.

Drugs have also been used in aversion therapy, where their action does not have to be as fast because the application is not contingent. In most cases, drugs like Apomorphine have been used in aversion therapy to produce nausea and vomiting. For example, Sansweet (1975) has reported a number of case studies in which Apomorphine was used in the treatment of sexual fetishism. In one case in which a patient experienced sexual arousal in relation to women's handbags and baby carriages, he was hospitalized and given Apomorphine every 2 hours around the clock for a full week. He was not allowed to eat, and amphetamines were used to keep him awake at night. Just before the onset of nausea he was shown a collection of handbags and baby carriages. Following the intensive treatment, the patient received outpatient treatment for 6 months, as well as a booster session. Reportedly, he did have a mild relapse after 6 years, for which he was again successfully treated with aversion therapy.

How the aversive stimulus is arranged will determine its effectiveness. Azrin and Holz (1966) summarized the circumstances that maximize the effectiveness of applying aversive stimuli to eliminate undesirable behaviors. Some of these circumstances apply to punishment procedures only, but others are of concern in aversion therapy as well. Among other things, Azrin and Holz noted that the aversive stimulus should be delivered in such a manner that unauthorized escape is impossible. In addition, the punishing (aversive) stimulus should be as intense as possible from the beginning and its frequency as high as possible (administered immediately after every response). Extended periods of aversive stimulation (punishment) should be avoided, and great care should be taken that it is not differentially associated with any reinforcement. Azrin and Holz also pointed out that, ideally, an alternative response should be available that offers the patient the same amount of reinforcement that was previously obtained from the undesired response. In the absence of such an alternative response, the patient should have access to a different situation in which some comparably reinforcing behavior can take place. When an aversive stimulus cannot be used, it may be possible to use in its place a conditioned stimulus that has been previously associated with the aversive stimulus, or it may be feasible to use a reduction of positive reinforcement as punishment.

Aversion Therapy

The application of aversion therapy requires the implementation of a basic classical conditioning procedure, which

> consists of pairing a neutral stimulus or event with a behavior that already elicits a particular reaction from a client. By repeatedly pairing stimuli and responses, separate events become associated in such a way that the client exhibits the same response when either stimulus is present. (Matson & DiLorenzo, 1984, p. 12)

Thus, the stimulus that produces the maladaptive behavior, the conditioned stimulus (CS), is repeatedly paired with an aversive (unconditioned) stimulus (UCS), so that the once pleasurable stimulus will eventually come to produce fear, an unconditioned response (UCR). Eysenck and Beech (1971) noted in this connection that although conventional wisdom states the CS should just precede the UCS, the most critical event is that the UCR follows the CS.

Because both aversion therapy and punishment are designed to decelerate specified aberrant behaviors, the first step in applying these procedures is to identify clearly the behaviors to be decelerated or eliminated. Generally, this identification involves a process of behavioral analysis, which is shared by all of the behavioral techniques discussed in this volume. If the behavior to be eliminated is, indeed, what Wolpe calls an "autonomic habit," aversion therapy may be appropriate. In addition to identifying the undesired response, a decision has to be made about the specific aversive stimulus to be used. As previously discussed, a number of stimuli have been used as aversive stimuli, although various researchers (for example, Morse & Kelleher, 1977) have cited considerable evidence to dispel the notion that some stimuli are aversive, and therefore effective in decelerating or eliminating behaviors, under all circumstances. These researchers have cited studies showing, for example, that under some circumstances electric shock can enhance certain behaviors. Consequently, a thorough behavioral analysis should include an assessment of whether an aversive stimulus is actually aversive to the patient who is a candidate for aversion therapy.

Another issue that has to be addressed as part of the behavioral analysis is the manner of presentation of the conditioned stimulus (CS)—the stimulus that provokes the undesired reaction (behavior) and that is to be paired with the aversive stimulus (UCS). Eysenck and Beech (1971) noted that the CS may be the actual behavior pattern that is to be eliminated, or it may be a picture, an object, or an imagined scene. Again, depending on the nature of the problem and characteristics of the patient, as well as on practical, legal, and ethical considerations, one method of presentation may be more appropriate and effective than another. Furthermore, the number of trials necessary for effective retraining is likely to vary along similar parameters.

Punishment Procedures

As mentioned previously, aversive stimuli can be used in operant procedures in a number of different ways, including escape training, avoidance training, preservation, or punishment (Church, 1963). To discuss the precise method of implementing each of these operant procedures is beyond the scope of this chapter. Instead, in discussing the operant use of aversive stimuli, we will focus on punishment procedures, and for the most part we will discuss the application of contingent electric shock in suppressing maladaptive behavior.

In discussing the specific procedures to be used in implementing contingent electric shock treatment, Carr and Lovaas (1983) felt compelled to reemphasize that the procedure is very involved and that a "cookbook approach" is not possible. They proceeded, however, to amplify the following points:

1. The elimination or suppression of the undesired behavior will be relatively permanent only if the patient is reeducated and helped to acquire appropriate alternative behaviors. The reason is that the undesired behavior, no matter how bizarre, serves some function and must be replaced by something else.

2. The therapist should experience the effect of the electric shock procedure at least once at the start of each treatment session in order to appreciate the effect of the aversive stimulus.

3. Behaviors to be punished should be specified precisely at the outset so as to preclude therapists' spontaneously enlarging the repertoire of punishable behaviors because of the positive reinforcement they obtain from initial success with the punishment procedure.

4. The electric shock must be applied immediately following occurrence of the undesired behavior.

5. It is always better to use a few strong and relatively painful shocks than a lot of milder ones, because patients may adapt to mild aversive stimulation so that the treatment becomes ineffective.

6. A shock duration of 0.5 to 2 seconds appears to be adequate.

7. Shock should always be applied to a fleshy area of the body and never to the face, abdomen, or chest.

8. The undesired behavior should be followed by a shock in each instance.

9. Unauthorized avoidance of shock must not be allowed. Proper staffing must be maintained to ensure that resistant, or aggressive, clients cannot simply leave, thereby avoiding the shock procedure and dooming it to fail.

10. Conditioned aversive stimuli, such as the word *no*, should be developed to replace the shock eventually.

Means and Conditions for Implementing Aversion Therapy and Punishment
The Therapist's Qualifications

The training of behavior therapists has been the subject of considerable discussion in recent years. For example, Linehan (1980) outlined the skills and competencies of well-trained behavior therapists, suggesting among other things that behavior therapists must learn overt motor skills as well as skills in the cognitive and affective areas. These skills include what have traditionally been considered basic clinical skills, as well as procedural skills. As a matter of fact, training in the specific techniques of behavior therapy should take place only in the context of a comprehensive and integrated graduate program that includes training in behavior theory and philosophy as well as in scientific methodology (Collins, Foster, & Berler, 1986).

With aversion therapy and punishment procedures, special therapist characteristics must be considered. Carr and Lovaas (1983) suggested that an individual supervising contingent shock treatment should be familiar with the research literature on punishment of humans, as well as of other organisms; have some experience with experimental design and evaluating treatment outcomes; have had hands-on supervised experience in administering shock treatment; and possess clinical judgment and sensitivity. In addition, Carr and Lovaas indicated that the therapist's personal limitations should also be scrutinized, with special emphasis on how the individual reacts to social pressures. For example, it is pertinent to know whether the therapist has a short temper or a history of reacting harshly or even sadistically under some circumstances. Although it is obviously difficult to make such determinations, the most practical and feasible approach may be use of a review committee to safeguard patients' interests, to review the appropriateness of aversion therapy or punishment techniques, and to screen out behavior therapists temperamentally unsuited to implement these procedures.

Conditions for Conducting Aversion Therapy and Punishment

Use of aversion therapy and punishment procedures in treating patients will very likely continue to be controversial, even when such procedures are shown to be beneficial. Because they quite naturally command a higher level of public scrutiny than therapeutic approaches perceived as more benign, extraordinary care needs to be exercised in implementing any kind of aversive or punishment procedure. This care must be reflected in the training and preparation of therapists, in the use of first-rate treatment facilities, and in the selection of the most advanced available methods and technologies. Of particular concern is how the aversive stimulation is produced.

Harris and Ersner-Hershfield (1978) reported that the most commonly used device used to administer contingent electric shock is operated with 1.5 volt flashlight batteries and produces 1400 volts at 0.4 milliamperes (mA). The device used to deliver the electric shock stimulus is called an inductorium, and it supplies the electric current through two electrodes. The electrodes may be located, about a half to three-quarters of an inch apart, at the end of a stick approximately a foot long; or they may be fastened directly to the patient with elastic strips or Velcro. Many considerations regarding the precise nature of the equipment used to deliver electric shock were discussed extensively by Butterfield (1975). Those include, for example, the specific device used, the precise output characteristics of the device, and the design and characteristics of the electrodes. These parameters may vary slightly from one situation to another depending on the physiological characteristics of the patient, as well as the manner in which the treatment schedule has been designed. Quite clearly, however, the proper specification and selection of the necessary instrumentation is critically important and requires a well-trained and experienced therapist.

Some applications of aversion therapy require hospitalization and the availability of emergency medical services in case of complications; an example is use of drugs such as Anectine (Blanchard, Libet, & Young, 1973) or Scoline (Farrar, Powell, & Martin, 1968) to produce traumatic respiratory paralysis. Needless to say, trained anesthesiologists should be involved when these kinds of procedures are administered. Proper medical supervision is also necessary for any treatment involving drugs that produce nausea, such as Apomorphine (for example, Glynn & Harper, 1961; Morganstern, Pearce, & Rees, 1965).

Limitations of Aversion Therapy and Punishment

Aversive procedures, including punishment interventions, involve administering unpleasant stimuli, or depriving patients of privileges, conveniences, possessions, and activities that they value. Under extreme circumstances, legitimate concerns may arise about whether some of these procedures involve depriving patients of basic human rights. Virtually all of these techniques are thus very controversial, and their use is tightly controlled and, in some circumstances, specifically prohibited. The most commonly endorsed position regarding these techniques is that they should be used as a last resort, after less objectionable procedures have clearly proved ineffective in addressing the undesirable behaviors. Moreover, Matson and DiLorenzo (1984) insisted that punishment procedures should not be used in lieu of reinforcement procedures, but rather as a supplement. These authors also pointed out that some professionals' objections to use of any aversive or punishment procedures under any circumstances is based on misunderstanding or ignorance of documented facts regarding the effectiveness of such procedures. Finally, some authors (for example, Warren, 1971) have recommended that only reinforcement and extinction procedures be used, claiming that these are more effective than punishment techniques. This sentiment has often been repeated, in part because of its emotional appeal. Punishment procedures, however, when used appropriately, can produce far greater improvement than reinforcement alone (for example, Meyer & Offenbach, 1962; Spence & Segner, 1967).

Carr and Lovaas (1983) suggested a sequence of treatment procedures that should precede the use of punishment, which in their case consisted of contingent electric shock as a treatment for severe behavior problems. This recommended sequence consists of first trying differential reinforcement of other behavior (DRO), which allows patients to earn various reinforcements for gradually increasing the frequency and duration of periods during which they refrain from the undesired behavior. If unsuccessful, Carr and Lovaas recommended that DRO be combined with extinction procedures, in which the previously applied reinforcement is withheld when the problem behavior recurs. Next in the recommended sequence, assuming that DRO combined with extinction is unsuccessful, is DRO combined with a time-out procedure, which involves removing the patient from all possible sources of reinforcement when the patient engages in the undesired behavior. Finally, Carr and Lovaas recommended that DRO may be combined with "positive practice over correction," in which "the individual is required to practice a more appropriate alternative behavior to the one being suppressed, each time the inappropriate behavior is exhibited" (p. 224).

Hazards

Applying any aversive stimulation to another human being carries some risk. Even when using aversive stimulation or punishment appropriately, with proper safeguards for patient and practitioner, practitioners need to be cognizant of certain hazards. Azrin and Holz (1966) pointed out that emotional concomitants may occur with any kind of aversive stimulation and may include disruptive and undesirable emotional states. They cited a number of studies, however, that show that chronic behavioral disruption or chronic negative emotional states are unlikely to result. On the other hand, they acknowledged that when the aversive stimulation is administered by an individual, the punished person may react negatively—that is, aggressively— toward the individual (therapist) and thereby disrupt the therapeutic relationship.

Punishment may be conceptualized as producing at least four different kinds of effects, which have been labeled primary, physical, social, and secondary (Newsom, Favell, & Rincover, 1983). In the therapeutic use of punishment, the primary effect is, of course, response deceleration or suppression. The physical effects of a punishing stimulus are the immediate physiological effects associated with its administration and are considered essential in the therapeutic application of punishment. Social effects are identified as others' reactions to the use of punishment procedures. Finally, Newsom, Favell, and Rincover defined secondary effects as the so-called side effects of any punishing stimulus, which may be undesirable or desirable. Undesirable side effects represent potential hazards in the application of aversion therapy and punishment procedures; of these, emotional reactions are perhaps most common. These may include grimaces, bodily movements that suggest fear, screaming, and crying. When properly administered, however, punishing stimuli are unlikely to produce any lasting emotional disturbance. Another possible negative side effect is that the application of aversive stimuli, either contingently or as part of aversion therapy, may result in aggression, either against the therapist or against others. Other possible negative side effects include response facilitation, in which a contingently punished response actually increases, and generalized suppression, in which the suppressive effect of the punishment on the targeted behavior may be generalized to other behaviors (Newsom, Favell, & Rincover, 1983). The therapist needs to understand these undesirable side effects so that they can be properly countered if they do occur.

Contraindications

Application of aversive stimuli either in contingent operant procedures or as part of aversion therapy has remained controversial for a number of reasons. Some view any use of punishment as unacceptable, in part because society at large has turned away from an emphasis on corporal punishment and become sensitized to issues of physical abuse and inhumane treatment. These changes have been reflected in numerous court decisions designed to protect patients from exposure to harmful conditions. Sheldon and Risley (1990) reviewed many of these legal issues and reported that some treatment procedures have been explicitly forbidden. They noted that aversive techniques have presented some particularly problematic issues for courts, as well as for practitioners. In particular, Sheldon and Risley stressed that such techniques should never be used for retribution, for the convenience or benefit of the staff or institution, or to "accommodate the individual to the existing environment" (p. 229). They also pointed out that aversive techniques of any kind should never be used as a simple substitute for less intrusive treatment. Moreover, in order to ensure that these protections are effective, a number of authors have proposed that human rights committees be established in all institutions where potentially harmful interventions, including aversion therapy and punishment procedures, might conceivably be used.

The Effectiveness of Aversion Therapy and Punishment

Aversion Therapy

Although disagreements have continued to exist about the precise mechanisms by which aversion therapy works (for example, Wolpe, 1990; McConaghy, 1990), most published outcome studies have reported considerable improvement in the treated conditions as a consequence of aversion therapy. Nevertheless, numerous studies have reported at least some success attributable to aversion therapy in the treatment of paraphilia (sexual deviation). For example, Killman, Sabalis, Gearing, Bukstell, and Scovern (1982) reviewed numerous studies and, while criticizing the methodology used, concluded that aversion therapy could be effective in the treatment of sexual dysfunction. Similar conclusions were reached by McConaghy (1975), McConaghy, Armstrong, and Blaszczynski (1981), and Feldman and MacCulloch (1964). Wolpe (1990) reported a number of case studies showing aversion therapy to be effective in treating a variety of disorders. Orleans, Shipley, Williams, and Haac (1981a, 1981b) offered a comprehensive review of aversion therapy in the treatment of smoking. Like most others reviewing the effectiveness of aversion therapy, they found that when applied optimally, aversion therapy is at least as effective as alternative approaches in suppressing a target behavior. Because aversion therapy is so controversial, it is likely that particular attention will be given to studies that demonstrate lack of success in its application. In the extensive literature on aversion therapy outcomes, however, most reports of inadequate success in the use of aversion therapy are based on procedures that were ill-conceived, poorly executed, or both.

Punishment

In evaluating the effectiveness of punishment procedures, it is useful to refer to the classic article by Azrin and Holz (1966). After examining many technical issues, they concluded that there is no question that punishment can reduce a target behavior. They noted, however, that the effectiveness of punishment in eliminating a behavior depends primarily on precise characteristics of the punishing stimulus and the circumstances under which it is administered. Moreover, Holz, Azrin, and Ayllon (1963) compared a variety of methods of eliminating behavior, including stimulus change, extinction, satiation, and punishment. They concluded that although all of these methods can result in the reduction of target behaviors, in the real world punishment may be most effective.

A key issue in the effectiveness of punishment procedures is maintenance of suppression. Carr and Lovaas (1983) cited a number of studies demonstrating that the suppressive effects of contingent shock treatment can be very durable, but they also noted that some failures of maintenance have been reported as well. They suggested that to maximize the chances that suppression of target behaviors is maintained, behavior therapists should whenever possible strengthen appropriate alternative behaviors. Moreover, Carr and Lovaas suggested that maintenance of suppression can be enhanced when booster sessions are routinely scheduled. Kazdin (1980) also addressed the issue of maintenance of behavior change, as well as issues of the transfer of training—that is, the problem of transferring newly learned (or unlearned) behaviors from the therapy session to other situations. He concluded that a whole series of behavior therapy techniques can ensure response maintenance and generalization of the desired treatment effects to situations and circumstances outside the treatment room.

A review of outcome studies using punishment procedures is beyond the scope of this chapter. Punishment procedures have been used in the suppression of a wide range of problematic behaviors, and many of these studies are reviewed in such volumes as Axelrod and Apsche (1983), Hadley (1985), Kazdin and Wilson (1978), and Matson and DiLorenzo (1984); Sansweet (1975) reported numerous case studies.

References

Adams, J. A. (1976). *Learning and memory: An introduction*. Pacific Grove, CA: Brooks/Cole.

Archer, T., & Nilsson, L. G. (1989). *Aversion avoidance, and anxiety perspective on aversively motivated behavior*. Hillsdale, NJ: Erlbaum.

Azrin, N. H., & Holz, W. C. (1966). Punishment. In W. K. Honig (Ed.), *Operant behavior: Areas of research and application* (pp. 380–447). New York: Appleton-Century-Crofts.

Axelrod, S., & Apsche, J. (Eds.). (1983). *The effects of punishment on behavior*. New York: Academic Press.

Blanchard, E. G., Libet, J. M., & Young, L. D. (1973). Apneic aversion and covert sensitization in the treatment of a hydrocarbon inhalation addiction: A case study. *Journal of Behavior Therapy and Experimental Psychiatry*, *4*, 383–387.

Butterfield, W. H. (1975). Electric shock: Safety factors when used for the aversive conditioning of humans. *Behavior Therapy*, *6*, 98–110.

Carr, E. G., & Lovaas, O. I. (1983). Contingent electric shock as a treatment for severe behavior problems. In S. Axelrod & J. Apsche (Eds.), *The effects of punishment on human behavior* (pp. 221–245). New York: Academic Press.

Church, R. M. (1963). The varied effects of punishment on behavior. *Psychological Review, 70*, 369–402.

Collins, F., Foster, S., & Berler, E. (1986). Clinical training issues for behavioral psychology. *Professional Psychology: Research and Practice, 17*, 301–307.

Eysenck, H. J., & Beech, H. R. (1971). Counterconditioning and related methods. In A. E. Bergin & S. L. Garfield (Eds.), *Handbook of psychotherapy and behavior change: An empirical analysis* (pp. 543–611). New York: Wiley.

Eysenck, H. J., & Rachman, S. (1965). *The causes and cures of neurosis.* Routledge & Kegan Paul.

Farrar, C. H., Powell, B. J., & Martin, L. K. (1968). Punishment of alcohol consumption by apneic paralysis. *Behavior Research Therapy, 6*, 13.

Feldman, M. P., & MacCulloch, M. J. (1964). A systematic approach to the treatment of homosexuality by conditioned aversion: A preliminary report. *American Journal of Psychiatry, 121*, 167–171.

Franks, C. M. (1963). Behaviour therapy: The principles of conditioning and the treatment of the alcoholic. *Quarterly Journal of Studies on Alcohol, 24*, 511–529.

Franks, C. M. (1966). Conditioning and conditioned aversion therapies in the treatment of the alcoholic. *The International Journal of the Addictions, 1*, 61–98.

Glynn, J. D., & Harper, P. (1961). Behavior therapy in transvestism. *Lancet, 1*, 619.

Hadley, N. H. (1985). *Foundations of aversion therapy.* New York: SP Medical & Scientific Books.

Harris, S. L., & Ersner-Hershfield, R. (1978). Behavioral suppression of seriously disruptive behavior in psychotic and retarded patients: A review of punishment and its alternatives. *Psychological Bulletin, 85*, 1352–1375.

Holz, W. C., Azrin, N. H., & Ayllon, T. (1963). A comparison of several procedures for eliminating behavior. *Journal of Experimental Analysis of Behavior, 6*, 399–406.

Kantorovich, N. V. (1930). An attempt at associative reflex therapy in alcoholism. *Psychological Abstracts,* No. 4282.

Kazdin, A. E. (1980). *Behavior modification in applied settings* (2nd ed.). Pacific Grove, CA: Brooks/Cole.

Kazdin, A. E., & Wilson, G. T. (1978). *Evaluation of behavior therapy: Issues, evidence, and research strategies.* Lincoln: University of Nebraska Press.

Killman, P. R., Sabalis, R. R., Gearing, M. L., Bukstell, L. H., & Scovern, A. W. (1982). The treatment of sexual paraphilias: A review of the outcome research. *Journal of Sex Research, 18,* 192–252.

Linehan, M. M. (1980). Supervision of behavior therapy. In A. K. Hess (Ed.), *Psychotherapy supervision: Theory, research, and practice* (pp. 148–180). New York: Wiley.

Matson, J. L., & DiLorenzo, T. M. (1984). *Punishment and its alternatives: A new perspective for behavior modification.* New York: Springer.

Max, L. W. (1935). Breaking up a homosexual fixation by the conditioned reaction technique: A case study. *Psychological Bulletin, 32,* 734.

McConaghy, N. (1975). Aversive and positive conditioning treatments of homosexuality. *Behaviour Research and Therapy, 13,* 309–319.

McConaghy, N. (1990). Sexual deviation. In A. S. Bellack, M. Hersen, & A. E. Kazdin (Eds.), *International handbook of behavior modification and therapy* (pp. 565–580). New York: Plenum.

McConaghy, N., Armstrong, M. S., & Blaszczynski, A. (1981). Controlled comparison of aversive therapy and covert sensitization in compulsive homosexuality. *Behaviour Research and Therapy, 19,* 425–434.

Meyer, W. J., & Offenbach, S. I. (1962). Effectiveness of reward and punishment as a function of task complexity. *Journal of Comparative and Physiological Psychology, 55,* 532–534.

Morganstern, F. S., Pearce, J. F., & Rees, W. (1965). Predicting the outcome of behavior therapy by psychological tests. *Behavior Research Therapy, 2,* 191.

Morse, W. H., & Kelleher, T. R. (1977). Determinants of reinforcement and punishment. In W. K. Honig & J. E. R. Stadan (Eds.), *Handbook of operant behavior* (pp. 174–200). Englewood Cliffs, NJ: Prentice-Hall.

Newsom, C., Favell, J. E., & Rincover, A. (1983). The side effects of punishment. In S. Axelrod & J. Apsche (Eds.), *The effects of punishment on human behavior* (pp. 285–316). New York: Academic Press.

O'Leary, K. D., & Wilson, G. T. (1975). *Behavior therapy, applications and outcome.* Englewood Cliffs, NJ: Prentice-Hall.

Orleans, C. T., Shipley, R. H., Williams, C., & Haac, L. A. (1981a). Behavioral approaches to smoking cessation. 1. A decade of progress 1969–1979. *Journal of Behavior Therapy and Experimental Psychiatry, 12,* 125–129.

Orleans, C. T., Shipley, R. H., Williams, C., & Haac, L. A. (1981b). Behavioral approaches to smoking cessation. 2. Topical bibliography 1969–1979. *Journal of Behavior Therapy and Experimental Psychiatry, 12,* 131–144.

Pavlov, I. P. (1927). *Conditioned reflexes* (G. Anrep, Trans.). Oxford University Press.

Rachman, S. (1961). Sexual disorders and behavior therapy. *American Journal of Psychiatry, 118,* 235–240.

Rachman, S. (1965). Studies in desensitization, I: The separate effects of relaxation and desensitization. *Behavior Research Therapy, 3*, 245–251.

Rachman, S., & Teasdale, J. (1969). *Aversion therapy and behaviour disorders: An analysis.* Coral Gables, FL: University of Miami Press.

Sansweet, S. J. (1975). *The punishment cure.* New York: Mason/Charter.

Sheldon, J. B., & Risley, T. R. (1990). Balancing clients' rights: The establishment of human rights and peer review committees. In A. S. Bellack, M. Hersen, & A. E. Kazdin (Eds.), *International handbook of behavior modification and therapy* (2nd ed., pp. 227–249). New York: Plenum.

Spence, J. T., & Segner, L. L. (1967). Verbal versus nonverbal reinforcement combinations in the discrimination learning of middle and lower-class children. *Child Development, 38*, 29–38.

Ullman, L. P., & Krasner, L. (1975). *A psychological approach to abnormal behavior* (2nd ed.). Englewood Cliffs, NJ: Prentice-Hall.

Urban, H. B., & Vondracek, F. W. (1977). Delivery of human intervention services: Past, present and future. In S. Goldberg & F. Deutsch (Eds.), *Life-span individual and family development* (pp. 429–448). Pacific Grove, CA: Brooks/Cole.

Warren, S. A. (1971). Behavior modification: Boon, bane or both? *Mental Retardation, 9*, 2.

Wolpe, J. (1958). *Psychotherapy by reciprocal inhibition.* Stanford, CA: Stanford University Press.

Wolpe, J. (1990). *The practice of behavior therapy* (4th ed.). New York: Pergamon Press.

■

PART III

···

Cognitive
Approaches

···

■

CHAPTER 7

....

Rational-Emotive
Therapy

....

■

Rational-emotive therapy (RET) is a psychotherapeutic approach aimed at helping people live longer, happier, and more fulfilling lives. RET focuses on helping people think more rationally, feel more appropriately, and act more functionally (Ellis & Bernard, 1986). Ellis (1991, p. 9) stressed that as clients progress, they

1. Give up their presenting symptoms
2. Give up or reduce other dysfunctional symptoms
3. Maintain progress
4. Through using RET, reduce their long-term chances of becoming seriously disturbed again
5. Use RET promptly when problems occasionally recur
6. Keep looking for maximally enjoyable but nondefeating paths to personal enjoyment

It is *not* a purpose of RET to get people to become less emotional; instead, RET encourages clients to have strong but, most of all, appropriate feelings.

History of Rational-Emotive Therapy

Rational-emotive therapy was initially founded and developed by Albert Ellis. Ellis's earliest writings about RET (1957, 1958, 1962) attracted a substantial following, and during the past three decades RET therapy has become one of the dominant approaches in the practice of psychotherapy. Ellis himself has reported that he founded RET in 1955 when, as a clinical psychologist, he became dissatisfied with practicing psychoanalysis (Ellis & Dryden, 1987). Bernard and DiGiuseppe (1989) traced the beginnings of rational-emotive therapy to Ellis's personal life in the 1920s and 1930s, when he was trying to cope with his own problems, particularly his shyness toward females and his significant anxiety about speaking in public. Ellis became a prolific reader of many leading philosophers of his own time, as well as those of antiquity. He credited in particular the writings of the Greek philosopher Epictetus, the Roman Marcus Aurelius, and psychotherapists such as Alfred Adler and George Kelly.

One result of Ellis's deep interest in philosophy was his early conclusion that if people acquired a sane philosophy of life, they would be unlikely to become unhappy or emotionally disturbed. Moreover, as Ellis and Bernard (1986) reported, RET was from the beginning highly philosophical and disputatious, in the sense that it challenged clients' irrational beliefs. Ellis stated that RET is an extension of the logico-empirical methods of science (1962), and as such it opposes dogmas and rigid absolutism, while favoring flexibility and antidogmatism. In addition to various philosophers, a number of psychologists also influenced Ellis's formulations of RET. Having been trained by a psychoanalyst of the Karen Horney school, Ellis was particularly impressed by Horney's concept of the "tyranny of the shoulds" (Ellis & Dryden, 1987). Adler also influenced many of the emerging concepts of RET (Ellis, 1981), by virtue of his stress on self-rating, goal-directedness, and social interest, as well as his use of a very cognitive-persuasive form of psychological intervention.

Range of Applicability

Ellis (1979) differentiated between two main forms of RET—inelegant and elegant RET. Inelegant RET—which represents its more general form, incorporates a large variety of cognitive, affective, and behavioral methods, whereas elegant RET emphasizes cognitive restructuring according to the ABC theory of emotional disturbance and personality change, which will be discussed in more detail below. Because RET, especially in its inelegant form, employs a great number of cognitive behavioral techniques, it has been applied to an immense range of problems and to a large variety of different populations.

Relatively early in the development of RET, Ellis expanded RET to include not only the original method of individual psychotherapy, but also a group therapy procedure. In group RET, all group members are trained to use RET with one another. RET can also be applied to large-scale group processes, such as lectures, workshops, courses, and so on. In addition, RET may be used in connection with bibliotherapy, self-help procedures, and the use of various media. As early as 1979, Ellis reported that it had been applied to the treatment of anxiety, depression, hostility, character disorder, and psychosis. Furthermore, it had been used in assertion training and self-management and in addressing problems in the areas of sex, love, marriage, child-rearing, and adolescence. Ellis and Grieger (1986) edited a volume that documented application of RET to discomfort anxiety, anger problems, motivational deficits, self-acceptance problems, and women's issues. Special attention has also been given to applying RET in the workplace (DiMattia, 1991) and in working with children and adolescents (Bernard & Joyce, 1991). In a recent volume (Walen, DiGuiseppe, & Dryden, 1992), applications of RET to problems of love, sex, relationships, children and adolescents, procrastination, anger, anxiety, and depression are discussed. Examples are also given of how RET can be used to deal with women's issues, assertiveness, habit control and addiction, and in family therapy.

Theoretical Foundations

Assumptions About Human Nature and Personality

Ellis has been quite explicit about his views on human nature. The theory of personality he has developed focuses primarily on personality change (Ellis, 1989). Ziegler (1989) evaluated Ellis's RET theory by examining its position on nine basic dimensions. Since Ellis (1989) expressed agreement with the substance of Ziegler's review, a summary of Ziegler's discussion will provide the most comprehensive assessment of RET's basic underlying assumptions that is possible in the limited space available.

Freedom versus determinism.   Ellis has viewed individuals as having considerable freedom of choice in their overall conduct. This freedom of choice is circumscribed, however, by Ellis's acknowledgement that both biological-constitutional predispositions and environmental factors may limit the range of choices available to a particular individual at a given time. One objective of RET is to help people, through cognitive restructuring, to increase their freedom of choice and to limit the impact of biological, as well as environmental, constraints.

Rationality versus irrationality.   Ellis has strongly contended that humans are both uniquely rational and uniquely irrational. Rationality and irrationality share equal weight and importance in influencing behavior. Ziegler made the particularly important point that Ellis's use of these terms is relativistic and does not necessarily correspond exactly to their standard meaning in the English language. Thus, the term *rational* in RET refers to the use of efficient, flexible, logical, and scientific ways to pursue important values, goals, and ideals. The term *irrational* refers to the use of dogmatic, illogical, and ineffective thoughts, behaviors, and emotions that lead to self-defeating and self-destructive consequences.

Holism versus elementalism.   This dichotomy deals with whether humans are better understood as complex whole organisms or instead when (conceptually) broken down into constituent parts. Ellis has generally taken the view that humans are best understood when one fully appreciates the complex interplay of the various parts and components of human functioning. Consequently, for example, he has viewed cognition, emotion, and behavior as interrelated and difficult to separate. Ziegler pointed out that while appreciating the utility of examining separate components of human functioning, Ellis has believed that their holistic interrelatedness is more central in understanding humans.

Constitutionalism versus environmentalism.   Ellis has been a strong constitutionalist. He has maintained that the biological tendency of humans to think irrationally can be inferred from the prevalence of such thinking among individuals from all possible backgrounds, including among individuals raised rationally. Moreover, Ellis wrote that humans also have the basic biological tendency "to exercise the power of human choice and to work toward changing their irrational thinking" (Ellis & Dryden, 1987, p. 7). While asserting that human personality and human behavior have a biological basis, Ellis also has acknowledged the impact of environmental influences. Ziegler pointed out, however, that Ellis has not yet articulated the precise biological and neurological processes that represent the basis of these constitutional dispositions, nor has Ellis been explicit about the mechanisms by which environmental influences may affect the development and maintenance of various behaviors.

Changeability versus unchangeability.   To claim a strong constitutional basis for behavior, and yet to also claim that people almost always can significantly change their behaviors, as Ellis has, may seem a contradiction. Ellis, however, has seen no contradiction, and his well-documented success in helping people change tends to validate his position. Ellis has claimed that if people really want to change, and work hard to do so, their chances to succeed are excellent.

Subjectivity versus objectivity.   In Ellis's theory of RET, individuals' subjective beliefs—their subjective construction of the world—represent the most potent influence on their behavior. In other words, it is not the objective events and features of the external world that determine behavior, but rather how people choose to interpret them. Ziegler pointed out that as a consequence of taking this position, RET theory currently lacks an explanation of how objective factors participate in personality development and functioning. This subjectivist, phenomenological approach, however, paves the way for making the individual's beliefs about him- or herself and the world a central focus for therapeutic intervention.

Proactivity versus reactivity.   Ellis has been clearly committed to the view that people have the power to shape their lives and that they can thus be viewed as predominantly proactive. This position is related to the view of humans as goal-directed and purposeful, as well as the view that behavior is determined primarily through factors inside the individual (such as beliefs, values, and perceptions) and not by external circumstances. Ziegler pointed out, however, that although Ellis has come down on the side of proactivity, he recently made significant progress in exploring the complex interrelationships between people's reactions to external events and their more powerful proactive tendencies, which together help shape human behavior.

Homeostasis versus heterostasis.   Are humans motivated primarily toward reducing tensions and maintaining an internal state of equilibrium (homeostasis) or instead toward growth and stimulation (heterostasis)? Ellis's position is that people may aspire to both. Thus, although people are viewed as wishing to be relatively happy and to get along with others (essentially homeostatic tendencies), they also are said to be short-range hedonists, and they want to actualize their potential for growth (heterostatic tendencies).

Knowability versus unknowability.   Despite his strong commitment to scientific and logico-empirical methods, Ellis has realized that humans are so complex that it may be difficult, even in principle, to gain a full and complete understanding—to know all there is to know about human functioning. Ellis is fundamentally opposed to any kind of absolutist thinking, and thus he concluded that even science and reason are not necessarily the answer to all questions about humans. Ellis's unknowability assumption, however, has not kept him or his followers from pursuing knowledge and theory relevant to RET.

Assumptions About Conducting Rational-Emotive Therapy

Both Ellis and his students have written extensively about RET's theoretical basis. A recent summary of these writings sets out six principles of RET theory (Walen, DiGiuseppe, & Dryden, 1992, pp. 15–17).

1. The first principle is that "*cognition is the most important proximal determinant of human emotion.*" Basically, although external events may contribute to what we feel, internal events, especially our cognitive evaluations of how we perceive things, are the most powerful sources of our emotional responses.

2. The second principle indicates that "*dysfunctional thinking is a major determinant of emotional distress.*" Among these dysfunctional thought processes are "exaggeration, oversimplification, overgeneralization," and others.

3. The third principle suggests that "if distress is a product of irrational thinking, *the best way to conquer distress is to change this thinking.*"

4. The fourth principle asserts that "*multiple factors*, including both genetic and environmental influences" represent the antecedents of irrational thinking and thus of psychopathology.

5. The fifth principle of RET theory "*emphasizes present* rather than historical influences on behavior." This important principle underscores that although genetic and environmental conditions may contribute to development of irrational thinking, disturbed behavior is typically maintained by what people do in the present, often including continued self-indoctrination in irrational thinking.

6. Finally, the sixth principle is that change in irrational beliefs "will *not necessarily come about easily*," but that it can be accomplished through persistent efforts to change one's thinking.

The foregoing underscores a key assumption underlying RET—the importance it places on distinguishing between rational and irrational beliefs. Rational beliefs are preferential in nature, whereas irrational beliefs are absolute and dogmatic. Both are evaluative cognitions with personal significance to those who hold them. Rational beliefs are expressed in the form of preferences—that is, wishes, desires, likes, and dislikes. Irrational beliefs are expressed in the form of "musts," "shoulds," "oughts," and "have-to's." Positive feelings are associated with getting what one desires (rationally), and negative feelings with not getting what is desired (rationally). The consequences of irrational beliefs, on the other hand, are invariably negative emotions that generally interfere with pursuing and attaining one's goals. For example, sadness may be the negative feeling (consequence) associated with the rational assessment of an event as an unfortunate loss or failure, whereas depression would be the feeling (consequence) associated with irrational beliefs that the loss or failure should not have occurred and that it is terrible and awful rather than too bad or simply unfortunate (Ellis & Dryden, 1987).

A cornerstone of Ellis's RET theory is his assumption that rational beliefs are the basis of functional behaviors and that irrational beliefs represent the basis of dysfunctional behaviors. Put another way, "the essence of human emotional disturbance . . . consists of the absolutistic 'musts' and 'must nots' that people think *about* their failure, *about* their rejections, *about* their poor treatment by others, and *about* life's frustrations and losses" (Ellis & Dryden, 1987, p. 17).

The basic framework for intervention was presented by Ellis (1962) as the ABC framework. In this framework, *A* represents the *activating* event, *B* the person's *belief* about that event, and *C* the emotional and behavioral *consequences* (responses) for the person of holding belief B. According to Mahoney, Lyddon, and Alford (1989), two basic assumptions about human change processes are implicit in Ellis's ABC model: the idea that thought can determine feeling and action; and the assumption that emotional distress, disorder, and dysfunction reflect instances of irrational thinking. The RET therapist attacks the client's irrational beliefs by disputing, contradicting, and denying them. Thus, reason, logic, and persuasion represent the RET therapist's most formidable weapons.

The client's dogmatic and unconditional *musts* and *must nots* lead to what Ellis has called a philosophy of "musturbation." Ellis and Dryden presented a fairly extensive (though by no means complete) list of illogicalities at the core of musturbatory thinking:

1. *All-or-none thinking*: "If I fail at any important task, as I *must* not, I'm a *total* failure and *completely* unlovable!"
2. *Jumping to conclusions and negative non sequiturs*: "Since they have seen me dismally fail, as I *should* not have done, they will view me as an incompetent worm."
3. *Fortune-telling*: "Because they are laughing at me for failing, they know that I *should* have succeeded, and they will despise me forever."
4. *Focusing on the negative*: "Because I *can't stand* things going wrong, as they *must* not, I can't see any good that is happening in my life."
5. *Disqualifying the positive*: "When they compliment me on the good things I have done, they are only being kind to me and forgetting the foolish things that I *should* not have done."

6. *Allness and neverness*: "Because conditions of living ought to be good and actually are so bad and so intolerable, they'll *always* be this way and I'll *never* have any happiness."

7. *Minimization*: "My good shots in this game were lucky and unimportant. But my bad shots, which I *should* never have made, were as bad as could be and were totally unforgivable."

8. *Emotional reasoning*: "Because I have performed so poorly, as I *should* not have done, I feel like a total nincompoop, and my strong feeling proves that I *am* no damned good!"

9. *Labeling and overgeneralization*: "Because I *must* not fail at important work and have done so, I am a complete loser and failure!"

10. *Personalizing*: "Since I am acting far worse than I *should* act and they are laughing, I am sure they are only laughing at me, and that is *awful!*"

11. *Phonyism*: "When I don't do as well as I *ought* to do and they still praise and accept me, I am a real phony and will soon fall on my face and show them how despicable I am!"

12. *Perfectionism*: "I realize that I did fairly well, but I *should* have done perfectly well on a task like this and therefore really am incompetent!" (1987, pp. 15–16)

Since the initial presentation of the ABC framework, different RET therapists have developed a variety of expanded versions. Ellis suggested that one may quickly teach not only the ABC framework, but also what he calls the ABCDEs of RET. In addition to the *activating events* (As) and their emotional and behavioral *consequence* (C), he suggested that it is important to differentiate between *rational beliefs* (rBs) and *irrational beliefs* (iBs) in order to "actively Dispute (at point D) their irrational Beliefs (iBs) and thereby arrive at E, an Effective New Philosophy and the Effective New (self-helping) Feelings and Behaviors that normally accompany strongly believed preferential, undogmatic philosophy" (Ellis, 1991, p. 2). Others have expanded the ABC framework to allow for distinctions among different types of cognitive activity. For example, Grieger (1986) presented what he calls a "contextual" ABC model, which attempts to better capture the complexities of human cognitions and the diverse interrelationships among the As, Bs, and Cs. Grieger stressed that it is important to address not only situation-specific beliefs but also enduring beliefs that might represent life positions, values, and interpretational habits. He also proposed that the self be viewed as context rather than as an object in order to facilitate clients' liberating themselves from self-assessment. Other authors, including Ellis (1984), Moore (1988), Raitt (1988), and Wessler and Wessler (1980) have also proposed further elaborations and refinements in the ABC framework. In principle, however, that framework continues to represent the basic theoretical model for RET.

Implementing Rational-Emotive Therapy

Although RET has been applied to different types of clients, with different kinds of problems, using a large variety of specific methods, one process is basic to RET and has been outlined by Grieger (1986, pp. 204–211). This process has four steps:

1. *Rational-emotive psychodiagnosis.* The basic focus of this step is on identifying and explicating the client's disturbance-producing beliefs or philosophies, since they are assumed to form the basis of the client's emotional problems. To accomplish this, the therapist has to determine that the client indeed has internal problems that include emotional disturbance and dysfunctional behavior and therefore require psychotherapeutic rather than some other form of intervention. Grieger called this the chore of "categorizing problems." A second chore of rational-emotive psychodiagnosis is "detecting irrational beliefs." This may be the most important step in the diagnostic process because the irrational beliefs that are detected will become the focus of the actual intervention process. The third chore involved in rational-emotive psychodiagnosis Grieger called "detecting problems about problems." It involves the identifying of secondary symptoms of emotional disturbance, which may exacerbate the original or primary symptoms. In other words, people often develop emotional problems about their emotional problems. The final chore of rational-emotive psychodiagnosis consists of "goal setting." This procedure rounds out the psychodiagnostic process by delineating for the client different options available for determining priorities for subsequent psychotherapy. For example, clients may choose to work on environmental concerns (having to do with the external circumstances related to their problems), an option that usually is not recommended. The preferred option presented to clients would be to work on emotional-behavioral problems about other emotional-behavioral problems, if present, or to work on emotional-behavioral problems directly.

2. *Rational-emotive insight:* Grieger listed five different kinds of insight that clients had better acquire in the process of RET. First, clients must understand the basic conceptualization of activating events, irrational beliefs, and emotional-behavioral consequences, as presented in the ABC theory. This basic concept provides insight about the real cause of emotional problems. Second, clients are encouraged to accept responsibility for their emotional problems by realizing that whatever the events surrounding their original acquisition of irrational beliefs, clients continue to be miserable because they continue to hold these irrational beliefs. Third, clients need to be aware of, acknowledge, and appreciate the specific irrational ideas or beliefs that cause

their emotional problems. Fourth, clients must be helped to understand that they can accept themselves in spite of their newfound realization that they have created and maintained their emotional problems themselves. The fifth and final insight clients must have is that they must work hard, now and in the future, to relinquish their irrational beliefs and to thereby get over their emotional problems.

3. *Rational-emotive working through, Part I—teaching a rational knowledge base:* During this process, the rational-emotive therapist assumes the role of educator or teacher. A large part of the therapist's effort is directed toward helping clients to give up their irrational ideas in spite of fears they may have about giving up something familiar and, in a way, comfortable—a task made more difficult because many clients may be "allergic to thinking" (Ellis, 1967). If successful, the therapist can help clients to understand what is illogical about their ideas or philosophies, show them the self-defeating consequences of their irrational ideas, teach them new ideas contrary to their irrational ones, and convince them of the benefits of such new ideas as a means to motivate them to take responsibility for adopting those new ideas.

4. *Rational-emotive working through, Part II—facilitating a new philosophy:* According to Grieger, Parts I and II of rational-emotive working through are somewhat overlapping and complement each other. The focus in Part II, however, is to instill in clients a new rational way of thinking, a new philosophy that eventually will allow them automatically to act rationally. Primarily, this end is accomplished through disputation and habit strengthening. Disputation involves questioning irrational ideas and philosophies, as well as facilitating clients' discriminations between rational and irrational parts of their ideas; between their wishes and desires on the one hand, and their musts on the other; between doing bad things, and being a bad person. Many different specific techniques may be used as part of disputation. They will be discussed in more detail below. The final aspect of RET, habit strengthening, simply involves encouraging clients to strengthen their newfound rational philosophy of life by thinking about it, practicing it, encouraging others to embrace it, rewarding themselves for being rational, and punishing themselves for being irrational.

Specific Techniques

Practitioners of RET use an extensive array of specific techniques, many borrowed or adapted from other therapeutic approaches. Dryden (1986b) called this "theoretically consistent eclecticism." Presenting all the dozens of techniques used by RET practitioners is beyond the scope of this chapter. Instead, what has been called the "most important and distinctive RET intervention strategy," disputation, will be discussed in some detail (Bernard & Joyce, 1984, pp. 82–89).

Cognitive disputation.   This technique consists of a set of direct verbal statements designed to convince clients of the irrationality of their beliefs. A central feature is articulating, when appropriate, the reasons certain beliefs are irrational. Different means of applying cognitive disputation have been presented by Walen, DiGiuseppe, and Wessler (1980), including the following:

1. Questioning, which forces clients to challenge the logical consistency and semantic clarity of their beliefs
2. Didactic presentations, which may feature mini-lectures, analogies, and parables
3. Humor, including exaggeration and, selectively, paradoxical intention
4. Vicarious modeling, which involves demonstrating that others have successfully coped with similar circumstances

Bernard and Joyce (1984) suggested two additional techniques of cognitive disputation:

5. Cognitive homework assignments, consisting of readings that will help clients to dispute their irrational beliefs, or questionnaires such as the *Rational Self-Help Form*, published by the Institute for Rational-Emotive Therapy
6. Cognitive modeling, in which the RET practitioner models verbally the kinds of rational self-statements that can be used to counter emotional distress arising from the client's use of irrational self-statements

Emotional disputation.   One key difficulty in helping clients achieve their goals through RET is to help them not only to achieve intellectual understanding of their irrational beliefs and how these beliefs contribute to clients' unhappiness, but also to gain the emotional changes that will assist clients to make meaningful changes in the ways they think, feel, and behave. Bernard and Joyce stated:

> Emotive disputational strategies, while overlapping somewhat with behavioral and cognitive strategies, have in common the goal of evoking in the client emotions (desirable and undesirable) which the client can link up with the detection and cognitive disputation of irrational beliefs. (1984, p. 86)

Ellis (1979) suggested that passionate self-statements, repeatedly made by clients to themselves and to others, can be effective in helping clients gain an emotional understanding of what they may already accept at a cognitive level. Essentially, passionate self-statements are rational self-statements made in a particularly dramatic and strong manner. Another emotional disputation technique recommended by Ellis (1979) is shame-attacking exercises— particularly effective with people upset about the shameful consequences of their failures. Essentially, these exercises involve clients' doing something deliberately that they consider ridiculous or shameful, but doing it without feeling ashamed and without considering it particularly risky. Finally, Maultsby and Ellis (1974) suggested the use of rational-emotive imagery as a technique of emotional disputation. In this technique, the RET practitioner asks clients to imagine themselves in a specific problem situation but feeling much better and behaving more adaptively—in other words, to envision positive imagery. Clients are then asked to report the rational self-statements that enabled them to feel better. Dryden (1986a) described numerous additional methods of emotional disputation, calling them vivid disputing methods. These typically involve vividly portraying activating events (the A in the ABC method described above) to help clients tune into their emotional reactions and the cognitive determinants of these reactions.

Behavioral disputation.   Use of behavioral disputation methods is based on the notion, central to RET, that thoughts, feelings, and behavior are very closely linked. Consequently, instructing clients to engage in specific behaviors can serve to encourage clients to give up their irrational beliefs and adopt rational ones. For example, Walen, DiGiuseppe, and Wessler (1980) suggested that clients should be given homework assignments to practice behaviors that will challenge the validity of their irrational beliefs. Such exercises may include clients' deliberately placing themselves in situations that they find frightening, anxiety-producing, embarrassing, or problematic in some other way. These exercises are frequently described as shame-attacking and risk-taking exercises.

Means and Conditions for Implementing Rational-Emotive Therapy
The RET Therapist's Qualifications

Ellis and Dryden (1987) outlined the characteristics and personal qualities of effective RET therapists. Ellis has repeatedly emphasized that the role of the RET therapist is that of an "authoritative (but not authoritarian!) and encouraging teacher" (Ellis & Dryden, 1987, p. 28). They also pointed out that RET therapists tend to be appropriately humorous in order to discourage clients from taking themselves and their problems too seriously. Ellis has underscored that RET involves genuine collaboration between therapist and client. He suggested:

> Therapists had better always give clients unconditional acceptance, and not merely *tell* but *show* their clients that they are accepted by the therapist, *whether or not* they perform adequately and *whether or not* they are nice and lovable.

Moreover, in addition to offering unconditional acceptance, RET therapists teach their clients how to accept themselves. Ellis underscored that such a "double-barrelled approach uniquely emphasizes people's ability to *choose* and *construct* their own self-acceptance" (Ellis, 1992, p. x).

Ellis (1978) made a number of observations about what RET therapists should be like. Among other things, he suggested that effective RET therapists should be comfortable with structure and the intellectual, cognitive, and philosophical orientation of RET. Thus, they should be at ease with conducting themselves in a very strong, actively directive manner, which may involve providing direct behavioral instruction and assuming a teaching role. Ellis suggested, in particular, that effective RET practitioners should "have their acts together" in the sense of not fearing failure, not needing client approval, tolerating both their own and their clients' errors, and having a high tolerance for frustration. Finally, Ellis noted that effective practitioners should strive to be scientific, empirical, and "undevout" in their overall approach to therapy.

Several avenues are open to those who wish to become RET therapists. Basic education and training for becoming a therapist is, of course, available through numerous university-based programs leading to graduate degrees in psychology and counseling, and through professional schools in medicine, social work, and nursing. Many of these educational programs offer training in a variety of therapeutic approaches, often including RET or, at least, training in a variety of cognitive-behavioral methods. To become certified as an RET therapist, however, an individual with the requisite educational background would need to participate in special training programs offered by the Institute for Rational-Emotive Therapy in New York City or any of its numerous affiliates located in all parts of the world.

At the Institute for Rational Emotive Therapy, individuals can earn a primary certificate, advanced certificate, and associate fellowship. Completion of a relatively brief 2 1/2- to 3-day program leads to the most basic certification in RET, the primary certificate, and the more advanced 5-day program leads to the advanced certificate. Both of these must be earned before trainees are eligible to move on to the associate fellowship program, which involves the supervision and evaluation of actual therapy sessions conducted by the trainees over a period of a year. When successfully concluded, this training course leads to associate fellowship membership at the Institute for Rational Emotive Therapy. The Institute also offers fellowship and internship programs that involve prolonged training and supervision at the Institute (Walen, DiGiuseppe, & Dryden, 1992).

Conditions for Conducting Rational-Emotive Therapy

RET, as a verbal intervention method, requires no special equipment and relatively little in the way of facilities. RET does not require the kind of intensive concentration necessary in, for example, hypnotherapy. Consequently, a reasonably quiet and comfortable office suffices. Such an office must offer privacy and protect the confidentiality of all material disclosed within its walls.

Limitations of Rational-Emotive Therapy
Contraindications

There are no absolute contraindications to the conduct of RET. Nevertheless, for some conditions RET would be inadvisable because its successful application is very difficult or because alternative treatments may be far superior. For example, severely developmentally disabled individuals may be unable to comprehend the irrationality of their beliefs despite competent efforts to demonstrate the superiority of rational beliefs. Severely paranoid individuals may perceive RET as a devious effort at brainwashing, and acutely psychotic individuals may be incapable of the reality testing necessary to behave rationally. These are examples of rather extreme states, however, and very few potential clients are likely to be and to remain so dysfunctional that RET is contraindicated.

Hazards

The conduct of RET has relatively few hazards; however, Ellis and Dryden (1987) pointed out that therapists must be careful not to show undue warmth in their relationships with most clients. Through being unduly warm and providing attention, caring and support, therapists may unwittingly reinforce an illogical idea that represents a major source of difficulty for many clients—namely, their dire need for love and approval. Thus, although clients may temporarily improve because one of their irrational needs is being met, their improvement will be achieved at the cost of becoming dependent on the therapist.

Although Ellis acknowledged that RET may be used in conjunction with many other therapeutic interventions, he warned against using what he calls "insufficient" and "inelegant" procedures (Ellis, 1991, pp. 5–8). Among other things, he suggested generally avoiding free association and dream analysis. He also indicated that it may be counterproductive for clients to engage in very detailed and prolonged accounts of their activating events, to engage in compulsive talking about feelings, or to engage in "too much positive thinking." Finally, Ellis warned against "overstressing practical changes."

Another potential hazard that Ellis (1985) addressed in some detail is resistance. Ellis considered it one of the most important aspects of almost any psychotherapeutic intervention. Client resistance to therapeutic change is assumed by Ellis to result from both biological predispositions and learning. Thus, specific reasons for client resistance to therapeutic change are likely to vary significantly, even for the same client at different times. Just as Ellis favors using a large variety of cognitive, emotive, and behavioral techniques in RET proper, he also favors using the same techniques to overcome resistance in clients. He also proposed, however, that very rarely and under unusual and special circumstances and with due caution, some inherently hazardous methods may be used. These methods could include "inducing clients to become devoutly and dogmatically religious or cultish," or convincing "them that they will undoubtedly wind up in heaven—or hell" (p. 188).

Ellis is also aware, however, that therapists may be resistant or inefficient for a number of reasons. The same kinds of irrational beliefs that may cause a client to seek help may also be held by therapists with regard to their therapeutic endeavor. For example, a therapist may feel a need to be successful with all clients virtually all of the time. Ellis warned that such absolutist ideas can significantly interfere with therapists' effectiveness and therefore represent a hazard to the client seeking help. Finally, Ellis stressed that therapy has distinct limitations and shortcomings, and that therapists should be aware that they can do harm as well as good.

The Effectiveness of Rational-Emotive Therapy

Summarizing the research on RET's effectiveness is relatively difficult because RET encompasses so many specific techniques and because the volume of research generated over the years is quite overwhelming. Individuals interested in more closely examining the broad range of research available can refer to the *Journal of Rational-Emotive & Cognitive-Behavior Therapy* and numerous other publications concerned with psychotherapy and counseling. For present purposes, it should suffice to note that Mahoney reviewed the research literature on rational-emotive therapy in 1974, and DiGiuseppe and Miller reviewed 22 outcome studies on rational-emotive therapy in 1977. Generally, these reviews offered qualified support for the efficacy of RET in dealing with a wide variety of clients using a broad range of techniques. A subsequent review by McGovern and Silverman (1984) examined 47 studies, of which 31 had significant results favoring RET over other approaches. Moreover, in all the studies they reviewed, the RET treatment group showed improvement, and "in no study was another treatment method significantly better than RET" (p. 99).

Finally, a recent review of outcome studies in rational-emotive therapy by Haaga and Davison (1989) served to confirm the overwhelmingly positive assessment of RET, while underscoring the diversity and complexity of the procedures used in modern applications of RET. These authors pointed out that RET consists of much more than simply telling a client that he or she is thinking irrationally and would be better off thinking differently. They noted that, as a consequence, it is not always easy to tell how well a given researcher has implemented Ellis's principles regarding personality and personality change. Interestingly, Haaga and Davison reviewed the application of RET not just to clinical subjects but also to nonclinical ones. They found RET effective in reducing self-reported irrationality, neuroticism, test anxiety, and trait anxiety (p. 158) in children. They reported similar findings with nonclinical adults. In treating a variety of symptoms including anxiety, obsessions, stuttering, psychosexual dysfunctions, depression, obesity, and antisocial behavior, RET either was most effective when compared with other treatments or else showed considerable promise. For some other symptoms and conditions, such as anger, headaches, obsessions, agoraphobia, and simple phobia, results were frequently more difficult to interpret and did not clearly favor RET over other approaches.

References

Bernard, M. E., & DiGiuseppe, R. (Eds.). (1989). *Inside rational-emotive therapy: A critical appraisal of the theory and therapy of Albert Ellis*. New York: Academic Press.

Bernard, M. E., & Joyce, M. R. (Eds.). (1984). *Rational-emotive therapy with children and adolescents: Theory, treatment strategies, preventative methods*. New York: Wiley.

Bernard, M. E., & Joyce, M. R. (1991). RET with children and adolescents. In M. E. Bernard (Ed.), *Using rational-emotive therapy effectively: A practitioner's guide* (pp. 319–347). New York: Plenum.

DiGiuseppe, R. A., & Miller, N. J. (1977). A review of outcome studies on rational-emotive therapy. In A. Ellis & R. Grieger (Eds.), *Handbook of rational-emotive therapy* (pp. 72–95). New York: Springer.

DiMattia, D. J. (1991). Using RET effectively in the workplace. In M. E. Bernard (Ed.), *Using rational-emotive therapy effectively: A practitioner's guide* (pp. 303–317). New York: Plenum.

Dryden, W. (1986a). Vivid methods in rational-emotive therapy. In A. Ellis & R. M. Grieger (Eds.), *Handbook of rational-emotive therapy* (Vol. 2, pp. 221–245). New York: Springer.

Dryden, W. (1986b). A case of theoretically consistent eclecticism: Humanizing a computer "addict." *International Journal of Eclectic Psychotherapy, 5*, 309–327.

Ellis, A. (1957). Rational psychotherapy and individual psychology. *Journal of Individual Psychology, 13*, 38–44.

Ellis, A. (1958). Rational psychotherapy. *Journal of General Psychology, 59*, 35–49.

Ellis, A. (1962). *Reason and emotion in psychotherapy.* Secaucus, NJ: Lyle Stuart.

Ellis, A. (1967). Talking to adolescents about sex. *Rational Living, 2*, 7–12.

Ellis, A. (1978). Family therapy: A phenomenological and active-directive approach. *Journal of Marriage and Family Counseling, 4*(2), 43–50.

Ellis, A. (1979). The practice of rational-emotive therapy. In A. Ellis & J. M. Whiteley (Eds.), *Theoretical and empirical foundations of rational-emotive therapy* (pp. 61–100). Pacific Grove, CA: Brooks/Cole.

Ellis, A. (1981). The place of Immanuel Kant in cognitive psychotherapy. *Rational Living, 16*(2), 13–16.

Ellis, A. (1984). *Rational-emotive therapy and cognitive behavior therapy.* New York: Springer.

Ellis, A. (1985). *Overcoming resistance: Rational-emotive therapy with difficult clients.* New York: Springer.

Ellis, A. (1989). Comments on my critics. In M. E. Bernard & R. DiGiuseppe (Eds.), *Inside rational-emotive therapy: A critical appraisal of the theory and therapy of Albert Ellis* (pp. 199–233). New York: Academic Press.

Ellis, A. (1991). Using RET effectively: Reflections and interview. In M. E. Bernard (Ed.), *Using rational-emotive therapy effectively: A practitioner's guide* (pp. 1–33). New York: Plenum.

Ellis, A. (1992). Foreword. In Walen, S. R., DiGiuseppe, R., & Dryden, W., *A practitioner's guide to rational-emotive therapy* (2nd ed., pp. i–xiii). New York: Oxford University Press.

Ellis, A., & Bernard, M. E. (1986). What is rational-emotive therapy (RET)? In A. Ellis & R. M. Grieger (Eds.), *Handbook of rational-emotive therapy* (Vol. 2, pp. 3–30). New York: Springer.

Ellis, A., & Dryden, W. (1987). (Eds.). *The practice of rational-emotive therapy (RET)*. New York: Springer.

Ellis, A., & Grieger, R. (1986). *Handbook of rational-emotive therapy* (Vol. 2). New York: Springer.

Grieger, R. M. (1986). From a linear to a contextual model of the ABC's of RET. In A. Ellis & R. M. Grieger (Eds.), *Handbook of rational-emotive therapy* (Vol. 2, pp. 59–80). New York: Springer.

Haaga, D., & Davison, J. (1989). A review of outcome studies in rational-emotive therapy. In M. E. Bernard & R. DiGiuseppe (Eds.), *Inside rational-emotive therapy: A critical appraisal of the theory and therapy of Albert Ellis* (pp. 155–197). New York: Academic Press.

McGovern, T. E., & Silverman, M. (1984). A review of outcome studies of rational-emotive therapy from 1977 to 1982. *Journal of Rational Emotive Therapy, 2*, 1–22.

Mahoney, M. J. (1974). *Cognition and behavior modification*. Cambridge, MA: Ballinger.

Mahoney, M. J., Lyddon, W. J., & Alford, D. J. (1989). An evaluation of the rational-emotive theory of psychotherapy. In M. E. Bernard & R. DiGiuseppe (Eds.), *Inside rational-emotive therapy: A critical appraisal of the theory and therapy of Albert Ellis* (pp. 69–94). New York: Academic Press.

Maultsby, M. C., Jr., & Ellis, A. (1974). *Techniques for using rational-emotive imagery*. New York: Institute for Rational-Emotive Therapy.

Moore, R. H. (1988). Inference as 'A' in rational-emotive therapy. In W. Dryden & P. Trower (Eds.), *Developments in rational-emotive therapy* (pp. 3–11). Philadelphia, PA: Open University Press.

Raitt, A. (1988). Weight control: A rational-emotive approach. In W. Dryden & P. Trower (Eds.), *Developments in rational-emotive therapy* (pp. 197–209). Philadelphia, PA: Open University Press.

Rogers, C. R. (1957). The necessary and sufficient conditions of therapeutic personality change. *Journal of Consulting Psychology, 21*, 95–103.

Walen, S. R., DiGiuseppe, R., & Dryden, W. (1992). *A practitioner's guide to rational-emotive therapy* (2nd ed.). New York: Oxford University Press.

Walen, S. R., DiGiuseppe, R., & Wessler, R. L. (1980). *A practitioner's guide to rational-emotive therapy*. New York: Oxford University Press.

Wessler, R. A., & Wessler, R. L. (1980). *The principles and practice of rational-emotive therapy*. San Francisco: Jossey-Bass.

Ziegler, D. J. (1989). A critique of rational-emotive theory of personality. In M. E. Bernard & R. DiGiuseppe (Eds.), *Inside rational-emotive therapy: A critical appraisal of the theory and therapy of Albert Ellis* (pp. 27–45). New York: Academic Press.

CHAPTER 8

....

Reality
Therapy

....

■

The overriding purpose of reality therapy is to help people improve their ability to live responsibly. As far as William Glasser, the founder of reality therapy, is concerned, all pathological behavior, whether neurotic or delinquent, represents irresponsibility. People can fulfill their own long-term needs and be better members of society as a whole if they learn to behave more responsibly. Those identified as patients have one common characteristic: "They all deny the reality of the world around them" (1965, p. 6). Glasser proposed that therapy is most likely to be successful when patients are able to give up denying the real world and understand that they must fulfill their needs within the framework of that world. Perhaps most important, Glasser insisted that individuals, in spite of emotional problems, delinquent or antisocial behaviors, or personality problems, must learn to accept responsibility for their own behavior in order to live more responsible and therefore more satisfying lives. The ultimate goal of reality therapy is to help people to accomplish this acceptance of responsibility.

History of Reality Therapy

Reality therapy grew out of the dissatisfaction of one psychiatrist, William Glasser, with the characteristic ways his profession treated patients. Glasser's dissatisfaction became focused toward the end of his psychiatric residency when he realized the severe limitations of classical psychoanalysis and began to formulate what he eventually called reality therapy. In particular, he objected to the insistence of psychoanalysis and other conventional therapy methods that therapists had to remain impersonal, aloof, and objective to be effective. Glasser went even further in repudiating traditional approaches by calling into question the entire concept of mental illness (Glasser, 1960). Working at the Ventura School for Delinquent Girls in California, he developed and instituted his new approach to treatment, which proved so promising and successful in that setting that he also introduced it, with the collaboration of G. L. Harrington, at the Veteran's Administration Neuropsychiatric Hospital in Los Angeles, to treat hospitalized psychotic patients.

In 1962, Glasser felt sufficiently confident about the effectiveness of reality therapy to present it to the National Conference on Crime and Delinquency. In 1965, Glasser reported these early beginnings of reality therapy in his now classic book, *Reality Therapy: A New Approach to Psychiatry*. In it he described the basic concepts of reality therapy and its application to delinquent girls and psychotic patients, in outpatient therapy, and as a means to mental hygiene in the public schools. Glasser's initial book on reality therapy was enormously successful and hailed by the distinguished psychologist O. H. Mowrer as extraordinarily important (Glasser, 1965). Less than ten years later, Glasser was reported to be in tremendous demand on the lecture circuit, and he was helping communities set up teacher-training centers (Berges, 1976). In addition, as president of the Institute for Reality Therapy, Glasser has continued to elaborate reality therapy, to extend its influence, and to train others in its use.

Range of Applicability

Glasser stated his belief that almost any individual can benefit from being taught to live life responsibly. He disputed the reality of mental illness considering the numerous psychiatric diagnoses to simply describe various kinds of irresponsible behavior. Reality therapy is therefore applicable to all the conditions covered by those diagnoses. Glasser wrote that "using reality therapy there is no essential difference in the treatment of various psychiatric problems. . . . The treatment of psychotic veterans is almost exactly the same as the treatment of delinquent, adolescent girls" (1965, p. 48). Glasser has encouraged others to apply the principles of reality therapy to other populations in other settings (Karrass & Glasser, 1980). Clearly, he has viewed reality therapy as something anyone can use to help themselves and others to live more successful lives. Reality therapy is thus not exclusively for people with serious problems, but also for anyone who wishes to gain a successful identity or help others become successful (Glasser, 1975).

Being particularly intrigued with the broad potential of reality therapy in school settings, in 1969 Glasser published his book *Schools Without Failure*, an elaboration and extension of his previously published principles of reality therapy as they apply to school settings. As already noted, much of Glasser's original work in developing reality therapy was accomplished at California's Ventura School for Delinquent Girls. One reason for extending the application of reality therapy to the public schools has been Glasser's conviction that its application in such settings could have important preventative outcomes. Consequently, Glasser proposed that reality therapy be applied in a public school–based mental hygiene program. He has also offered one-semester courses designed to teach the principles of reality therapy to schoolteachers, including those in nursery school, elementary school, and junior and senior high schools, as well as other school personnel, such as nurses and counselors. More recently, Glasser (1986), expanded his ideas about application of his insights in the school system through the publication of *Control Theory in the Classroom*.

Theoretical Foundations
Assumptions About Human Nature

A basic assumption in Glasser's formulation of reality therapy is that "in their unsuccessful effort to fulfill their needs . . . all patients have a common characteristic: *they all deny the reality of the world around them*" (1965, p. 6). According to Glasser, people have "two basic psychological needs: the need to love and be loved and the need to feel that we are worthwhile to ourselves and to others" (1965, p. 9). The need to love and be loved is lifelong and must be satisfied in both its essential respects. Glasser emphasized, in particular, that we must maintain a satisfactory standard of behavior in order to feel that we are worthwhile. Individuals must learn to appraise their behavior realistically, thus allowing them to correct themselves when they do wrong and credit themselves when they do right. Glasser pointed out that substandard behavior, left uncorrected, prevents people from feeling worthwhile.

Individuals who do not learn to fulfill their basic needs will suffer all their lives. Glasser suggested that if one learns to satisfy one's needs early in life, chances for a satisfactory life are enhanced, although there is no guarantee that the ability to satisfy one's needs will persist amid changing circumstances. At times, people have to relearn how to satisfy their needs. They can succeed in doing so if they have what Glasser has called the single most important factor for fulfilling their needs—namely, a relationship of mutual caring with at least one other person. Moreover, this critical involvement must occur with individuals who are in touch with reality and able to satisfy their own needs. Glasser stated that at least one such relationship of mutual caring is essential, because without it and the resulting encouragement to cope with reality, people resort to unrealistic ways of meeting their needs.

In *The Identity Society*, Glasser (1975) made some important additional points about human nature. Basically, he proposed that society is in the process of accomplishing a fundamental shift from what Glasser called a civilized survival society to a civilized identity society. In an identity society, people struggle to find themselves and to enjoy the pleasures of their own humanity. Glasser stated that "almost everyone is personally engaged in a search for acceptance as a person" (1975, p. 2). Integrating his earlier views on human needs, Glasser proposed that when individuals are unsuccessful in their attempts to satisfy their need to be loved and to feel worthwhile, they develop a failure identity. A failure identity can result in virtually all the problems that have been labeled as delinquency, criminality, and mental illness. Individuals develop a success identity, however, when their need for love and self-worth is satisfied. Helping people to change their failure identity to a success identity is thus a major objective of reality therapy.

Assumptions About Conducting Reality Therapy

The fulfillment of a person's needs takes place in the person's present life. Glasser has taken the position that this fulfillment is independent of the person's past, regardless of how difficult or miserable that past has been. Consequently, reality therapy involves ignoring the past, for the most part, and focusing on the present. Glasser stated that nothing that happened to a person in the past will make any difference once the person learns to satisfy his or her needs in the present. As will be discussed later, in reality therapy a person's past may be used in some specific ways, but for the most part history is ignored in favor of concentrating on the present.

Another underlying assumption in conducting reality therapy is that concern with the person's unconscious mental processes is unnecessary to successfully help the person fulfill important needs. This assumption represents a major departure from most traditional psychiatric therapies, and particularly from psychoanalysis. Glasser has gone to some length in differentiating reality therapy from conventional therapy. Specifically, Glasser has listed six ways that are important in making this differentiation:

1. Reality therapy does not accept the concept of mental illness because that concept portrays patients as having no responsibility for their behavior.

2. Reality therapy does not focus on the patient's history because it cannot change what has happened to the patient in the past and it does not accept that the patient is limited by past experiences.

3. Reality therapists relate to patients as themselves, not as transference figures.

4. Reality therapy ignores unconscious conflicts because patients may be prevented from becoming involved with the therapist by using unconscious motivations as an excuse for their behaviors.

5. Reality therapy emphasizes the morality of behavior by encouraging therapists to make the distinction between right and wrong. Glasser stated that moral behavior can be defined as individuals acting in such a way that they give and receive love and feel worthwhile to themselves and others.

6. Reality therapy does not focus on promoting insight; instead, it focuses on teaching patients better ways to fulfill their needs. (Glasser, 1965, pp. 44–45)

Another important feature underlying the use of reality therapy is that along with throwing out the concept of mental illness, reality therapy denies the necessity for psychiatric diagnosis. In particular, Glasser pointed out that psychiatrists' attempt to follow the medical model in treating their patients has not worked because, basically, no brain pathology has been shown to exist. In reality therapy the treatment approach does not differ across the various and diverse manifestations of psychiatric problems or personality disorders. According to Glasser, all these different manifestations represent irresponsibility and failure to satisfy basic needs on the part of the patient, and they can all be treated using the basic framework of reality therapy. When people are able to fulfill their needs, and to do so in a way that does not interfere with others' ability to fulfill their needs, they are acting responsibly. The concept of responsibility is so central to Glasser's approach that he has suggested that the term *responsibility* be used instead of *mental health* and *irresponsibility* instead of *mental illness* (Glasser, 1965, p. 15). Finally, in disavowing adherence to the prevalent medical model used in psychiatry, Glasser has defined the role of the reality therapist as that of a teacher, who teaches better ways to fulfill needs, more effective ways to become more involved, and more effective (responsible) ways to live in general.

Implementing Reality Therapy

Glasser indicated that, in contrast to conventional psychiatry, in which the theory is easy but the practice difficult, reality therapy has a relatively simple theoretical base but a difficult treatment procedure (cf. Bassin, 1976a).

Nevertheless, reality therapy appears to involve three specific, closely interrelated procedures (Glasser, 1965, p. 21). The first consists of the therapist's developing involvement with the patient. The second procedure consists of the therapist's challenging unrealistic patient behaviors in a way that will not undermine the relationship between therapist and patient. The third set of procedures involves the therapist's teaching the patient better ways to fulfill important human needs.

Glasser has lectured and written extensively about the practice of reality therapy, always emphasizing that therapy is a special kind of teaching, which tries to accomplish in a concentrated, intense period what should have occurred during normal growing up (1965, p. 20). Over the years Glasser has repeatedly written about the most important principles to be implemented in conducting reality therapy. Initially, he focused on therapist involvement and the teaching of responsibility (1965). He then further refined and elaborated reality therapy and proposed seven principles of reality therapy (for example, Glasser & Zunin, 1972). More recently, he spoke of 8 steps involved in the conduct of reality therapy (Glasser, 1981). Others have distilled more than 8 steps from their reading of Glasser's approach. For example, Rachin (1976) proposed 14 steps and explained that the principles of reality therapy are "common sense interwoven with a firm belief in the dignity of man and his ability to improve his lot" (p. 324).

Glasser's seven principles describe how the therapist becomes responsibly involved with patients in order to guide them toward a success identity (Glasser & Zunin, 1972). Since they represent the most readily recognized substance of reality therapy, the seven principles are briefly described below. They represent the most significant features implemented (although not sequentially) in reality therapy. It has always been Glasser's intention to make reality therapy straightforward and easily understood; he has not been concerned with building a formal theory. Consequently, the number of principles or steps used to represent the basic ideas of reality therapy is not critical; what is important is to capture and present the ideas as clearly and simply as possible.

Principle I: Personal. This principle signifies that the therapist is warm, friendly, and personally involved with the patient. Understanding and realistic concern are expressed by the therapist who uses personal pronouns such as *I* and *me* and *you* as a means to facilitate involvement. The personal principle means that therapists' traditional aloofness is discarded; anything, including the therapist's personal life, is open for discussion. As a matter of fact, patients are discouraged from dwelling on their misery and are encouraged to talk about whatever may be important to them. Perhaps most important, the therapist conveys to the patient his or her belief that the patient is capable of achieving happiness and fulfillment in life.

Principle II: Focus on behavior rather than feelings. This principle acknowledges, basically, that behaviors can be much more readily changed than feelings. In other words, it can be rather straightforward to help patients to behave differently; it is not nearly as apparent how one can help patients to feel differently. Moreover, the underlying theory of reality therapy tells us that if patients act responsibly, they are able to fulfill their needs and will very likely feel better as a consequence.

Principle III: Focus on the present. The focus on the present is mandated by the realization that only the immediate present and the future can be changed—never the past. The person's past need not be ignored; but when it is discussed, focus is on the strengthening and character-building experiences in the patient's past that may be related to the patient's current attempts to be successful. Discussion may involve exploring constructive alternatives that the patient might have taken at the time. It may also focus on what the patient did right then, thus avoiding even greater problems.

Principle IV: Value judgments. This principle addresses the requirement that all patients must make value judgments in order to appreciate how they contribute to their own failures, as a prerequisite to being able to accept meaningful help in their efforts to change. Bassin (1976a) has called this principle the most important single component of reality therapy, next to the principle of involvement. He suggested that patients must be pressed, again and again, to evaluate their behaviors in order to determine how those behaviors may or may not be helping them meet their needs, and whether those behaviors are interfering with other people's meeting their needs. In short, patients must constantly make value judgments about whether they are behaving responsibly. Therapists must not impose their value judgments but rather insist that patients make their own.

Principle V: Planning and commitment. A significant feature of reality therapy is that it involves making realistic plans for change. Generally, simple and easily implemented plans are favored because they increase the likelihood of success and thereby contribute to the patient's achievement of a success identity. Frequently, plans are formalized as written contracts, which may enhance patients' strength, responsibility, and degree of commitment. In addition to the patient's commitment to honor and pursue what is planned, the therapist must also be committed to stay with the patient no matter how difficult the process. Glasser has exhorted therapists to never, ever, give up.

Principle VI: Evasions. If plans fail, the patient must understand that excuses are simply not acceptable. Excuses allow patients to evade responsibility. It is far better for therapists to work with patients on developing new, more realistic plans than to discuss reasons for a plan's failure. Therapists must not put patients down for failing, but instead motivate them to work with their therapists on developing a better plan.

Principle VII: Eliminate punishment. Punishment works poorly with most people. It works particularly poorly with individuals who have a failure identity, because it simply reinforces their belief that they are no good. Glasser has made a distinction between punishment and the natural consequences of failure, which may help patients to make realistic plans and to have the commitment to follow through. Moreover, punishment is likely to interfere in the therapist's efforts to be perceived by the patient as a genuine, concerned person committed to helping the patient to understand and deal with reality. (Adapted from Glasser & Zunin, 1972, pp. 58–61)

Glasser's (1981, pp. 267–269) statement of the steps of reality therapy is slightly different from his presentation of the seven principles, although the seven principles are clearly represented within the eight steps. The following briefly summarizes Glasser's eight steps so as to permit comparison with the originally formulated seven principles.

Step 1: Make friends. This first step focuses on helping the patient enter into a warm, concerned relationship with the therapist and experience a sense of belonging. This step also involves the therapist's asking patients what they want in order to assist the therapist in understanding the patient's internal world.

Step 2: What are you doing now? This step involves helping patients to focus on the "doing" component of their present behavior rather than on their past history. Glasser has stressed the point that any feeling patients experience, such as depression, needs to be conceptualized as a feeling behavior; patients must change that behavior if they wish to feel better.

Step 3: Is this behavior helping you? In negotiating this step, therapists ask their patients to evaluate whether their behavior is working for them. Invariably, patients discover that their problem behaviors (symptoms, in the vocabulary of traditional psychiatry) are not working for them in their efforts to satisfy their needs. This realization leads right into Step 4.

Step 4: Make a plan to do better. This step incorporates much of what goes on during reality therapy. The therapist takes an active role in helping patients figure out better behaviors. During this process, the therapist fully implements the teaching role of reality therapy by offering patients behavioral choices, pointing out behaviors patients may not have considered, and even suggesting specific behaviors. Ultimately, patients will thus have a behavioral repertoire filled with behaviors more likely to get them what they want than their old behaviors were.

Step 5: Get a commitment. In this step, the therapist works on getting patients to commit to trying new behaviors and to plan to behave better. One danger is that, despite making a commitment, the patient does not carry out the plan. Glasser suggested that this problem is generally avoided in reality therapy if the therapist ensures that commitments are made only to plans that are reasonable and possible.

Step 6: No excuses. Throughout years of writing about reality therapy, Glasser has stressed the necessity of therapists' turning down excuses offered by their patients. Therapists need to be tough sometimes in not accepting excuses and in letting patients suffer the natural consequences of failure. Equally important, at the same time, is that therapists reconfirm their faith in the patient's ultimate ability to behave better, including a return to Steps 4 and 5 in order to develop a new plan, to get a new commitment, and to keep on trying.

Step 7: No punishment. Reality therapy does not include punishment (or criticism) of patients for having inadequate behaviors or for any other reason. Basically, punishment contributes to what Glasser has previously called a failure identity. Although punishment is viewed as not only inappropriate but harmful, reality therapy does allow patients to suffer reasonable consequences of their failures, which may include being restrained from behaving in ways that hurt others.

Step 8: Don't give up. Many of Glasser's case histories include critical periods when patients realize that the therapist is unlikely to give up trying to help them. Usually, such a critical period represents a turning point in the therapeutic process. Glasser has maintained that a patient's recognition that a therapist will not give up solidifies the patient's feeling of belongingness and commitment to learn better behaviors.

Means and Conditions for Implementing Reality Therapy
The Reality Therapist's Qualifications

Glasser (1965, p. 20) maintained that, in principle, anyone can learn to use the general principles of reality therapy. Teachers, counselors, parole officers, ministers, athletic coaches, and others who work with people may employ therapeutic principles. Psychiatrists and other social scientists, however, have the special responsibility of working with the most irresponsible people, necessitating their work as therapists, which is differentiated from common guidance merely by its intensity. The most important attribute of reality therapists is their ability to get involved and to do so relatively quickly. Glasser has stated a number of therapist qualities likely to facilitate the therapist's ability to develop the desired involvement:

> The therapist must be a very responsible person—tough, interested, human, and sensitive. He must be able to fulfill his own needs and must be willing to discuss some of his own struggles so that the patient can see that acting responsibly is possible though sometimes difficult. Neither aloof, superior, nor sacrosanct, he must never imply that what he does, what he stands for, or what he values is unimportant. He must have the strength to become involved, to have his values tested by the patient, and to withstand intense criticism by the person he is trying to help. Every fault and defect may be picked apart by the patient. Willing to admit that, like the patient, he is far from perfect, the therapist must nevertheless show that a person can act responsibly even if it takes great effort.
>
> The therapist must always be strong, never expedient. He must withstand the patient's requests for sympathy, for an excess of sedatives, for justification of his actions no matter how the patient pleads or threatens. Never condoning an irresponsible action on the patient's part, he must be willing to watch the patient suffer if that helps him toward responsibility. (1965, pp. 22–23)

One of the more controversial characteristics of reality therapists, according to Glasser, is their ability to become emotionally involved with all patients, to be affected by them, and to suffer with them. Glasser has maintained that posttherapy friendships between therapists and patients should be neither discouraged nor dismissed, for they are natural consequences of the kind of involvement that therapists must have with their clients in order to help them to become responsible individuals. Gutsch, Sisemore, and Williams (1984) concluded that although Glasser is not explicit about so doing, he relies not only on the therapist's personal characteristics but also to a certain extent on modeling and positive reinforcement to influence change in patients.

Conditions for Conducting Reality Therapy

Reality therapy is a multifaceted approach that can be applied in many different settings. Bassin (1976a) stated that it is less a technique than an existential philosophy that can be translated into clear-cut procedures to help people. Glasser (1965) originally described a number of different facilities in which reality therapy was developed. For example, he spoke of organizing the entire environment at the Ventura School for Girls around the principles of reality therapy. The treatment environment included not only the physical facilities, but the entire staff, from custodians through psychiatrists. It even included volunteers from the community, who took girls out of the institution and treated them like family members in their own homes. Another setting Glasser described was a whole building of a large neuropsychiatric hospital— essentially a ward for chronic psychiatric patients. In that setting, as at the Ventura School, the entire staff created a reality therapy environment, which depended far more on a properly trained staff than on any specific physical facilities. Glasser (1969, 1986) reported extensively on implementation of reality therapy in schools. Again, the focus was on creating a total environment that implemented the principles of reality therapy. Physical facilities are much less important than proper training of teachers in reality therapy innovations, such as Circles of Learning and learning teams.

Reality therapy can also be applied in the more traditional settings of the counselor's or therapist's office. There, facilities requirements are the same as those for most other forms of verbal intervention—namely, a reasonably quiet and comfortable environment that offers privacy. Glasser has maintained throughout his writings, however, that reality therapy should be practiced in group sessions when possible. Groups are particularly appropriate for delinquents and students because they may have an easier time relating to one another and accepting one another's perceptions than they would accepting an authority figure's views. With other groups of individuals, too, group procedures may accelerate members' acceptance of responsibility, as well as members' involvement with one another. Consequently, practice of reality therapy frequently requires the availability of a group room large enough for a meeting of 10 to 12 individuals, the size of the average therapy group.

Limitations of Reality Therapy
Contraindications

Reality therapy is based on the premise that everyone is capable in principle of satisfying his or her needs and living responsible and fulfilling lives. Consequently, all individuals who have been unable to fulfill their needs—as manifested in irresponsible conduct, including delinquency, criminal behavior, alcoholism, drug addiction, and so-called mental illness—are proper candidates for reality therapy. Only those individuals who have some form of organic pathology that keeps them from fulfilling their needs may be inappropriate for reality therapy.

Hazards

The most important hazards involved in the conduct of reality therapy involve therapists' not adhering to the principles of reality therapy. According to Glasser, fatal errors in reality therapy involve therapists' giving up on patients or giving in to patients' attempts to obtain therapist approval for irresponsible behaviors. Moreover, because of the requirement for personal involvement with patients, therapists leave themselves open to criticism and to continual testing by patients. Ultimately, such testing is designed to find out whether the therapist is, indeed, the responsible person that he or she wants the patient to be. If therapists are found vulnerable and can be shown to have acted irresponsibly themselves, their demands that patients act responsibly may fail.

Many therapists, as compassionate and caring individuals, have a natural tendency to want to comfort their patients and to empathize with them about how unfair life has been. These therapist behaviors are hazardous to patients' ultimate ability to satisfy their needs and simply help patients accept their irresponsible behaviors and become more comfortable with them. Glasser (1965, p. 148) stated; "*It is important that depressed patients do not get sympathy because sympathy emphasizes their worthlessness and depresses them even more.*" Therapists must be vigilant in implementing the principles of reality therapy, which require them to be tough taskmasters who insist that patients cease dwelling on past problems and symptoms and accept responsibility for fulfilling their needs in the real world.

The Effectiveness of Reality Therapy

Glasser has taken the position that meaningful experimental studies of reality therapy's effectiveness cannot be accomplished because they are too difficult to conduct. Instead, Glasser's preference has been to emphasize single case study methods to demonstrate the effectiveness of reality therapy. Indeed, his books are filled with examples of such successful cases. Although the evidence in favor of reality therapy that has been accumulated in this manner is quite impressive, it does not represent the kind of scientific evidence required to support an unqualified endorsement of reality therapy as a treatment method. Nevertheless, many of Glasser's ideas have been met receptively by psychiatrists and psychologists eager to embrace an alternative to psychoanalysis, on the one hand, and strictly behavioral approaches, on the other.

Glasser's position has been criticized as unnecessarily radical in its complete rejection of psychodynamic and other insight-oriented approaches to counseling (Tosi, Leclair, Peters, & Murphy, 1987). Glasser has also offended some by rejecting the concept of mental illness. Glasser nevertheless has been praised for his courage in advocating positions that were, and are, controversial. For example, some have found his position on the importance of moral values and responsibility in the therapy process disconcerting. Others have been concerned about Glasser's apparent willingness to generalize from his experience in working with delinquents to psychiatric patients in general. In spite of some shortcomings, however, Glasser's position has been sufficiently provocative and apparently successful that reality therapy continues to be practiced widely in many different settings.

References

Bassin, A. (1976a). IRT therapy in marriage counseling. In A. Bassin, T. E. Bratter, & R. L. Rachin (Eds.), *The reality therapy reader: A survey of the work of William Glasser, M.D.* (pp. 181–204). New York: Harper & Row.

Bassin, A. (1976b). The reality therapy paradigm. In A. Bassin, T. E. Bratter, & R. L. Rachin (Eds.), *The reality therapy reader: A survey of the work of William Glasser, M.D.* (pp. 265–280). New York: Harper & Row.

Bassin, A., Bratter, T. E., & Rachin, R. L. (Eds.). (1976). *The reality therapy reader: A survey of the work of William Glasser, M.D.* New York: Harper & Row.

Berges, M. (1976). A realistic approach. In A. Bassin, T. E. Bratter, & R. L. Rachin (Eds.), *The reality therapy reader: A survey of the work of William Glasser, M.D.* (pp. 6–13). New York: Harper & Row.

Bratter, T. E. (1976). Something old, something new, something borrowed: Introduction. In A. Bassin, T. E. Bratter, & R. L. Rachin (Eds.), *The reality therapy reader: A survey of the work of William Glasser, M.D.* (pp. 74–80). New York: Harper & Row.

Glasser, W. (1960). *Mental health or mental illness? Psychiatry for practical action.* New York: Harper & Row.

Glasser, W. (1965). *Reality therapy: A new approach to psychiatry.* New York: Harper & Row.

Glasser, W. (1969). *Schools without failure.* New York: Harper & Row.

Glasser, W. (1975). *The identity society* (rev. ed.). New York: Harper & Row.

Glasser, W. (1981). *Stations of the mind: New directions for Reality Therapy.* New York: Harper & Row.

Glasser, W. (1986). *Control theory in the classroom.* New York: Harper & Row.

Glasser, W., & Zunin, L. M. (1972). Reality therapy. *Current Psychiatric Therapies, 12,* 58–61.

Gutsch, K. U., Sisemore, D. A., & Williams, R. L., Sr. (1984). *Systems of psychotherapy: An empirical analysis of theoretical models.* Springfield, IL: Charles C Thomas.

Karrass, C. L., & Glasser, W. (1980). *Both-win management: A practical approach to improving employee performance, using the 8-step RPM program.* New York: Lippincott.

Rachin, R. L. (1976). Helping people help themselves. In A. Bassin, T. E. Bratter, & R. L. Rachin (Eds.), *The reality therapy reader: A survey of the work of William Glasser, M.D.* (pp. 313–325). New York: Harper & Row.

Tosi, D. J., Leclair, S. W., Peters, H. J., & Murphy, M. A. (1987). *Theories and applications of counseling: Systems and techniques of counseling and psychotherapy.* Springfield, IL: Charles C.Thomas.

CHAPTER 9

Cognitive-Behavioral Therapy

■

Cognitive-behavioral therapy is a term applied to a wide variety of interventions and therapies with certain common features. Most of them represent relatively brief, time-limited interventions usually applied to limited targets of change (Dobson & Block, 1988). Most were developed as part of a markedly increased emphasis on cognition in psychology, which some authors have referred to as a cognitive movement or cognitive revolution (Mahoney, 1974, 1988). Whereas many leading behaviorists (for example, Skinner, 1971) essentially denied the importance of cognitive processes, cognitive-behavioral approaches are distinguished by their reintroduction of cognition into models of behavioral change. Thus, as Dobson and Block (1988) argued, cognitive-behavioral theorists do not deny that overt reinforcement contingencies (such as operant conditioning) can alter behavior. They simply maintain that overt reinforcement contingencies represent only one of several methods that can accomplish behavior change, and they choose to concentrate on cognitive mechanisms in the production of such change. Thus, efforts to alter behavior center on changing the "clients' interpretations of themselves and their environments, as well as the manner by which they create these interpretations" (Lehman & Salovey, 1990, p. 243). Most approaches to cognitive-behavioral therapy emphasize the acquisition of new and better coping skills. Behavioral approaches are typically used to help clients acquire these skills—hence the hybrid designation of the therapy as cognitive-behavioral.

History of Cognitive-Behavioral Therapy

Cognitive-behavioral approaches to therapy were formulated, for the most part, beginning in the 1970s. Contributing to their development was the focus by social psychologists on attributional processes and Bandura's (1977) introduction of self-efficacy as an important cognitive mediational process in behavior change. Important early articulations of cognitive-behavioral perspectives were produced by Mahoney (1974, 1977) and Meichenbaum (1977). The rational-emotive therapy of Ellis (1962) and the cognitive therapy of Beck (1976) are also often cited as seminal in the development of cognitive-behavioral approaches to therapy, although rational emotive therapy may be more aptly described as a cognitive restructuring approach that assumes that behavioral change will follow automatically and without the teaching of new behavioral skills.

Range of Applicability

The range of problems that can be addressed by cognitive-behavioral therapy is quite broad. Illustrations of its range of applicability include its use in the treatment of depression (Beck, 1967; Beck, Rush, Shaw, & Emory, 1979), sexual problems (Steger, 1978), mood disorders (Beck, 1976; Burns & Beck, 1978), somatic disorders (Gentry, 1978), and personality disorders (Beck, Freeman, & associates, 1990), as well as in pain management (Turk, 1978) and stress management (Meichenbaum, 1993). In addition, it has been used in the framework of so-called brief therapy (Bloom, 1992) and with children (Braswell & Kendall, 1988), as well as adults. It has also been used in problem-solving training with families (Blechman, Olson, & Hellman, 1976).

Theoretical Foundations
Assumptions About Human Nature and Change

Cognitive-behavioral therapy's basic assumption about human nature is that humans are, more than anything else, defined by functioning cognitively. Humans are assumed to have expectations, to anticipate, to conceptualize, to remember, to evaluate and to appraise events, and to engage in a large variety of cognitive functions. Cognition is thus seen as mediating behavior, a perspective affirmed by a significant body of research (Dobson & Block, 1988). This mediational model proposes that various cognitive processes are able to shape the way a person experiences and reacts to events. This view is in sharp contrast to the strictly behavioristic model, in which humans respond directly and more or less automatically to environmental stimuli. Theorists of a cognitive-behavioral persuasion do not deny the significance of external stimuli; they simply believe that their impact is mediated by cognition. The logical extension of this position is that intervention into a person's cognitions represents a most efficient and effective means of changing the person's behavior.

Assumptions About Conducting Cognitive-Behavioral Therapy

Three fundamental propositions are shared by most cognitive-behavioral therapies:

1. Cognitive activity affects behavior.
2. Cognitive activity may be monitored and altered.
3. Desired behavior change may be affected through cognitive change. (Dobson & Block, 1988, p. 4)

Meichenbaum (1977) described mechanisms by which these fundamental propositions may be assumed to operate in the course of therapy. He proposed that clients have to develop a certain amount of self-awareness, which acts, in turn, as a cue for the production of internal dialogue (the client's own internal talk). Initially, the client's internal dialogue may consist primarily of negative self-statements and negative evaluations, and in fact the client may not be aware of the role of these thought processes in producing and maintaining the presenting problems. With the therapist's help, the client learns to use new language that represents new conceptualizations and new understanding of problems and of the role played by these cognitions; in other words, the client develops new cognitive structures. Meichenbaum maintained that if an individual is to make changes, he or she must engage in specific intentional mediational processes:

> The mediational process involves the recognition of maladaptive behavior (either external or internal) and this recognition must come to elicit inner speech that is different in content from that engaged in prior to therapy. The altered private speech must then trigger coping behaviors. (1977, p. 218)

Meichenbaum explicitly recognized that some clients may need to be taught such coping behaviors.

Another way to view the theoretical framework of cognitive-behavioral therapy is as an integration of strictly behavioral approaches, on the one hand, and cognitive-interpersonal or cognitive-semantic therapies, on the other (Lehman & Salovey, 1990). Indeed, cognitive-behavioral therapy embraces a combination of behavior therapy techniques while recognizing the crucial importance of mediational cognitions. Moreover, rather than insisting that behavior is determined mostly internally (as did Freud) or that it is determined mostly externally (as did Skinner), cognitive-behavioral approaches integrate these two perspectives. They acknowledge that the person's behaviors and the reactions those behaviors elicit from others (external factors) play an important part in changing behavior, as do the person's self-evaluations or internal dialogue and the person's cognitive structures (internal factors) (Meichenbaum, 1977).

Implementing Cognitive-Behavioral Therapy
Preliminary Considerations

Describing the specific procedures of cognitive-behavioral therapy per se is impossible because cognitive-behavioral therapies vary significantly in their specific approaches. In offering a chronology of the development of cognitive-behavioral therapies, Dobson and Block (1988, p. 12) list no fewer than 12 different approaches. They divide them into three categories, identified as cognitive restructuring therapies, coping skills therapies, and problem-solving therapies. Included in their chronology are, for example, the cognitive restructuring approaches of Ellis (1962—rational-emotive therapy), Beck (1963—cognitive therapy), and Meichenbaum (1971—self-instructional training). Also included are the coping skills approaches of Suinn and Richardson (1971—anxiety-management training) and Meichenbaum (1973—stress inoculation training), and the problem-solving approaches of D'Zurilla and Goldfried (1971—problem-solving therapy) and Mahoney (1974—personal science).

Because cognitive-behavioral approaches are typically formulated to address specific problems, they almost always start by conceptualizing the problem to be addressed, and defining target cognitions and behaviors. Virtually all these approaches recognize features of the client-therapist relationship as important in the change process, and most are time-limited in nature. Many cognitive-behavioral approaches embrace an educative approach in the actual conduct of the intervention, and some focus on prevention or "inoculation" (for example, Meichenbaum, 1985, 1993). All share the belief that clients are more or less responsible for their problems, and consequently, clients can also be responsible for solving their problems (Dobson & Block, 1988).

Despite significant similarities across various cognitive-behavioral approaches, there are also important differences. For the most part, the differences center around the relative importance assigned to behavioral methods as opposed to "cognitive restructuring" (the latter being stressed, for example, in Ellis's rational-emotive therapy). Important differences also emerge when one examines the specific, step-by-step procedures employed in conducting various cognitive-behavioral approaches. In recognition of this last observation we have chosen one particular approach—namely, Meichenbaum's (1985, 1993) stress inoculation training (SIT)—to illustrate the actual implementation of a cognitive-behavioral method.

Stress Inoculation Training (SIT)

SIT was developed as a comprehensive approach that incorporates three major integrated components. Each is considered an important contributor to the change process (Meichenbaum, 1993), although the specific procedures used in each of the phases will differ depending on the specific nature of the problem addressed, the characteristics of the client, and the clinical circumstances. The three phases are designed, basically, to help clients to think in more adaptive and self-helping ways about their problems and about their capabilities for coping, to teach them new and better skills for coping and problem-solving, and to use what they have learned in "real life." Meichenbaum (1985) labeled them (1) conceptualization, (2) skills acquisition and rehearsal, and (3) application and follow-through.

Conceptualization.   One key component of this phase is to "collaboratively formulate with the client and significant others a reconceptualization of the client's distress" (Meichenbaum, 1993, p. 383). With regard to the reported problem or distress, the client is asked to report what is happening, when, where, and how, under what circumstances, and within what time frame. Essentially, this involves helping clients to become better and more sophisticated reporters of what they experience and how they interpret it. Among other things, clients are encouraged to engage in self-monitoring, to disaggregate problems, and to consider behavioral components of their presenting difficulties, rather than vague global descriptions. Using information provided by the client, as well as the therapist's expertise, client and therapist collaborate in reconceptualizing the problem. Throughout this process, the therapist is mindful of creating a positive atmosphere. Clients are encouraged to think not only of their weaknesses, but also of their strengths, so that they can recover a measure of hope that they will be able to meaningfully recover from their problems as a consequence of their own actions, albeit with the time-limited help of a therapist.

Skills acquisition and rehearsal.   "The major objective of the second phase of SIT training is to help clients develop and consolidate a variety of intrapersonal and interpersonal coping skills" (Meichenbaum, 1985, p. 75). The particular skills taught during skills acquisition training typically depend on the client's needs and the length and intensity of the anticipated training period, although Meichenbaum (1985) noted that in most cases, skills acquisition begins with relaxation training. SIT focuses on teaching a large variety of coping- and problem-focused skills in order to expand the client's repertoire of such skills and enhance the client's ability to respond flexibly in future problem situations. The skills rehearsal portion of this phase of SIT is designed to encourage clients to integrate their newly learned coping and problem-solving skills into their overall behavioral repertoire and to consider any remaining barriers to implementing the skills. Modeling procedures and self-instructional training are favored ways to accomplish this. Among the coping skills that may be taught in the skills training are "anxiety management, cognitive restructuring, self-instructional training, communication, assertion, problem-solving, anger control, relaxation training, parenting, study skills, using social supports" (Meichenbaum, 1993, p. 383). In addition to these instrumental skills, affectively based coping skills, such as perspective-taking and humor, may also be taught.

Application and follow-through.   The use of imagery in order to expose clients to increasingly stressful life situations, as well as other means of graded exposure to stressors, are designed to facilitate in vivo responding and actual application of their newly acquired coping skills. Such exposure is particularly important because the transfer of these skills from the training situation to real life involves overcoming well-established old response habits and expectations (Meichenbaum, 1985). In addition to promoting the steadily, gradually increased use of various coping skills, SIT trainers pay special attention to preventing relapse. Training in relapse prevention is necessary because lapses are likely to occur when clients first face new and stressful life circumstances after SIT. The basic purpose of relapse prevention is to prevent lapses from resulting in relapses and consequent client disillusionment and discouragement. The final objective of the follow-through portion of this phase is maintenance and generalization. Among other things, clients may be encouraged to help others with similar problems and to involve significant others in training (Meichenbaum, 1993). In addition, booster sessions may be planned at regular intervals following the initial training, and clients may also be taught to determine when they may be in need of some follow-up training (Meichenbaum, 1985). These procedures help ensure that SIT does not just represent a temporary improvement, but that lasting gains are achieved by all who participate and stick with the whole training program. Most failures are expected when clients do not adhere to the treatment program; hence, the problem of treatment adherence requires special attention (Meichenbaum & Turk, 1987).

Means and Conditions for Implementing Cognitive-Behavioral Interventions

The Therapist's Qualifications

Above all, the therapist (whom Meichenbaum calls the trainer) "needs to be a sensitive, caring, thoughtful clinician" (Meichenbaum, 1985, p. 30). These characteristics are essential so that clients are not hurried or pushed to progress at a faster pace than they might be able to handle. Moreover, the therapeutic relationship represents the context for nurturing the discovery of new ideas about old problems and the acquisition and integration of novel and powerful coping skills, to deal not just with current problems but with the forthcoming challenges of life. Most cognitive-behavioral approaches recognize that technical proficiency is essential, in addition to clinical sensitivity and relationship skills. Nevertheless, the client-therapist relationship is typically characterized as a special collaborative relationship—what Beck, Freeman, and associates have called "collaborative empiricism," or "working with the patient to test the validity of the patient's beliefs, interpretations, and expectations" (1990, p. 80). In a similar vein, Mahoney and Kenigsberg's (1980) personal science views the therapist as a consultant who teaches clients self-assessment and self-management intervention skills.

Conditions for Conducting Cognitive-Behavioral Therapy

Various forms of cognitive-behavioral therapy have been used in many different settings, ranging from more traditional treatment settings like outpatient clinics and therapists' offices, to work settings, schools, and other organizational contexts. Whatever the specific context of the intervention, the treatment setting must offer an ambience conducive to the development of confidence and trust in the therapist or trainer. More often than not, individuals seeking cognitive-behavioral interventions experience significant distress and may require the calming influence of a pleasant, reasonably quiet, and friendly atmosphere. When special types of coping skills are addressed, such as in relaxation training, special types of furniture and instrumentation may also be necessary. These requirements, however, vary widely depending on the specific cognitive-behavioral method being implemented. Finally, many of these methods may be used with groups, therefore requiring facilities appropriate for group sessions.

Limitations of Cognitive-Behavioral Therapy
Contraindications and Cautions

Although there are virtually no contraindications to cognitive-behavioral therapy based on any concern about potential harm to clients, the possibility nevertheless exists that a given cognitive-behavioral method may be contraindicated for a particular population (Meichenbaum, 1993). Also, clients who lack the necessary self-observational and cognitive abilities to engage in such therapy must be referred to other treatment modalities. Nowhere is this more apparent than in therapy conducted with children. In working with children, it is particularly important to ascertain whether the child possesses the necessary pre-skills for a given cognitive-behavioral intervention to be applied. In addition, client variables such as age, type of disorder, cognitive level, and attributional style may all play important, though frequently neglected, roles in determining whether clients can successfully participate in various cognitive-behavioral interventions (Braswell & Kendall, 1988).

Some additional cautions must be observed in applying cognitive-behavioral therapy. Perhaps most important is the "danger of failing to recognize when other intervention methods are necessary or more appropriate for a particular case" (D'Zurilla, 1988, p. 116). D'Zurilla (1988) also noted that in certain crisis situations a deviation from the course of therapy may be necessary in order to deal more directly with the crisis. Another potential danger involves focusing on rational and intellectual forms of the therapy to the neglect of emotional and behavioral factors. Finally, the critical importance of developing and maintaining a positive therapeutic relationship must be borne in mind, particularly in working with clients who are skeptical about any psychological treatment or who lack a commitment to making changes (D'Zurilla, 1988).

The Effectiveness of Cognitive-Behavioral Therapy

Most of the research regarding the effectiveness of cognitive-behavioral therapies is, by its very nature, focused on the treatment of specific problems or dysfunctions, using very specific cognitive-behavioral techniques. Moreover, most proponents of cognitive-behavioral approaches maintain that the application of specific procedures must not proceed from a rigidly uniform, sequential perspective, but instead should be individually tailored as necessary to fit clients' particular circumstances and needs (Meichenbaum, 1993). Nevertheless, cognitive behavioral methods have been the subject of a good deal of attention from researchers seeking to examine their efficacy. Such research has frequently been conducted within the framework of controlled outcome studies, although many other studies have represented clinical and anecdotal reports or single-case designs.

Keeping in mind these limitations, evidence is accumulating in support of the observation that cognitive-behavioral interventions are at least as effective as other types of therapy (Lehman & Salovey, 1990). Miller and Berman (1981, as reported by Lehman & Salovey, 1990) conducted a quantitative review of the literature on the effectiveness of cognitive-behavioral therapy. Their conclusions prompted Lehman and Salovey to observe that "cognitive-behavior therapy's efficacy remained stable across a wide range of diagnostic categories, regardless of whether it was administered in individual or group formats" (1990, pp. 254–255). They also noted, however, the difficulties involved in drawing conclusions about the relative efficacy of cognitive-behavioral interventions because of the broad range and diversity of specific techniques.

Some cognitive-behavioral methods have been subject to more extensive outcome research than others. Meichenbaum (1985, pp. 24–25) summarized several dozen studies dealing with SIT and related stress management procedures. He concluded that the outcome research on SIT is "encouraging and improving." At the same time, he noted that long-term follow-up studies are still missing and that other methodological limitations need to be addressed before more definitive conclusions can be reached about SIT's efficacy. Beck, Freeman, and associates (1990) examined the evidence regarding the effectiveness of cognitive-behavioral interventions in the treatment of personality disorders. They acknowledged that such research is in its infancy, but concluded that initial evidence provides "grounds for optimism," with almost all studies reporting some improvement in most patients. D'Zurilla (1986, 1988) reviewed a number of outcome studies of problem-solving therapy. He concluded that positive treatment effects had generally been reported for a variety of patients, including psychiatric patients with severe social-skills deficits, alcoholism, depression, stress and anxiety, and agoraphobia, although the usual disclaimers regarding methodological shortcomings apply to most research in this field.

References

Bandura, A. (1977). Self-efficacy: Toward a unifying theory of behavioral change. *Psychological Review, 84,* 191–215.

Beck, A. T. (1963). Thinking and depression. I: Idiosyncratic content and cognitive distortions. *Archives of General Psychiatry, 9,* 36–46.

Beck, A. T. (1967). *Depression: Clinical, experimental, and theoretical aspects.* New York: Hoeber.

Beck, A. T. (1976). *Cognitive therapy and the emotional disorders.* New York: International Universities Press.

Beck, A. T., Freeman, A., & associates. (1990). *Cognitive therapy of personality disorders.* New York: Guilford Press.

Beck, A. T., Rush, A. J., Shaw, B. F., & Emory, G. (1979). *Cognitive therapy of depression.* New York: Guilford Press.

Blechman, E., Olson, D., & Hellman, I. (1976). Stimulus control over family problem-solving behavior: The family contract game. *Behavior Therapy, 7,* 686–692.

Bloom, B. L. (1992). *Planned short-term psychotherapy: A clinical handbook.* Boston, MA: Allyn & Bacon.

Braswell, L., & Kendall, P. C. (1988). Cognitive-behavioral methods with children. In K. S. Dobson (Ed.), *Handbook of cognitive-behavioral therapies* (pp. 167–213). New York: Guilford Press.

Burns, D. D., & Beck, A. T. (1978). Cognitive-behavior modification of mood disorders. In J. P. Foreyt & D. P. Rathjen (Eds.), *Cognitive behavior therapy: Research and application* (pp. 109–134). New York: Plenum.

Dobson, K. S., & Block, L. (1988). Historical and philosophical bases of the cognitive-behavioral therapies. In K. S. Dobson (Ed.), *Handbook of cognitive-behavioral therapies* (pp. 3–38). New York: Guilford Press.

D'Zurilla, T. J. (1986). *Problem-solving therapy: A social competence approach to clinical intervention.* New York: Springer.

D'Zurilla, T. J. (1988). Problem-solving therapies. In K. S. Dobson (Ed.), *Handbook of cognitive-behavioral therapies* (pp. 85–135). New York: Guilford Press.

D'Zurilla, T. J., & Goldfried, M. R. (1971). Problem-solving and behavior modification. *Journal of Abnormal Psychology, 78,* 107–126.

Ellis, A. (1962). *Reason and emotion in psychotherapy.* New York: Lyle Stuart.

Gentry, W. D. (1978). Cognitive treatment of somatic disorders. In J. P. Foreyt & D. P. Rathjen (Eds.), *Cognitive behavior therapy: Research and application* (pp. 175–187). New York: Plenum.

Lehman, A. K., & Salovey, P. (1990). An introduction to cognitive-behavior therapy. In R. A. Wells & V. J. Giannetti (Eds.), *Handbook of the brief psychotherapies* (pp. 239–259). New York: Plenum.

Mahoney, M. J. (1974). *Cognition and behavior modification.* Cambridge, MA: Ballinger.

Mahoney, M. J. (1977). Personal science: A cognitive-learning therapy. In A. Ellis & R. Grieger (Eds.), *Handbook of rational psychotherapy* (pp. 3–33). New York: Springer.

Mahoney, M. J. (1988). The cognitive sciences and psychotherapy: Patterns in a developing relationship. In K. S. Dobson (Ed.), *Handbook of cognitive-behavioral therapies* (pp. 357–386). New York: Guilford Press.

Mahoney, M. J., & Kenigsberg, M. (1980). A strategy for generating self-help. In G. L. Martin & J. G. Osborne (Eds.), *Helping in the community: Behavioral applications* (pp. 333–344). New York: Plenum.

Meichenbaum, D. (1971). A self-instructional approach to stress management: A proposal for stress inoculation training. In C. Spielberger & I. Sarason (Eds.), *Stress and anxiety* (Vol. 1., pp. 237–263). Washington, DC: Hemisphere.

Meichenbaum, D. (1973). Cognitive factors in behavior modification: Modifying what clients say to themselves. In C. M. Franks & G. T. Wilson (Eds.), *Annual review of behavior therapy, theory, and practice, 1973* (pp. 416–431). New York: Brunner/Mazel.

Meichenbaum, D. (1977). *Cognitive behavior modification: An integrated approach.* New York: Plenum.

Meichenbaum, D. (1985). *Stress inoculation training.* New York: Pergamon Press.

Meichenbaum, D. (1993). Stress inoculation training: A 20-year update. In P. M. Lehrer & R. L. Woolfolk (Eds.), *Principles and practice of stress management* (2nd ed., pp. 373–406). New York: Guilford Press.

Meichenbaum, D., & Turk, D. C. (1987). *Facilitating treatment adherence: A practitioner's guidebook.* New York: Plenum.

Miller, R. C., & Berman, J. S. (1981). *The efficacy of cognitive behavior therapy: A quantitative review of the research evidence.* Paper presented at the annual meeting of the American Psychological Association, Los Angeles, CA.

Skinner, B. F. (1971). *Beyond freedom and dignity.* New York: Knopf.

Steger, J. C. (1978). Cognitive behavioral strategies in the treatment of sexual problems. In J. P. Foreyt & D. P. Rathjen (Eds.), *Cognitive behavior therapy: Research and application* (pp. 77–108). New York: Plenum.

Suinn, R. M., & Richardson, F. (1971). Anxiety management training: A non-specific behavior therapy program for anxiety control. *Behavior Therapy*, 2, 498–510.

Turk, D. C. (1978). Cognitive behavioral techniques in the management of pain. In J. P. Foreyt & D. P. Rathjen (Eds.), *Cognitive behavior therapy: Research and application* (pp. 199–232). New York: Plenum.

PART IV

Humanistic Approaches

....

CHAPTER 10

The Person-Centered Therapy
of Carl Rogers

....

■

Few personality theorists have chronicled their own personal growth as it relates to their attempts at theory building and the practice of psychotherapy as meticulously or as publicly as Carl Rogers. As a result, Rogers's theory of personality development and psychotherapy according to the person-centered approach, have been the subject of constant scrutiny and revision. Rogers was a prolific author who produced highly readable and comprehensive volumes chronicling his work as a theoretician and clinician. This chapter will examine Rogers's person-centered approach to psychotherapy.

Rogers has summarized his evolution as a therapist as follows:

> One brief way of describing the change that has taken place in me is to say that in my early professional years I was asking the question, How can I treat, or cure, or change this person? Now I would phrase the question this way: How can I provide a relationship which this person may use for his own personal growth? (Rogers, 1961, p. 32)

General Purpose of Person-Centered Psychotherapy

The general purpose of Rogers's approach to therapy is to provide the essential conditions that will facilitate the client's personal growth. In broad terms, Rogers saw as the purpose of therapy to promote "the growth, development, maturity, improved functioning, improved coping with life of the other" (Rogers, 1961, p. 40). Person-centered psychotherapy aims to provide an atmosphere in which the individual becomes fully aware of his or her experience as a person. As therapy progresses, clients replace their distorted self-image with a more congruent self-image that contains all aspects of experience.

History of Person-Centered Psychotherapy

After receiving his Ph.D. from Columbia University in 1931, Carl Rogers began his work as a clinician at the Rochester Society for the Prevention of Cruelty to Children. According to Rogers, he began during this time to develop his own views on treatment out of his day-to-day working experience. Rogers's attempts to treat the children at the clinic with the Freudian methods he had been taught were often unsuccessful. In addition, the approach itself, which positioned the therapist as the expert on another individual's experience, did not match Rogers's experience of the therapeutic relationship. So Rogers began to follow his intuition in treating patients. His main criteria seemed to be how effective his methods were and how comfortable as a person he was with his methods. Rogers's thinking took a major shift during his years in Rochester. He realized that "it is the *client* who knows what hurts, what directions to go, what problems are crucial, what experiences have been deeply buried" (Rogers, 1961, pp. 11–12).

From Rochester, Rogers took an academic post at Ohio State University in 1940. He became keenly aware that he had developed a distinctive point of view regarding counseling, as his graduate students pushed him to explain his counseling and treatment techniques. Rogers had clearly departed from the dominant psychoanalytic view and was placing less emphasis on the diagnosis of disorders and labeling of patients—in fact, he referred to patients as clients. He set forth his views in *Counseling and Psychotherapy,* published in 1942. Much to his surprise, Rogers's non-directive approach was considered quite controversial. In these early years, the emphasis was on technique, and the technique of the non-directive approach was reflection. Critics of Rogers's technique saw the therapist as a rather passive individual who merely repeated what the client said and occasionally nodded or said "uh huh" to let the client know the therapist was being attentive. Today, those who have not studied Rogers's theory and method often voice the same misunderstanding of the person-centered approach.

Rogers's next academic position was at the University of Chicago, where he established a counseling center and began to work in earnest on research that focused on both the process and outcome of psychotherapy. During this time, Rogers's non-directive approach became known as the client-centered approach. This label offered the clear message that the client, rather than a particular theory, should be considered paramount in the therapist's work. Although Rogers insisted that the client should decide the content and direction of therapy, he saw a lawfulness in the process of therapy and a commonality in the experience of clients. Encouraged by his students and colleagues, Rogers set to work on elucidating his theory of personality; the result was his 1951 publication of *Client-Centered Therapy*.

Rogers moved to California in 1964 to join the Western Behavioral Sciences Institute. Rogers became interested in expanding his ideas with applications to group dynamics, education, and international politics. The client-centered approach ultimately became the person-centered approach. *Person-centered* is the most appropriate term, since Rogers believed that both client and therapist must be authentically and deeply involved in the therapeutic relationship and that both change as a result of the relationship. In this way, client and therapist share the responsibilities and rewards of the therapeutic relationship. Rogers left the Western Behavioral Sciences Institute with a number of other members to found the Center for the Study of the Person, where he remained until his death in 1987.

Range of Applicability

Generally, textbook discussions of the person-centered approach advocate that its use is limited to highly motivated, highly verbal individuals who, in psychiatric terms, might be diagnosed as neurotic but not psychotic, and that individuals with a more severe diagnosis are not candidates for this approach. Rogers would disagree. He and his colleagues have successfully worked with a wide variety of clients with diagnoses as severe as schizophrenia.

Rogers eschewed diagnostic labels and preferred to speak of neurotic individuals as exhibiting defensive behaviors and psychotic individuals as exhibiting disorganized behaviors. Rogers considered a diagnostic label both unnecessary and harmful. Labels are unnecessary for two reasons. First, using the person-centered approach, treatment will proceed in the same manner regardless of the specified condition of the client. Second, according to Rogers's theory, all maladaptive behavior, however it is manifested, results from a distorted self-concept formed out of particular childhood experiences that Rogers called "conditions of worth."

Since the major goal of the person-centered approach is to help individuals to rely on their own evaluations of their own experience and to cast off others' judgments and evaluations, it follows that imposing diagnostic labels on individuals would be harmful (and contradictory). Rogers maintained that the client is always in the best position to select the experiences, thoughts, behaviors, and emotions that are the source of his or her difficulties.

Theoretical Foundations
Assumptions About Human Nature and Key Concepts

The major assumption underpinning the person-centered approach is that the innate force that drives human behavior is "positive, forward moving, constructive, realistic, and trustworthy" (Rogers, 1957, p. 199)—a force that Rogers called the actualizing tendency. Contrary to Freudian theory, we are not born with an unruly host of biological drives that must be gradually brought under control. Instead, a person's nature is to develop in a positive direction. The unconscious, then, is a positive force, and the purpose of therapy is to allow the unconscious to surface and operate as the intelligent, creative, autonomous force it is. Rogers saw this tendency toward growth in a positive direction as operating at all levels in the universe. Humans, then, are not alone in possessing this innate force. It is a "tendency which permeates all of organic life—a tendency to become all the complexity of which the organism is capable" (Rogers, 1980, p. 134).

The notion that the individual possesses a positive and trustworthy core is in direct contrast to our beliefs as a society. Rogers pointed out that "in our institutions the individual is seen as untrustworthy [and it is believed that] persons must be guided, corrected, disciplined, and punished, so that they will not follow the pathway set by their inherent natures" (Rogers, 1987, p. 180). Whereas Freudian theory depicts human nature as hostile, antisocial, and potentially destructive, Rogers viewed human nature as full of glorious potential.

Students who hear about Rogers's positive view of human nature frequently ask the following question: if we have an innate tendency to develop in a positive direction, then how do people get into such difficulties? Rogers asserted that people exhibit defensive (neurotic) or disorganized (psychotic) behavior because they possess distorted self-concepts. The self-concept becomes distorted as a result of interactions with significant others in which the others make judgments about the individual's worth as a person. Rogers called these judgments conditions of worth—evaluations made by significant others that set up criteria the developing individual must meet in order to feel lovable and worthy. To gain the acceptance of the significant other, the individual assimilates or introjects the criterion set up by the significant other (for example, "you must never feel rage") into the individual's concept of self. In so doing, the individual negates or represses her or his true experience because it is inconsistent with the information the individual is perceiving from the other. Experience with others plays a crucial role in developing a sense of self, with parental influence an extremely powerful agent in this process.

The following is an example of how a significant other sets up conditions of worth that a developing individual feels she must meet. Kelly (age 6) is angry with her sister, Molly (age 4), because Molly ate the last cookie. Kelly tells Molly she hates her. Mother overhears, races into the kitchen, and says, "Kelly! You must never say you hate your sister. You don't hate her. You love her. All we have in this world is family. I don't ever want to hear you say that again! Now apologize to your sister." Molly smiles smugly as Kelly grits her teeth and says tearfully, "I'm sorry." More than likely, mother has a judgment that one must never hate anyone, and the lesson of never hating will be repeated between mother and daughter. At age 6, Kelly does not yet possess the ego strength to say to herself, "I do hate Molly at this moment, and I can certainly have any feeling I want. Mother seems to be uncomfortable with feelings of anger. I, on the other hand, am comfortable with my feelings, and I will ignore what she says." Instead, Kelly incorporates her mother's evaluation into her concept of self, and in the future she will deny experiencing any feeling of rage toward another. In other words, her feelings of rage will be inconsistent with her structure of self and will be denied.

When Kelly experiences a visceral sense of rage but denies that experience to awareness, her unconscious experience is incongruent with her conscious experience. The result is a distorted concept of self. In other words, a discrepancy exists between what one truly feels and how one presents oneself. According to Rogers, this predicament thwarts the actualizing tendency, and the result is psychological tension. Any experience inconsistent or incongruent with the sense of self is perceived as a threat. The more threatened one feels, the more rigid one will become in order to defend oneself from the perceived threat. The more numerous the conditions of worth, the more a person is at risk psychologically to be maladjusted. None of us escapes being exposed to conditions of worth, and as a consequence all of us exist with some degree of psychological tension.

Rogers stated that one's sense of self must be unified or made whole by bringing unconscious experiences into conscious experience so that the self-concept can be revised, so to speak, to include all experience. Such revision can be accomplished only when certain conditions are present that result in a complete absence of threat to the structure of the self. The absence of threat enables the individual to perceive and examine experiences that are incongruent with the sense of self and incorporate those experiences into the sense of self. Threat is absent when the individual experiences unconditional positive regard from an empathic and congruent individual. Unconditional positive regard involves total acceptance of another's thoughts and feelings without evaluation or judgment. When one is congruent, one's inner experience is consistent with one's outer expression of the experience. Communications are genuine and are so perceived. When one is empathic, one accurately senses another's thoughts and feelings so that the other feels understood. Empathy does not involve interpretation or prodding the individual to admit to feelings the other thinks he or she may be experiencing, for only the individual has access to his or her true experience.

The notion that only the client has access to her or his true experience is a key assumption in the theoretical foundations of person-centered psychotherapy and has its roots in the phenomenological perspective. According to the phenomenological perspective, the accurate point of view for understanding an individual's experience is from the individual's internal frame of reference. In addition, what determines an individual's responses to and experience of present and future events is the individual's perception of past events. In other words, whether or not an individual was well loved as a child does not matter as much as how the individual presently perceives childhood experiences of love. One individual can never know the past experience of another. In fact, a therapist's interpretations and preconceptions about another individual's experience may destroy the therapist's ability to assist the individual in bringing salient unconscious material into consciousness.

Assumptions About Conducting Person-Centered Psychotherapy

According to Rogers, the source of psychological maladjustment is a distorted self-concept, which occurs when the individual is exposed to conditions of worth during his or her formative years. The more numerous the conditions of worth, the more rigid the individual becomes in how he or she experiences the world. This rigidity stems from the individual's sense that various rules must be followed and particular feelings must or must not be experienced for the person to feel that he or she will be accepted by a significant other, first, and ultimately by others in general. Examples of such conditions of worth include the following: "I must not feel rage," "I must not feel proud," "I must never offend anyone." Rogers spoke of therapy as a process that moves the individual from "fixity to flowingness" (Rogers, 1961, p. 132). When an individual is flowing rather than fixed or rigid, she or he is said to be congruent. Congruence exists when the individual's inner experience is perceived in awareness and that experience is willingly and openly expressed. As a result, there is no distortion or inconsistency in the self-concept.

Rogers provided a detailed account of his "seven stages of process" in his book *On Becoming a Person* (1961). The seven stages may be viewed as a process of personality change that exists along a continuum beginning with fixity and ending with flowingness. Rogers stated that by "sampling the qualities of experiencing and expressing in a given individual, in a climate where he feels himself to be completely received, we may be able to determine where he is in this continuum of personality change" (Rogers, 1961, p. 132). This statement is as close as Rogers came to providing a diagnostic tool for assessing an individual's condition. Of course, therapy would proceed in the same manner regardless of which stage marked the client's ability to "express and experience."

1. *Stage One*: The individual communicates in a superficial way about external matters. She or he is uncomfortable with intimate relationships in which one is expected to share feelings. As is typical of a rigid person, she or he is out of touch with the inner experience of an event and, therefore, unable and unwilling to express feelings. Generally, this person comes to therapy involuntarily. Typical statements might include the following: "I really don't see how it can help to talk about it." "I don't know how I feel about that." "I don't think it matters how one feels about their job, you simply go to work and do it."

2. *Stage Two*: In this stage, the individual is still rather rigid but an opening appears as she or he makes statements about the experience of others. Generally, problems are seen as imposed upon the individual. In other words, there is no sense of responsibility in the creation of one's reality. Feelings may be expressed, but at a rather superficial level. Typical statements might include the following: "My mother seems to be unhappy in her marriage to my father." "Why am I here? Well, people get depressed now and then." "Things just don't go my way. I can't do much about that."

3. *Stage Three*: In stage three, people talk more freely about themselves and yet apparently do not understand their own responsibility in creating their day-to-day experiences. People experience their feelings as unacceptable and choices they have made as wrong. They are more comfortable talking about past feelings rather than present feelings. Also, they recognize that components of their experience are contradictory. Rogers felt that people entering therapy are most often at stage three. Some typical statements at stage three are as follows: "My life has really been a mess so far." "I can't really quit this job now. I'm not trained for anything else so I'll just have to live with it." "I was pretty angry at my father for a long time. I know that's not a very nice thing

to say." "I always wanted loving relationships, but I seem to do things to turn them sour."

4. *Stage Four*: As people move along the continuum, their expression of feelings takes on a consistently freer flow. Now the individuals express feelings in the present and begin to accept some of those feelings. They begin to comprehend various aspects of their self-concept and, as this occurs, begin to question the validity of various aspects of the self. The contradictions about self that have begun to surface in stage three are now examined and become a source of concern. In addition, people begin to get a sense of their responsibility in the creation of their present experience of living. Clients will now begin to accept the close relationship that is available with the therapist and begin to relate to the therapist on a personal level by disclosing feelings they have about the relationship. The following are some examples of statements made at stage four: "I am feeling hurt by the remarks my boss makes. Angry and hurt." "I always thought I was honest . . . yet, as I think about it now, well . . . I hate to say it, but I am not honest with my husband." "So am I an optimist or a pessimist? I can't decide . . . I think I'm a pessimist . . . no . . . I don't know." "I have always blamed my wife for not being attentive enough to me . . . but I'm beginning to see that maybe I haven't allowed her to be." "I'm wondering if I can trust you."

5. *Stage Five*: At this stage people freely express their present feelings and feel them in a deeper way, with more intensity than previously expressed. In addition, people may experience feelings that have no referent in consciousness. In other words, a person may experience sadness and not know why she or he is feeling sad. At this stage, though, individuals know that they are themselves the source of these feelings and that the referent lies within them. Although a person may not have a handle on the particular experiences evoking these feelings, the person experiences feelings with more immediacy than in the previous stage. The individual longs to discover the real self and to communicate that reality to the therapist. The individual continues to discover inconsistencies in the self-image and yearns to examine them and sort them out. In addition, there is a greater differentiation in feelings, a kind of fine-tuning of one's experience of the world. At this stage, self-acceptance is increasing, as is acceptance of responsibility for the problems being faced. Typical statements include these: "I have an overwhelming feeling of sadness right now and I don't know why." "I know I have the answer, I just don't have a handle on it yet." "Who am I? That's what I need to find out." "If I am really kind at my core than why do I feel like I want to make my wife wrong?" "I'm having

this conversation with myself and I'm asking myself why are you putting me through this ordeal?" "I do feel angry at my father for being so
uncommunicative and there's nothing wrong with my feeling that
way." "I suppose I've expected to be rejected and, in that way, I've
made sure I was."

6. *Stage Six*: Rogers stated that rather dramatic changes take place in this
stage. "A present feeling is directly experienced with immediacy and
richness" (Rogers, 1961, p. 145). This richness can be found in people's
ability to experience the feeling within them at the moment rather than
intellectualize about the feeling as if it were one step removed. The
person has moments of experiencing congruency (that is, feeling like
the real self) as inner experiences are communicated openly and accepted. Clients look less to the therapist to evaluate the rightness of
their feelings. The feelings simply are as they are, and clients live their
experience of feelings in the moment. At this point clients are developing unconditional positive regard for themselves. Out of experiencing
unconditional positive regard for oneself, one is able to begin to view
others with unconditional positive regard. Rogers noted that during this
stage the person exhibits "moistness in the eyes, tears, sighs,
[and]muscular relaxation" which he terms "physiological loosening"
(Rogers, 1961, p. 147). Rogers considered these physiological signs to
be evidence that emotions are indeed being experienced at a very deep
level. The following are some typical statements at stage six: "I'm feeling
vulnerable at this very moment as I think about losing my mother at
such a young age." "I want someone to take care of me . . . now . . . at
this moment . . . that's just how I feel. Yet I do feel a strength within
me at the same time. I think it's fine to feel lost at times." "I have a
feeling of tenderness for myself . . . love even."

7. *Stage Seven*: Rogers said of stage seven:

> The client often seems to go on into the seventh and final stage
> without much need of the therapist's help. This stage occurs as much
> outside of the therapeutic relationship as in it, and is often reported,
> rather than experienced in the therapeutic hour. (Rogers, 1961,
> p. 151)

For the most part, stage seven involves a deepening of the experiences
of stage six. The individual lives in the moment of his or her experience, trusting his or her intuition, and is not locked into a rigid structure of self. One's sense of self becomes more fluid, in that the individual responds to events in the environment, not out of past patterns,
but rather out of how the event is experienced and interpreted in its

newness. Statements made by an individual in stage seven might include these: "Although I felt angry at my husband, at the same time I could feel how difficult the decision was for him to make and my anger kind of dissipated into understanding." "Although I knew some people wouldn't like my decision, I simply knew that I had to do what I felt I had to do without checking it out against some other criterion other than myself."

The Therapist's Qualifications

Rogers stated that when the therapist "provide[s] a certain type of relationship, the other person will discover within himself the capacity to use that relationship for growth, and change and personal development will occur" (Rogers, 1961, p. 33). In other words, therapeutic growth will occur when a client comes in contact with a therapist who creates a very specific context that serves as a catalyst for change. According to Rogers, the "certain type of relationship" that fosters personal growth is characterized by unconditional positive regard, empathy, and congruence. These three conditions are the necessary precursors for initiating the process of therapy outlined in the previous section.

Unconditional positive regard.   According to Rogers, the desire for the positive regard of others is a strong and enduring drive from infancy onward. We seek others' love and acceptance to such a degree that we are willing, especially during infancy and childhood, to deny our own emotional experience in order to please another. For example, a mother might say to her child: "Be a big boy and stay here with the baby-sitter. Big boys aren't afraid when their mommies leave." The child's choice to hold back his tears and put on a brave face is an indication that his mother's positive regard is more important to him than expressing fear in the moment. For most of us, significant others' positive regard was offered with some conditions we had to meet. When the therapist offers positive regard without any conditions, the therapist provides the client with unconditional positive regard. The therapist's respect for the individual, then, does not depend on the client behaving or feeling a particular way. One feeling or action is not valued over another. The therapist maintains a warm and accepting attitude without possessiveness, judgment, or restriction.

Empathy.   Rogers (1980, p. 142) experienced empathy as "temporarily living in the other's life, moving about in it delicately without making judgments." Empathy involves the ability to accurately sense another's feelings and attitudes and to communicate that information to the other in such a way that the other feels understood. Empathy does not involve interpreting the condition of another or attempting to uncover unconscious material. Empathy is offered to clients so that they may listen to themselves more clearly. As with unconditional positive regard, empathy is a tool that enables clients to rely on themselves as the frame of reference for self-understanding. Empathy characterized by accuracy and depth provides an expanded frame of reference, which clients can use to "unblock a flow of experiencing and permit it to run its uninhibited course" (Rogers, 1980, p. 156).

Congruence.   To be congruent is to be genuine in the sense that the individual's outward expression is in accord with her or his inner experience. Congruent therapists are aware of their own feelings, whether pleasing or not, and are willing to express that reality. A congruent therapist enables clients to have the courage to present themselves in a congruent fashion also. Rogers stated: "It is only by providing the genuine reality which is in me, that the other person can successfully seek the reality in him" (Rogers, 1961, pp. 33). For Rogers, to be real is the crucial thing. Only then can the therapeutic relationship have reality. In other words, the therapist does not present a facade of friendliness, toughness, ignorance, or calm that misrepresents his or her real feelings. Therapy is not a manipulation, but rather a letting go. Person-centered therapists are not passive, aloof individuals but, instead, expressive and fully human.

Means and Conditions for Implementing Person-Centered Psychotherapy

The following is a case illustration of the application of person-centered therapy. The therapist's responses consist of empathic statements in which the therapist attempts to capture the client's experience and, through the use of reflective responses, to demonstrate acceptance of the client as a unique individual. The client begins therapy with a degree of self-expression, indicated by her statements, that place her at stage three of the therapeutic process. Rogers stated that "many people who seek psychological help are at approximately the point of stage three" (Rogers, 1961, p. 136). The present example will include a portion of the first session. The client, a 39-year-old-woman, has entered therapy because over the past few months she has been experiencing anxiety attacks characterized by heart palpitations, shallow breathing, and a free-floating fear that arises without warning.

Client: I don't know what's been happening to me. I feel like I'm losing it.

Therapist: Like you're out of control at times.

Client: Yeah . . . this fear just comes over me . . . out of the blue. It's awful. I hate it and I just can't figure out why this is happening to me.

Therapist: It's unpredictable . . . and you don't understand where it's coming from.

Client: I don't know where to start talking about this. I suppose I should talk about my childhood. . . . (*Laughs nervously.*)

Therapist: It feels a little uncomfortable to be sitting here trying to begin to figure things out.

Client: Well, new situations are sometimes hard for me. I try to be relaxed but I guess I worry about what people will think of me.

Therapist: Whether or not they'll like or accept you.

Client: Right. That's so much like my mother. Why am I so much like her when that's exactly what I don't want to be?

Therapist: I can hear your frustration.

Client: You bet . . . but don't get me wrong . . . I do love her . . . I mean I wouldn't want to say anything against her. Or my father. He was pretty overbearing . . . a real disciplinarian. Well, I should say how I feel. So there's nothing wrong in saying something against my father but, at the same time, I should be understanding of him.

Therapist: You feel torn between being true to yourself and how you think a good daughter should be.

Client: How my father thinks a good daughter should be.

Therapist: Oh . . . how your *father* thinks a good daughter should be. You and he think differently on the subject.

Client: You bet. I raise my daughters very differently from how my father and mother raised me. I let them make their own decisions now that they're young adults. I don't interfere with their lives . . . I'm there if they need me.

Therapist: So you feel that a good parent allows her children a degree of freedom when they are old enough to handle it. And your father is the interfering kind.

Client: Right. How is one ever supposed to learn to handle responsibility if one is not given the opportunity to make one's own choices, if someone's always trying to run one's life? I guess I should say that I feel like my father is still trying to run my life. One must speak the truth.

Therapist: You feel certain about that . . . you have a sense of rightness about speaking the truth.

Client: Yes . . . yes, I do.

Therapist: And it feels good to say it.

Client: Absolutely.

A congruent therapist who expresses unconditional positive regard using empathic responses enables clients to listen to themselves so that experiences previously blocked become unblocked. In this way, clients come "in closer contact with a wider range of their experiencing [which] gives them an expanded referent to which they can turn for guidance in understanding themselves and directing their behavior" (Rogers, 1980, p. 156). It follows that the client, rather than the therapist, will determine when the goals of therapy have been reached.

Limitations of Person-Centered Psychotherapy
Contraindications

Critics of Rogers's approach have suggested that person-centered psychotherapy is inappropriate for individuals incapacitated in such a way that their ability to make responsible decisions is impaired. Individuals suffering from severe forms of mental illness, developmentally disabled individuals, and individuals living in poverty are said to be poor candidates for person-centered psychotherapy because (1) mentally ill individuals are not able to make decisions about their care; (2) poor people need services before they can grow psychologically; and (3) developmentally disabled individuals cannot make informed decisions.

Challenging this position, a wide spectrum of practitioners have maintained that mentally ill individuals should indeed be making decisions about their care. The same could be said for developmentally disabled individuals. In addition, one could argue that there is no reason a person living in poverty should not receive services while engaged in psychotherapy. Although critics agreed that "every client can be treated with respect," they stated that "it often doesn't make sense to treat the client as an equal" (Schmolling, Youkeles, & Burger, 1993, p. 158). Rogers would disagree emphatically.

Rogers did not set forth any criteria that would have to be met in order for an individual to be a candidate for person-centered psychotherapy. Although the evidence regarding the effectiveness of person-centered psychotherapy may be conflicting, there is no evidence that this approach inflicts harm.

Hazards

The necessary conditions for implementing person-centered psychotherapy are present when an empathic, congruent therapist receives a client with unconditional positive regard. The greatest threat to a client's well-being is a therapist who strays from Rogers's approach by being either incongruent or judgmental. Although Rogers has said that a therapist need not be completely congruent in order to foster psychological growth within a client, it is generally accepted that the more congruent the therapist, the greater the success of treatment. Evaluative statements and the use of sympathy rather than empathy by the therapist would run counter to the basic assumptions of the person-centered approach and, therefore, would undermine the process of therapy.

The Effectiveness of Person-Centered Psychotherapy

According to Rogers, "one of the most important characteristics of [person-centered psychotherapy] is that from the first it has not only stimulated research but has existed in a context of research thinking" (Rogers, 1961, p. 244). Rogers stated repeatedly that his theory of personality must be viewed not as dogma but as a series of testable hypotheses. Through the years Rogers, his colleagues, and his students have conducted research on the person-centered approach in psychotherapy and education. In fact, Rogers's theory and approach to psychotherapy have been the subject of empirical study for nearly 40 years. There is general agreement among scholars that Rogers was a productive scientist, and his work is held in high esteem.

A number of volumes contain bibliographies of research conducted on Rogers's therapy and theory of personality (for example, Rogers, 1961; Raskin & Rogers, 1989). The general findings offer support for his theory and the effectiveness of his method of psychotherapy. As such, the research is impressive. Although studies generally demonstrate that clients tend to improve using the person-centered approach, the level of growth or improvement falls short of the projected stages of the therapeutic process set forth earlier in the chapter. Rarely do clients emerge from therapy as the fully functioning individual characterized in stage seven of the therapeutic process.

References

Raskin, N. J., & Rogers, C. R. (1989). Person-centered therapy. In R. J. Corsini & D. Wedding (Eds.), *Current Psychotherapies* (4th ed., pp. 155–194). Itasca, IL: F. E. Peacock.

Rogers, C. R. (1942). *Counseling and psychotherapy: New concepts in practice.* New York: Houghton Mifflin.

Rogers, C. R. (1951). *Client-centered therapy.* Boston: Houghton-Mifflin.

Rogers, C. R. (1957). The necessary and sufficient conditions for therapeutic personality change. *Journal of Counseling Psychology, 21,* 95–103.

Rogers, C. R. (1961). *On becoming a person: A therapist's view of psychotherapy.* Boston: Houghton Mifflin.

Rogers, C. R. (1980). *A way of being.* Boston: Houghton Mifflin.

Rogers, C. R. (1987). Rogers, Kohut, and Erickson: A personal perspective on some similarities and differences. In J. Zeig (Ed.), *The evolution of psychotherapy* (pp. 179–187). New York: Brunner/Mazel.

Schmolling, P., Youkeles, M., & Burger, W. (1993). *Human services in contemporary America* (3rd ed.). Pacific Grove, CA: Brooks/Cole.

■

CHAPTER 11

. . . .

Child-Centered or Nondirective
Play Therapy

. . . .

■

Six-year-old Kevin stood in silence as he looked around the room. John Nesbitt, Kevin's therapist, looked around the room also and said, "There sure are a lot of toys in here. You're wondering what to do." Kevin nodded without looking at Dr. Nesbitt. He fidgeted with his shirt, looked at the clock, and began to edge toward the door. "You're not so sure you want to be here," said Dr. Nesbitt. Kevin nodded again and turned toward the table where toy soldiers, clay, puppets, and various other toys were displayed. He walked over to the table, tentatively gathered up the toy soldiers, sat on the floor and began dividing them into two piles. "You've picked the soldiers out of all the toys," said Dr. Nesbitt. Kevin nodded again and said, "These are for you." Dr. Nesbitt sat on the floor next to Kevin, picked up one of the toy soldiers and said, "You'd like me to play with you."

On the surface, Dr. Nesbitt's comments may appear neutral, but his expertise as a nondirective play therapist enabled Kevin to face his own discomfort, stay in the playroom, and engage his therapist in a direct interaction.

History of Nondirective Play Therapy

Child-centered or nondirective play therapy is a counseling technique based on the client-centered, nondirective approach developed by Carl Rogers (1942) and adapted for children by Virginia Axline (1947). Play has been used as a component of therapy with children since the early 1900s. Prior to the advent of nondirective play therapy, play in psychoanalytic therapy was used in two ways: first, to establish the therapeutic alliance between therapist and child; and second, to assist the child in working through emotional disturbance by directing the child to recreate traumatic or disturbing events through play (O'Conner, 1991). Play was substituted for direct verbalization, and the therapist took responsibility for directing the child's play so that the child would ultimately cathect an emotionally disturbing event. Generally, play sessions were structured by the therapist with specific materials set out for the child in order to direct play toward a specific outcome. The primary value of the child's play was seen in the information it offered the therapist for interpreting the child's intrapsychic difficulties. Therapists, then, could be characterized as participant-observers, gathering information to support or refute their hypotheses about the child's mental status. Play was more a medium from which the therapist gathered information than the essence of therapy. From the interpretation of play activity, the therapist took the lead in directing play sessions toward the ultimate goal of catharsis.

Carl Rogers took issue with the prevailing notion that the therapist was the expert about both the nature of the client's problems and the direction therapy should take. Both Rogers and Axline espoused a deep conviction, born out of clinical experience, that human beings are motivated primarily by an innate tendency or drive toward self-actualization, and dysfunctional behavior is the result of environmental conditions that hinder or distort that tendency. They believed that, given the proper environment, individuals can uncover and activate the tendency toward self-actualization and, in essence, direct themselves in resolving inner conflicts, eliminating problem behaviors, and achieving a coherent identity. Within a nondirective framework, play is more the essence of therapy than a medium to be used by the therapist to gather information.

Range of Applicability

The range of applicability of nondirective play therapy encompasses a wide variety of emotional disorders. According to Guerney (1982), a respected practitioner and teacher of nondirective play therapy, nondirective play therapy is an appropriate intervention for any child who has the capacity to achieve self-actualization. Guerney reported that nondirective play therapy has proved successful with every possible diagnostic category, with the exceptions of only "completely autistic and out-of-contact schizophrenic" children. O'Connor (1991) agreed that this method is suitable with children "exhibiting a wide variety of psychopathologies." He also asserted that nondirective therapy generally is "not considered very useful with very aggressive children or children who engage in considerable acting out." He suggested that these children require more limits and structure than what is generally offered by nondirective play therapists. O'Connor appears to be in the minority in his thinking on aggressive and acting-out children. The majority of clinicians who contribute to the literature on nondirective play therapy (Axline, 1947; Ginott, 1961; Guerney, 1982; Moustakas, 1953) agree on the method's efficacy for these children.

Theoretical Foundations
Assumptions About Nondirective Play Therapy

The Rogerian model holds great appeal for many clinicians and students of human development because of its positive perspective on the way individuals develop. Rather than viewing the individual as waging an internal battle against opposing forces destined to be at odds, humanistic theory, as set forth by Carl Rogers (1942, 1953), posits that the individual is predisposed to behave in a mature, rewarding, and generally positive manner. When individuals exist in an environment characterized by acceptance and understanding, their natural inclination toward positive growth is nurtured, and a congruent self-concept is free to develop.

Rogers himself did not consider that he had set forth a definitive theory of personality development, nor would he consider nondirective therapy a method. With regard to theory, Rogers would have had it known that the assumptions he set forth will surely change with time and new information, and ultimately these assumptions will be transformed. With regard to therapy, Rogers continually reminded us in his writings that nondirective therapy is not a technique, but a philosophy of living and a set of beliefs about human nature. The following paragraphs are a condensation of the major theoretical assumptions that guide the Rogerian model of personality development.

Self-Actualizing Tendency

Every individual possesses an innate drive or tendency toward self-actualization. Self-actualization in Rogers's model may be defined as the constructive, creative, and essentially positive trend that moves a person to become all that the person is able to be. Although a person is free to develop in any direction, the person will select positive and beneficial pathways if this tendency is not thwarted. According to Rogers, "Individuals have within themselves vast resources for self-understanding and for altering their self-concepts, basic attitudes, and self-directed behavior" (Rogers, 1980, p. 115). The actualizing tendency can be trusted to move the individual in a positive direction toward acceptance of self (and others), creativity, and fulfillment of positive potentials. As such, this innate drive is selective, directional, and constructive.

For the child, mature behavior becomes more rewarding than immature behavior. As the child experiences freedom of expression in a safe and accepting environment, the child will ultimately learn to "think for himself, to make his own decisions, to become psychologically more mature, and, by so doing, to realize selfhood" (Axline, 1947, p. 16). This basic trust in human nature echoes Jean-Jacques Rousseau's notion of the noble savage. Rousseau believed that children are naturally good, but are perverted by an environment that denies them the opportunity to act and develop in accordance with their true nature.

Unconditional Positive Regard

The self-actualizing tendency flourishes in an environment characterized by an unconditional positive regard on the part of the other or others present. The particular qualities or facilitative attitudes that compose unconditional positive regard are acceptance, genuineness, and empathy. Those qualities must be present in order to release or activate the drive toward positive growth. Harsh judgments, rejection, and disingenuousness defeat and ultimately stifle the individual's ability to achieve self-understanding and self-directed behavior.

Conditions of Worth

Rather than receiving the unconditional positive regard of others, individuals generally develop in an atmosphere of conditional regard. In other words, we are aware that certain aspects of ourselves are met with acceptance and others are not. Rogers said that "a condition of worth arises when the positive regard of a significant other is conditional, when the individual feels that in some respects he is prized and in others not" (Rogers, 1959, p. 209). The self-concept is composed of aspects of one's experience in the world that are accepted into awareness. The aspects of experience we hold in awareness are modified by two sources of information. The first source is one's own inner experience of an event; and the second source consists of the values surrounding the event that are introjected or taken over from others. When one's experience of an event is rejected by a significant other whose love and acceptance is necessary for healthy development, or for survival, the developing individual will repress the actual experience of an event and, as a result, become disconnected from the true or genuine self. The significant other's judgment about the developing individual's experience of an event becomes a condition of worth, which the individual must meet in order to feel lovable or worthy, or in some cases to survive physically. When the individual's reconstruction of self according to this condition of worth is altered to meet the demands of the environment, one's self-concept is distorted in the process. The distortion is created as a result of the incongruency between the individual's genuine experience of an event, and the significant other's criteria for acceptance (conditions of worth).

If, for example, a small boy is told that he should not feel fear when attacked by a bully but rather be a man and be stoic, the boy will disown or repress his true feelings of fear and attempt to act accordingly when attacked in the future. The condition of worth in this situation is this: "If you are to be accepted (and lovable), you must not admit feeling fearful." The child will deny or block from consciousness this aspect of himself and, therefore, be disconnected from his true self. Fear, in future events, will become an unacceptable emotional experience. The result, as previously stated, is a distorted self-concept that blocks the child from experiencing a congruent self. According to Rogers, congruence is a necessary condition for experiencing "realness" and achieving self-actualization.

Congruence

The source of psychological health is congruence; conversely, the source of psychological maladjustment is incongruence. When individuals behave in ways that maintain and enhance the self-actualizing tendency, they are behaving congruently. When they behave in ways that maintain a self-concept formed to satisfy others' conditions of worth (rather than behaving in a way that allows genuine experience to enter one's awareness), they are behaving incongruently. According to Rogers, an individual can be said to be congruent when "he is genuine, without 'front' or facade, openly being the feelings and attitudes which at that moment are flowing in him" (Rogers, 1961, p. 61). Anxiety results from the perception, usually below the level of consciousness, that one's experience is at odds with one's self-concept. Because this perception is not in the individual's immediate awareness, anxiety is experienced as a state of tension with unknown causes. Anxiety, then, is a red flag of sorts, which alerts the individual to a discrepancy between one's genuine experience of an event and one's outward behavior.

Means and Conditions for Implementing Nondirective Play Therapy
The Therapist's Qualifications

The nondirective play therapist's primary role is to provide an environment that will foster the child's positive growth by removing the barriers that make it difficult for the child to move toward self-actualization. The conditions and conduct of therapy will be presented as much as possible in the words of Virginia Axline, who has become well known for her clear articulation of the therapeutic process. According to Axline, eight basic principles guide the conduct of therapy:

1. The therapist must develop a warm, friendly, relationship with the child, in which good rapport is established as soon as possible.
2. The therapist accepts the child exactly as he is.
3. The therapist establishes a feeling of permissiveness in the relationship so that the child feels free to express his feelings completely.
4. The therapist is alert to recognize the feelings the child is expressing and reflects those feelings back to him in such a manner that he gains insight into his behavior.
5. The therapist maintains a deep respect for the child's ability to solve his own problems if given an opportunity to do so. The responsibility to make choices and to institute change is the child's.
6. The therapist does not attempt to direct the child's actions or conversation in any manner. The child leads the way; the therapist follows.
7. The therapist does not attempt to hurry the therapy along. It is a gradual process and is recognized as such by the therapist.
8. The therapist establishes only those limitations that are necessary to anchor the therapy to the world of reality and to make the child aware of his responsibility in the relationship. (Axline, 1969, pp. 73–74).

These principles manifest themselves in the therapist's verbalizations. Four categories of responses are available to the nondirective play therapist: structuring, empathic responding, personal statements, and setting limits.

Structuring

The first session typically begins with an introductory remark by the therapist that gives the child information about what to expect in the play-room. The therapist says: "This is a very special room. In here, you can say anything you want and do just about anything you want. If there's something you may not do, I'll let you know." The vast majority of therapeutic comments are empathic reflections. The introductory remark is a category of therapeutic response called structuring. Most structuring takes place in the first session and involves both providing the child with information (such as how long sessions will last, what the child can do, and so on), and arranging the room so as to prevent the child from suffering injuries—putting away objects that are not for the child's use and generally making the room safe for therapy, while providing the least restrictive environment.

At first, children tend to behave in the playroom as they would in the "outside world." They ask questions and speak in a conversational way. In general, they expect the adult to set the pace of the interaction. Structuring comments help the child to understand the nature of interactions in the play room. For example:

Child: (*Looking at two games*) Which one do you want to play?
Therapist: (*Structuring*) In the playroom you can decide about things. I'll play whichever game you want me to play.

If the child persists in asking the therapist to choose a toy, the therapist would reflect empathically by saying "You really want me to be the one to choose." If the child responded by saying, "Yes! That's what I want," the therapist would oblige the child by choosing a game.

Empathic Responding

Empathic responses are statements the therapist makes that reflect either the content of the child's behavior, or the child's thoughts or feelings about the present experience. An empathic reflection of the child's feelings or thoughts should not be confused with the therapist's interpretation of the child's feelings or thoughts. According to Axline,

> Reflection and interpretation are two different things. However, it is difficult to differentiate between them. The child's play is symbolic of his feelings, and whenever the therapist attempts to translate symbolic behavior into

words, she is interpreting because she is saying what she thinks the child has expressed in his actions. . . . A cautious use of interpretation, however, would seem the best policy, with the therapist keeping the interpretation down to a minimum, and, when using it, basing it upon the obvious play activity of the child. (Axline, 1969, p. 98)

The following example may be helpful in differentiating between empathic responding and interpretation. In the first, the therapist is interpreting.

Child: (*Playing with dolls*) Bad boy! Give her back her toy! (*Child manipulates dolls so that the boy doll is stealing the girl doll's toy.*)
Therapist: (*Interpreting*) You're angry with your brother because he bullies you. You'd like to see him punished.

In the second example, the therapist responds empathically to the same words and behavior from the child.

Therapist: (*Empathic responding*) That boy doll is a bully. He's stealing her toy and you're going to stop him.

Axline's advice to therapists is to avoid getting ahead of children with interpretations. Although the interpretation may be on target, the child may not be ready to receive it. Instead, the therapist should focus on reflecting the child's feelings accurately, and letting the child know that they have been understood and accepted. The child is thus enabled to go on to express deeper feelings. Axline stated: "When the therapist catches the feeling that is expressed and recognizes the feeling, the child goes on from there and the therapist can actually see the child gain insight" (Axline, 1969, p. 99). In this way, the therapist follows the lead of the child, and the child proceeds at a pace that is tolerable for him or her.

Personal Statements

The first response in any situation in nondirective play therapy is generally an empathic response. From time to time, a child will ask the therapist a question of a personal nature. A child may ask a question because the child has a need to know the answer or the child may simply be wondering out loud with no particular need to hear a response. The generally accepted response to an inquiry from the child is as follows:

Child: I have a dog. My mom doesn't really like dogs. Do you have a dog?
Therapist: (*Empathic response*) You're hoping that I like dogs too.
Child: That's right. Do you like dogs?
Therapist: (*Personal statement*) Yes. I like dogs and I have two of them.

Often, a child asks a question without the need for a reply.

Child: I have a dog. My mom doesn't really like dogs. Do you have a dog?
Therapist: (*Empathic response*) You're hoping that I like dogs too.
Child: Yeah. I wish my mom liked my dog.
Therapist: (*Empathic response*): You'd feel a lot better if she did.

Once it has been established that the child has a clear need to know particular information about or from the therapist, it should be offered. Personal information should not be volunteered. Personal statements are made only to the extent that they are of interest to the child as evidenced by his or her insistence on knowing.

Setting Limits

Limits are set on the child's behavior in the playroom for a variety of reasons. First, setting limits ensures the physical safety of both child and therapist. Children may not endanger themselves or the therapist in any way—this grounds them in the world of reality. Setting limits provides children with the opportunity to strengthen their ego control. The limit-setting procedure allows children the choice of either controlling their dangerous or unacceptable behavior, or experiencing external controls because the therapist ends the play session. Some limits are set because of monetary considerations. A child may not destroy toys, furniture, or equipment in the playroom simply because these things would be too costly to replace. Children have many opportunities to express aggressive feelings in the playroom without destroying objects. Finally, it is difficult for therapists to maintain an empathic and caring attitude when they are threatened with violence or physical discomfort. Limits permit the therapist to continue to offer unconditional positive regard to the child and remain congruent in so doing.

When setting a limit, the therapist's attitude is of utmost importance. The limit should be presented to the child in a way that will minimize defensiveness or resentment in the child. In other words, limits are presented in a nonjudgmental tone that conveys helpful authority. Guerney (1982) stated: "Playroom limits should be few, but very clear, definable, and enforceable" (p. 38). Ginott suggested the following four-step sequence for setting limits:

1. The therapist recognizes the child's feelings or wishes and helps him to verbalize them as they are;
2. He states clearly the limit on a specific act;
3. He points out other channels through which the feelings can be expressed;
4. He helps the child to bring out the feelings of resentment that are bound to arise when restrictions are invoked. (Ginott, 1961, p. 107)

This approach is illustrated in the following example. Kevin, age six, was threatening to pour a pitcher of water onto the therapist.

Therapist: (*Empathic response*) You feel like you'd like to show me who's the boss. You're thinking about pouring water on me.

Kevin: Yeah! I just might do that.

Therapist: (*Setting a limit*) Remember when I told you if there was something in the playroom you could not do, I would tell you? You may not pour water on me.

Kevin: Rats!

Therapist: (*Empathic response*) You wish that weren't the rule. You'd like to do that.

Kevin: Yeah. Where can I pour it?

Therapist: (*Empathic response*) You're wondering where you could pour it that wouldn't be breaking a rule.

Kevin: Right.

Therapist: (*Structuring*) You may pour it in the sink or into some of the dishes.

Kevin: (*Smiling*) O.K. I won't break the rule.

Therapist: (*Empathic response*) That makes you feel good inside.

Sometimes a child persists in behaving in a way that is unacceptable, and a decision must be made regarding the consequences of breaking a rule or limit. There is some disagreement in the field about whether the child should be removed from the room (thus ending the play session) or the offending object should be removed instead. The therapist must consider that removing the offending object from the room will not necessarily stop unacceptable behavior. For example, if a child was throwing a toy at a window and the therapist, after setting the limit, removed the toy from the room, the child might continue to attempt to throw various other toys at the window. Guerney (1982) advocated ending the play session when it is clear that a child is refusing to accept a limit in the playroom. She suggested the following sequence in enforcing limits.

1. *First infraction:* The rule is stated: "Remember when I told you if there was something you could not do in the playroom I would tell you? You may not throw anything at the window."
2. *Second infraction:* "Remember, I told you that you may not throw anything at the window. If it happens again, we will need to end the play session."
3. *Third infraction:* "Remember, I told you that if you chose to throw something at the window that we would have to end the play session. Now we will have to end the session."

The statements made by the therapist after each infraction would include a reflection of the child's feelings. The child's desire to break a limit is the important aspect of the therapeutic situation and, as such, should be expressed. In the example just given, the therapist might say, "You're so mad that you feel like breaking the rule about the window." By acknowledging and accepting the child's underlying feelings, further limit testing is often avoided. In this way, through verbalizing feelings of anger, instead of throwing toys at the window, the child may learn to express hostility with words rather than deeds. Hostile words, of course, would be acceptable in the playroom.

The Therapist's Characteristics

In *Play Therapy*, Axline wrote directly about the "personality qualifications" of the therapist. It is unusual in reading a text on a particular method to find such a direct and clear enumeration of particular traits considered essential to the conduct of successful therapy. In considering the characteristics of the therapist, we are reminded of Rogers's admonition that nondirective therapy is more a philosophy of living than a method to be followed.

Axline stated that the therapist "must like children and really know them" (1947, p. 63). According to Axline, the following characteristics must be an integral part of the therapist's personality, rather than attitudes assumed for the play sessions. The therapist must be sincere, genuinely interested in the child, permissive, accepting, respecting of the child, straightforward, relaxed, mature, empathic, consistent, kind, patient, and supportive. Axline warned that the therapist must not become emotionally involved with the child "because when that happens the therapy bogs down and the child is not helped by the complicating circumstances" that might accompany an emotional involvement (1947, p. 65). She likened the therapist to a "favorite teacher" (1947, p. 63) and, by so doing, defined the role of the therapist as one that is of great importance to the child, yet carries with it a certain emotional and therapeutic distance.

Professionals generally obtain training in the methods of nondirective play therapy in one of two ways. As a student working toward a professional degree, one obtains training in a clinical course under the supervision of a counseling psychologist, clinical psychologist, or psychiatrist. This work involves both didactic and experiential components. Generally, the student engages in role playing prior to actual work with a child in therapy, so as to gain experience and become comfortable with the method. As a professional or paraprofessional, one could receive training by taking an intensive workshop, which would also involve both didactic and experiential elements. Generally, play sessions in this type of situation involve working with children who are free of a clinical diagnosis.

Guerney (1982) stated that "whereas the play therapist typically will have a general background in a clinical area of some sort, there is nothing inherent in the method which mandates that such a background is necessary" (1982, p. 28). Rogers was adamant that nonprofessionals and paraprofessionals were as adept as professionals in their performing the role of a nondirective therapist. In fact, he felt nonprofessional or paraprofessional therapists had something of an advantage in that they would be unencumbered by the psychoanalytic notions that sometimes dominate professional training and thinking.

Teachers, day-care workers, nurses, and parents have been trained in the methods of nondirective play therapy for a number of years with impressive results (see Guerney, 1982; Hornsby & Appelbaum, 1978; Kraft, 1978). Guerney (1982) stated that the most important factor in the outcome of training is an openness to the approach itself. Because of the popularity of behavioral methods in dealing with children, a resistance may be present on the part of professionals. The resistance is rooted in the assumption that the therapist must take responsibility for the direction, pace, and content of therapy.

Conditions for Conducting Nondirective Play Therapy

The toys available for the child's use in the playroom are selected using particular criteria, rather than simply as a hodgepodge of randomly selected items. If possible, the playroom itself should be constructed so that it facilitates the child's unhampered play and provides optimal conditions for training and supervising therapists.

With regard to toys, Axline's (1969) original list of toys continues to guide most therapists' selection of toys. Her list included such items as water; nursing bottles; a doll family; a doll house with furniture; toy soldiers and army equipment; toy animals; playhouse materials, including table, chairs, cot, doll bed, stove, dishes, and pans; spoons; various dolls; puppets; drawing paper; fingerpainting material; cutting paper; crayons; a telephone; a toy gun; a sandbox; and games such as checkers. Toys should be kept on shelves so that the children can readily see all the toys available and make their choice. Ginott (1961) and Guerney (1982) discussed the criteria for selecting toys for play. The following list includes the criteria of both:

1. Choose toys that permit children to test reality and express their needs symbolically.

2. Choose toys that may be used in a variety of ways. For example, in Guerney's playroom, the toy gun that is included can be used for target shooting. It comes with rubber darts, and thus allows the child to play a game of cops and robbers, or shoot at a target alone or in competition with the therapist.

3. Choose toys that allow the child to express the feelings that are difficult to deal with in real life, such as dependence, fear, and aggression. Guerney's room includes such items as a punching bag, rubber knives, frightening masks, and nursing bottles, which serve as vehicles for these deeper feelings.

4. Choose toys that allow the child to play alone or with the therapist. Playroom toys should allow the opportunity both for play alone and for joint play. Guerney's playroom includes two telephones rather than one. The games (involving a ring toss or a bean bag with a target) in her playroom can be played by one or two people.

With regard to the construction of the playroom, Axline suggested that the playroom be soundproofed and that the floors and walls be constructed of easily cleaned materials. In this way, the child's loud and messy play can be tolerated. Recording equipment and a one-way mirror facilitate therapist training and supervision. Although these conditions are ideal, effective play therapy can be carried out in a corner of a schoolroom or office, with the therapist transporting toys to the location.

Limitations of Nondirective Play Therapy
Contraindications

Nondirective play therapy is indicated for use with children between about 3 and 10. Some immature 12-year-olds can still benefit from the experience. There are few limitations with regard to the types of childhood disorders that can be treated using this method. When the diagnosis is autism or a severe form of schizophrenia, however, the likelihood of the child benefiting from play sessions is diminished.

Hazards

No hazards are associated with the implementation of play sessions. Essentially, the child experiences another individual's unconditional positive regard in the context of relatively unrestricted play. The environment is characterized by safety, predictability, and compassion. As such, the child is not at risk for any harmful effects resulting from this type of experience.

The Effectiveness of Nondirective Play Therapy

The general criteria used to assess the effectiveness of nondirective play therapy are essentially the same as those for any other form of play therapy. In other words, therapy may be considered a success and terminated once the child is functioning at a developmentally appropriate level. Specifically, the therapist would be alert to the cessation of the problem behavior or behaviors that brought the child to therapy. If, for example, the presenting problems of a 10-year-old were lying and aggressive behavior, the necessary conditions for termination would be both the disappearance of those behaviors and the presence of functional behavior appropriate for a child of 10.

Nondirective play therapy has been subjected to the scrutiny of empirical assessment perhaps more than most therapeutic methods. The results of the majority of studies indicate that it renders positive treatment effects. Outcome studies of nondirective play therapy conducted in the late 1940s and early 1950s provide evidence of positive results with diverse problems such as allergies (Miller & Baruch, 1948), mental deficiencies (Axline, 1949), personality problems (Bloomberg, 1948; Fleming & Snyder, 1947), physical disabilities in children (Axline, 1947; Cowen & Cruickshank, 1948), race conflicts (Axline, 1948), and reading difficulties (Axline, 1947; Bills, 1950). Although the results of such studies generally indicated the efficacy of nondirective play therapy for treating such problems, these early studies were criticized for their general failure to provide control groups for purposes of comparison. According to Lebo (1953), "play therapy should stand or fall on the results of experimental studies investigating its effectiveness in relation to other procedures" (p. 430).

In general, more recent empirical assessments of the efficacy of nondirective play therapy have employed careful methodologies including the use of control groups and random assignment of subjects to control and treatment groups. Guerney (1982) conducted a thorough examination of such studies. In her review of the empirical research on the effectiveness of non-directive play therapy, Guerney examined the effectiveness of the method as used by professional therapists, nonprofessionals, and parents as therapists. Studies conducted to test the effectiveness of nondirective play therapy over-whelmingly demonstrated positive results. When nonprofessionals (under-graduate students) were trained in the methods of nondirective play therapy and allowed to treat actual clinical cases under the supervision of graduate students, the results indicated that the children receiving nondirective play therapy from nonprofessionals exhibited decreases in problem behaviors (as reported by their parents and teachers). No significant changes in problem behaviors were reported for children in a control group who received simple play time with untrained undergraduates (Stollak, Scholom, Green, Schreiber, & Meese, 1975).

These generally positive findings suggest that the potential of play therapy in preventing adult psychopathology deserves to be considered in future research.

References

Axline, V. (1947). *Play therapy*. Cambridge, MA: Houghton Mifflin.

Axline, V. (1948). Play therapy and race conflict in young children. *Journal of Abnormal Social Psychology, 43*, 300–310.

Axline, V. (1949). Play therapy: A way of understanding and helping reading problems. *Childhood Education, 26*, 156–161.

Axline, V. (1969). *Play therapy* (rev. ed.). New York: Ballantine.

Bills, R. (1950). Non-directive play therapy with retarded readers. *Journal of Counseling Psychology, 14*, 140–149.

Bloomberg, C. (1948). An experiment in play therapy. *Childhood Education, 25*, 130–177.

Cowen, E., & Cruickshank, W. (1948). Group therapy with physically handi-capped children. *Journal of Educational Psychology, 39*, 193–215.

Fleming, L., & Snyder, W. (1947). Social and personal changes following non-directive group play therapy. *American Journal of Orthopsychiatry, 17*, 101–116.

Ginott, H. (1961). *Group psychotherapy with children: The theory and practice of play therapy*. New York: McGraw-Hill.

Guerney, L. (1982). Child-centered (nondirective) play therapy. In C. Schaefer & K. O'Connor (Eds.), *Handbook of play therapy* (pp. 21–64). New York: Wiley.

Hornsby, L., & Appelbaum, A. (1978). Parents as primary therapists: Filial therapy. In L. Arnold (Ed.), *Helping parents help their children* (pp. 126–134). New York: Brunner/Mazel.

Kraft, P. (1978). The play therapist: The student, the struggle, the process. *Journal of Psychiatric Nursing and Mental Health Services, 16,* 29–31.

Lebo, D. (1953). The relationship of response categories in play therapy to chronological age. *Child Psychiatry, 2,* 330–336.

Miller, H., & Baruch, D. (1948). Psychological dynamics in allergic patients as shown in group and individual psychotherapy. *Journal of Consulting Psychology, 12,* 111–115.

Moustakas, C. (1953). *Children in play therapy.* New York: McGraw-Hill.

O'Connor, K. (1991). *The play therapy primer.* New York: Wiley.

Rogers, C. R. (1942). *Counseling and psychotherapy.* Boston: Houghton Mifflin.

Rogers, C. R. (1953). The interest in the practice of psychotherapy. *American Psychologist, 8,* 48–50.

Rogers, C. R. (1959). A theory of therapy, personality, and interpersonal relationships as developed in the client-centered framework. In S. Koch (Ed.), *Psychology: A study of science, Vol. III: Formulations of the person and the social context* (pp. 184–256). New York: McGraw-Hill.

Rogers, C. R. (1961). *On becoming a person: A therapist's view of psychotherapy.* Boston: Houghton Mifflin.

Rogers, C. R. (1980). *A way of being.* Boston: Houghton Mifflin.

Stollak, G., Scholom, A., Green, L., Schreiber, J., & Meese, L. (1975). Process and outcome of play encounters between undergraduates and clinic-referred children: Preliminary findings. *Psychotherapy: Theory, Research, and Practice, 13,* 327–331.

CHAPTER 12

Existential Psychotherapy

In *The Culture of Narcissism*, social critic Christopher Lasch (1979) examined the changes that have taken place in the form of psychiatric complaints in the United States since the Second World War. He stated that an increasing number of patients presented themselves for treatment describing themselves as demoralized, unable to feel deeply, uncertain about their experience of living, indecisive, and fearful of dying and death. Lasch stated that capitalism ultimately reduces human beings "to interchangeable objects" (1979, p. 132). As a result of capitalism's dominance in the United States, Americans possess a "self-consciousness that mocks all attempts at spontaneous action or enjoyment" (p. 165). The individual seeks solace in cults and the egocentric notions of pop psychology—"anything to get his mind off his own mind" (p. 178).

The idea that modern men and women lack the courage to confront their experience of living and that, as a result, they give up much of their freedom, is a root assumption of existential philosophy. Clients who present themselves without specific symptoms, but with a vague sense of purposelessness and alienation accompanied by boredom and transient feelings of dread, would be diagnosed by existential psychotherapists as suffering from an existential neurosis. The existential therapist's goal would not be to alleviate these clients' symptoms. Instead, the therapist's aim would be to enable them to expand their awareness of what it is to be fully human and, by so doing, to increase their ability to make choices based on knowledge of their own potential.

According to Rollo May, a prominent existential psychologist, existential therapy emphasizes "meaning rather than mechanics [and is] against the epiphany of mechanics and techniques. Existential therapy could well be called existential-humanistic, for it stands against the worship of techniques" (1987, pp. 214–215).

General Purpose of Existential Analysis

Sartre (1960, p. 15) stated that the essence of existential philosophy is the notion that "man is nothing else but what he makes of himself." According to existential thinking, the primary task of living is to find meaning in one's life (although this quest may not always be a conscious one). Ultimately, we must realize that each of us is alone and, in that way, responsible for the content of our existence. Life, then, is a series of choices made by the individual, and the circumstances of that individual's life are the result of those choices.

The general purpose of existential analysis is to assist individuals in coming to terms with their existence and in taking responsibility for the direction and quality of their lives. This goal is accomplished by existential psychotherapists' assuming the role of an active participant in facilitating the "unfolding beingness of the other person" (Kruger, 1979, p. 168). In other words, the therapist is available to clients so that, in the process of disclosing the meaning of their own lives, they are able to grasp fully what it is to be themselves.

History of Existential Analysis

Existential analysis has its roots in phenomenology and existential philosophy. Existential philosophy grew in prominence in Europe after the Second World War as people became acutely aware of the destructive consequences of political ideologies, which required individuals to sacrifice their personal values and beliefs for the purported good of the nation. In the process of sacrificing self, individuals were reduced in significance and, as a result, suffered a loss of personal identity and sense of control over their own destiny. Albert Camus and Jean Paul Sartre, two of the existential movement's foremost spokesmen, brought existential notions to the attention of the general public and hastened the spread of existentialism to the United States. Other notable writers and philosophers who were powerful figures in the existential movement include Nietzsche, Dostoyevsky, Kafka, Heidegger, Jaspers, Buber, and Kierkegaard.

During the postwar years, a growing number of psychiatrists and psychologists found that their patients' complaints centered around feelings of isolation, alienation, loneliness, and a lack of meaning in their lives. Behaviorism, as well as Freudian psychoanalysis, failed to provide an understanding of these patients' experience. As psychology became less the domain of university-based psychologists, and applied psychologists increased in numbers, a search began for more relevant knowledge about the person and human values. Existentialism offered an approach to understanding people that was more rooted in experience, with a firm philosophical base that rejected positivism and determinism.

In addition, a number of researchers and clinicians felt that the tools of empirical science seemed inadequate to uncover and explain the nature of human beings. According to existentialists, a principal limitation of the empirical sciences is an "exclusive interest in facts" without concern for their "ontological significance and consequences" (Hanly, 1979, p. 8). The behavioral psychology that dominated the United States in the 1950s obscured that which is essentially human by insisting that internal processes, such as cognition and emotion, could never be known and should thus be disregarded. In an attempt to find a theory or philosophy that would explain their patients' experience, and a method that would allow them to investigate psychological phenomena, these practitioners sought answers in existential philosophy and phenomenology.

Existential philosophy and phenomenology are wedded in existential psychology, in that "existential psychology may be defined as an empirical science of human existence that employs the method of phenomenological analysis" (Hall & Lindzey, 1978, p. 313). The data of phenomenology are descriptions of immediate experience. The goal is to understand, rather than explain, phenomena as they are subjectively experienced by the individual.

Although Martin Heidegger is generally acknowledged as the individual who joined existential thought with the methods of phenomenology, Ludwig Binswanger and Medard Boss are considered the leading figures in applying existential ideas to the field of psychiatry. In the United States, Rollo May has been the foremost advocate of existential analysis.

Range of Applicability

Existential and humanistic therapies are often viewed in college textbooks as treatments appropriate only for the articulate, neurotic individual, a brand of therapy for the so-called worried well. Existential therapists do not set any limitations on the applicability of this method. Since the early years of existential analysis, practitioners of existential therapy such as Ludwig

Binswanger (1963) have published the results of their work with deeply disturbed patients. In addition, the noted British psychiatrist and existential therapist, R. D. Laing, has written extensively on his work with schizophrenic individuals (Laing, 1969a, 1969b).

According to existential psychotherapy, one's behavior and psychic life are an expression of one's existence. As viewed by the dominant medical model, psychiatric symptoms reflect the individual's maladaptive behavior or failure to adjust to his or her circumstances of life. The person is diseased, and the therapist makes a diagnosis by observing the outward behavior or symptoms that the patient displays. The verbal responses of, for example, a psychotic or schizophrenic patient are generally considered a series of disconnected sentences that are useless except as indicators or signs of disease; therefore the patient's words are ignored. To the existential therapist, the verbal responses of schizophrenic patients express their existence, and thus constitute useful information. Existential psychotherapy with schizophrenic patients involves listening on a deep level to the schizophrenics' communications in order to understand what they say about their existence, and to respond to those communications as one human being to another.

For an interesting account of a psychotic episode as reported by an existential therapist, the reader is referred to Laing's *The Politics of Experience* (1967). Laing referred to the psychotic episode as a "voyage" and stated: "This voyage is not what we need to be cured of, but . . . it is itself a natural way of healing our own appalling state of alienation called normality" (p. 167). Laing's use of the term *voyage*, rather than *psychotic episode*, is not an attempt to romanticize or minimize the suffering involved in such an experience. Instead, his language is an attempt to personalize what has been depersonalized as a result of the popularity of a science that studies organisms rather than people. Whatever diagnosis is applied to a particular client, the existential psychotherapist would proceed in the same broad fashion with all individuals—meeting them where they are in an attempt to "reveal the undisclosed structures of consciousness" (Hanly, 1979, p. 17).

Theoretical Foundations

Assumptions About Human Nature

Existential writers in general seek to describe and understand the nature of being a person. Since a basic assumption of existential therapists is that each person is unique and thus experiences the world in a unique way, no general theory that explains the lives of individuals is possible. Some basic assumptions about the experience of being human, however, are generally shared by existential therapists. Before proceeding to discuss existential therapists' assumptions about human nature, an understanding of the phenomenological approach to studying human lives will be helpful; that approach underpins existential psychotherapy.

As we have seen, existential thinkers reject the reductionistic tendencies of quantitative approaches that seek to understand people by studying them as objects. A basic assumption of empirical science is that everything in existence exists to a particular degree and therefore can be measured. Psychologists have clung to the notion that we can understand human beings better if we measure them. This notion persists, in part, because researchers believe that quantifying data is scientific in the sense that our understanding of ourselves will be revealed through mathematical equations, just as Descartes saw science as resolving itself into mathematics.

According to R. D. Laing (1969a), "many psychologists feel that if psychology is not a branch of natural science it is not a science at all" (p. 13). He argued that studying the person as an organism rather than as a person will not lead to a valid understanding of people. If one is studying the behavior of an organism, one is studying behavior pure and simple and not the person. When conceiving of the person as an organism, scientists take a very different point of view from studying the person as a person. Phenomenologists believe that the natural sciences should not dictate methods of studying human beings. "The science of persons is the study of human beings that begins from a relationship with the other as a person and proceeds to an account of the other still as a person" (Laing, 1969b, p. 20). The phenomenological and existential viewpoints hold that "existence is absolutely original and unrepeatable, radically personal and unique" (Kruger, 1979, p. 22). As a result, one must employ a method of study that allows the researcher to grasp the uniqueness and depth of experience. This is the aim of phenomenology.

Phenomenology stems from the thinking of Edmund Husserl, who said that the way to understand a phenomenon is to let the phenomenon speak for itself. An assumption of phenomenology is that consciousness is an intentional act of individuals, during which they allow the world to appear to themselves. It is in our nature as humans to reveal the world to ourselves. The world is illuminated or made known by consciousness. Since consciousness always involves an object (the world), it does not exist by itself, nor can the object exist without consciousness to reveal it. In this way, phenomenology bridges the split between subject and object that Descartes proposed. The term for this consciousness in the language of phenomenology is *being-in-the-world*.

Individuals experience the world in their own unique ways; each life is a series of unique experiences that can never be replicated or repeated. These experiences of being can be described and comprehended when individuals are approached in such a way that their true being shows itself. The individual must be approached by another who has no preconceptions about the individual's experience of being and who thus remains open to the individual's description of experience. Phenomenology is the study of the structure of existence as revealed by lived experience.

The fundamental assumption of existential analysis is that the structure of human existence is based on being-in-the-world, or *Dasein*. Heidegger first used *Dasein* to denote human existence. Literally translated, *Dasein* means "to be *the* there." Note that the expression is not "to be there" but "to be *the* there"—a phrase that implies a oneness with the world. Although this notion is an awkward one for Western thinkers, "to be the there" implies a state of being in the world. The world in this sense is not the external world, but rather a state of being in the world in which an individual's existence appears and is present. Humans do not exist apart from the world, and the world does not exist apart from humans. This view does not state that individuals interact with events in the world, but rather that individuals are their experience in the world, and the world is in the experience of the individual. Thus, the world is disclosed in the experience of being-in-the-world. The therapist's role within this framework is to assist clients in articulating their experience of being-in-the-world.

According to existentialists, we can conceive of the world of existence as having three spheres or spaces of existence (Binswanger, 1963). Those three spheres consist of *Umwelt, Mitwelt,* and *Eigenwelt. Umwelt* refers to the "landscape-world," or the world of nature that would exist without the awareness of humans. *Umwelt* also includes natural forces and, therefore, includes our biological drives, such as the need for food and for sleep. Although *Umwelt* includes those things in nature that would exist without our being conscious of them, an individual's *Umwelt* is seen as the individual's subjective experience of, say, feeling hungry or seeing a tree. Once, during a winter walk with a friend, one of the authors stopped to admire the beauty of a large gnarled tree. The friend said, "How can you possibly think that tree is beautiful? It's barren and looks dead!" The author was struck by the discrepancy between her and her friend's experiences of "catching" the world as it had shown itself.

Mitwelt refers to the "person-world," or the world of being in relationship with others—the individual's social experience. The conception of *Mitwelt* is quite similar to the basic assumption of Harry Stack Sullivan's interpersonal theory of psychiatry. We make meaning of our world by drawing on our experience of being in relationship with others. Kruger (1979) wrote: "it is not possible for me to make explicit in word, image or sound, any feeling, thought or any other psychic structure other than in dialogue with someone else" (p. 29). Each of us assumes the possibility of being understood by another (whether that person is present or not), and this possibility of being understood is a necessary condition for us to be reflective. According to existential thinking, a true encounter with another person involves a "letting-beness of the things-that-are as they present themselves to a person in a shared world" (Kruger, 1979, p. 76)—an idea that will be discussed in the section on conducting existential therapy. Once again, the language of existentialists involves hyphenated expressions meant to express both the flow of existence and the absence of a split between subject and object. In a true encounter, both people can reveal themselves as they are without anxiety.

Eigenwelt is the "thought-world," or the sphere in which persons see the world with reference to their self-identity. As a person I have self-awareness and, in the world of *Eigenwelt,* I grasp who I am in the sense of how I perceive the world, what my preferences are, and so on. *Eigenwelt* is the world of inner life. Existential psychologists feel that this sphere has been largely ignored by psychology as a discipline.

While the individual's existence consists of being-in-the-world, each individual also possesses the desire and ability to get beyond the world. The human possibility of getting beyond the world is expressed in the existential concept of being-beyond-the-world. Being-beyond-the-world is a particular form of awareness and being that involves transcending the world as one actualizes one's potentialities. A genuine or authentic life is possible only when the individual exercises the freedom to choose to realize the full potential of the individual's being. The responsibility for that choice lies with the individual. Choosing not to exercise this freedom means that the individual will be "caught in the narrowed-down mentality of an anonymous, inauthentic 'everybody'" (Boss, 1963, p. 48). Freedom for humans comes in accepting and embracing life with an attitude of "letting-be-ness of things-that-are." When one accepts life with an attitude of letting-be-ness, one is not apathetic, but rather the opposite, in that one is open to life's possibilities. Letting-be-ness of things-that-are involves not fighting against that which is and that which shows itself in the world. Letting-be-ness of things-that-are includes accepting one's ground of existence.

Each of us has a ground of existence onto which we are thrown. One's ground of existence is the circumstances of one's life, which include the individual's personal characteristics, the characteristics of the individual's social situation, and the inevitable fact of death. Our ground of existence constitutes our destiny (although not in the sense of a predetermined future, since in existential thinking the future always exists in possibility). Our ground of existence includes characteristics such as intelligence, size, genetic predisposition for certain illnesses, gender, talents, and other psychological and cultural factors. For example, because I am a woman I have a different ground of existence than if I were a man. I am the daughter of my mother and not the daughter of your mother, which also contributes to my ground of existence.

In various ways my ground of existence places certain limitations on my existence, but these limitations must be accepted, since they are not in my power to change. These limitations, then, are not to be confused with the limitations people set for themselves as a consequence of the choices they make in life. Our ground of existence brings to our being-in-the-world a feeling of being "determined, limited, placed in time and space" and fixed "without its consent" (Binswanger, 1963, p. 98). One's sense of having been determined or destined is conceptualized as "being thrown." Out of our thrownness, we sense our finitude and limitedness. To the extent that we fight against or refuse to recognize our ground of existence, we will live in an inauthentic manner and experience guilt and anxiety as a result of our inauthenticity. Binswanger stated that "the more stubbornly the human being opposes his being-thrown into his existence . . . the more strongly this thrownness gains in influence" (1958, p. 340). When one fights one's thrownness, one becomes alienated from oneself. Although one has no choice about the characteristics that constitute one's thrownness (for example, being a woman, the certainty of death), the many opportunities in life present individuals with the freedom of choice. The ability to choose—which always implies responsibility for the choices we make—holds a position of great importance in existential thinking.

The most important task of existence is becoming. Existence is everchanging and, because our being is dynamic, the possibility of transcendence is ever-present. To be fully human is to transcend. To transcend, according to Boss, involves "a state of being suffused with a mood of serenity; a pervasive letting-be-ness is a state of being in which all the significances and meaningful coherences of everything that is encountered is allowed to become clear" (Kruger, 1979, p. 67). In this state, individuals are able to respond to the world with their fullest capacity. The individual, in the language of existentialists, is attuned to the world. This experience of transcending or being-attuned corresponds to the peak experience described in humanistic writings.

Earlier in this discussion it was stated that humans are aware of their existence in the world. Just as we are aware of our being-in-the-world, we are aware of the possibility of nonbeing or death. Existential writers believe that in order to grasp what it means to exist, we must grasp the fact that death is inescapable; the moment when we cease to exist will one day arrive. Nonbeing also takes the form of denying our ability to make choices based on what we want and who we are. In such a state of nonbeing, we become less self-aware, and our being-in-the-world becomes extremely limited. For some of us, our fear of nonbeing is so overwhelming that we withdraw from life.

That withdrawal can take forms as extreme as a psychotic break or as mundane as becoming an automaton, giving up freedom of choice in favor of conforming to society's expectations. The latter is not without its price, for existentialists believe that the automaton lives a life of quiet desperation, characterized by anxiety and hostility. Becoming an automaton is something of a paradox in that, out of our fear of nonbeing, we become that which we fear.

Existential writers continually remind us that we live in an age of anxiety. Anxiety is viewed in existential writings as both a constructive and destructive force. As we move through life transitions, we experience a degree of anxiety that is considered normal. A normal amount of anxiety serves us in that it motivates us to change. Too much anxiety cripples us and stands in the way of our ability to behold the world with a fresh outlook. When anxiety is appropriate or proportionate to an experience, it is constructive; exaggerated or disproportionate anxiety is destructive. Guilt, too, can be constructive or destructive—constructive when it motivates us to live in harmony with others and to use our abilities in a creative fashion; destructive when we dwell on our actions or inaction to such a degree that we become frozen and ineffectual.

Assumptions About Conducting Existential Therapy

Existential therapists assume that individuals who present themselves for treatment are suffering from an existential dilemma. Clients are people who have not come to terms with their destiny (their ground of being) and are stuck in a mode of being-in-the-world in which they deny their responsibility for the flow of their lives and are closed to their possibilities. Thus they experience their existence as inauthentic and meaningless. Although symptoms and their severity differ from individual to individual, the cause of all symptoms may be traced to the same source, the existential dilemma. The diagnosis, then, is the same for all individuals—as is, in a broad sense, the approach to treatment (it should be noted that existential therapists generally shudder at the word *treatment*). The approach involves

> a situation in which one human being (therapist) is available to another human being (client) as a fellow human being in the attitude of . . . let-be-ness . . . aimed at grasping those relational meaning coherences of the world that are specifically the client's. (Kruger, 1979, p. 168)

As the therapist assists the client in uncovering the structure of meaning that characterizes the client's life, the client moves toward an authentic existence and, thus, the ability to live more fully in the world. The aim of existential therapy, simply stated, is to help people to become aware of and to experience their possibilities, and to take responsibility for living. It is assumed that, as clients understand their being-in-the-world, symptoms present at the onset of treatment will lessen or disappear.

The writings on existential therapy do not offer any specific directions concerning the conduct of therapy. Instead, case studies are used to demonstrate the unfolding of the client's existence and the outcomes of therapy. Most case studies in the literature are presented from the therapist's point of view. M. D. Eppel (1978) provided a client's own retrospective account of her 2-year experience of existential psychotherapy. The client, a woman named Sara, emphasized that the valuable part of therapy was not in being taught how to change particular behaviors or how to relieve her depression—indeed, those kinds of things were not discussed. For Sara, therapy enabled her to take responsibility for the life that was essentially hers and to confront all that presented itself to her in the world. Sara stated that the crucial experiences for her were not so much what happened in therapy as how she lived her life between sessions as a result of her awakening to herself. As this occurred, Sara began the process of confronting her existence, making choices, and taking responsibility for those choices. The therapist facilitated Sara's understanding of her existence by being open to her world and participating fully in the relationship as one human being to another.

Most clients come to therapy with the expectation that the therapist will provide answers. Existential therapists believe that providing answers disempowers individuals, because providing answers exempts people from taking responsibility for their own lives. More to the point, existential therapists believe that no one individual has the answers for another individual's dilemmas, nor can one individual explicate the lived experience of another individual. One can only receive the other in an attitude of letting-be-ness.

Letting-be-ness is the essential attitude of the therapist. Binswanger (1963) described this attitude as "letting beings—all beings—be as they are in themselves" (p. 252). When one is able to experience letting-be-ness in the immediate moment when one encounters another, one has no sense of urgency about changing the other. Binswanger takes care to note that letting-be-ness is not a passive or apathetic state, but rather a highly active and empathic one. He stated that "a revolutionary spirit who seeks to overthrow things of the world actually resides in undisturbed immediacy among them; otherwise he could not overthrow them" (p. 252). The essence of letting-be-ness is to experience a sense of harmony and understanding with the other, with the circumstances, and with ourselves.

As the existential therapist holds an attitude of letting-be-ness with the client, the client is engaged in the process of becoming. The goal is to become fully human and to realize as many of the possibilities of being-in-the-world as one can. To refuse the freedom that is ours as human beings is to deny our existence. Individuals who suffer from neurotic and psychotic symptoms are those who have become stuck in the process of becoming.

Means and Conditions for Implementing Existential Therapy
The Therapist's Qualifications

Kruger (1979) stated that "the therapist already has a hold on what his life is uniquely about" (p. 168) as a result of experience and training. Just as in psychoanalysis, it is assumed that existential therapists will have undergone their own existential analysis. Existential therapists generally hold an advanced degree such as a Ph.D. or an M.D., and typically they have received training at an institute specializing in existential analysis. Rollo May (1961) stated that "rigorous clinical study and thought" (p. 28) are necessary for the clinician who engages in existential analysis.

Conditions for Conducting Existential Therapy

Existential therapy requires no special equipment and may be practiced in any space that offers privacy.

Limitations of Existential Therapy
Contraindications and Hazards

As is true with many other methods, any limitations on the use of existential therapy exist as opinion rather than fact. The literature on existential therapy places no limits on its applicability. Rollo May (1961) has warned against the "wild eclecticism" (p. 28) that may be present in the therapy of those who practice without having received rigorous clinical training. The literature on existential therapy is vast and complex; it is not a method that one can acquire in a weekend workshop. Existential therapy is not a brief therapy. Case studies generally reveal a period of therapy lasting 1 to 2 years.

The Effectiveness of Existential Therapy

Research on the effectiveness of existential therapy consists of clinical case studies such as Binswanger's Case of Ellen West (1958) and Case of Lola Vass (1963). Because existential psychotherapy attempts to help clients become aware of their uniquely lived experience and, out of this awareness, to experience their possibilities, whether therapy is a success or failure is really the decision of the individual receiving the therapy. No specific criteria can be used as standards to measure therapeutic outcomes; in fact, it would contradict the essence of existential psychology to set up some criterion, apart from a client's own determination, of whether therapy was successful. A basic tenet of existential psychology is that people are free to choose what they want to be and how they want to live. Numerous possibilities for success or failure therefore exist. While existentialists see the aim of psychotherapy as assisting individuals to become aware of and experience their possibilities, no operational definition of this goal, except the definition given by the client, is possible. The primary purpose of case studies in the existential literature is to describe and understand the client's lived experience in the framework of existential thinking.

References

Binswanger, L. (1958). The existential analysis school of thought. In R. May, E. Angel, & H. F. Ellenberger (Eds.), *Existence: A new dimension in psychiatry and psychology* (pp. 191–213). New York: Basic Books.

Binswanger, L. (1963). *Being-in-the-world: Selected papers of Ludwig Binswanger*. New York: Basic Books.

Boss, M. (1963). *Psychoanalysis and daseinsanalysis*. New York: Basic Books.

Eppell, M. D. (1978). *A phenomenological explication of a client's retrospective experience of psychotherapy*. Unpublished master's thesis, Rhodes University.

Hall, C. S., & Lindzey, G. (1978). *Theories of personality* (3rd ed.). New York: Wiley.

Hanly, C. M. T. (1979). *Existentialism and psychoanalysis*. New York: International Universities Press.

Kruger, D. (1979). *An introduction to phenomenological psychology*. Duquesne University Press.

Laing, R. D. (1967). *The politics of experience*. New York: Pantheon.

Laing, R. D. (1969a). *Self and others*. New York: Pantheon.

Laing, R. D. (1969b). *The divided self*. New York: Pantheon.

Lasch, C. (1979). *The culture of narcissim: American life in an age of diminishing expectations*. New York: Norton.

May, R. (1961). (Ed.). *Existential psychology*. New York: Random House.

May, R. (1987). Therapy in our day. In J. Zeig (Ed.), *The evolution of psychotherapy* (pp. 212–220). New York: Brunner/Mazel.

Sartre, J. P. (1960). *Existentialism and humanism*. London: Methuen.

Family Therapy Approaches

■

··

CHAPTER 13

Structural
Family Therapy

··

■

Ageneral assumption underlying psychotherapy is that the family exerts a
powerful influence on an individual's developmental trajectory. Although
clinicians agree that the family is a powerful agent in the formation of
personality, they disagree about the level at which intervention should take
place—the individual or the family. By intervening at the level of the individual,
clinicians make certain assumptions about diagnosis and treatment. First, they
assume that an individual is an adequate source of information about his or her
experience and behavior in the world. Second, they assume that the individual
is the site of pathology. Third, they assume that the changes brought about in
the individual will endure as the individual interacts in the various contexts of
daily life. Each of these assumptions is challenged by the tenets of structural
family therapy.

General Purpose of Structural Family Therapy

The broad goal of structural family therapy is to change the family unit's
structure or organization so that family functioning moves from a dysfunctional to a functional state of being. The therapist directs attention to altering
the roles and experience of each individual in the context of the family. When
the organization of family dynamics is changed, the position and therefore the
experience of each family member is changed; as a result, the context of

family life begins to provide an environment that promotes healthy development. In other words, the family changes from a pathogenic system to a
growth-supporting system. In a broad sense, healthy development is fostered
by each individual's sense of being securely connected to, yet separate from,
the family. In this way, each individual experiences a sense of place or
belonging within the family system and a sense of the uniqueness of his or
her self, both in the family and in the world.

History of Structural Family Therapy

The notion that the family is the most potent source of influence on an
individual's development, and provides the context in which individuals shape
their self-concepts, forms the basis for most theories of human development.
This notion is clearly at the heart of Harry Stack Sullivan's *Interpersonal Theory of
Psychiatry*, in which Sullivan defined personality as "the relatively enduring pattern of recurrent interpersonal situations which characterize a human life"
(1953, p. 111). In texts outlining various approaches to family therapies, Sullivan is rarely, if ever, recognized for his influence in the conceptualization of the
family as a group whose members interact in a reciprocal fashion to influence
one another's experience. Instead, family therapy's beginnings are traced to a
monograph by John Bell (1961) and the work of an interdisciplinary team of
researchers in Palo Alto led by Gregory Bateson. Sullivan's influence is apparent
in a statement by the founder of structural family therapy, Dr. Salvador
Minuchin, that "the individual influences his context and is influenced by it in
constantly recurring sequences of interaction" (1974, p. 9).

Structural family therapy was developed by Salvador Minuchin and his
associates at the Philadelphia Child Guidance Clinic. Minuchin's work has
been extremely influential and is set forth in his classic *Families and Family
Therapy* (1974). The impetus for Minuchin's shift from working with individuals to working strictly with families grew out of his experience in the late
1950s as he counseled delinquent boys from extremely disadvantaged circumstances. In Minuchin's words, "we were faced with the irony and hope-
lessness of dramatic failures despite intensive, individualized treatment of
these children" (Minuchin, Montalvo, Guerney, Rosman, & Schumer, 1967,
p. 5). Conventional psychotherapy, with its focus on either insight or
behavior modification techniques, failed to produce lasting change in these
children. At that time, the notion that the family, rather than the individual,
was responsible for the development and maintenance of pathology in its
members was gaining recognition. As a result, a number of practitioners
began working with families rather than individuals to correct dysfunction.
Minuchin followed suit and began using the techniques of family therapy at

the Wiltwyck School for Boys. In the early 1960s, Minuchin began intensive study of the methods of leading figures in family therapy. As he moved to the Philadelphia Child Guidance Clinic and continued his work with impoverished families, he began formulating what eventually became his pioneering contribution to the field of family therapy.

Range of Applicability

Structural family therapy views individuals' behavior and psychic life as governed by the characteristics of their social system. As previously stated, individuals influence, and are influenced by, the various settings in which they interact with the family, which is seen as the most powerful setting. Pathology, then, is located in the ongoing or recurrent patterns of interactions of the family system. In other words, the transactional patterns present in the family system are responsible for regulating the behaviors and experiences of its members and, therefore, for maintaining the disorder. Each member stresses the system and is stressed by the system in patterned ways. In this way, the identified patient's dysfunctional behavior is viewed as a symptom of family dysfunction rather than in isolation, a piece of the puzzle rather than a thorn to be removed. This basic assumption holds for all diagnoses of psychotic and neurotic symptoms; therefore, all psychiatric diagnoses would be amenable to treatment with family therapy. Minuchin and his colleagues successfully treated families with such diverse disorders as schizophrenia; conduct disorders; phobias; depression; and disorders that have both physical and psychological symptoms, such as anorexia nervosa, diabetes, and asthma (Minuchin, Rosman, & Baker, 1978). In the language of family therapy, these families would be considered, for example, schizophrenic families or anoretic families. In naming a family as schizophrenic, rather than as a family with a schizophrenic member, the point is brought home that the site of the pathology is considered to be in the family, rather than in the individual.

Theoretical Foundations
Assumptions About Human Nature

Just as context affects an individual's development, the conceptual development of a particular therapeutic technique is influenced by the thinking of the times. Minuchin's formulation of structural family therapy contains elements of Talcot Parsons's structural functionalist theory (Parsons & Bales, 1955), Harry Stack Sullivan's interpersonal theory (1953), Ludwig von Bertalanffy's general systems theory (1975), and the notion of embeddedness found in the ecological perspective of Urie Bronfenbrenner (1979).

Most family therapists fail to acknowledge the influence of various theoretical frameworks on their work, and Minuchin is no exception. As Leupnitz stated, this failure to trace the origin of theory as it relates to practice is "simply part of the pattern of [family therapists'] concentrating on clinical and methodological issues and minimizing issues of theory and intellectual roots" (1988, p. 65). The language and conceptual organization of structural family therapy are laden with systems thinking, references to function, the impact of interpersonal relations, and the embeddedness of the individual in various dynamic contexts.

Minuchin has been careful to set forth "axioms" about the functioning of the family system and the conduct of therapy, but he has been less explicit about his notions of how humans develop. Nonetheless, certain assumptions about human development are implicit in his thinking.

A guiding assumption of structural family therapy is that individuals influence and are influenced by the various contexts or settings in which they live. In other words, the individual's development is viewed as a result of the influence of, and the individual's influence on, the various settings that the individual encounters in daily life. These settings include the family, various settings within the community, and the larger societal or cultural setting. Relationships involving individuals and their various settings are seen as reciprocal. Both developing individuals and the settings or contexts in which they interact are seen as powerful agents of influence and change.

A second assumption involves the stability of personality. A frequent theme in studies of human development is the relative influence of personality as a stable entity versus situational influences. In other words, does the behavior of individuals generally remain stable across situations, or is their behavior significantly influenced by the properties of a specific setting? In structural family therapy, the environment or setting is seen as the more powerful force in guiding the individual's behavior. Minuchin stated: "The family therapist does not conceive of an 'essential' personality, remaining unchanged throughout the vicissitudes of different contexts and circumstances" (1974, p. 9). In addition, Minuchin stated that "context directly influences the internal processes of the mind" (1974, p. 5).

According to Minuchin, the individual's identity is hammered out of experience. Identity contains two vital elements: a sense of belonging and a sense of being separate. The sense of belonging is formed in the context of the family; the sense of being separate develops as the individual participates in various family subsystems (that is, two or more family members whose presence does not constitute the whole family) and in extrafamilial groups. In Minuchin's view, the family is the most powerful influence on the individual's psychosocial development. The "family structure is the invisible set of functional demands that organizes the ways in which family members interact" (Minuchin, 1974,

p. 51). Each individual, then, has particular roles or functions within the family system, and those roles are reinforced through repetitive transactional patterns. Thus, each individual experiences family life in a particular way. The functional family accommodates to the individual's developmental needs and ever-expanding range of activities outside of the family system. Conversely, the dysfunctional family resists developmental changes and fails to integrate the changes that occur as a result of extrafamilial interactions.

Assumptions About Conducting Structural Family Therapy

Despite the present popularity of family therapy, it is generally the individual who comes in for treatment or, in the case of a child or adolescent, who is brought in for treatment. The family therapist considers this person the "identified client" or "index client;" the first order of business is to insist that the entire family present itself for treatment. As previously stated, the identified client's presenting problem is seen as a symptom of a dysfunctional system. Treating the individual alone would be akin to prescribing aspirin for a headache that is being caused by a dietary problem. The pain may be subdued, but the problem will persist until the source of the dysfunction is uncovered and treated. It is also assumed that the therapist becomes part of the system; as a consequence, the therapist's behavior is instrumental in bringing about change by changing the experience of the system.

Transactional patterns indicate "how, when, and to whom to relate, and these patterns underpin the system" and "regulate family members' behavior" (Minuchin, 1974, p. 51). A family's transactional patterns can be seen by observing the boundaries that exist between subsystems in the family. Therefore, transactional patterns (or family organization) are fully developed and clear only when all family members are present. Boundaries are a key concept in the vernacular of family therapy, and can be thought of as the rules defining who participates in a subsystem and how they participate. The concept of boundaries is both a useful parameter in evaluating family functioning and the focus of intervention in the therapist's attempts to change dysfunctional transactional patterns.

Key Concepts

Minuchin provided a detailed account of the key concepts and conduct of structural family therapy in *Families and Family Therapy* (1974). The key concepts provide the basis for conducting therapy and are presented in the following paragraphs.

Joining.   Joining is the action taken by the therapist, that results in the therapist becoming a part of the family system. In Minuchin's words, "to join a family system, the therapist must accept the family's organization and style and blend with them" (1974, p. 123). In other words, in order to learn about family functioning, the therapist must experience it firsthand. By encouraging family members to interact with one another, the therapist is able to observe and experience the transactional patterns that govern family functioning. By joining with the family, the therapist uncovers the family's particular channels of communication and learns "which ones are open, which are partly closed, and which are entirely blocked" (Minuchin, 1974, p. 123).

Subsystems.   The family system is divided into a number of subsystems that have various purposes in the functioning of the family and make particular demands on members. Each family member is considered a subsystem and, in addition, belongs to several subsystems. According to Minuchin, "subsystems can be formed by generation, by sex, by interest, or by function" (1974, p. 52). For example, the executive subsystem is generally composed of mother and father, and is the most powerful subsystem in the family. Parents are responsible for child-rearing, maintenance of the marital dyad, and major decisions in the course of family life. The sibling subsystem has less power than the executive subsystem and provides the context in which children can learn to negotiate with authority figures, compete for affection, and cooperate with peers.

As children grow, the executive or parental subsystem must meet the developmental demands of children for autonomy. In turn, the executive subsystem must maintain clear boundaries that allow children access to parents but exclude children from taking on the role of a wife or husband. An older child may be given parental responsibilities from time to time, but it is clearly understood that these duties are assigned by parents and are limited in scope. A family is seen as dysfunctional if its transactional patterns do not allow for the healthy development of its members. A therapist, then, must be well informed about children's developmental needs and alert to the possibility that a child may be used as a buffer in parental conflict. A parent who uses a child as a confidant to complain to about marital conflict is said to have an enmeshed relationship with that child. Such complaints must be kept inside the spousal subsystem, so that the child does not bear the burden of being a pseudo-husband or -wife.

Boundaries.   Boundaries are the rules that dictate who participates in particular subsystems and how. Three types of boundaries can characterize a particular subsystem. Each type represents a particular transactional style or preference for interacting. Boundaries exist along a continuum, with extreme poles of rigid and diffuse boundaries. Dysfunction occurs when the boundaries of any particular subsystem become either enmeshed (weak or diffuse) or disengaged (rigid), as opposed to clear. The result of enmeshed or disengaged boundaries can be maladaptive functioning of that subsystem and dysfunction in the transmission of information to and from surrounding subsystems. The degree of clarity of boundaries is a useful parameter to evaluate family functioning and, therefore, can be thought of as a diagnostic tool.

Enmeshed boundaries are characterized by extreme proximity and intensity in family interactions. Family members are seen as overly involved in and overly concerned with one another's lives. This type of boundary blocks the developmental tasks of separation and individuation and results in extreme family loyalty. The individual is engulfed by the larger entity of the family, and any attempts by the individual to attain privacy or autonomy are seen as disloyal acts, rather than a healthy striving for a clear sense of self.

Disengaged boundaries are inappropriately rigid. Communication and supportive interactions among members are infrequent, and family loyalty is low. The family with disengaged boundaries can be thought of as a group of individuals living under the same roof, but leading quite separate lives. When a situation occurs that would generally call for a response from other family members, such as a child's failing in school, the disengaged family is slow to respond, if they respond at all. The general attitude is that individuals must fend for themselves and handle their own business. A family member may be in extreme distress—for instance, clinically depressed—but other family members react with little concern. The family members' sense of belonging in a family characterized by disengaged boundaries is jeopardized, while their sense of self is distorted, in part because they are poorly prepared for supporting and being supported by others.

Clear boundaries allow for proper family functioning. The individual is able to maintain a clear sense of self while establishing a sense of family unity that is not overwhelming (as it is when boundaries are enmeshed). Members of particular subsystems are able to carry out particular functions without interference from members outside that subsystem. For example, husband and wife resolve marital problems without involving the children in their disputes. Adolescent children make age-appropriate decisions (for example, accepting a date or deciding to spend the night with a friend) without undue interference from parents. While members have a certain degree of independence, if a situation arose that called for other family members' concern and involvement—such as an illness or the discovery of an adolescent's poor school performance—members would respond with appropriate support and involvement.

Diagnosis.   Diagnosis is generally thought of as the labeling of an individual according to information received from performing a psychiatric assessment of the person's past and present functioning. Diagnosis, in turn, dictates treatment, and treatment would take place at the level of the individual. Family problems are not adequately addressed in the current diagnostic classification system used by mental health professionals. Thus, according to Minuchin, "diagnosis is the working hypothesis that the therapist evolves from his experiences and observations upon joining the family" (1974, p. 129). The diagnostic label that results from an assessment using structural family therapy is applied to the whole family. In addition, the diagnosis is conceived of as a working hypothesis, subject to change as more information is obtained from involvement with the family.

The family, with its orientation to a traditional medical model, may expect the therapist to view the family member whose behavior is unmanageable or troubling as the patient and other family members as present to bear testimony to the identified patient's behavior. The patient, according to the family, is the site of pathology. In addition, the family may expect the therapist to change the troubled family member and return family functioning to the way it was before the symptoms of the troubled family member became problematic.

The therapist holds a different view of the site of pathology. The therapist "regards the identified patient merely as the family member who is expressing, in the most visible way, a problem affecting the entire family" (Minuchin, 1974, p. 129). As such, the entire family is seen as creating and maintaining dysfunctional transactional patterns and, thus, is the focus of therapeutic intervention.

The therapist enters the family system as it exists in the present and assesses certain properties of the system in order to diagnose family functioning and arrive at a strategy for intervention. Diagnosis involves several steps:

1. Identifying the family's preferred transactional patterns.
2. Evaluating the family's potential for change, which involves assessing the family's flexibility or potential for responding in ways that vary from their preferred transactional patterns.
3. Evaluating the family's responses to individual member's behaviors and communications. At this particular step, the therapist assesses the boundaries which exist in various family subsystems.
4. Identifying the various settings external to the family that serve as resources or stressors.
5. Evaluating the family's performance of developmental tasks that are appropriate to the developmental stage of the family.
6. Exploring ways the identified patient's symptoms serve to maintain family functioning as it exists in the present.

Minuchin pointed out that diagnosis is interactional, in the sense that it is accomplished by the therapist's interacting with the family; assessments are made on the basis of transactional patterns as observed and encouraged by the therapist. For example, the therapist might say to the family, "Who would like to talk about why we are here?" This question is aimed at discovering who is in charge. If the father responds and, as he speaks, checks with his eldest daughter to verify his words while the mother remains silent, the evidence suggests that an enmeshed subsystem exists between the father and eldest daughter, and that the mother has little power in the family. If this pattern persists, the therapist might turn to the mother and ask, "When did you give up your position as mother in this family?" Using this probe, the therapist is able to evaluate the family's response to challenging their preferred transactional patterns.

Restructuring.   Minuchin defined restructuring as "the therapeutic interventions that confront and challenge a family in the attempt to force a therapeutic change" (1974, p. 138). Restructuring requires that a family give up old transactional patterns and adopt new, and therefore uncomfortable, patterns. For restructuring to be successful, the family must accept the therapist's leadership. The therapeutic unit is composed of the therapist and the family, and must be solidly formed for restructuring to be successful. Thus, joining the family system is a necessary first step toward restructuring. Minuchin stated that numerous categories of restructuring operations exist; the reader is referred to his *Families and Family Therapy* for a more complete treatment of this key concept.

One example of restructuring is directing certain family members to interact with one another in a way that is not a preferred transactional pattern, but is desired in order to achieve a therapeutic goal. For example, noting that father and eldest daughter form an enmeshed subsystem (having formed an alliance that involves tasks usually performed by the parental subsystem), and father and mother form a disengaged subsystem (having abandoned their partnership in tasks usually performed by the parental subsystem), the therapist might direct the mother and father to discuss issues of child-rearing involving their youngest daughter without interference from the eldest daughter. This directive reinforces the notion that the parental subsystem is responsible for particular tasks and pulls the mother back into a position of power in the family. If the eldest daughter attempted to interrupt her parents' conversation, the therapist would not allow the interruption and might direct her to sit beside the therapist and keep silent. The therapist might reframe her overinvolvement with her father by telling her she does not have to save her mother, that she can trust her mother to be a responsible parent, and that she needs to be a teenager and not a wife. After the therapist has restructured transactional patterns a number of times to require mother and father to form a solid parental subsystem, the family members will accept this new alliance as a component of the therapeutic system.

In a broad sense, restructuring is directed at defining both individual boundaries and subsystem boundaries. Returning to the notion presented earlier, the family should function in such a way that each family member maintains both a clear sense of self and a sense of belonging within the family system. Each family member should be involved in subsystems that have clear boundaries, are appropriate to the individual's developmental status, and promote healthy development.

Implementing Structural Family Therapy

The following case, illustrating the application of structural family therapy, is taken from sessions conducted by one of the authors. While typifying the general form of structural family therapy, this case illustration by no means exhausts the range of procedures available to the family therapist. It does, however, provide a general view of some common maneuvers of a structural family therapist. The dialogue among therapist and family members will be presented, with an explanation of the therapist's and family members' actions in parentheses.

The family system includes Mr. and Mrs. Butler, both in their mid 40s, and their children, Julia and Dan. Mr. Butler is an engineer, and Mrs. Butler is a housewife. They have been married 19 years. Julia, who is 16, is the identified patient. Her brother, Dan, is 17 years old. If the medical model were applied, Julia would be given the diagnosis of an adjustment disorder or oppositional defiant disorder and receive individual psychotherapy. She is rebellious, uncommunicative, disobedient, and has recently received criminal charges of DUI (driving under the influence) and underage drinking. She has been ordered by a court to receive counseling. Her therapist has asked that the family accompany Julia to therapy. After a brief discussion about the difficulty the Butlers had in finding a parking space, the first session commences.

Therapist: Although I have received material from Julia's intake, I'd really like to hear from the family about what's going on. Who would like to start? (*The therapist indicates that she is starting fresh with the family rather than relying on previous information. She directs her question to the whole family, which will allow her to hypothesize about who holds the power in the family, depending on who responds. In addition, she is challenging the notion that Julia is the only problem. The therapist has taken note of the seating arrangement. Mr. and Mrs. Butler sit to the left, with Dan sitting between them. Julia takes* *the chair to the right of the therapist and pulls it back so that she is somewhat removed from the group.)*

Mrs. Butler: *(Mrs. Butler speaks after a rather long silence in which Julia and Mr. Butler look at the floor, while Mrs. Butler and Dan exchange glances.)* We're here because of Julia. She's unmanageable and we simply don't know what to do. We don't understand her at all. I don't know why the whole family is here, but you said it would help if we'd all come.

Therapist: I certainly appreciate your concern and your willingness to come. What do you see going on in the family, Mr. Butler? *(Mrs. Butler responded with an extremely concerned attitude; her manner was rather stiff with an undercurrent of anger. The therapist responded in turn with a polite comment and acknowledged her concern. The term for this action is* mimesis, *which means accommodating to the family's affective style in order to join. The therapist directs her question to Mr. Butler, to explore his position in the family and his style of communicating.)*

Mr. Butler: I guess the same thing. Julia is a good girl. She's unhappy and I don't know why. We want to do what we can to help her.

Therapist: You sense her unhappiness. How about you, Dan? How does this family seem to you? *(Again, the therapist acknowledges Mr. Butler's apparent sensitivity to his daughter, viewing her as unhappy rather than as the belligerent daughter Mrs. Butler sees. The therapist now includes Dan in the conversation to join and explore his position in the family.)*

Dan: I don't know. Everything seems pretty normal except for Julia.

Therapist: Normal in what way? *(The therapist is probing the structure of the family. Dan is quiet and obviously uncomfortable. The therapist leans toward him to indicate she is really interested in what he has to say.)*

Dan: I really don't know. *(Laughs nervously.)*

Therapist: This feels kind of weird, sitting in this room talking about your family. *(Dan smiles and nods. The therapist makes contact with Dan in an age-appropriate way. She does not pursue questioning him so as to continue to explore the family's preferred transactional style. Thus far, everyone is uncomfortable, and it is becoming clear that their discomfort stems from having to address an issue directly rather than simply being in the therapy room.)* Julia, what do you see happening in your family? *(Once again, the therapist intentionally avoids focusing on Julia as the identified patient, instead holding to her position that the family is in therapy.)*

Julia: I'll tell you what's going on. I'm the black sheep. Dan is the good boy. I'm always the problem, and I just don't belong in this family.

Therapist: So, you say you're always the problem. Do *you* think you're the problem? *(The therapist's question encourages Julia's doubt about herself as the problem, which is a restructuring maneuver.)*

Julia: I know I've gotten into trouble, so I guess I am the problem.

Therapist: Don't be so sure. (*The therapist is challenging Julia's and the family's assumption that Julia is the problem.*)

Mrs. Butler: Well, she is the one who was caught drinking underage. (*At this point, the therapist notices that Mr. Butler and Julia exchange glances and Mr. Butler rolls his eyes as if disgusted with Mrs. Butler's comment.*)

Therapist: I'm getting the sense that there could be some disagreement between you (*indicating Mr. and Mrs. Butler*) about the motives for Julia's behavior. Am I correct? (*The therapist is exploring the cohesiveness of the parental subsystem and setting the stage for an investigation of the boundaries of this subsystem.*)

Mrs. Butler: I don't think we do agree about Julia. I think there are a number of things we don't agree about.

Therapist: Is that how you see it, Mr. Butler?

Mr. Butler: Yes, we don't agree about Julia, but I don't know about not agreeing on a lot of things.

Therapist: Why don't you ask your wife for an example of some of the other things she thinks you don't see eye to eye on? Go ahead and do that now. (*The therapist is directing the action so that she can witness the Butlers' transactional style in the context of the marital dyad.*)

Julia: She's always complaining, and Dad gets tired of it.

Therapist: Julia, come sit next to me. Your mother and father are talking to each other now about their relationship. You don't need to speak for anyone else. Your father can voice his own opinions and take care of himself. Go ahead, Mr. Butler. (*The therapist has discouraged Julia's talking for her father, which reinforces the rule that family members should talk for themselves without an intermediary. In addition, she has implied that Julia is defending her father against her mother and that she need not take on this task, which is inappropriate. Seating Julia next to her, she increases the stress in the spouse subsystem by removing their buffer and creating clear boundaries.*)

Mr. Butler: I should ask her what she thinks we disagree on? (*The therapist nods.*) What else do we disagree on besides Julia?

Mrs. Butler: Well, for one thing, how much time you should spend on the golf course and how much time we should spend together.

Mr. Butler: (*Looks at the therapist.*) I don't spend that much time on the golf course, and we're together as much as any married couple.

Therapist: Talk to your wife, please. (*The therapist continues to reinforce the boundaries of the subsystem and encourage direct communication.*)

Mr. Butler: We've been over this before. I work all week, and I like to play golf. (*He looks at the floor and shrugs.*)

Mrs. Butler: You think that's an answer? I don't know why we're married! I can't seem to make you understand how I feel! (*She breaks down in tears.*

A long silence ensues with every family member looking at the floor except Julia who glares at her mother.)

Therapist: What do you do when your wife gets upset, Mr. Butler?

Mr. Butler: I don't know what to do.

Therapist: Why don't you try to comfort her—right now. *(The therapist is challenging the preferred transactional pattern of the spouse or marital subsystem by directing Mr. Butler to engage with his wife rather than withdraw from her.)*

The therapist tentatively hypothesized that the spouse subsystem was defined by disengaged boundaries, father and daughter were enmeshed and involved in a coalition against the mother, and the son was disengaged from the family. As the sessions progressed, the Butlers' disengagement from each other became the focus of therapy and, for a short period of time, the children were excluded from sessions. Julia's symptoms had served to deflect the parents' attention away from their marital problems, and allowed them to focus on her rebellious behavior. The goal of therapy became to strengthen the spouse subsystem so that Mr. and Mrs. Butler could resolve their marital conflicts and function as mature partners and effective parents. As a result, Julia would be relieved of the responsibility of creating a problem to distract her parents, and both she and Dan could become engaged in family life in a functional, age-appropriate manner. Dan was supported in sharing more of himself and his extrafamilial experiences with the family. As Julia experienced a cohesive parental subsystem and an appropriate degree of autonomy in her experience of family life, she became less rebellious and, therefore, more cooperative in accepting the rules that her parents imposed regarding reasonable curfews and activities with friends. Mr. Butler continued to enjoy his game of golf along with evenings spent alone with his wife or with other couples. Mr. Butler, from a therapeutic standpoint, became a more active family member, which resulted in greater intimacy in the spouse subsystem and provided the children with a more functional model of a satisfying marital dyad.

Means and Conditions for Implementing Structural Family Therapy

The Therapist's Qualifications

The initial clinical application of structural family therapy was with families living in poverty. These families were seen as disorganized and even chaotic; imposing structure therefore was the immediate goal of therapy. The therapist is not concerned about family members' ability to see the relationship between their present functioning and each spouse's respective family of origin. The therapist joins a family to modify its functioning rather than to educate, psychoanalyze, or socialize it. Reorganization of family structure, rather than insight, is the goal of therapy.

The use of structural family therapy does not require the expertise of a trained analyst, nor is clinical experience a prerequisite. In fact, seasoned clinicians who choose to use this method must do a great deal of unlearning of traditional methods. The style of interactions, rather than the content of interactions, is stressed, and the history of a disorder is viewed as less important than the family's present functioning. Many structural family therapists are, in fact, paraprofessionals. Salvador Minuchin has a long-standing commitment to social issues and began a program at the Philadelphia Child Guidance Clinic to train African-American men and women from the community as family therapists. During the 1970s, the Philadelphia Child Guidance Clinic initiated a program that sent teachers to interested community mental health centers to train paraprofessionals in the methodology and practice of structural family therapy. Those paraprofessionals, in turn, trained fellow caseworkers as family therapists.

Conditions for Conducting Structural Family Therapy

Structural family therapy requires no special equipment and may be practiced in the practitioner's office, the family's home, or any other space that offers privacy.

Limitations of Structural Family Therapy
Contraindications

Any limitations on the use of structural family therapy exist as opinion and are therefore not unequivocal. Many respected practitioners, such as Aponte and Van Deusen (1981), have observed that the clinical applicability of structural family therapy is limitless. Structural family therapy is perhaps best known for its effectiveness with families whose identified patients are children, adolescents, and young adults still living at home. In addition, Minuchin and his colleagues have reported success with families who have a member suffering from an illness with a psychosomatic component. And although other therapies, based on a psychodynamic model, might prove ineffective with a family containing a mentally retarded family member, structural family therapy, with its emphasis on structure and function, would be appropriate for such a family.

Hazards

The greatest hazard associated with structural family therapy is the focus of a caveat for the therapist to observe. According to Minuchin, the therapist must avoid being "sucked into the family system" (1974, p. 139). Structural family therapists have two overarching tasks. They must join the family system and, by joining, accommodate to the family. In addition, therapists must maintain a position of leadership, so that they can challenge the system and so that the family accommodates them at critical times to facilitate positive movement. If therapists join the family in such a way that they perpetuate the dysfunctional organization of the family, their efforts will, in fact, reinforce negative functioning.

As a student of structural family therapy, one of the authors was headed toward being sucked into the family system during a particular interaction. Working with the spouse subsystem (a disengaged husband and wife), a critical moment came when Mrs. X began to cry. As Mr. X looked at the floor and shifted nervously in his chair, the therapist reached over and put her arm around Mrs. X. At that moment the telephone rang in the therapy room. (All sessions were conducted with live supervision through a two-way mirror; a telephone connected supervisor and therapist for just such moments.) The supervising therapist said, "What are you doing? Mr. X should be soothing his wife, not you. Now direct him to do that!" The therapist returned to her seat and said, "Mr. X, your wife is quite upset. She needs you to comfort her." Mr. X then moved closer to his wife and awkwardly, but successfully, held her. Mrs. X laid her head on his shoulder and cried. Had the therapist been the one to provide comfort to the family member in pain, the dysfunctional distance that characterized the spouse subsystem would have been reinforced.

The Effectiveness of Structural Family Therapy

A number of research articles and books have explored the effectiveness of structural family therapy. The majority of work thus far has focused on the application of structural family therapy techniques to families with a wide array of problems. There has been consistent evidence of improvement in the treatment of families with such varying presenting problems as drug and alcohol addiction, psychosomatic illnesses, and disorders of childhood and adolescence.

The majority of research reports are clinical case studies, which outline the specific procedures used and the results obtained. Studies that compare the effectiveness of structural family therapy to other therapies have been less numerous. Although the majority of such comparative research reports contain methodological shortcomings—such as failure to use established, reliable, and valid measures—their usefulness for demonstrating specific techniques and the versatility of this method is admirable. The interested reader can refer to journals such as *Family Process, Journal of Marital and Family Therapy*, and *Journal of Family Therapy* for studies of the effectiveness of structural family therapy and other family therapy techniques.

Minuchin and his associates provided a readable and vivid account of the remarkable effectiveness of structural family therapy in alleviating both the symptomatic and psychological aspects of the psychosomatic illnesses of asthma and diabetes (Minuchin, Rosman, & Baker, 1978). In addition, Minuchin's classic book, *Families and Family Therapy* (1974), contains impressive reports regarding the rise in levels of free fatty acid (a reliable measure of emotional arousal) in two diabetic siblings as they witnessed stressful family interactions. The sibling identified as the patient in the family had elevated free fatty acid levels for $1\frac{1}{2}$ hours after the family interview. In Minuchin's words, "the interdependence between the individual and his family is poignantly demonstrated in the experimental situation, in which behavioral events among family members can be measured in the bloodstream of other family members" (1974, p. 9). Aponte and Van Deusen (1981) summarized the findings of 20 studies involving 201 families and concluded that approximately 73% of families were effectively helped by practitioners using structural family therapy.

References

Aponte, H., & Van Deusen, J. (1981). Structural family therapy. In A. S. Gurman & D. P. Kniskern (Eds.), *Handbook of family therapy* (pp. 310–360). New York: Brunner/Mazel.

Bell, J. E. (1961). *Family group therapy.* Public Health Monograph No. 64. Washington, D.C.: Government Printing Office.

Bronfenbrenner, U. (1979). *The ecology of human development.* Cambridge, MA: Harvard University Press.

Leupnitz, D. (1988). *The family interpreted: Feminist theory in clinical practice.* New York: Basic Books.

Minuchin, S. (1974). *Families and family therapy.* Cambridge, MA: Harvard University Press.

Minuchin, S., Montalvo, B., Guerney, B., Rosman, B., & Schumer, F. (1967). *Families of the slums*. New York: Basic Books.

Minuchin, S., Rosman, B., & Baker, L. (1978). *Psychosomatic families: Anorexia nervosa in context*. Cambridge, MA: Harvard University Press.

Parsons, T., & Bales, R. (1955). *Family socialization and interaction process*. Glencoe, IL: Free Press.

Sullivan, H. S. (1953). *The interpersonal theory of psychiatry*. New York: Norton.

von Bertalanffy, L. (1975). *Perspectives on general systems theory*. New York: Braziller.

CHAPTER 14

．．

Strategic
Family Therapy

．．

■

The general aim of strategic family therapy is to alleviate the presenting concern of a family system, generally construed by the family as a problematic behavior displayed by a family member. This particular approach to family therapy is noteworthy because the course of therapy is brief and the therapist accepts responsibility for change in the family system by providing directives. According to the strategic family therapist, change occurs as a result of directives issued by the therapist, rather than through the family's acquiring understanding or insight.

History of Strategic Family Therapy

Prior to the 1950s, the dominant view of the etiology and treatment of emotional disturbance was that pathology developed within the individual as a result of difficult early life experiences; hence, the individual was encouraged to work through and cathect those painful experiences. In the late 1940s and early 1950s, research conducted into the etiology of schizophrenia suggested that particular styles of family communication were associated with families with schizophrenic members. The most noteworthy of findings came from the Palo Alto group, which included Gregory Bateson, Jay Haley, Don Jackson, John Weakland, and Virginia Satir. The group found that a particular style of communicating, the double bind, seemed to induce schizophrenic behavior. Individuals caught in a double bind receive conflicting messages about what is expected of them and, as a result, become anxious, confused, and ultimately unable to respond.

In the early 1960s, Satir and Haley, having left the Palo Alto group, developed their respective ideas about the contribution of family communications to individual pathology. At the same time, Murray Bowen set forth his notions of enmeshment, triangularization, and intergenerational transmission of traits and patterns as contributing to the development of schizophrenia. Satir, Haley, and Bowen agreed that treatment should be directed toward the family rather than the individual. All saw the identified patient's problematic behavior as a symptom of family dysfunction. Each family member was seen as contributing to, and maintaining, the presenting problem.

During the 1970s, Salvador Minuchin's structural family therapy was the most widely used method of treating families. In the 1980s, strategic family therapy emerged as a preferred method of intervention among family therapists, with Jay Haley (1976) and Cloe Madanes (1981) as its leading advocates.

While Haley and Madanes's conceptualization of dysfunctional families was clearly influenced by Haley's work with the Palo Alto group, another significant influence on their thinking was the work of Milton Erickson. Erickson, a psychiatrist who worked primarily with individuals, used hypnotic directives to induce change in his clients. Erickson maintained that the therapist must carry full responsibility for choosing the specific therapeutic strategy to be used with a particular client and, ultimately, for the client's success or failure in therapy. Erickson's methods were brief, involved a specific course of action for each problem, and were remarkably successful.

Haley stated that "a therapy can be called strategic if the clinician initiates what happens during therapy and designs a particular approach for each problem" (1973, p. 17). Strategic family therapists advocate treatment of the entire family, and although they attend to and use communication patterns existing in the family system, the focus of therapy is to remove the presenting concern (the symptomatic behavior) of the family.

Range of Applicability

As with other forms of family therapy, the presenting problem of a family or family member is conceived of as a symptom of an underlying systemic or family problem. In strategic family therapy, the symptom is thought of as a pathological attempt on the part of a family member to control familial relationships. Moreover, a symptom is only a part of the picture. A symptom is part of a "sequence of acts between several people" (Haley, 1976, p. 2), because in a family system each member influences and is influenced by the behavior of every other member. In this way, every family member has a part to play in the symptomatology of a problem.

The following is an example of a child's behavior that is a symptom of a dysfunctional family system. In a family composed of mother, father, and a 12-year-old son, the parents are experiencing marital difficulties, which, rather than being addressed and resolved, are worsening. The son senses the tension in the marital dyad and is aware that a family rule is that no one is to speak about the trouble that the mother and father are having. As the parents' tension persists, the son's tension becomes acute and he develops a symptom (a school phobia) in order to release the tension he is experiencing. The parents, who have become disengaged as a result of their marital difficulties, pull together in order to help their child through his difficulties. As the child's tension is relieved through the parents' united efforts, he loses his fear of going to school and, as he resumes a normal pattern of attending school, the parents must once again face their own marital difficulties. As they do so, they return to their disengaged state; as their tension increases, the child's tension increases and his school phobia reappears. Thus, the cycle is repeated. The symptom of school phobia serves the purpose of making the marital dyad a cohesive unit.

The symptom then is not the cause of dysfunction, but the manifestation of dysfunction. With this assumption in mind, the range of applicability of strategic family therapy is vast, and the generally used psychiatric diagnoses become relatively meaningless. Strategic family therapists view diagnostic labels as an impediment to treatment. Their preference is to relabel a psychiatrically defined problem (school phobia) in more common terms (unwillingness to leave the house), for two reasons. First, by stating the problem in behavioral and outwardly identifiable terms, the problem becomes more precise. Second, by rejecting psychiatric labels, the problem is made less clinical, less imposing, and more amenable to change.

Whether the symptom is anxiety, depression, anorexia nervosa, delinquency, or any other diagnostic classification, the therapist's job is to determine what function the symptom serves in the family system, and to assist the family to function so that the symptom becomes unnecessary.

Theoretical Foundations
Assumptions About Human Nature

According to Madanes (1981), the theoretical foundations of strategic family therapy can be traced to what she identifies as the "communication approach" (p. 15) of the Palo Alto group headed by Gregory Bateson and the cybernetic science of the 1950s. The focus of this approach is on the communication aspects of systems, with an emphasis on the homeostatic nature of such systems. Madanes stated that "the approach suggested that the inter-change of messages between people defines relationships, and these relation-ships are stabilized by homeostatic processes in the form of actions of family members within the family" (1981, p. 15). According to the communications approach, problem behavior is an attempt on the part of a family member to cope under adverse circumstances within the family; in this way, the problem behavior can be viewed as an adaptive and therefore appropriate response to a difficult situation. In addition, the problem behavior of a particular family member is seen as only one component in a sequence of behavioral patterns initiated and maintained by the family system. This view, of course, relieves the family member with the presenting problem of receiving the label of patient. Instead, the family system is viewed as the patient.

Based on the communications approach, the following assumptions are made regarding family functioning:

1. The problem is manifest in the family system, and therefore the sys-tem must be present in order to identify and alleviate the problem.
2. The problem can be seen in the way family members communicate and behave.
3. Because the family is a homeostatic system, family members will per-sist in functioning in a particular fashion. In addition, as a homeo-static system, the family possesses feedback processes, which will ena-ble the system to be self-correcting.
4. In order to change a dysfunctional family system to a functional fam-ily system, one must change the way family members communicate—a task accomplished by introducing new behaviors or ways of com-municating into the system.

Assumptions About Conducting Strategic Family Therapy

A general assumption of family therapies based on a psychodynamic, or experiential, model is that awareness of repressed material is a necessary pre-cursor to change. This assumption leads the therapist to use interpretation of past experience extensively in practice. Behavioral family therapies, on the other hand, use learning theory and assume that learning new ways of behaving, rather than insight, will lead to change. Strategic family therapy resembles the behavioral approach to therapy in a number of ways. First, the focus of therapy is on treating the presenting problem, rather than eliciting awareness or insight about the origin of the presenting problem. Second, both therapies assume responsibility for providing directives for behavior, both inside and outside the treatment room. Third, early childhood experiences are of no interest to behavioral therapists or strategic family therapists. Both deal exclusively with present behaviors, and both design interventions for the pre-senting problem rather than using a particular predetermined method.

Strategic family therapy departs from the behavioral approach in a number of important ways. Generally, behavioral family therapies enlist another family member to assist the identified patient in reinforcing a new behavior or extinguishing the problem behavior. The level of intervention, then, is most often with two family members, rather than the family system. Practitioners of strategic family therapy include the family system in treatment and, in many cases, include "a social network wider than the family, particularly professionals who have power over the person with the pre-senting problem" (Madanes, 1981, p. 20). In the case of a child with a school phobia, the strategic family therapist might include teachers in the treatment of the presenting problem.

Next, the strategic family therapist is concerned with hierarchies. As an organization, the family system necessarily involves members who are not of equal status. In other words, the balance of power within the family is unequal. According to Madanes, "parents are expected to be in charge of their children, and cross-generational coalitions, such as one parent's siding with a child against another parent, are blocked" (1981, p. 22). Although the strategic family therapist does not assume there is one, and only one, healthy hierarchical organization, it is assumed that a functional hierarchical structure exists for a particular family.

A functional hierarchy, according to Haley (1976), is formed along the lines of power, as indicated by such things as generation membership, the skills one possesses, the resources one brings to the family, and so on. The family constructs rules about who is in charge; most often the parents are in charge of the children. When there is confusion about who is in charge, the hierarchy is dysfunctional, and pathology is the result. Pathology is most often found when a coalition exists between two family members who do not belong to the same hierarchical level—for example, a parent and a child. A dysfunctional hierarchy can be seen in the following example. A father behaves in a disengaged fashion toward the mother by refusing to address what the mother perceives as marital difficulties. The mother complains to the father with no result. After a period of time, the mother expresses symptoms of depression and her adolescent daughter takes over the mother's role as housewife by cooking the meals, doing the laundry, and so on; in addition, the daughter has regular sessions with her mother during which she listens to her mother's complaints. The daughter develops a great deal of anger toward her father and teams up with her mother to complain about him in his presence. The mother and daughter have formed a coalition against the father, and the father and mother are not defining a clear, functional hierarchy within the family. In addition, the daughter is being denied a healthy relationship with both of her parents.

This example contains what Haley terms a sequence. According to Haley, "one of the ways we can map out a hierarchy is by observing the sequences that occur in an organization" (1976, p. 104). Using a communications approach, any one family member's behavior is never viewed in isolation. Instead, any member's behavior is both the result of, and the catalyst for, other members' behaviors. All members participate in particular ways to keep a sequence of behavior in motion. In the example just given, the daughter's coalition with the mother against the father was the result of the father's disengaged style and the mother's depression. At the same time, the daughter's behavior served to further alienate the father and assist the mother in remaining depressed. The sequence of the father's withdrawal, the mother's depression, and the daughter's behaviors to save the mother and punish the father continue in a circular fashion.

The strategic family therapist's job is to discern the hierarchical organization within the family, uncover the sequence of behaviors that maintain the symptom, and formulate a prescription for the family to behave so as to alleviate the symptom. In order for a symptom to disappear, the family must function in a nonpathological manner. For example, for the mother in the example just given to find relief from her depression, she and her husband must address the issues of marital conflict; thus, the family will be reorganized so that the daughter is no longer needed in the marital subsystem and may return to a different level in the family hierarchy.

Strategic family therapists are problem-focused and less interested than any other family therapists in using insight as a mechanism for change. Haley stated that the therapist "should not try to persuade the family that the *real* problem lies in the family and not in the person" and that "the goal is not to teach the family about their malfunctioning system, but to change the family sequences so that the presenting problems are resolved" (1976, pp. 129–130).

Removing the symptom involves giving directives to the family. Haley made a clear distinction between giving advice and giving directives. Advice involves telling people how they ought to behave, and Haley insisted that people generally know how they ought to behave. Telling a family to listen to one another, or to be fair about assigning housework, is futile, since people generally know that listening and fairness are desirable ways to behave. Families are not behaving in desirable ways because they are trapped in dysfunctional sequences of behaviors, and not because they lack the knowledge of how people ought to behave in their situation. They will ultimately sabotage their own attempts to behave in desirable ways because, according to Haley, they are unable to behave in a rational manner.

Giving a directive involves telling, rather than asking, the family to perform a particular task. In other words, directives involve action on the part of the family, rather than discussion. A directive is essentially an assignment or task to be performed. Directives are given for behavior both during a session and outside of a session.

In an enmeshed family consisting of a mother, a father, and an adult son living at home, the therapist might direct the son to make his own meal on a Friday evening and the parents to go out by themselves for a meal on that evening. Directives are precise and should involve all family members; the therapist should go over the task with the family to ensure that it is clearly understood.

Directives are often designed to break up coalitions within the family hierarchy by changing the way family members communicate. For example, in the example of the detached father, depressed mother, and overinvolved daughter, a directive might be given to the parents to set aside an evening just for themselves when they would plan a dinner party for themselves and some friends. The daughter would be directed to stay out of the planning. In addition, a directive might be given that the father and daughter go out to lunch on a Wednesday afternoon, while the mother sees one of her friends. This directive would assist the father and daughter in restoring their relationship, and the mother in acting in a less depressed way. An overarching goal of all directives is to achieve a functional hierarchy.

Key Concepts

As we have seen, strategic family therapy is a problem-oriented approach that uses directives to solve problems. Directives, then, are the main therapeutic technique. Directives may be straightforward or paradoxical. A paradoxical directive is used when a straightforward directive has not been effective. A paradoxical directive is indicated when it is evident that a family is resisting the help being offered to them. In essence, this therapeutic maneuver makes use of the family's resistance.

A commonly used paradoxical directive is prescribing the symptom. The therapist might direct a depressed husband, who would be relabeled unhappy or lazy in strategic terms, to gather the family around him between 7 and 8 p.m. every evening to tell them about his troubles. The success of the intervention depends on the family's responding in one of two ways. First, the family might defy the therapist's directive because of their resistance to help and, as a result of their defiance, abandon the symptom. Second, they might cooperate and, as they do so, the symptom will diminish when controlled. In addition, a sense of the absurd comes into play as the symptom is elicited in contrived situations.

Another type of directive is a metaphorical directive. A metaphorical directive involves directing behavior in one domain that will affect the behavior in another domain. Madanes (1981) provided the example of a young child's fear of abandonment being treated metaphorically by directing the family to adopt a puppy. Although the child's fear was not treated directly, Madanes reported that it was alleviated as the child experienced the family's devotion to the care of the puppy.

Implementing Strategic Family Therapy

Strategic family therapy is generally considered a brief therapy. Strategic therapists often pride themselves on therapy being accomplished in as few sessions as possible. Most accounts of cases using strategic family therapy involve a description of the presenting problem, and the tactic or strategy used to alleviate the problem. A more explicit account of the steps involved in this type of family therapy can be found in Haley's (1976) *Problem-Solving Therapy*, in which he described the four stages of the first interview. The four stages are as follows:

1. *The social stage*: The social stage involves essentially the same step as the task of joining in structural family therapy. Although the therapist intends to make the family comfortable during this stage of the first session, it is also a time when the therapist observes the communication style of the family. The therapist's observations and the conclusions about family functioning that are drawn during this stage should be considered tentative hypotheses, awaiting further confirmation as the session continues. For example, the therapist might observe that a son constantly watches his father as he replies to the therapist's questions. A tentative hypothesis about family functioning from this observation would be that the son and the father have formed some sort of coalition within the family.

2. *The problem stage*: During this stage, the therapist asks the family to state the presenting problem. Haley extensively discussed which family members might be asked to contribute to this statement of the problem, and why. For example, Haley suggested that a father who is a reluctant participant in therapy might be asked to contribute his opinion first in an attempt to involve him in therapy. As with most family therapies, the individual with the presenting problem is generally asked to contribute last—or at least not first—so as to avoid placing blame on that individual. The focus of this stage is to obtain a clear statement of the presenting problem.

3. *The interaction stage*: During the problem stage, everyone in the family is asked to discuss the problem. During the interaction stage, the goal is to have family members interact with one another. The therapist must thwart any attempts on the part of the family to engage the therapist in their conver-

sation at this point. Haley insisted that the family cannot tell the therapist about their sequences of behavior patterns because they do not know what they are. The therapist can discern the sequences only by observing the communication style of the family system. Everyone must talk, and each family member, at some point, must talk to every other family member. Two forms of interaction among family members are possible at this stage. First, since disagreement will surely be present, the therapist can instruct family members to talk about their disagreements. Second, the family can be instructed to demonstrate the presenting problem for the therapist. For example, if the presenting problem is a disobedient, rebellious adolescent, the therapist can instruct the parents to make a request of the adolescent and instruct the adolescent to disobey. The therapist's hypotheses about the family's hierarchical structure, and the sequences of behavior patterns that support the hierarchy, can be tested during this stage.

4. *The goal-setting stage*: With the presenting problem having been defined in the previous stage, the family is asked at this stage to state what changes they seek in therapy. Haley insisted that goals must be perfectly clear. He stated, in fact, that "goals should be something one can count, observe, measure, or in some way know one is influencing" (pp. 40–41). The goals must also be ones that everyone in the family can agree on. For example, if the presenting problem is an agoraphobic family member, who has been relabeled "unwilling to leave the house" to fit the purposes of strategic family therapy, the agreed-upon goal might be for the agoraphobic family member to be willing to leave the house. The goal must be clear, and all members must agree on it, in order to ensure the family's cooperation in following directives the therapist issues in order to solve the problem.

Subsequent sessions will involve the strategy selected by the therapist to solve or eliminate the presenting problem. As stated earlier, the therapist is solely responsible for creating a directive that will lead to disappearance of the symptom that brought the family to therapy.

Means and Conditions for Implementing Strategic Family Therapy
The Therapist's Qualifications

Both professionals and paraprofessionals are presently trained in the methods of strategic family therapy. As with structural family therapy, students of strategic family therapy must abandon any traditional training that included a psychoanalytic or humanistic orientation. The strategic family therapist must be dedicated to the following beliefs:

1. Symptoms represent a struggle for power in relationships.
2. When a symptom is no longer useful, it will disappear.
3. Symptoms can be made to disappear through deliberately planned directives on the part of the therapist.
4. The therapist is ultimately responsible for devising the proper directives that will result in a functional, rather than dysfunctional, hierarchy within the family.
5. Insight, understanding, and interpretation are ineffectual forms of intervention with families.

Haley and Madanes have continued to teach the methods of strategic family therapy to both professionals and paraprofessionals. Those professionals and paraprofessionals become teachers who, in turn, train other mental health practitioners.

Conditions for Conducting Strategic Family Therapy

Strategic family therapy requires no special equipment and may be practiced in the practitioner's office, the family's home, or any other space that offers privacy.

Limitations of Strategic Family Therapy
Contraindications

As with other forms of family therapy, the limitations of strategic family therapy are a matter of opinion rather than hard evidence. According to practitioners of structural family therapy, since virtually all mental disorders are viewed as symptoms or destructive sequences of behavior, and all psychiatric labels are rejected, all forms of emotional disturbance or psychological dysfunction are amenable to this type of treatment. Case studies include successful treatment of such problems as anxiety neurosis, depression, anorexia nervosa, bed-wetting, delinquency, agoraphobia, and many other disorders. Nowhere in the literature of strategic family therapy is it suggested that a particular disorder would be best treated by another method. Madanes stated that "there are no contraindications in terms of patient selection and suitability" (1981, p. 27).

Hazards

Strategic family therapy begins with two crucial questions:

1. What is the presenting problem as identified by the family?
2. What circumstances exist that make the presenting problem necessary?

With the answers to these questions in mind, the therapist sets out to change the sequence of behaviors that make the problem necessary in such a way that the problem becomes unnecessary. The greatest hazard to a successful outcome is a therapist's becoming distracted from the task of solving the presenting problem. The distraction may take the form of the therapist's attempts to educate the family about the real problem.

A common thread that runs through the philosophy of family therapy in general is that the presenting problem is never the real problem. Rather, the presenting problem is a symptom of a malfunctioning family system caught in a destructive pattern of communication. All family therapists would agree that a symptom should be removed as a result of therapy. Most therapists, however, see as the overarching goal of therapy the growth and development of the whole family. Not strategic family therapists. Instead, insight is viewed as countertherapeutic. Haley stated that the therapist should not attempt to educate the family about family dynamics, nor should the therapist attempt to elicit insight from the family about the cause of the presenting problem. Straying from the goal of fixing the presenting problem by entering into discussions of a reflective nature with the family would jeopardize the goal of strategic family therapy. According to Haley, "to discuss issues insightfully leads only to a change in the client's ability to discuss things insightfully. . . . People are more cooperative and less resistant to change if one does not make interpretations or give insight" (Zeig, 1987, p. 26).

The Effectiveness of Strategic Family Therapy

Most information about the effectiveness of strategic family therapy is based on clinical studies that contain anecdotal accounts of successful resolutions of presenting problems (Conoley, 1987; Madanes, 1981). Watzlawick and his colleagues (Watzlawick, Weakland, & Fisch, 1974), at the Brief Therapy Center, asked clients (97 cases in all) to rate the success of therapy 3 months after its termination. Clients responded according to three categories: (1) complete relief, (2) considerable but not complete relief, and (3) little or no change. In addition, clients were asked whether new symptoms had appeared to replace the original presenting symptom. Reporting complete relief were 40% of respondents; 32% reported considerable relief. Little or no change was reported by 28%. None reported any symptom substitution.

Although the majority of strategic therapists consistently report remarkable success with this method, the results of the more systematic studies of strategic family therapy are generally consistent with the success rate reported for other types of family therapy. In general, the empirical research evaluating the success of strategic family therapy provides promising support for its success; but, to date, strategic family therapy remains a relatively unproven method for treating family dysfunction.

References

Conoley, J. (1987). Strategic family intervention: Three cases of school-aged children. *School Psychology Review, 16,* 469–486.

Haley, J. (1973). *Uncommon therapy.* New York: Norton.

Haley, J. (1976). *Problem-solving therapy.* New York: Harper & Row.

Madanes, C. (1981). *Strategic family therapy.* San Francisco: Jossey-Bass.

Minuchin, S. (1970). The use of an ecological framework in the treatment of a child. In E. J. Anthony & C. Kauperaik (Eds.), *The child in his family* (pp. 41–57). New York: Wiley.

Watzlawick, P., Weakland, J., & Fisch, R. (1974). *Change: Principles of problem formation and problem resolution.* New York: Norton.

Zeig, J. (1987). *The evolution of psychotherapy.* New York: Brunner/Mazel.

CHAPTER 15

Family
Sculpting

Family sculpting is a therapeutic tool or technique that can be used as an adjunct to therapy in a wide variety of therapeutic and educational contexts. In order to create a family sculpture, family members are asked to arrange themselves in such a way as to form a living sculpture, which represents their relations to one another at a particular moment in time. In the case of an individual in group therapy, other members of the group are called upon to represent the individual's family. Although family sculpting is generally presented as an adjunct to family therapies, it can be used in various therapeutic milieus and educational settings as a powerful and enlightening experience for those seeking understanding about family processes. One of the authors has used family sculpting successfully as a teaching technique in the classroom to demonstrate family dynamics.

General Purpose of Family Sculpting

Family sculpting is a metaphorical representation of family members' relations to one another at a particular point in time. The purpose of family sculpting is to demonstrate the dynamics of family functioning in order to provide family members, or the individual, with an immediate and intense affective experience of family life. The intention of the therapist using family sculpting is to offer the family or individual an avenue of expression into past and present family functioning that is nonverbal and experiential. L'Abate and his colleagues stated that family sculpting provides "a concrete way to refer to something normally too abstract for words" (L'Abate, Ganahl, & Hansen, 1986, p. 168). For example, one of the authors used family sculpting as an adjunct to group therapy in order to assist a young woman who was having difficulty verbalizing the source of her depression. Her sculpture revealed the tremendous pressure she was experiencing as the result of constant conflict between her husband and daughter (her husband's stepdaughter). She felt as though she were being torn apart by their respective demands that she take a stand for one side or the other. This feeling was demonstrated in her sculpture by two group members, representing her husband and daughter, who tugged and clawed at her from each side. When asked to place her young son in the sculpture, it became evident to her that his needs were being ignored, since the group member representing her son could only stand back and watch her as she struggled with her husband and daughter.

In addition to providing the opportunity to explore present or past conditions of family dynamics, family sculpting may also be used to explore a potential beneficial change in family dynamics. Once a family or individual has sculpted the present dysfunctional dynamics of family relations, the sculpture can be rearranged to demonstrate potentially healthy ways of functioning. For example, in the case of the depressed young woman, the family sculpture was rearranged so that she could free herself from the conflict between her husband and daughter and attend to the needs of her young son. The other family members, in turn, had to respond to her unwillingness to stay in the position of mediator of their conflict.

History of Family Sculpting

In the early 1970s, as the community mental health movement was strengthened by access to federal funds, the number of paraprofessionals in the field of human services increased. Paraprofessionals soon outnumbered professional clinicians as direct service providers in both inpatient and outpatient facilities. They became a vocal majority who shared a preference for a particular method of treating clients. That method was family therapy—in particular, the methods of structural family therapy and Virginia Satir's communications approach to family therapy. Mental health practitioners were eager to acquire therapeutic techniques that would emphasize both the profound effects of family dynamics on the present psychological condition of the individual, and the circular causality believed to be present in family functioning. Family sculpting was being used at that time by highly respected family therapists such as Peggy Papp, Bunny and Fred Duhl, and Virginia Satir, who emphasized the importance of experiential awareness as a catalyst for change. The majority of mental health practitioners immediately accepted family sculpting as a dynamic and valuable adjunct to family therapy.

Virginia Satir gave an account of her intuitive creation of family sculpting as she described working with a schizophrenic young woman and her family:

> Since I am very visually minded, I saw these people in exaggerated stances to themselves and to each other. That was the beginning of my sculpting technique. In this family I saw the son standing on a chair with the other three below worshipping him, hands outstretched. My patient was obscured from contact with the parents because she was pushed behind them. This was my initial attempt to manifest communication through body postures. (1987, pp. 67–68)

Satir understood from her experience that if she placed people in particular stances representing their communication style within the family, they could recognize the dynamics of their particular communication style and experience the feelings that accompanied the stance. Family sculpting became an often-used tool for accessing information not readily available to conscious thought and, in addition, a technique that held the family's interest in a nonthreatening way. Satir stated that sculpting is "a quick, reliable, and interesting way to get to the feelings" (1987, p. 68), which, according to Satir, are to be trusted when the affective and verbal parts of a message are congruent.

Range of Applicability

Family sculpting is an appropriate modality whenever the goal is to uncover past or present dynamics of family member relationships. As we have seen, although family sculpting was originally developed as a therapeutic tool to be used in the context of family therapy, this technique has been used successfully in group therapy with diverse psychiatric populations such as schizophrenics, alcoholics, and juvenile delinquents. In addition, family sculpting has been used as a method to enhance an individual's understanding of self in sensitivity training sessions and also as a teaching tool in counselor education programs and in the training of marriage and family therapists.

Theoretical Foundations
Assumptions About Human Nature

Family sculpting grew out of both the communications and the experiential approaches to family therapy, which have their roots in the tenets of humanistic and phenomenological psychology. The focus of family sculpting, then, is on creating conditions that will facilitate personal growth by eliciting insight regarding the individual's (or family's) perceptions of and feelings surrounding their present experience of family life.

Experiential therapists generally view theory and intellectual interpretations as blocks to change. They believe that change instead occurs as a result of a growth experience. Change results from a kind of "eureka experience," in which the individual (or family) is spontaneously flooded with insight into their present situation. Past experiences may also be illuminated in a growth experience, but experiential therapists do not dwell on past experiences or believe it is necessary to uncover past experiences to change the present.

According to Costa (1991), experiential therapists "shun theory as a hindrance" and, instead, seek to create a therapeutic experience characterized by "openness, self-awareness, spontaneity, freedom of expression, creativity, action, intuition, self-fulfillment, process, confrontation, and personal integrity" (pp. 121–122). These characteristics are also defining qualities of the therapeutic goals and conditions of humanistic psychology.

The communications approach, based on the work of Virginia Satir (1964), stresses the importance of clarifying communication between family members. The goal of clarifying communication is to achieve congruency. For Satir, congruency is present when one's internal experience of an event, and one's external behavior and words reflect the internal experience. According to Satir,

> Instead of double-level communication, there is this: I feel angry in my guts—I say I am angry and I look angry. You don't have any trouble getting the message—a nice straight message—I am angry. I have sexy feelings, my voice softens, and I tell you I feel sexy. Nice and straight. I feel helpless, I look helpless, and I say that I am helpless. A nice straight message. Nothing is crossed out. It is all there. (Satir, Stachowiak, & Taschman, 1975, p. 47)

Satir, in her usual informal and straightforward manner, stated the assumptions of her method as "looking at people from a positive point of view, connecting with them as people, and minimizing emphasis on pathology in order to work for their growth" (1987, p. 66). In addition, Satir believed that in their families of origin, people learn particular rules, both overt and covert, about how one should behave and the extent to which one may express one's true feelings.

Communication, according to Satir, is composed of a verbal component that originates in the cognitive part of oneself and an affective component that originates in the body itself. When the verbal and affective components are disparate, Satir believed that the affective component is the true message and the message that others receive. Once individuals experience and acknowledge the affective component of their communications, communicate in a congruent manner, and have their communications accepted, their personal growth will follow.

Assumptions About Conducting Family Sculpting

It is assumed that a sculpture can be created from the vantage point of only one individual. When sculpting is used in family therapy, then, only one person's view of family relations can be expressed in any one sculpture. The therapist might sculpt the family from the therapist's point of view, and ask the family to react to the sculpture. Family members, in turn, might sculpt the family from their own perspectives. When individuals in group therapy sculpt their families, each sculpture represents each individual's experience, not necessarily how other family members would have sculpted the family.

Since it is assumed that the reality of an experience lies in the individual's perception of the experience, each person's sculpture is a valid representation of that person's experience and, therefore, should not be denied. No one family member's experience takes precedence over another's. Rather than to arrive at some single, accurate sculpture of the family, the goal of family sculpting is to elicit and clarify each family member's experience in order to move forward from that clarification in a positive direction.

Key Concepts

While the process of sculpting involves a dialogue between the therapist and the sculptor, the sculpture generally does not include verbalizations on the part of the individuals who are arranged into a sculpture. Sculpting is used precisely to avoid verbalization and to cut through to the emotional experience of family living. As the sculptor places individuals in a specific metaphorical position, particular indicators represent the sculptor's perception of the family. Those indicators are body position, facial expression, and individuals' proximity to one another in the sculpture.

Body position.   The sculptor is instructed to place each individual in the position that best represents the individual's attitude and stance. For example, in Satir's sculpture of the young schizophrenic woman's family, Satir placed the brother on a chair with other family members in pleading positions below him. In order to demonstrate the brother's attitude and stance, she might have asked him (if appropriate) to turn away from the family and fold his arms across his chest to indicate his disdain for the family's pleading. The family members in the pleading positions might have been placed on their knees with their arms extended and hands in a prayer-like position, all stretching in the direction of the brother to capture his attention.

Facial expression.   The sculptor is instructed to provide the individuals being sculpted with information concerning facial expression. The brother on a chair in Satir's sculpture might be asked to avert his eyes from the family's gaze and to tighten his mouth in defiance of their pleading. He might be asked to look as if annoyed at their groveling, or instead to look pleased at their attention. The pleading family members might be asked to gaze directly at the brother with a look of fear on their faces. Perhaps the mother might be asked to look at the brother adoringly.

Proximity.   The sculptor is instructed to place family members in space with regard to distance or closeness to one another. Family therapists recognize this instruction as conveying information about the boundaries present in the family. A great distance between family members would indicate disengaged boundaries, whereas placing family members in extreme proximity would indicate enmeshed boundaries. In Satir's sculpture, the mother might be placed closest to the son (brother). In order to depict extreme enmeshment between mother and son, the mother might be directed to kiss her son's hand while clinging tightly to his legs. Satir placed the sister behind the parents to represent her inability to engage the parents in communicating with her and their disengagement from her.

Implementing Family Sculpting

The following steps are generally followed in creating a family sculpture:

1. Because family dynamics change over the course of the family life cycle, the sculptor is asked to sculpt the family during a particular time period (for example, during the client's adolescence or after the divorce of the client's parents) or in a particular situation (for example, in the conflict that

brought the family to therapy, or reflecting how a family member feels at the moment).

2. If sculpting is being conducted with people who are not family members, the sculptor is asked to choose people to represent each member of the family. Family members play themselves when family sculpting is being used in family therapy.

3. The sculptor is instructed to sculpt the family by placing each family member in space with regard to characteristic body position, facial expression, and proximity in relation to the sculptor and other family members. The instruction might be offered as follows: "Position your family members in ways that would best depict their attitudes and ways of communicating in the family as *you* perceive them to be." The author generally begins with the marital dyad and asks the sculptor to depict the husband and wife's relationship to one another. Particular questions that facilitate sculpting include these: "How close is your mother to your father? Is he looking at her? Should they be touching? How close are they? Is she looking at him? What is the expression on your mother's face? On your father's face? Who is closest to your mother of all the children? How close are they? Should they be touching?"

4. The sculptor places him- or herself in the sculpture and adopts a characteristic body position, facial expression, and proximity in relation to other family members.

5. When the sculpture is complete, the therapist (who remains outside of the sculpture) comments on the meaning of the sculpture from the *sculptor's* perspective. Family members (or participants representing family members) are asked how it feels to be in their respective places in the family. The therapist facilitates with comments such as the following: "It looks to me as if your father feels separated from the family. How do you feel in relation to your parents? What do you feel like saying to your mother?"

6. Finally, the therapist might ask the sculptor to rearrange the family in such a way that family relations are improved. The therapist might say, "How could you change this sculpture so that it would feel better to be a part of this family?" The sculptor would then go about rearranging the family sculpture so as to indicate what changes would be needed to improve the family's functioning.

In particular circumstances, the process of family sculpting is especially useful to move a family or individual forward in therapy. Those circumstances may include the following:

1. Therapy seems to have lost its momentum. Group or family members appear to be at a standstill.

2. Members are having difficulty expressing their feelings about a particular family issue.
3. Members are intellectualizing issues and, as a consequence, are ignoring the affective component of their communications.
4. Members' feelings are being rationalized, denied, or otherwise excluded from conscious experience.
5. The therapist feels that members are having difficulty comprehending verbal descriptions of family functioning.
6. A tool is required to explore possible solutions to seemingly unresolvable conflict.

Means and Conditions for Implementing Family Sculpting
The Therapist's Qualifications

Family sculpting is a technique used by both professionals and paraprofessionals. Since the guidelines for conducting family sculpting are relatively simple, one can acquire training by attending a workshop on family sculpting. Many practitioners have added family sculpting to their therapeutic repertoire after reading about the technique or observing a colleague sculpt a family. The most effective learning comes out of an experiential encounter with the method, during which one is required to sculpt one's own family. Family sculpting is often included in the curricula of graduate programs that train marriage and family therapists.

Conditions for Conducting Family Sculpting

Family sculpting requires no special facilities or equipment and may be used in the practitioner's office or in the family's home. A few pieces of sturdy furniture should be available, since participants are often required to stand on a piece of furniture in order to indicate their place in the family constellation.

Limitations of Family Sculpting
Contraindications

The therapist must exercise caution with families or individuals so as not to push them too quickly into particular emotional experiences that can result from family sculpting. As is true for many other forms of therapy, the practitioner must exercise judgment about a family's or an individual's readiness to face particular issues. Some questions have been raised in the literature on family sculpting about its use with the families of schizophrenics, since these families are often particularly rigid and fragile.

Hazards

As we have seen, family sculpting is a relatively straightforward technique, and because no certification is required for its use, one can incorporate family sculpting into practice immediately. The greatest hazard associated with family sculpting, then, is that a therapist will use the technique prematurely, before the therapist gains the experience that enhances one's skill as a practitioner of family sculpting. It is suggested that before implementing family sculpting, one become part of a group of practitioners interested in incorporating the technique into practice. As a group, members can sculpt fictitious families, families of past or present clients, and practitioners' own families of origin, enhancing practitioners' awareness of the process and allowing them to acquire some practical experience.

The Effectiveness of Family Sculpting

To date, articles on the subject of the effectiveness of family sculpting generally offer detailed case studies of the use of this method with particular populations. For example, Kates-Julius (1987) provided evidence in the form of case studies that sculpting can be used with psychotic individuals—a population generally considered too disturbed to find sculpting useful. Other articles have described variations on the traditional method of family sculpting. Lawson and Hebert (1991) found sculpting to be time-consuming; they also found that some families are reluctant to engage themselves in the process of sculpting because of self-consciousness. Lawson and Hebert suggested that sculpting can be more expedient and less threatening if a flannel board with figures of family members is used instead.

Despite the impressive array of case studies reporting the success of family sculpting as an experiential technique, its effectiveness from an empirical perspective remains unproven. Family sculpting has not been systematically investigated, nor have comparative studies pitted family sculpting against other techniques in order to assess its reliability as a diagnostic tool. Nevertheless, most authors have concluded that sculpting is an effective assessment tool in family counseling, and many practitioners find sculpting extremely useful in moving stuck families forward in therapy and as a method to provide insight for individuals in group therapy or educational settings.

References

Costa, L. (1991). Family sculpting in the training of marriage and family counselors. *Counselor Education and Supervision, 31*, 121–131.

Kates-Julius, E. (1987). Family sculpting: A pilot program for a schizophrenic group. *Journal of Marriage and Family Counseling, 4*, 19–24.

L'Abate, L., Ganahl, G., & Hansen, J. (1986). *Methods of family therapy.* Englewood Cliffs, NJ: Prentice-Hall.

Lawson, D., & Hebert, B. (1991). Family sculpting using a flannel board. *Journal of Mental Health Counseling, 13*, 405–409.

Satir, V. (1964). *Conjoint family therapy.* Palo Alto, CA: Science and Behavior.

Satir, V. (1987). Going behind the obvious: The psychotherapeutic journey. In J. Zeig (Ed.), *The evolution of psychotherapy* (pp. 58–68). New York: Brunner-Mazel.

Satir, V., Stachowiak, J., & Taschman, H. (1975). *Helping families to change.* New York: Aronson.

CHAPTER 16

Relationship Enhancement

In his 1977 volume *Relationship Enhancement*, Bernard Guerney, Jr. suggested that *therapy* be abandoned as a term to describe the "kinds of services that mental health professionals provide when they are not dispensing drugs" (p. 6). He stated that the vast majority of clients who seek counseling are not ill or sick, but rather stuck in dysfunctional patterns of behavior or styles of communicating. These clients need education, not therapy; therefore, mental health professionals are in the business of providing information, rather than producing cures. Guerney stated that the client who seeks counseling and who is not suffering from some biochemical imbalance "is no more sick than someone who wants to play tennis and does not know how, and the professional is no more providing 'therapy' or 'curing' his or her client than a tennis coach is 'curing' his clients" (p. 5). The medical model, then, is appropriate when the problem is biochemical in nature, but inappropriate when the problem is not a biochemical one. Guerney saw the role of the mental health professional as that of an educator or teacher. Through his use of an educational approach, Guerney developed an intervention program that involves different strategies and a different philosophical outlook from what students are generally taught.

As we shall see, Guerney's approach to intervention stands in direct contrast to the approach of family therapists such as Jay Haley, who believed that individuals know how they should behave but have a deep resistance to behaving that way. In other words, clients know they should try to understand the other's point of view, but are unwilling to do so because of a deep-seated resistance that may not have originated in the present relationship. As a result, Haley believed that teaching people how to communicate with one another would be treating a symptom rather than the cause of dysfunction. Therapists such as Haley, then, work with the client's resistance, rather than teaching particular skills. Guerney, on the other hand, believed that teaching people communication skills provides them with the tools that allow them to rid themselves of any resistance they have.

General Purpose of Relationship Enhancement

Relationship enhancement (RE) is a method of intervention that involves a number of programs designed to teach participants specific interpersonal skills, which will ultimately "enhance relationships between intimates, especially family members" (Guerney, 1977, p. 1). The programs are highly structured and task-oriented. Whatever type of program is in use, the principles that are taught remain the same. In other words, whether the program is aimed at a single individual, a parent-child dyad, marital counseling, family counseling, or a workshop designed to assist the staff of a particular institution, the content will consist of specific communication skills taught in a highly specific and systematic fashion.

History of Relationship Enhancement

Bernard Guerney, Jr. received his Ph.D. in clinical psychology from Pennsylvania State University in 1956. Before returning as a professor to Pennsylvania State University in 1969, Guerney was a psychologist at the Lafayette Clinic in Detroit, Michigan, for 1 year and served as director of the Psychological Clinic at Rutgers University for 12 years. During his tenure at Rutgers, Guerney collaborated with other prominent family therapists, among them Salvador Minuchin and Braulio Montalvo, on a large intervention and research effort involving dysfunctional inner-city families and their disturbed children. Their efforts culminated in the highly regarded text *Families of the Slums* (Minuchin, Montalvo, Guerney, Rosman, & Schumer, 1967), in which the authors presented both their theory of family dynamics and therapeutic techniques designed specifically for intervention with unstable families of urban slums.

Guerney shared the view, which emerged in the 1960s, that psychotherapies that focused solely on insight or behavior modification failed to produce lasting change in the individual. His clinical experience led him to adopt an interpersonal approach to intervention, which focused on the quality and content of interpersonal communication in family groups. In the early 1960s, Guerney and his colleagues began to develop the assumptions and methods of what would become known as relationship enhancement.

Range of Applicability

Relationship enhancement is applicable to all individuals who are experiencing everyday problems in living and who have not been diagnosed as having an organically based mental illness. Although Guerney and his colleagues acknowledged that certain individuals are mentally ill due to some imbalance in body chemistry, they believed that the overwhelming majority of people seen by mental health professionals are not mentally ill. Instead, these individuals are experiencing difficulties in interpersonal relationships, which can be alleviated through learning particular communication skills. Guerney (1977) stated that for these people, "the role of interpersonal relations is central to the problem and to the solution" (p. 4).

Unless an individual is suffering from some mental illness (defined as having an organic cause), Guerney believed diagnosis to be a useless endeavor for many of the same reasons given by other family therapists and those who follow a humanistic perspective—namely, that the vast majority of people who seek service on an outpatient basis are not ill, but instead are caught up in dysfunctional patterns of relating to other people. In essence, individuals' psychological well-being is governed by the characteristics and quality of their interpersonal relationships. Because of the absence of illness and the presence of the common condition of dysfunctional interpersonal communication patterns, a psychiatric diagnosis is of little value and, in fact, inappropriate. Diagnosis, then, is useful only when an illness is present that can be treated with specific medication. Guerney (1977) stated that relationship enhancement programs are "applicable whether one is highly troubled or very happy, and whether the relationship in question is highly precarious or extremely stable" (p. 168).

Theoretical Foundations
Assumptions About Human Nature

Guerney (1977) summed up the main assumption underlying the philosophy of relationship enhancement as follows: "We believe that the strength and stability of an individual's intrapsychic life is largely determined by the quality of his interpersonal relationships with significant others, particularly his family and other intimates" (p. 3). Relationship enhancement, according to Guerney (1983), "draws upon and integrates a variety of previous psycho-therapeutic theories and practices" (p. 44). In some instances, relationship enhancement accepts certain assumptions of a particular theory but rejects the therapeutic methods derived from that theory. In addition, the general orientation and technique of a particular method may be accepted, while the theoretical base is rejected. Although the theoretical foundations of relationship enhancement have not been published, the basic assumptions concerning human nature made by Guerney and his colleagues have been addressed in various writings (Guerney, 1977, 1983).

Relationship enhancement depends, to a great extent, on Harry Stack Sullivan's interpersonal theory of psychiatry. Sullivan's notion that personality is "the relatively enduring pattern of recurrent interpersonal situations which characterize a human life" (1953, p. 111) corresponds with Guerney's statement that an individual's psychic life is determined by the quality of the individual's interpersonal relationships. Although Guerney accepted Sullivan's notion that anxiety is a major force in determining one's interpersonal behavior, he disagreed that it is the primary cause of emotional disturbance. Sullivan maintained that individuals can be understood only in the context of their interpersonal relationships, and Guerney accepted this position. Personality, then, is the product of interpersonal relationships; in turn, one's personality influences the quality of one's present and future interpersonal relationships.

Relationship enhancement also involves an unusual wedding of Rogerian and Skinnerian theory. Although Guerney accepted the Rogerian techniques of empathy and unconditional positive regard, he rejected the Rogerian assumption that individuals possess a self-actualizing tendency that is activated by these conditions. Guerney took the view that psychological growth follows empathy and unconditional positive regard as a result of conditioning and deconditioning processes. Relationship enhancement involves methods proposed by both Skinner and Bandura; relationship enhancement therapists are taught to model behavior for clients and give praise as a contingent reward for appropriate behavior.

Relationship enhancement also draws from the psychoanalytic theories of both Adler and Freud. Relationship enhancement accepts Adler's notion that any attempt to understand an individual's present behavior must consider the individual's goals in life and anticipation of future events. It is assumed, then, that individuals construct their present behavior, in part, out of their anticipated future. Other assumptions drawn from psychoanalytic theory are that the unconscious is a repository for thoughts and feelings that have been kept from awareness, and that positive change can occur when some of these feelings and thoughts are brought into awareness. Catharsis is seen as a positive experience and a powerful force in bringing about change.

Although Guerney accepted the essence of Freud's views on the role of the unconscious and the desirability of catharsis, he rejected the methods of psychoanalysis: "We reject most of the therapeutic techniques used by Freudian or other psychodynamic therapists, because we believe that probing, interpretation, and the like generally are counterproductive to making the unconscious conscious and to therapeutic gains in general" (1983, p. 44). The techniques that Guerney felt best brought the unconscious to awareness and fostered personal growth are the Rogerian techniques of empathy, genuineness, and acceptance.

In summary, the following assumptions are part of the theoretical perspective of relationship enhancement:

1. Individuals' intrapsychic life and personality are determined by the quality and content of their interpersonal relationships, both past and present. A reciprocal relationship exists between one's personality and one's interpersonal relationships.

2. An individual's present behavior is constructed by both past experience and the anticipated future.

3. Anxiety in large amounts is a destructive force in interpersonal relationships. Anxiety results from an anticipated threat to the self. This threat is alleviated when one experiences unconditional positive regard.

4. The unconscious contains repressed material that can interfere with satisfying interpersonal relationships. It is desirable to cathect, or bring into awareness, particular repressed material in order to improve interpersonal relationships.

5. Catharsis can be brought about in an interpersonal relationship with another who expresses empathy and acceptance in a genuine manner.

6. Those interpersonal communications that are desirable can be developed and maintained by the technique of modeling and through the use of verbal and experiential rewards. In other words, an individual can gain access to appropriate interpersonal skills necessary for satisfying relationships through learning.

Assumptions About Conducting Relationship Enhancement

Since relationship enhancement is an educational approach, sessions begin with instruction. The therapist's first task is to present the rationale of the program to the client in such a way that the client, in determining whether the program is suitable, can "make the best decision in light of his own needs, judgment, and experience" (Guerney, 1977, p. 91). Guerney prefers to call the therapist the "leader." Leaders, in turn, see their clients as "students" or "participants." Leaders adopt the attitude that they possess particular skills that participants will find useful in solving their own problems. The leader, then, will not be solving the participants' problems but, instead, will be teaching skills and supervising participants' use of those skills. This manner of presenting the program's objectives is crucial in conveying to participants that they are not, and will not be, dependent on the leader to solve their problems. Participants simply lack information; once they have acquired that information, they will be self-sufficient in solving their problems and fostering their own personal growth.

The leader's task is to help participants see that personal growth can occur and disagreements can be resolved when one's needs and feelings are communicated to the other in such a way that they will not only be heard but also be given careful consideration. In addition, the leader explains that when one fails to communicate needs and feelings, or masks them with hostility, conflict and estrangement can escalate. According to Guerney, "except for establishing rapport, generally, [the leader's] use of therapeutic methodology is limited to the direct [demonstration] of these methods in order that the participants may consciously model themselves after him in the use of these techniques" (1977, p. 77).

Participants are given written material that outlines the major components of the four basic skills at the heart of the relationship enhancement program. The four basic skills include three modes of communicating (the expressive, empathic, and facilitator modes) and instructions for switching between modes. These skills will be explained in the following section. The leader discusses each skill with participants as follows:

1. The rationale for the skill is presented along with the guidelines for using the skill.
2. The leader demonstrates the skill through role playing or the use of audio or video tapes.
3. The leader supervises the participant's use of the skill in a very detailed fashion.
4. Once the leader and participant feel that the participant has reached a comfortable level of skill use, the participant is provided with assignments that involve use of the skill at home.
5. The participant returns to sessions with records of use of the skill at home. The records may involve either self-reports or audio tapes. The participant and leader discuss using the skill outside sessions.

6. The leader provides assignments that involve using the skill in every-day living. Once again, the participant is asked to keep some sort of record of this use.
7. The leader and participant discuss using the skill in everyday living.

When participants have mastered the basic skills of relationship enhancement, they are ready to begin their training in problem-solving, which involves mode-switching skills.

Key Concepts

The skills taught to participants that enable them to resolve conflicts and work toward personal growth involve self-expression, empathic responding, facilitation of others' attempts to use self-expression or empathy, and switching between the three modes of communication. These four basic skills are labeled expressor mode, empathic mode, facilitator mode, and mode switching. The expressor and empathic modes are highly specific ways of communicating, while the facilitator mode is a skill used to help others to learn the skills in relationship enhancement. Mode switching is a technique one uses when engaged in a dialogue with another person. Guerney provided an excellent and detailed discussion of these skills in his volume *Relationship Enhancement* (1977, pp. 26–44). That volume also captures the respect and empathy that Guerney and his colleagues feel toward those who participate in relationship enhancement programs.

Expressor mode.   The expressor mode provides participants with the opportunity to express their needs, wishes, thoughts, and feelings without interruption and in such a way that the words accurately capture the intended message. In relationship enhancement, only one person speaks at a time during a conversation—there are no interruptions. When one individual is using the expressor mode, the other individual may respond only in the empathic mode. In this way, full attention is given to the concerns of the individual who is speaking in the expressor mode.

When one is speaking in the expressor mode, one uses "I" statements. Since the intention of speaking in this mode is to make one's inner world known to the other, the statements must reflect the individual's experience. For example, one might say, "In my estimation, work doesn't get done quickly enough around our house," rather than, "Work doesn't get done quickly enough around our house." Guerney's rationale for using "I" statements is that one can only be an authority on one's own perceptions of events or people. He warned participants against claiming that an objective reality surrounds any situation or any person's actions. In essence, Guerney said that expressor statements should contain the following elements:

1. The subjectivity of perceptions and judgments should be acknowledged; in other words, the participant states what he or she perceives, believes, or feels. As a result, the listener is likely to feel less challenged by the expressor's words.

2. Expressors should include their feelings about the situation in the statement. Sometimes individuals are not aware of their feelings surrounding an issue. This element offers the participant the opportunity to bring those feelings into awareness and communicate them to the other.

3. The expressor is asked to find a positive element in the issue under discussion. Since participants have come to relationship enhancement to solve problems, it is assumed that the relationship must have some positive features for participants to want to save it.

4. Expressor statements should be specific. In other words, if participants are feeling hurt because they think their partner is ignoring them, they are asked to describe specifically the other's behaviors. The expressor statement might be something like, "I feel hurt when I think you are ignoring me. Earlier this evening when you were reading the newspaper, I asked you a question and you didn't respond."

5. In addition to being specific about the behavioral components of the issue at hand, expressors should include a statement about what they would like to have happen. For example, "I would like you to put down your newspaper and respond to my question."

Empathic mode.   When a participant is speaking in the empathic mode, the participant is being asked to "put yourself inside the skin of another person and . . . share the world that he sees and feels" (Guerney, 1977, p. 27). In other words, the participant is being asked to demonstrate empathy for the partner's feelings and viewpoint. Once again, this technique is used to defuse defensive feelings on the part of the partner. In the expressor mode, participants are asked to acknowledge that their viewpoint is a subjective one that the other may not share. Conversely, in the empathic mode, participants are asked to make an attempt to understand the other. Guerney stated that kindness encourages kindness in the other, and understanding encourages understanding from the other.

According to Guerney, empathic statements should be used only if the participant is truly attempting to understand the partner, and this understanding is based on previous conversations. In addition, the participant must make a sincere effort to be accepting and understanding. In other words, the empathic mode is not an opportunity to make hostile or competitive attributions about the partner's motives and needs. For example, it would be inappropriate to say, "You always need to be right." Instead, one could say, "I know you're used to making important decisions in your work, and, as a result, you feel a sense of responsibility for how things turn out."

The empathic responder demonstrates a respect and acceptance for the other's thoughts and feelings, whether the participant agrees with them or not. In essence, participants are asked to give their partner the same respect and acceptance that they would like to receive themselves. It is expected that when one employs empathic responding, one's partner will be encouraged to share at a deeper level because of the sense of trust that results from this type of communication.

Guerney (1977) presented a number of guidelines to be followed when speaking in the empathic mode:

1. The responder may not ask questions of the partner. Questions tend to interrupt the flow of communication and are viewed as the responder's attempt to direct the conversation. When one is listening empathically, one responds only to the communications that the speaker intends to address.

2. The responder does not interpret what the other is saying, because interpretation would express the responder's point of view rather than the speaker's. In addition, the responder does not present an opinion about what the speaker is saying. The responder's only goal is to understand the feelings, thoughts, perceptions, and viewpoints of the speaker.

3. The responder will refrain from making any suggestions about how the speaker should resolve a problem or view a situation. Although suggestions are a normal response in an everyday conversation, they are forbidden while one is in the empathic mode.

4. Most important, the responder will not make any judgments about what the speaker is saying. Judgments would clearly defeat the purpose of encouraging honest expression and deep sharing on the part of the partner.

Mode Switching.   After participants are familiar with the two modes of communicating discussed above, they will receive instruction in how to move back and forth between those modes in order to engage in a constructive dialogue with their partners. Mode switching generally occurs when the person who is responding empathically would like an opportunity to speak in the expressor mode, although it can occur when the expressor is at a point in the conversation when he or she wishes to hear from the other. The guide-lines for moving from one mode to another are as follows:

1. Both the expressor and the responder agree to switch modes.

2. Before the responder can switch to the expressor mode, the responder must provide an empathic response to the expressor's last statement that the expressor feels is accepting and accurate.

3. Mode switching is appropriate when the expressor feels that the major feelings and thoughts on the subject at hand have been expressed or when the expressor is interested in hearing the responder's views on the issue.

4. Mode switching is appropriate when the responder feels that the expressor's view is fully understood and nothing new remains to be said. Also, the responder may feel that further thoughts on the issue are begin-ning to hamper the ability to be empathic and, as a result, the responder's reflections may be bordering on insincere. Responders may request a mode switch if they have something to say that may alter the conversation in a positive way.

Facilitator mode.   The facilitator mode involves a skill that enables the par-ticipant to coach another in using the expressor and empathic modes or switching modes. As a facilitator, the participant is essentially a teacher who uses praise to encourage another to persist in using the skills and to provide an incentive for dealing with thorny issues. Just as a leader would do, the participant using this mode takes responsibility for assisting others in fol-lowing the guidelines for communicating in each mode. The participant who is taking on the role of facilitator must be comfortable with and skilled in communicating in the expressor and empathic modes. A participant would use the facilitator mode only after receiving careful supervision from the leader. As a facilitator, the participant may suggest ways that the other can improve upon their expressor or empathic statements. Therefore, the partici-pant must reach a certain level of skill before communication in the facilitator role is appropriate.

The facilitator mode is appropriate in various situations. For example, a mother may act as a facilitator for her husband and son during a discussion at home; in this situation, it is assumed that all three individuals have been participants in a relationship enhancement program. It is also possible to use facilitative skills with individuals who have not taken a relationship enhance-ment program. For example, if a friend or relative says, "You're driving me crazy with your questions," a participant might say, "You're frustrated because I ask so many questions. It doesn't seem to me that I ask a lot of questions. If you could give me some examples it might help me to understand what you mean."

Implementing Relationship Enhancement

Guerney (1977) included a number of clear examples of the use of relationship enhancement skills in his text *Relationship Enhancement*. The following is a fictitious conversation between a husband, Ed, and a wife, Jane, who have received training and are therefore well versed in the basic skills of relationship enhancement. The leader is participating in the facilitator mode in order to deepen the participants' statements and responses.

Ed: I'd like to talk about an issue that's been bothering me for quite some time now. I have been feeling angry when I think that you're spoiling the kids.

Jane: You've been feeling frustrated with the way I'm handling the kids.

Ed: Right. I really blew my stack the other night when you let Susan go to bed without putting her laundry away.

Jane: That was the last straw for you.

Ed: Yeah. And Jimmy seems to be able to slack off whenever he wants without any kind of consequences.

Jane: *(She hesitates and seems to be at a loss.)* Hm-m-m. I can really hear your anger.

Leader: What is he saying, Jane?

Jane: You're saying that you're angry because the kids aren't pulling their weight with the household chores.

Leader: Good!

Ed: That's right! And when I don't do something you ask, you jump all over me. I understand the kids have homework or other things to do at times and sometimes they're just tired. Well, so am I.

Jane: So you're angry that I let the kids get away with things but not you.

Leader: Good. And he's also saying, I think, that he feels somewhat hurt that you don't give him the same consideration that you give the kids.

Jane: You feel hurt when you see the kids getting better treatment than you, and you want me to be as understanding with you as I am with the kids when I ask you to do something.

Ed: Right. Sometimes I wonder how much you appreciate me as a person.

Leader: Good, Ed. Sounds like you're getting down to a deeper feeling.

In this example, what began as Ed's anger at Jane for spoiling the kids turned out to be quite a different issue. Ed's real concern was his perception of Jane's lack of appreciation and concern for him. He saw how tenderly Jane treated the children and felt he was not receiving the same compassion from her. Ed was able to reveal his deeper concern because Jane responded in an empathic way and was making real attempts to understand the issue. Without the structure of the basic skills, this conversation might have remained simply an argument about how Jane was spoiling the children. Apparently, though, Ed was less concerned about the children carrying their weight than about the discrepancy between Jane's treatment of the children and her treatment of him.

After praising her effort at responding, the leader assisted Jane in catching the deeper meaning of Ed's statement about the discrepancy in Jane's responses to her husband and children. Because the leader is not acting as a therapist, the leader simply shared this observation with Jane so that she could test that observation with Ed through empathic responding. The leader praised Ed for his courage in exposing the deeper issue of his feeling of a lack of caring on Jane's part. Although the leader is assisting Ed and Jane in their efforts to talk about this issue, the problem-solving effort remains a dialogue between husband and wife.

Means and Conditions for Implementing Relationship Enhancement
The Therapist's Qualifications

As is true with Carl Rogers's person-centered approach and Salvador Minuchin's structural family therapy, the methods of relationship enhancement are taught to both professionals and paraprofessionals through workshops taught by Guerney and his colleagues. Whether the relationship enhancement leader has a high school diploma or a Ph.D., he or she will be highly skilled in a number of techniques based on such diverse approaches as social learning theory, behaviorism, humanistic theory, and social psychology.

Guerney (1977, 1983) stated that two attitudes are extremely helpful to individuals learning the methods of relationship enhancement. First, individuals must give up the notion that they understand the problems of the couple or family better than the couple or family themselves. Traditionally, family therapists proceed with the notion that they know what changes to make in a family and how to make those changes after a few sessions. Relationship enhancement leaders believe that they have specific communication skills that will facilitate the family's ability to solve problems, but they do not believe that they know the dynamics of the family better than the family itself. In other words, the family, rather than the leader, selects the issues to be addressed in sessions.

Second, the relationship enhancement leader must be willing to trust in others' ability to work through their problems in ways that are best for them.

The leader, then, teaches the skills and follows the family's lead in the use of the skills. The leader's only obligation is to monitor the skills and hone their use.

Conditions for Conducting Relationship Enhancement

Relationship enhancement programs are generally taught in a comfortable setting that ensures privacy for the participants. Guerney and his colleagues offered a wide array of materials to assist leaders in running relationship enhancement programs. These materials include video and audio tapes and forms to be used with participants, all of which are useful in demonstrating relationship enhancement skills to clients.

Limitations of Relationship Enhancement
Contraindications and Hazards

There is no evidence to suggest that the application of relationship enhancement would be contratherapeutic in an educational or clinical setting. Although Guerney made the distinction between mental illness and problems of living as a rationale for the application of relationship enhancement, he stated that "even in the cases of true diseases [such as schizophrenia or other severe disorders], when psychological intervention of any kind does seem appropriate, clinical experience has shown that marital and family RE [relationship enhancement] therapy can be helpful" (1983, p. 42).

The Effectiveness of Relationship Enhancement

Relationship enhancement has been extensively researched with regard to its effectiveness as a treatment, participants' satisfaction with the treatment process, and its efficacy as compared to other treatments. Guerney provided the reader with detailed discussions of the research conducted on relationship enhancement and bibliographies of research articles (see, for example, Guerney, 1977, 1983). In reviewing the research, Guerney found that relationship enhancement "consistently has been found to be superior to no-treatment and to alternative treatments . . . including a behavioral therapy approach, a Gestalt approach, a traditional eclectic group approach, and the therapist's own preferred form of treatment" (1983, p. 42).

The research design most commonly used to test the effectiveness of relationship enhancement is a controlled experimental study. Participants are randomly assigned to one of three groups: a control group receiving no treatment, a group receiving the treatment under study, and a group receiving an alternative treatment. A typical study testing the effectiveness of relationship enhancement against a control group and an alternative approach was conducted by Guerney and two of his doctoral students (Guerney, Coufal, & Vogelsong, 1981). In this study, mother and daughter dyads (N = 61 pairs) from a lower-level socioeconomic group were assigned to one of the three groups. The alternative method chosen for the study had a group discussion format; participants were directed to choose important issues for discussion, and encouraged to develop an attitude of openness and trust. These attitudes were modeled by the therapist and reinforced in the clients when they appeared, but specific skills were not taught. The measures used in this study were designed to test empathic and expressive skills, general communication skills, and the quality of the relationship. Whereas the group that was not treated showed no improvement on all measures, the alternative treatment group showed some improvement in all areas. The relationship enhancement group showed significant improvement in all areas, and improvement was to a higher level than that of the alternative treatment group.

References

Guerney, B., Jr. (1977). *Relationship enhancement*. San Francisco, CA: Jossey-Bass.

Guerney, B., Jr. (1983). Marital and family relationship enhancement therapy. In P. Keller & L. Ritt (Eds.), *Innovations in clinical practice: A sourcebook*, Vol. II (pp. 40–53). Sarasota, FL: Professional Resources Exchange.

Guerney, B., Jr., Coufal, J., & Vogelsong, E. (1981). Relationship enhancement versus a traditional approach to therapeutic/preventative/enrichment parent-adolescent program. *Journal of Consulting and Clinical Psychology*, 49, 927–939.

Minuchin, S., Montalvo, B., Guerney, B., Rosman, B., & Schumer, F. (1967). *Families of the slums*. New York: Basic Books.

Sullivan, H. S. (1953). *The interpersonal theory of psychiatry*. New York: Norton.

PART VI

Expressive Approaches

C H A P T E R   1 7

··

Gestalt
Therapy

··

■

In introducing the first comprehensive book on Gestalt therapy, Frederick (Fritz) Perls and his coauthors stated that it was designed "to assist you to discover your self and to mobilize it for greater effectiveness satisfying the requirements both as a biological organism and social human being" (Perls, Hefferline, & Goodman, 1951, p. 3). In a posthumously published book, Perls (1973) stated simply that the goal of Gestalt therapy is to give the patient the means to solve both present and future problems. Perls viewed becoming mature, responsible, complete as a person, and integrated as the ultimate objectives of Gestalt therapy. He proposed that these ends be accomplished by helping people become more aware of their experience in the here and now. Another author expressed the goal of Gestalt therapy slightly differently, stating that "therapy consists of the *reintegration of attention and awareness*" (Enright, 1970, p. 108).

History of Gestalt Therapy

The development of Gestalt therapy benefited from the work of many different individuals. There are also many ways of doing Gestalt therapy and of applying Gestalt therapy principles in different areas. One person whose name is virtually synonymous with the development of Gestalt therapy is Fritz Perls. After receiving his medical degree, Perls was originally trained in

Freudian psychoanalysis. He underwent training analysis and was supervised by Wilhelm Reich, one of the pioneers of psychoanalysis, who made a number of important contributions but whose later work was very controversial. Perls also was exposed to the influential work of Kurt Goldstein, whose research on brain-injured World War I soldiers led to his "organismic theory," essentially an application of Gestalt psychology's formulation of perception to the functioning of the whole person (Goldstein, 1939). Perls left Germany in 1934, immigrating to South Africa, where he worked as a practicing psychoanalyst. Even before leaving Germany, however, Perls began to question psychoanalytic doctrine, a process that would eventually lead him to formulate Gestalt therapy.

Perls left South Africa in 1948 to come to the United States. During his stay in South Africa, he wrote his first book, *Ego, Hunger, and Aggression*, originally published in 1947 in Great Britain with the subtitle *A Revision of Freud's Theory and Methods* (a subtitle dropped for the 1969 edition) (Perls, 1969a). This book contained many themes that were later to be of central importance in Perls's formulations of Gestalt therapy (Wheeler, 1991). Smith (1976) documented the development of Perls's views, concluding that they were strongly influenced by at least five traditions: psychoanalysis, Reichian character analysis, existential philosophy, Gestalt psychology, and Eastern religion. Perls's most important departures from orthodox psychoanalysis were that he embraced a holistic or organismic concept of the person and that he accepted Gestalt psychology as a more effective theoretical underpinning for his views on personality functioning than the association psychology that Freud used as a foundation of psychoanalysis. Perls was particularly critical of Freud's emphasis on infantile and early childhood experiences. Eventually, Perls promoted a viewpoint directly opposed to Freud's historical emphasis, declaring that a focus on anything but behavior in the here and now is a waste of time (Smith, 1976).

The influence of Wilhelm Reich began early in Perls's career when he was in analysis with Reich. Although Reich was discredited later in his career, Perls benefited from several of Reich's early insights. First, Perls found a great deal of appeal in Reich's assertions that remembrances produced in therapy must be accompanied by the appropriate affect in order to have maximum therapeutic value. Second, Reich was the first psychoanalyst to call attention to the role of the body in psychopathology and psychotherapy. Reich suggested that muscular armor—in other words, muscular rigidity—represents a protective mechanism invoked by individuals to bind free-floating anxiety. This particular emphasis in Reich's system eventually found its way into Gestalt therapy through Perls's emphasis on patients' psychosomatic language. Moreover, Perls eventually encouraged his patients to engage in exercises, in order through "enhanced body awareness and bodily involvement to facilitate organismic completion of emotion" (Smith, 1976, p. 8). Reich's influence may also be seen in Perls's emphasis on the importance of the form and style of communication in therapy, an emphasis that placed the *how* of communication over the *what*, or the content of the communication.

Perls was influenced by the Gestalt psychology of Köhler and Wertheimer, as well as by the field theory of Lewin. Although Perls was acquainted with many aspects of Gestalt psychology, the most important idea to him was the idea of the unfinished situation, the incomplete Gestalt. Associated with this idea is the notion that individuals have a strong need to complete the Gestalt, to come to a closure. Completing the Gestalt, in turn, represented to Perls the essence of personal responsibility, a concept to which he already had a strong commitment because of the influence of existentialism (Smith, 1976). Another feature of Gestalt psychology that has been influential in the emergence of Gestalt therapy has been the emphasis on *wholes*—in other words, emphasis on the notion that behavior is understood best by considering the entire situation, person, and environment. In a sense, this notion was a reaction against the reductionism apparent in early behaviorism, but also in the formulations of Freud. By adopting Gestalt psychology's view of the person, Perls found a framework that allowed him to address the whole person in his therapeutic efforts. It has been noted, however, that Perls's appreciation of Reich and Goldstein's holistic or organismic notion may have been rather limited, in that he focused primarily on the implication of these notions with regard to body, or body functioning (Wheeler, 1991).

A final influence on the development of Gestalt therapy was Perls's interest in Eastern religion, particularly Taoism and Zen Buddhism. In particular, Perls focused on the paradox that one can grow only by becoming more of what one is, not by trying to be different. Moreover, Perls emphasized the importance of focusing on realizing one's true nature rather than on attaining goals or fulfilling ambitions. He often instructed his patients not to think too much, but to allow themselves to be fully seeing, hearing, tasting, smelling, and touching. Reportedly, he was fond of telling patients that "you must lose your mind to come to your senses" (Smith, 1976, p. 35).

Perls's wife Laura, who was a psychoanalyst herself, has been credited with participating in the early development of Gestalt therapy (Hardy, 1991). Following Fritz Perls's death in 1970, other individuals have become leaders in the field of Gestalt therapy. To this day, however, Perls's powerful personality and individuality are clearly reflected in what Gestalt therapy has become and the ways it is continuing to evolve.

Range of Applicability

Fritz Perls popularized Gestalt therapy by leading demonstration work-shops in which he was the featured performer. These workshops led to some misconceptions about the applicability of Gestalt therapy in circumstances other than those demonstrated by Perls. Further misunderstanding has resulted from statements Perls apparently made in which he took the position that individual therapy was obsolete and group processes represented the wave of the future (Rosenfeld, 1978). In fact, whether Gestalt therapy is offered as individual psychotherapy, conducted in group settings, or carried out in organizational settings depends on the therapist's personal preference (Van De Riet, Korb, & Gorrell, 1980). When Gestalt therapy is used in groups, it may cover a continuum from doing individual work within a group to focusing on Gestalt group process (Harman, 1989). Both extremes are accepted as legitimate applications of Gestalt therapy and simply represent the therapist's preferences, as well as time limitations and other constraints imposed by the group's circumstances.

Gestalt therapy has also been applied to larger systems, including busi-ness organizations (for example, Nevis, 1987; Wallen, 1970) and couples and families (for example, Hardy, 1991; Harman, 1989; Kempler, 1974). It has been used in the treatment of many different types of problems, including all kinds of relationship problems and sexual dysfunctions. Because Gestalt therapy aims to help people become more aware, mature, and responsible, it is not limited to remedial intervention and may be used by anyone wishing to achieve these objectives.

Theoretical Foundations

Assumptions About Human Nature

The Gestalt therapy view of human nature is firmly based in existen-tialism, which focuses on a process approach to understanding human behavior. It is assumed that by attending to and becoming more aware of the processes underlying experience, human beings can discover the essentials of their existence. Passons (1975, p. 14) outlined several "pivotal assumptions" about Gestalt therapy's views of human nature, which may be paraphrased as follows:

1. The person is a whole who is—rather than has—a body, emotions, thoughts, sensations, and perceptions, all of which are interrelated.

2. The person is part of the environment and cannot be understood outside of it.
3. The person is proactive rather than reactive.
4. The person is capable of being aware of his or her sensations, thoughts, emotions, and perceptions.
5. The person, through self-awareness, is capable of choice and is thus responsible for covert and overt behavior.
6. The person possesses the wherewithal and resources to live effectively.
7. Personal experience takes place only in the present. The past and the future can be experienced only in the now through remembering and anticipating.
8. The person is neither intrinsically good nor bad.

Gestalt therapy assumes that lack of awareness is usually at the root of human problems, because people may lose touch with the what and the how of behavior and thus be unable to live effectively. Such people tend to exist rather than to be, and thus experience a sense of helplessness and despair. Associated with this sense of helplessness may be refusal to take responsibility and efforts to manipulate the environment. Conversely, in Gestalt therapy the emotionally healthy person is defined as "one who has given up manipulation of the environment, and is self-supporting" (Smith, 1976, p. 130).

Assumptions About Conducting Gestalt Therapy

The roots of Gestalt therapy in Gestalt psychology have been discussed briefly in the section dealing with theory. Fundamental to understanding the significance of this relationship is the meaning of the German word *Gestalt*, which has no direct translation in English. Essentially, the term refers to an object within its context, as well as to the relationship between the two. A Gestalt is perceived when we see the object as it relates to a particular context—when we see the whole. Being able to experience the whole is critical to human functioning; that experience is constituted by the person's awareness of self, the environment, and the relationship between the two. Because this awareness represents a meaningful pattern, it constitutes a Gestalt. The formation of *Gestalten* represents a natural process. Experiences that are successfully completed fade into the background, and the person focuses attention on things that emerge in the foreground. If the individual is totally aware and able to function in the here-and-now, life represents a series of emerging *Gestalten* and the completion of those *Gestalten* (Korb, Gorrell, & Van De Riet, 1989).

Experiences that are held over from the past, as well as anticipations about the future, are thought to diminish the awareness of the person in the present. Moreover, those distractions from the here and now distort the present here-and-now experience, resulting in distorted interpretations of what is happening instead of allowing the person to experience what is happening "as it is." Clearly, therefore, what an individual attends to is of critical importance in this process of Gestalt formation. Gestalt therapy postulates that attention is related to "organismic need and need reduction, as well as the need for wholeness" (Korb, Gorrell, & Van De Riet, 1989, p. 6). The most pressing need will produce the clearest figure and thus command the most focused attention. Once a need is satisfied, it recedes, only to have another need emerge, thereby leading to a new Gestalt. The overall process of need reduction takes place as part of the spontaneous self-regulation of the organism—that is, organismic self-regulation. Rather than achieving a relatively stable equilibrium, however, a process of continual rebalancing takes place (Perls, Hefferline, & Goodman, 1951, p. 43).

One particular need that has received considerable attention in Gestalt therapy is individuals' commonly observed tendency to seek closure—to strive to finish unfinished tasks and to complete their experiences, particularly their interpersonal situations. Apparently, most individuals tend to dwell on incomplete experiences, to relive them, and to be preoccupied by unresolved emotions related to them. Those activities, of course, detract significantly from the person's ability to be fully present in the here and now and thus from the person's equilibrium-seeking activities (Korb, Gorrell, & Van De Riet, 1989). The early evidence supporting the existence of this tendency came from the research of Zeigarnik (1927), who found that individuals experienced a need to complete incomplete perceptual experiences. In Gestalt therapy it is assumed that this need for closure, for the completion of *Gestalten*, encompasses not only perceptual experiences but all areas of human functioning.

The need for closure may be conceptualized as a special case of the need for wholeness, which is another important concept in Gestalt therapy. This need, which resides in every person, is recognized in Gestalt therapy by an uncompromising refusal to be reductionist—that is, to address only aspects of the person's functioning or to allow the person to avoid feeling whole. Recognition of the person's wholeness is complemented in Gestalt therapy by recognition of the wholeness of the moment. The whole is more than the sum of its parts. For example, intellectual understanding of wholeness, while useful, cannot fully grasp the full experience of being whole. Thus, Gestalt therapy rejects the intellectual exercise of logical analysis in favor of the kind of intuitive or organismic knowing pursued in Eastern philosophy (Korb, Gorrell, & Van De Riet, 1989).

The theoretical foundations of Gestalt therapy cannot be adequately described in one brief section. Although the most important concepts have been described, it should be clear that Perls and his followers have freely borrowed various concepts from Freudian psychoanalysis, from Reich's teachings, from Moreno's psychodrama, and from other approaches to therapy. The defining feature of Gestalt therapy may be captured best by the following statement: "The greatest value in the Gestalt approach . . . lies in the insight that the *whole determines the parts*, which contrasts with the previous assumption that the whole is merely the total sum of its elements" (Perls, Hefferline, & Goodman, 1951, p. xi).

Implementing Gestalt Therapy
Basic Principles

The conduct of Gestalt therapy is frequently described as an art that has as many forms of expression as there are therapists. Consequently, Gestalt therapists have resisted efforts to systematize their art, fearing that it could thereby be reduced to the mechanical application of a set of procedures that ultimately would have consequences diametrically opposed to the objectives of Gestalt therapy. Nevertheless, Levitsky and Perls (1970, pp. 140–144) spelled out some of the rules governing the conduct of Gestalt therapy:

The principle of the now.   This idea is described as the most potent, but also the most elusive, principle of Gestalt therapy. It refers to the priority of the immediate moment and present experience in Gestalt therapy. Historical material is dealt with by bringing it into the present as fully as possible. Questions such as "What is your present awareness?" and "What do you feel at this moment?" are used in order to facilitate communications in the present tense.

I and thou.   This principle emphasizes the notion that true communication involves the aware presence of both the sender and receiver. At the root of this concept is the distinction between talking to and talking at the listener.

"It language" and "I language."   Essentially, this principle requires that patients be encouraged to use personal pronouns, foregoing the relatively impersonal "it language" in favor of "I language."

Use of the awareness continuum.   The use of this continuum is designed to help patients to focus on the *what* and the *how* of behavior instead of the more common focus on the *why*, which is emphasized by many other types of therapy.

No gossiping.   This rule of Gestalt therapy prohibits talking about an individual who is present, rather than talking to the person. The aim of this rule is to facilitate the direct confrontation of feelings.

Asking questions.   In the context of therapy, as well as in everyday life, questions are often not simply requests for information, but are intended to manipulate or make a point. In keeping with the Gestalt emphasis on directness, therapists typically ask clients to change a question into a statement (which usually more clearly reflects the questioner's intent).

Margaret Korb and her associates have attempted to create a more comprehensive and updated statement that systematically describes the basic principles guiding the conduct of modern Gestalt therapy (Korb, Gorrell, & Van De Riet, 1989, pp. 16–18). In brief, they described seven principles of therapy that they consider the key concepts of the Gestalt approach:

1. *Contact* represents a process of focusing on important intrapersonal and interpersonal aspects of *interfunctioning* between client and environment, and between therapist and client. The latter is often referred to as an I–Thou relationship—a phrase that signifies the complete presence of both therapist and client in the therapy environment.

2. *Change processes* occur "through present-centered, spontaneous concentration on any figural aspect of the client's experience." Consequently, changes may occur not only in the problem areas the client identifies, but in any area of the client's experience.

3. *Affirmation*, considered an important ingredient in the contact experience, consists of the acknowledgement (by the therapist) of a personal truth discovered by the client, thereby facilitating positive change.

4. *Clarity* emerges out of the client's confusion and conflict as a consequence of affirmation.

5. *Appropriateness* refers to the nature of the interventions the therapist makes in the therapeutic context as a consequence of being aware of the client's resources for change.

6. *Respect* is demonstrated by the therapist for all client behaviors, whether healthy behaviors or ones that block healthy functioning. One important dictum of Gestalt therapy is that the client, not the therapist, represents the ultimate authority in the client's life.

7. *Experimentation*, designed to increase awareness and remove obstacles to self-regulation, is encouraged in therapy.

Although this summary presentation of key concepts is a useful cognitive map for understanding Gestalt therapy, further elaboration of some of these concepts is necessary. One difficulty in writing about Gestalt therapy is that Perls was not nearly as productive as, for example, Freud or Jung, who presented systematic and periodically updated views on their contributions. According to some writers, Perls did not have the work habits of some of his colleagues. He spent the last several years of his life giving occasional demonstrations and sitting in a hot tub at the Esalen Institute in California. In addition, his own presentation of the principles of Gestalt therapy (particularly that in Perls, Hefferline, & Goodman, 1951), although containing many of the basic ideas of Gestalt therapy, have been somewhat difficult to understand, especially for those not steeped in the language and traditions of Gestalt therapy.

Change Processes

The process of change in Gestalt therapy is conceptualized somewhat differently than in most other therapeutic approaches. Of particular concern in Gestalt therapy are two common ways in which people often prevent themselves from growing and changing. The first of these might be called the quest for self-improvement, or the quest for perfection. In questing after perfection, individuals continuously search outside themselves for what they might become and are always dissatisfied with what they are, thus effectively preventing self-actualization. The second way people often prevent themselves from growing and changing is to frighten themselves with dire expectations of what might happen if they allowed themselves to be themselves, to act in ways that will satisfy their needs, and to express their true feelings and thoughts (Van De Riet, Korb, & Gorrell, 1980, pp. 71–72).

In Gestalt therapy, the presenting problem (as initially defined by the client) is typically not the focus of attention. Rather, the Gestalt therapist attempts to be fully aware of the underlying processes that cause the client to experience a problem. Key features of the client's functioning attended to by the therapist are body tensions, voice quality, speech patterns, posture, peculiar forms of expression, and the like. Moreover, therapeutic change cannot be achieved through simply talking about a problem or conflict, because completion of the Gestalt can be achieved only through experience. This experience must include "allowing oneself to feel, or to say, or to do whatever is necessary for the unfinished business to be finished." The therapist's behaviors are designed to facilitate this experience. Moreover, the therapist is a full participant "as a catalyst, frustrator, or clarifier." Giving advice and solving problems are considered counterproductive in the therapy situation (Van De Riet, Korb, & Gorrell, 1980, pp. 74–75).

Completion of Gestalten

The completion of *Gestalten* that have been incomplete is of central importance in the ongoing process of therapy. Frequently, this process is conceptualized as the process of finishing unfinished business or of reaching closure. Four steps (see Korb, Gorrell, & Van De Riet, 1989, pp. 95–99) are thought to be necessary in this overall process:

1. *Expression*: This first step involves an initial overt expression reflecting the client's inner experience. This expression may be verbal or nonverbal, and it may involve body language or any other sign that the therapist may call to the client's awareness. The objective of the therapist's action in each case will be to bring out the inner experience at the root of the problems the client is subjectively experiencing.

2. *Differentiation*: The Gestalt therapist realizes that conflicting aspects of the client's situation may be expressed in different ways through different expressive modalities. In the differentiation stage, the therapist acts to facilitate the client's recognition of the fragmented selves within. For example, a client may be reporting on some aspect of his or her life situation, while at the same time providing evidence of inner conflict by displaying bodily tensions such as foot-tapping or fist-clenching. The therapist's role is to facilitate awareness of these fragmented expressions and what they mean, thus differentiating in the client's awareness thoughts and behaviors manifested by these various expressive modes.

3. *Affirmation*: In this step the therapist encourages clients to accept the often conflicting parts that have been emerging into their awareness in the differentiation stage. Part of the self-affirmation encouraged during this stage involves clients' acceptance of responsibility for all that they are.

4. *Accommodation and choice*: Once the client is aware of and accepts different parts of the self and owns them, the client is free to choose behaviors that fit. The problem presented by the client may be resolved through the choices made. "Awareness and conscious acknowledgement facilitates choice by enabling the individual to be what he or she is, without trying to be what he or she is not" (Korb, Gorrell, & Van De Riet, 1989, p. 99).

Intervention Strategies

Many references in Perls's work and the writings of other Gestalt therapists indicate that specific intervention strategies and techniques are limited
only by the therapist's imagination and personality. Most presentations of specific techniques focus primarily on what Perls has called the games of Gestalt
therapy. In addition, however, considerable attention has been given to the
importance of dream work and the utility of physical contact in the course of
Gestalt therapy.

Dream work.   Perls, referring to his work as a therapist, stated, "I especially
prefer to work with dreams. I believe that in a dream, we have a clear existential message of what's missing in our lives" (Perls, 1969b, p. 76). Thus, unlike
Freud, Perls considered dreams to be entirely projections of the dreamer. He
reasoned, "After all, you are the maker of the dream, and whatever you put
into it must be what is in you and therefore available for constructing the
dream" (Perls, Hefferline, & Goodman, 1951, p. 221). Many Gestalt therapists today consider dreams to be existential messages that reflect the nature
of the client's existence. A variety of techniques may be used to immerse the
client in dream work, including asking the client to recount the dream in the
first person, as if it were occurring now, or asking the dreamer to develop a
dialogue among the various actors in the dream (Harman, 1989).

Physical contact.   In contrast to many other kinds of therapeutic intervention, physical contact is acceptable under some circumstances between therapist and client. In response to the question of what psychotherapeutic
physical contact she would engage in, Laura Perls stated:

> I will use any sort of physical contact if I expect it to facilitate the patient's
> next step in his awareness of the actual situation and what he is doing (or
> not doing) in and with it. . . . I will light a cigarette, feed someone with a
> spoon, fix a girl's hair, hold hands or hold a patient on my lap—if that
> happens to be the best means of establishing the nonexistent or interrupted
> communication. I also touch patients or let them touch me in experiments
> to increase body-awareness: To point out tensions, malcoordination, rhythm
> of breathing, jerkiness, or fluidity in motion, etc. (1970, p. 128)

While making this broad statement, Perls acknowledged that such a stance
would be controversial but insisted that as a committed therapist one needed
to have the courage to take such risks.

Experiments or games.   Perls and colleagues (1951) conceptualized most of the conduct of Gestalt therapy as consisting of experiments designed around the tasks of orienting the self and manipulating the self. These initial attempts to identify experiments designed to facilitate contacting the environment and increasing awareness have since been refined and formalized as experiments or games of Gestalt therapy. Some of the more frequently used games (see, for example, Korb, Gorrell, & Van De Riet, 1989, pp. 103–104; Levitsky & Perls, 1970, pp. 144–148; Van De Riet, Korb, & Gorrell, 1980, pp. 83–84) that have demonstrated effectiveness may be briefly described as follows:

1. *Dialogue*: In what is often referred to as the empty chair experiment, dichotomies observed in the patient (for example, top dog versus underdog, nice guy versus scoundrel, and so on) result in the therapist's requesting that the patient have a dialogue with an aspect of his or her world that is not clear. The unclear or split aspect of the patient is imagined to sit in the empty chair, thereby separating it psychologically from the client so that the client can address it and have a dialogue with it.

2. *Making the rounds*: This experiment is conducted in group therapy sessions when the therapist feels that a particular theme or personal truth expressed by the patient should be expressed directly and individually to each member of the group. For example, if a person says, "I can't stand anyone in this group," he or she is asked to address each group member directly, saying, "I can't stand you," and perhaps adding some other remark that reflects feelings toward a particular group member.

3. *Unfinished business*: The basic notion in this experiment is to ask patients to complete unfinished business, which usually consists of unresolved feelings. Feelings of resentment toward parents are a common example of unfinished business.

4. *Exaggeration*: The game of exaggeration is used primarily to raise the patient's awareness of body language. For example, a patient may be asked to repeatedly perform in exaggerated fashion an unwitting gesture or movement that the therapist observes and assumes is an important communication of which the patient is unaware. A variation of this game can be used with verbal statements if the therapist notices that the patient glosses over an important statement. Asking the patient to repeat the statement with emphasis and conviction may help the patient to become aware of its significance.

5. *Reversal*: This game is based on Gestalt therapy's assumption that overt behavior often represents the reversal of underlying impulses or intentions. Thus, when the patient is asked to play a reversal, he or she is asked to make the reverse of a statement or play a role opposite to the one that has been

presented. For example, a person who is unassertive may be asked to play the role of an aggressive person.

6. *Rehearsal*: In Gestalt therapy it is assumed that people spend a great deal of their time in planning and rehearsing for their various social roles. The game of rehearsal consists of asking patients to share their rehearsals with others and thus to become more aware of these preparatory activities.

7. *Directed awareness*: When the therapist feels that a patient is ignoring certain sensory experiences, or is not clearly tuned in to bodily sensations, the therapist may design special experiments to heighten awareness of whatever appears to be confused or ignored by the patient.

Note that Perls himself was rather skeptical about the use of specific techniques that he considered gimmicks (Perls, 1969b, p. 1). To appreciate the full meaning of the Gestalt therapy approach, one must look beyond specific ways of applying Gestalt principles and focus on the therapy's overall objectives. Those objectives are to promote growth, to develop human potential, to release spontaneity, and to eliminate anxiety. Fritz Perls felt that virtually anything that would help people to accomplish these and related objectives would be consistent with the Gestalt approach. This idea explains why Gestalt therapists generally do not feel confined to specific techniques in the practice of their art. Gestalt therapy should be viewed as something that is becoming, emerging, and never finished—a perspective that would clearly meet with Fritz Perls's approval.

Means and Conditions for Implementing Gestalt Therapy
The Therapist's Qualifications

Throughout the literature of Gestalt therapy, the personal characteristics of Gestalt therapists receive more attention than their educational qualifications. One reason for this emphasis is the view that Gestalt therapy is more than any set of principles, techniques, or technical procedures. Gestalt therapy constitutes a deeply personal effort in which the Gestalt therapist tries to fully experience the existence of the patient. Only therapists who are authentic and who have achieved a high level of personal integrity can do this. Therapists must be able to integrate a high level of awareness, learned skills, and knowledge of theory with their personal characteristics. The Gestalt therapist is an instrument of change as well as an educator who helps patients to grow and mature through a process of discovery (Korb, Gorrell, & Van De Riet, 1989).

There are no firmly established criteria for the training of Gestalt therapists. In principle, anyone who is a qualified psychotherapist by virtue of having training in psychology, psychiatry, social work, or related areas may be considered a Gestalt therapist, as long as that person also has special training and experience in Gestalt therapy. How much of such special training is considered adequate has not been established and may vary considerably from one person to another. Since Gestalt therapists like to be considered creative artists, disagreements about who is truly qualified are likely to persist.

In the meantime, those who aspire to be Gestalt therapists might consult Brown, Mintz, Nevis, Smith, and Harman (1987) for a review of issues, methods, and criteria for the training of Gestalt therapists. In addition, it may be useful to consult the annual *Gestalt Directory,* published by the Center for Gestalt Development in Highland, New York. This directory lists the various Gestalt institutes, both in the United States and in foreign countries, that offer training in Gestalt therapy. All these institutes insist that prospective Gestalt therapists be well versed in Gestalt theory and undergo intensive training and supervised practice as a means to ensure the requisite level of personal and professional preparation.

Conditions for Conducting Gestalt Therapy

As is the case with most other psychotherapeutic approaches, the special requirements for the conduct of Gestalt therapy are minimal. Generally, Gestalt therapy is conducted in the customary office setting of the therapy practitioner. It is entirely possible, however, for therapy sessions to be conducted in naturalistic settings, outdoors, or even in a hot tub, depending on the specific circumstances of patient and therapist. Whatever circumstances permit the release of creative potential and the enhancement of awareness may be appropriate for the conduct of Gestalt therapy.

Limitations of Gestalt Therapy
Contraindications

Gestalt therapy is not the right approach for every patient. It is designed for people who are dissatisfied with the way they are and are willing to expend some effort to change, or to become more content with themselves (Enright, 1970, p. 121). This statement implies, of course, that individuals who do not meet these criteria may not be appropriate candidates for Gestalt therapy. Indeed, many techniques of Gestalt therapy require more of a commitment toward self-discovery than many patients are willing or able to give. Such patients may be better off in some other form of therapy that requires less responsibility and less commitment on their part than Gestalt therapy does.

Hazards

The most common hazard in Gestalt therapy is represented by the therapist's limitations. Skill, training, experience, and judgment are necessary in the competent therapist (Shepherd, 1970). Also, even when therapists are competent, Gestalt therapy is most effective when used with overly socialized, restrained, and constricted patients rather than with less organized, more severely disturbed individuals. Consequently, the therapist must select patients for whom Gestalt therapy is likely to be appropriate. Another possible hazard is that patients who are more in touch with themselves will experience increased dissatisfaction with the pretense and hypocrisy common in social interactions and institutions (Shepherd, 1970).

The use of Gestalt therapy with people who have a tendency to act out must be approached with caution. Such individuals typically have impulse control problems, which may create an explosive situation if their expression is encouraged in the course of Gestalt therapy. Such a situation may come about because the Gestalt therapist may be seen as an authority figure, and the presence of such a figure during the expression of impulse control problems may be seen as approval for inappropriate actions outside of the therapy situation (Hardy, 1991, p. viii). An additional concern in the conduct of Gestalt therapy is the extreme intensity of emotional expression that is often observed in the course of therapy. Although this phenomenon often has significant therapeutic value, it may be frightening and disconcerting to other patients in a group therapy session, or even to inexperienced therapists. This possibility underscores the necessity for extensive training and seasoning through experience as necessary qualifications for Gestalt therapists.

The Effectiveness of Gestalt Therapy

In 1970 Fagan and Shepherd noted that doing scientific research on Gestalt therapy was exceedingly difficult. They reported:

> Hard data are difficult to obtain; the important variables resist quantification; the complexity and multiplicity of variables in therapist, patient, and the interactional processes are almost impossible to unravel; and the crude-

ness and restrictiveness of the measuring devices available cannot adequately reflect the subtlety of the process. (p. 241)

Although they expressed optimism that these obstacles would not stand in the way of scientific research, more than 20 years later their comments still reflect the contemporary state of affairs.

One critical limitation of research on Gestalt therapy's effectiveness is that the therapy covers so much territory. Although this chapter has focused on the practice of Gestalt therapy as developed by Perls and his close associates, others have taken Gestalt therapy in still different directions—for example, Nevis adapted the Gestalt approach to organizational consulting. Also, the practice of Gestalt therapy ultimately involves in each instance a unique, joint experience of maturation and growth, in which both the therapist and the client change. Doing research on any particular outcome for the client only would not do justice to the Gestalt approach. Moreover, assessing the outcomes of Gestalt therapy requires the evaluation of a dynamic process that does not have any preconceived final state as its objective. Perls felt very strongly that there is no such thing as an ultimate outcome of therapy and that the processes of learning, integration, and maturation are continuous throughout each person's life. Ultimately, therefore, if people are able to function better in the here and now, accept themselves for who they are, and learn to enjoy life as it is rather than what it could be, therapy has been successful. How to establish scientifically that these ends have been accomplished as a consequence of Gestalt therapy remains a difficult and elusive task.

References

Brown, G., Mintz, E., Nevis, S. M., Smith, E. W. L., & Harman, R. (1987). The training of Gestalt therapists: A symposium. *The Gestalt Journal, 10,* 73–106.

Enright, J. B. (1970). An introduction to Gestalt techniques. In J. Fagan & I. L. Shepherd (Eds.), *Gestalt therapy now: Theory, techniques, applications* (pp. 107–124). Palo Alto, CA: Science and Behavior Books.

Fagan, J., & Shepherd, I. L. (1970). Applications of Gestalt therapy. In J. Fagan & I. L. Shepherd (Eds.), *Gestalt therapy now: Theory, techniques, applications* (pp. 239–242). Palo Alto, CA: Science and Behavior Books.

Goldstein, K. (1939). *The organism.* New York: American Book Company.

Hardy, R. E. (1991). *Gestalt psychotherapy: Concepts and demonstrations in stress, relationships, hypnosis, and addiction.* Springfield, IL: Charles C Thomas.

Harman, R. L. (1989). *Gestalt therapy with groups, couples, sexually dysfunctional men, and dreams*. Springfield, IL: Charles C Thomas.

Kempler, W. (1974). *Principles of Gestalt family therapy*. Oslo: Nordahls Taykkeri.

Korb, M. P., Gorrell, J., & Van De Riet, V. (1989). *Gestalt therapy: Practice and theory* (2nd ed.). New York: Pergamon Press.

Levitsky, A., & Perls, F. S. (1970). The rules and games of Gestalt therapy. In J. Fagan & I. L. Shepherd (Eds.), *Gestalt therapy now: Theory, techniques, applications* (pp. 140–149). Palo Alto, CA: Science and Behavior Books.

Nevis, E. C. (1987). *Organizational consulting: A Gestalt approach*. New York: Gardner Press.

Passons, W. R. (1975). *Gestalt approaches in counseling*. New York: Holt, Rinehart & Winston.

Perls, F. S. (1969a). *Ego, hunger, and aggression: The beginning of Gestalt therapy*. New York: Random House.

Perls, F. S. (1969b). *Gestalt therapy verbatim*. Moab, UT: Real People Press.

Perls, F. W. (1973). *The Gestalt approach and eye witness to therapy*. Palo Alto, CA: Science and Behavior Books.

Perls, F. S., Hefferline, R. F., & Goodman, P. (1951). *Gestalt therapy: Excitement and growth in the human personality*. New York: Julian Press.

Perls, L. (1970). One Gestalt therapist's approach. In J. Fagan & I. L. Shepherd (Eds.), *Gestalt therapy now: Theory, techniques, applications* (pp. 125–129). Palo Alto, CA: Science and Behavior Books.

Rosenfeld, E. (1978). An oral history of Gestalt therapy, part I: A conversation with Laura Perls. *The Gestalt Journal, 1*, 8–31.

Shepherd, I. L. (1970). Limitations and cautions in the Gestalt approach. In J. Fagan & I. L. Shepherd (Eds.), *Gestalt therapy now: Theory, techniques, applications* (pp. 234–238). Palo Alto, CA: Science and Behavior Books.

Smith, E. W. L. (1976). The roots of Gestalt therapy. In E. W. L. Smith (Ed.), *The growing edge of Gestalt therapy* (pp. 3–36). New York: Brunner/Mazel.

Van De Riet, V., Korb, M., & Gorrell, J. J. (1980). *Gestalt therapy: An introduction*. New York: Pergamon Press.

Wallen, R. (1970). Gestalt therapy and Gestalt psychology. In J. Fagan & I. L. Shepherd (Eds.), *Gestalt therapy now: Theory, techniques, applications* (pp. 8–13). Palo Alto, CA: Science and Behavior Books.

Wheeler, G. (1991). *Gestalt reconsidered: A new approach to contact and resistance*. New York: Gardner Press.

Zeigarnik, B. (1927). Das Behalten erledigter und unerledigter Handlungen. *Psychologische Forschung, 9*, 1–85.

CHAPTER 18

....

Psychodrama

....

■

On the evening of April Fool's Day, 1921, J. L. Moreno, the founder of psychodrama, walked onto a stage in Vienna in front of an audience of more than 1,000 people. Among the members of the audience were religious, political, and cultural leaders, who had come that evening to the Komoedien Haus for an evening of drama. Postwar Europe was in turmoil; Vienna was struggling with an extremely unstable government and a populace on the verge of revolt. Moreno stood alone in front of this audience beside a red chair that resembled a throne; on the chair was a crown. Although Moreno himself had no script and no cast, he knew his cast sat before him, and their scripts would emerge from their spontaneity. One by one, Moreno called upon certain members of the audience to "step upon the stage, to sit on the throne and to act like a king, unprepared and before an unprepared audience" (Moreno, 1946, p. 1). As each person took the royal seat, they spoke of a vision of a new order for Vienna. The audience acted as jury, but no one was judged competent to rule Vienna. Although the political problems of Vienna were not solved that evening, Moreno declared April 1, 1921, as the beginning of psychodrama.

General Purpose of Psychodrama

Psychodrama is a therapeutic approach that provides individuals with the opportunity to explore their inner life, or psyche, through an active, dramatic rendition of their experience. But rather than seeing this process as an imitation of life, psychodrama should be viewed as an extension of life in the sense that individuals have the "opportunity of recapitulation of unsolved problems within a freer, broader, and more flexible social setting" (Moreno, 1946, p. 15). In psychodrama, it is assumed that the acting out, or dramatization, of scenes from one's life, or inner life, is a more powerful and effective means for achieving insight, recalling forgotten experiences, and promoting catharsis than the general method of dialogue with a therapist. The psychodrama therapist believes that a reenactment of past or present events enables the client to experience the event in a fuller, more powerful way than by simply giving a verbal report. The curative process in psychodrama is achieved through spontaneity and role playing. Both these concepts will be explained in a later section.

History of Psychodrama

As a medical doctor in Vienna, Jacob Moreno began treating Viennese school children with behavior problems through the use of playacting. Moreno would compose plays about behavior problems, and the children would perform them. After a while, the children began to write their own plays, in which their experience was more directly and accurately represented. Moreno felt that the therapeutic element in the children's dramatic experience was the spontaneity of their performances. The stage, it seemed, "stirred [them] to a greater initiative and spontaneity" than they experienced in other settings (Moreno, 1945, p. 5).

In the early 1920s, Moreno formed his experimental Theater of Spontaneity, which was a haven for intellectuals, artists, and rebels in Vienna. Moreno (1946) claimed that the inspiration for what later became known as psychodrama rose out of his use of drama as a therapeutic tool in this setting. Moreno felt that the therapeutic benefits achieved from the spontaneous stage performances were deeper and more profound than those achieved in analysts' offices. The individuals involved in psychodrama faced their problems in a group rather than in isolation, and with action rather than simply verbalizations.

Moreno brought his ideas to the United States when he settled in Beacon, New York, and formed the Psychodramatic Institute. He felt that Americans were more accepting of the psychodramatic approach than were Europeans, because "a psychology of action is more akin to the Americans, a motorically minded people, trained by a history of pioneering" (Moreno, 1946, p. 11).

Range of Applicability

Psychodrama is an appropriate method of treatment for a variety of emotional disorders that range from mild to severe disturbances. Moreno wrote a number of monographs documenting the effectiveness of psychodrama in working with such diverse populations as psychotics (1945b) and couples experiencing marital problems (1945a). Adaline Starr (1977), a student of Moreno's and a prominent psychodrama therapist, has written about psychodrama as a form of treatment in working with children, adolescents, alcohol and drug abusers, depressed individuals, and hospitalized and outpatient groups.

Theoretical Foundations
Assumptions About Human Nature

Although Moreno took great exception to any identification of psychodrama with psychoanalysis, Freud's influence is clearly present in psychodrama's assumptions about the origin of emotional disturbance in the individual. Both psychoanalysis and psychodrama assume that dysfunctional behavior and emotional upset are the result of unresolved conflicts. In order for problems to be resolved, they must be brought to consciousness and worked out through catharsis. An emphasis on the role of unconscious and subconscious processes in driving outward behavior, then, is a central theme in both psychoanalysis and psychodrama. Moreno felt, however, that Freud's view of human nature was too narrow on the topic of the role of social relationships in both the individual's daily life and in the curative process.

Psychodrama's most noteworthy departure from psychoanalysis is its emphasis on treating the individual in the context of groups rather than in isolation. Moreno (1946) felt strongly that the individual's experiences "are not really his" (p. 11), but rather belong to the group, precisely because none of us lives in isolation. Sociology and anthropology appear to have had a greater influence on Moreno's thinking than psychology did. He denied the influence of the Viennese psychoanalysts on his thinking and instead, traced psychodrama's roots to "civilizations of the prehistoric period" (1946, p. 13) when shamans performed primitive rites to rid individuals of mental or physical illnesses, ensure the prosperity of the tribe, or drive away a curse. The essence of Moreno's thinking is that healing takes place within the powerful milieu of the group where everyone shares in, and contributes to, the experience.

The theory of psychodrama incorporates the tenets of sociometry. Sociometry explores the pattern of social relatedness that exists between individuals (Starr, 1977). This pattern is called a psychosocial network; it maps the individual's preferences for other people and objects, the feelings that flow between individuals, and the feeling an individual has for objects. In mentally healthy individuals, there is a positive balance in one's emotional expansiveness, which includes people and objects. In the mentally disturbed individual, that balance is disrupted. For example, a schizophrenic individual may develop an attachment to a piece of clothing rather than to a person. Various sociometric tests indicate the psychosocial network and pattern of social relatedness existing within an individual or a group. After diagnosis, psychodrama may be used as a way of acting on the information obtained from sociometric testing, since emotional disturbance is thought to result from a disturbance in role relationships.

Moreno claimed that one of psychodramatic theory's greatest contributions is its expansion of the concept of catharsis. He made the rather bold statement that "Breuer and Freud were ignorant of the therapeutic implications" (Moreno, 1946, p. 13) of catharsis as it was presented by Aristotle. Whereas Aristotle saw drama as an imitation of life, Moreno saw drama as life—not as a re-creation of circumstances, but rather as a continuation of circumstances. In the psychodramatic milieu, Moreno felt that as other members offered assistance and acceptance to the actor, they experienced a freedom of expression not ordinarily found in society. In psychodrama, catharsis is not simply a secondary phenomenon, a release or a by-product; instead, it is a primary phenomenon, the full experience of therapy. A fellow actor in psychodrama is not representing the client's father; he *is* the father. Once again, the experience of acting is not to re-create circumstances, but to live circumstances with the full range of emotion, spontaneity, and sincerity that can accompany real life.

Whereas Freud viewed the human dilemma as a struggle with our neuroses and conflicting drives, Moreno saw all people as potential heroes who could actualize that heroic potential in the midst of a crisis. He felt that the psychoanalyst's view of people as neurotic was crippling and demoralizing. He once told Freud: "You analyze their dreams. I try to give them the courage to dream again. I teach the people how to play god" (Moreno, 1946, p. 6). Moreno's idea of people's godhead quality rests on the notion that all people have the ability to create their own lives. Moreno believed, as did the existentialists, that responsibility for the quality of one's life rests with the individual.

The individual possesses the innate, fundamental quality of creativity, and creativity arises out of spontaneity.

Psychodramatic theory is complex and has been given extensive treatment elsewhere (Moreno, 1946; Starr, 1977). We encourage the interested reader to read Moreno in the original for a deeper understanding of psychodrama, and to experience the personality of this innovative thinker through his writing. Moreno's words are bold, dramatic, and forceful.

Key Concepts

Moreno was fascinated with the creative act, and out of his exploration of and experience with creativity he determined that creativity arose out of spontaneity. In teaching people to be creative, Moreno taught people to play god. The theory of psychodrama involves numerous key concepts; here, the concepts of spontaneity, creativity, warming up, roles, and role playing will be discussed.

Spontaneity and creativity.   Spontaneity is a self-initiated ability to respond to a situation, whether familiar or new, in the here and now, with vitality and creativity. Creativity is the manifestation of spontaneity in everyday life. The creativity that arises out of spontaneity must be productive rather than counterproductive—in psychological terms, functional rather than dysfunctional. For example, a schizophrenic patient who claims to be a secret agent on a mission to Mars is speaking spontaneously in a rather creative fashion, but this spontaneity is pathological, or dysfunctional. Existence tests the individual's spontaneity, because no two moments can be the same, and creative responses lead to a more satisfying, productive life. Moreno saw a positive correlation between the ability to be spontaneous, and therefore creative and godlike, and mental health.

Generally, we think of a spontaneous act as one that may arise out of unconscious impulses. Moreno saw spontaneity as a controlled act of will, and as such, he believed that people could be trained to be spontaneous. Part of that training process is called warming up.

Warming up.   Moreno described warming up as the "first basic manifestation of spontaneity" (1946, p. 52). When confronted with a novel situation, individuals spend a certain period of time warming up before they adjust and respond to the situation. According to Moreno, warming up involves both physical and mental processes, which he called starters. Physical starters might include a particular breathing pattern (for example, shallow breathing), arm or leg movements, or facial grimaces. Mental starters involve cognitions that prepare the individual for the situation. Essentially, warming up involves focusing one's attention on the task at hand and preparing for action. In psychodrama, the therapist, or director, may warm up an individual in the group by asking specific questions and discussing issues that will help the individual to confront and work on problems. In addition, specific exercises are used to warm up groups in preparation for dealing with a particular situation. The therapist must be sensitive to individuals' warm-up rates. As might be expected, some individuals require more warming up activity than others.

Roles.   Moreno viewed individuals as actors who play particular roles. As individuals develop, the number of roles they take on increases. Some roles are necessary to an individual's survival, and others are created out of a response to the social environment (Starr, 1977). Personality, in Moreno's theory, is a complex of roles. Some roles are functional and productive; others are dysfunctional and nonproductive. One's role repertoire may be expanded by the learning of new roles, which is often a goal of psychodrama. Conversely, one may have developed a role that is dysfunctional, so that the aim of psychodrama becomes unlearning that role.

Role playing.   Today the concept of role playing is widely understood and used among psychotherapists. Kipper (1986) acknowledged the work of George Herbert Mead, Ralph Linton, and Jacob Moreno as providing the basis for role theory as we know it today. Role playing is a technique used to assist individuals in gaining a sense of control by facilitating an encounter with the unknown. When role playing, an individual may rehearse a situation that is novel, has been unproductive in the past, or arouses anxiety in the present. In addition, the individual may take on another's role in order to gain a better understanding of the other or to assist another in role playing a particular situation. Starr (1977) stated that "role playing in a therapeutic situation is a reliable way to test and train spontaneity" (p. 30). The aim of psychodrama being to draw out individuals' spontaneity so that they may live more creative lives, role playing is a method used to elicit that spontaneity. When the individual causes something to happen out of a spontaneous moment, a new role emerges that can be added to the person's role repertoire.

Assumptions About Conducting Psychodrama

Psychodrama functions as a milieu in which patients are enabled to live through problems or confusion in an experimental setting that provides them with an opportunity to create new patterns of daily living, and thus to bring resolution to their problems or clarity to their confusion. The task of psychodrama is to assist the individual in developing the process necessary to effect a resolution. The therapist, or director, and group members act as "prompters and foils" (Moreno, 1945b, p. 4) as individuals work through their difficulties. In the experimental psychodramatic milieu, the boundaries and constraints of ordinary existence are left behind; individuals can act out their problems with a sense of freedom and lack of pressure from the outside world.

The psychodramatic experience is assumed to be a more powerful experience than talking about behavior in the abstract. The psychodramatist argues that meaning is lost when an individual sits in the artificial setting of a therapist's office and talks about particular events or feelings. Instead, events or feelings must be experienced in the context of scenes that allow the individual to continue the event or feeling. Moreno (1946) spoke of a *locus nascendi*, or place of birth. The idea contained in this expression is that the "true meaning of things unfolds only when they appear in their original context" (Kipper, 1986, p. 15). In addition, Moreno maintained that people can be aroused to a greater degree of spontaneity and initiative in the theater setting than in the drab confines of ordinary life settings.

Psychodrama assumes that the acting-out experience that takes place on the psychodramatic stage will have a lasting effect. Just as we incorporated into our lives the roles we learned as children, the roles we learn on the psychodramatic stage have the potential to become fixed components of our role repertoire. Note, however, that psychodrama is not a method that involves acting out everything and anything that comes to mind. Moreno likened the skill of the psychodramatic therapist to that of a surgeon who is aware of the patient's limitations. Therapists will limit the territory covered by the actors as they keep in mind the strain an exploration without limits would create for the actor.

Implementing Psychodrama

Psychodrama begins with an initial interview in which the client (or clients in the case of marital or family difficulties) describes the problem. According to Moreno, no elaborate case history is taken; instead, the therapist's aim is to uncover the psychodramatic situation that will become the subject matter of the first session. Before that first situation is dealt with on the psychodramatic stage, the therapist will talk with the client long enough to gain a clear understanding of the situation.

Once a situation has been set and described, the first session begins. For our purposes, we will assume that the presenting problem is marital conflict and the clients are a married couple. Psychodramatic sessions take place in a room containing a stage, which ideally will have various levels or tiers. This construction allows the various actors to be placed in particular relationship to other actors and to experience the distance and closeness of particular relationships, as well as the hierarchy often found in relationships. The people involved in psychodrama include the clients, other people who serve as auxiliary egos chosen by the clients (auxiliary egos are generally significant others in the clients' lives), other group members if it is group therapy, and the director (the therapist).

Initially, our married couple will be asked to go on stage and present the situation that will be used to build the action of the psychodrama. The couple will begin to discuss their situation in any way they choose, although the director will instruct them to experience and feel their situation more spontaneously than they have been. For example, they might be told specifically to include in their discussion feelings about the other that they have withheld when talking with each other at home. At this time, our married couple may begin an argument about the husband's lack of trust concerning his wife's activities outside the house. An auxiliary ego may be brought in to personify the wife's coworker, Mr. Jones, whom the husband suspects of having romantic feelings for his wife.

As the wife begins a conversation with Mr. Jones, she may start to realize that she in fact has some romantic feelings for him, which she has been denying. The safety of the experimental setting and the director's guidance allow her to express these feelings without the fear that would accompany them in daily life. The husband, stirred by his wife's honesty and concern, and at the therapist's urging, begins to examine his role in his wife's attraction as he questions Mr. Jones about what he offers the wife that he, the husband, does not.

In psychodrama, clients (actors) are encouraged to break out of their emotional isolation and identify with the problems and stances of others. In our example of the married couple, the husband was able to accept his wife's sincere admission of her attraction to Mr. Jones and move on to the business of exploring the marital relationship, because he was able to experience the problems of the other—in this case, his wife. The director (therapist) directs the action of the psychodrama at crucial junctures so that the actors are confronted with the purpose and ramifications of their behavior. It is the therapist's task to encourage—even to insist upon—the actor's examining, through live action, meaningful areas of past, present, and future behavior. The director fosters spontaneity in the actor by the director's own spontaneity.

Moreno published a number of monographs that provide great detail on the use of psychodrama to treat very specific problems (see, for example, Moreno, 1945a, 1945b). These monographs contain case histories that depict the action-oriented techniques of psychodrama, along with the theoretical assumptions that drive the action.

Means and Conditions for Implementing Psychodrama

The Therapist's Qualifications

It is generally assumed that anyone interested in becoming a psychodramatic therapist will first possess the credentials one usually associates with a qualified psychotherapist—that is, the individual will have received an advanced degree in psychiatry, psychology, counseling, or social work. Psychodrama is a highly complex, theoretically sophisticated technique that requires commitment from the student. Psychodrama should not be confused with the popular technique of role playing. Serious students who wish to pursue postgraduate training in psychodrama should be prepared to involve themselves in a course of study that extends far beyond a weekend workshop.

Conditions for Conducting Psychodrama

For the conduct of psychodrama, the client must be removed from both the settings of everyday life and the analyst's office; one must have access to a stage. Although an auditorium stage would suffice, the ideal stage would be constructed according to the Beacon model, which is the stage designed by Moreno and used at the Psychodramatic Institute in Beacon, New York. This model has three concentric circles, which form levels or tiers. A fourth level is provided by a balcony behind the stage. The stage is generally barren except for the presence of three or four chairs. Audience-style seating is recommended to capture the atmosphere of the theater. Those who are not participating in the particular scene would remain seated in the audience.

Limitations of Psychodrama

Contraindications and Hazards

Psychodrama, like any other therapeutic method, may not bring about the desired effect with every client. Common sense tells us that there must be some kind of fit between the client and the approach. Practitioners of psychodrama, however, view the approach as carrying no contraindications for particular populations. According to Moreno (1946), only clients who have some type of brain injury rendering them unable to communicate with the outside world are not candidates for psychodrama.

The greatest hazard associated with psychodrama involves the therapist's level of expertise. It is the psychodramatic therapist's responsibility to elicit from the client "an adequate re-enactment of the lived out and unlived out dimensions of his private world" (Moreno, 1946, p. 18). Moreno stated that whether this reenactment occurs depends on the therapist's artistry, imagination, and analytical skills. The successful psychodramatic therapist will be gifted in connecting with people on a deep level and in tapping the deep emotional well that exists within each individual.

The Effectiveness of Psychodrama

Although psychodrama has not attained the same level of acceptance in treating emotional disorders as, for example, humanistic psychology or behaviorism, it holds a great deal of appeal for a number of practitioners. The modest popularity of psychodrama among clinicians is most likely due to their positive, although sporadic, clinical experiences, rather than their acceptance of the theory underlying the approach. Concepts such as spontaneity and creativity are intuitively attractive to many clinicians. Psychodrama, then, generally holds greater appeal for clinicians than for academics. As a result, little research has been done regarding the effectiveness of psychodrama. Case studies that demonstrate the success of psychodrama abound in the literature (see for example, Moreno, 1945a, 1945b, 1946; Starr, 1977). In general, however, advocates of this method end up making a plea for empirical studies of the method's effectiveness.

Kipper (1986) believed that, although research on the effectiveness of this method is certainly desirable, establishing or failing to establish scientifically rigorous support for this approach does not carry the same weight for practitioners as it does for academicians. In other words, for clinicians, the decision to use a method will not rest solely on whether the method has well-established empirical support. Instead, their decision often rests on the method's intuitive appeal. The psychodramatic approach will continue to attract therapists interested in combining art and science in the practice of healing.

References

Kipper, D. (1986). *Psychotherapy through clinical role playing*. New York: Brunner/Mazel.

Moreno, J. (1945a). Psychodramatic treatment of marriage problems. *Psychodrama Monographs*, No. 7. Psychodramatic Institute. New York: Beacon House.

Moreno, J. (1945b). Psychodramatic treatment of psychosis. *Psychodrama Monographs*, No. 15. Psychodramatic Institute. New York: Beacon House.

Moreno, J. (1946). *Psychodrama*. New York: Beacon House.

Starr, A. (1977). *Rehearsal for living: Psychodrama*. Chicago, IL: Nelson-Hall.

■

....

CHAPTER 19

Art
Therapy

....

■

Jessica, a 6-year-old girl, sits at a small table intently drawing a picture of a family. The family consists of a mother, a father, two brothers, and a sister—reflecting the composition of Jessica's own family. The mother is holding the hands of both brothers, and these three figures take up most of the paper. The father, who has a sad look on his face, is quite small, and Jessica has placed him in the lower left-hand corner of the paper. The little girl is the smallest figure on the paper. She, like the father, is far away from the trio of mother and two brothers. Jessica has drawn her on the lower right-hand corner of the page. Unlike the other figures who have a head, a body, and two arms and legs, the little girl's arms and legs appear to extend from her head. In addition, while her face has two eyes and a nose, she has no mouth. Jessica completes her picture by adding a large dark cloud that looms over the entire family and hands the picture to the older woman sitting next to her. The woman smiles at Jessica and studies the picture. Drawing a picture of a family has enabled Jessica to converse with her therapist in a powerful way about feelings that she cannot put into words. In this way, Jessica has taken a first step toward healing by externalizing her distressing experiences.

General Purpose of Art Therapy

Art therapy may be broadly defined as the use of art in a therapeutic setting to foster an individual's psychological growth and well-being. Art in a therapeutic context is a nonthreatening avenue by which subconscious material may be brought into awareness and made concrete, thereby opening the door for perception and interpretation. Art, as a spontaneous creative act, can circumvent the difficulties often encountered in one's attempt to verbalize the feelings and circumstances of one's life. Art therapy affords individuals a source of immediate release through symbolic expression and an experiential encounter with their deepest feelings. Art therapy, then, is a symbolic verbalization of the material of the unconscious.

Although the majority of writing on art therapy has stressed the goal of making unconscious material conscious, art therapy is also used as a method to enhance and deepen one's understanding of conscious material. For example, an adolescent girl who is aware of her anger and frustration about her parents' divorce may be encouraged to express those feelings symbolically in a drawing. Through her drawing and subsequent dialogue with a therapist, she may discuss the depth of sadness surrounding the loss of regular contact with her father as he is placed far away from the rest of the family in the picture. As the therapist comments on her placing herself between the mother and father, the adolescent may begin to discuss conflicting loyalties and the fear of being asked to choose sides when her parents disagree. In this way, her drawing has become a catalyst for deepening therapeutic dialogue and, consequently, self-understanding.

History of Art Therapy

Although the birth of art therapy as it is practiced today is generally discussed with reference to the work of contemporary clinicians, art was perceived as a revealing and healing activity by a number of pioneering psychiatrists early in this century. Jung (1964), for example, encouraged his patients to draw in a spontaneous fashion their innermost feelings and fantasies. He was certain that symbols embodied unconscious material, and those symbols were the key to both the individual's unconscious and the collective unconscious. Although Freud did not include drawings as part of his technique, he believed that unconscious material could become conscious by eliciting visual images from his patients. On occasion he would make use of patients' drawings for interpretation and insight. In her clinical practice with children, Anna Freud consistently used drawings for diagnostic purposes.

Although they have found that drawings were useful media for establishing contact with patients' unconscious material, neither Jung nor the Freuds used art as their primary method of therapy.

Two women, Margaret Naumburg and Edith Kramer, are considered pioneers in bringing art therapy into prominence in clinical practice (Rubin, 1980). The therapies of both Naumburg and Kramer were founded on psychoanalytic technique, but their techniques differ in how they use art. These differences will be discussed in later sections.

Naumburg began her career as an art teacher. She had a keen interest in depth psychology and underwent analysis during the early 1900s. As an analyst and teacher, Naumburg was struck by the insight she obtained through drawings made as part of her own analysis, and by the spontaneous drawings of the children in her classes. During these years, Naumburg formulated her notion of art as a curative method for releasing unconscious material (Naumburg, 1966). Rather than viewing art therapy as an adjunct method, Naumburg proclaimed art therapy to be a primary therapy in its own right. Naumburg was able to realize the full potential of her methods during her association with the New York State Psychiatric Institute, under the direction of Dr. Nolan Lewis, an advocate of the use of art in psychoanalysis (Rubin, 1987).

Kramer, also an art teacher who was trained in psychoanalytic theory, taught at the Wiltwyck School for Boys in New York City, where her students were delinquent boys from extremely disadvantaged circumstances. Unlike Naumburg, Kramer saw art therapy as an adjunct method to be used in conjunction with a primary therapy; psychoanalysis was her method of choice and drove her approach to art therapy. She wrote a number of books on art therapy as a form of sublimation. She and Naumburg were the most influential practitioners of art therapy during the 1950s and 1960s, and their numerous books continue to be required reading for aspiring art therapists.

Range of Applicability

According to Judith Rubin, a prominent clinician, researcher, and past president of the American Art Therapy Association, art therapists work with children, adolescents, adults, and the elderly in a wide variety of treatment settings, "both in-patient and out-patient, [and] a substantial proportion work in schools for both normal and exceptional children, as well as in halfway houses, prisons, rehabilitation centers, [and] general hospitals" (Rubin, 1980, p. 7). Art therapy is used as both a diagnostic tool and a treatment modality, with both individuals and families. The circumstances of clients range from well populations, whose goal is insight, to deeply disturbed individuals, whose goal is recovery from mental illness.

Theoretical Foundations

Assumptions About Human Nature

For every theory of personality, there is an application of that particular theory in art therapy. Therapists apply art therapy as part of such diverse approaches as humanistic, cognitive, behavioral, developmental, psychoanalytic, and eclectic methods. A separate volume would be required to enumerate the theoretical foundations of art therapy in general. In fact, such a volume exists—*Approaches to Art Therapy: Theory and Practice*, edited by Judith Rubin (1987). In this chapter, the two major approaches of Naumburg and Kramer will be discussed. Although both these eminent clinicians based their respective work mainly on the psychodynamic approach of Sigmund Freud, each emphasized particular aspects of Freudian theory.

According to Freud, human nature is driven by the interaction of three distinct systems: the id, the ego, and the superego. In brief, the id is one's subjective experience of reality and operates from a basic principle that has as its aim to seek pleasure and avoid pain. Since the id has no awareness of objective reality, the ego arises to carry on transactions with the objective world. The ego, then, selects appropriate avenues in the environment to satisfy needs or instincts present in the id. The superego emerges to supervise the actions of the ego so that those actions do not go against society's moral order. The types of tensions that the id seeks to reduce with the help of the ego and the superego are "(1) physiological growth processes, (2) frustrations, (3) conflicts, and (4) threats" (Hall & Lindzey, 1978, p. 49).

The two general methods used to reduce tensions are identification and displacement. Simply stated, identification is the process by which one assimilates certain features of another's personality in order to achieve the goal of satisfying needs and reducing tensions. Displacement is the process of substituting an object for a desired original object that is inaccessible. Displacement involves a compromise. Individuals turn their instinctual drives toward a substitute object because the desired object is unavailable. When individuals are under extreme pressure to relieve tension, they will resort to defense mechanisms. Defense mechanisms are unconscious processes that serve the function of reducing tension; in serving that function, however, reality is distorted or denied.

As individuals attempt to cope with life's stresses while at the same time avoiding pain and finding pleasure, some interactions with the environment produce material that is too disturbing or disruptive to the psyche. This material is relegated to the realm of the unconscious. Although the disturbing material exists without the individual being conscious of it, the material of the unconscious continues to drive outward behavior. The goal of therapy becomes to bring unconscious material into conscious awareness. In so doing, individuals are able to work through chaotic feelings and impulses and, ultimately, to develop mastery over their conflicts.

Assumptions About Conducting Art Therapy

The basic assumption of art therapy is that art is a vehicle for tapping into the unconscious to facilitate the exploration of internal conflicts. The visual arts are assumed to be closer to the unconscious than verbalizations are because, according to Jung (1964), visual perceptions are more archaic than verbal expressions. Rubin stated: "Freud recognized early in his work that many of his patients' most important communications were descriptions of visual images" (Rubin, 1987, p. 7).

Naumburg based her approach primarily on Freudian psychodynamics while incorporating Jung's (1964) ideas about the universality of symbols. She firmly believed that the only appropriate interpretation of an individual's art was the individual's own (Naumburg, 1966). Naumburg treated the material produced in the patient's art as a psychoanalyst would treat dream material. Art therapy, then, is an insight-oriented approach, in which insight is generated through the dialogue between patient and therapist concerning the patient's art.

Kramer's approach differs from Naumburg's with regard to Kramer's emphasis on a particular form of displacement called sublimation. Kramer defined sublimation as made up of "processes whereby primitive urges emanating from the id are transformed by the ego into complex acts that do not serve direct instinctual gratification" (1987, p. 26). In other words, the primitive urges residing in the id seek release and, because these primitive urges are asocial (since the id has no sense of objective reality), the urges must be mediated by the ego. When the ego sublimates the primitive urge, it directs that energy toward socially productive behaviors. Since the primitive urge is transformed by the ego into an urge that can be carried out in objective reality, something is lost. Sublimation involves some sort of compromise as one abandons the primitive urge for a new activity. Nonetheless, Kramer stated that "the pleasure generated in the new activity [is] exceptionally great" (1987, p. 27).

Whereas Naumburg viewed art therapy as a vehicle for psychotherapy in which the art and subsequent discussion are emphasized, Kramer emphasized the curative aspect of the creative process in and of itself. Kramer saw the therapist's role as an assistant in the process of sublimation. Naumburg conceptualized the art product as a means to discussion, leading to increased insight; Kramer conceptualized the art product as an end. Kramer stated that it is during the process of creating the art product that unconscious material is reconciled in the conscious mind. In the process of sublimation, unconscious material becomes conscious, and integration and wholeness are achieved.

Implementing Art Therapy

Art therapy generally begins with the therapist's explanation to the client that the method is used to help clients better understand themselves. An array of simple art media are generally used so that the client may choose among them and so that the emphasis is on self-expression, rather than on technical skill. The therapist must create an environment of acceptance in order to make beginning sessions as comfortable as possible.

In the initial stage of therapy, clients familiarize themselves with the media, the clinician, and the method. As clients begin to feel comfortable and secure with the therapist, they will develop the trust necessary to reveal themselves to the therapist through artwork and discussion.

Like free association, the process of art therapy is unstructured and open in the sense that clients are free to create whatever they wish. In the beginning stages of art therapy, the therapist's comments are minimized in order to encourage a relaxed flow of thoughts. The therapist pays close attention to any remarks a client makes, viewing that information as material for tentative hypotheses about the client's developmental level, internal conflicts, and defense mechanisms. Although the art therapist is aware of the reasons for referral, questions and comments are limited to the client's artwork, much as an analyst would limit comments to dream material.

Once the client has developed trust in the therapist and is engaged in the process of symbolic communication through art, the therapist increases the therapeutic dialogue with the client. As the interaction between client and therapist increases, the therapist tests and revises the tentative hypotheses arrived at in initial sessions. Since it is assumed that unresolved conflicts are the source of the client's difficulty, the therapist will now begin to explore unresolved conflicts with the client. This stage can be thought of as a working-through stage. The client's artwork continues to be the focus of expression and the catalyst for insight.

Means and Conditions for Implementing Art Therapy
The Therapist's Qualifications

In 1969, the American Art Therapy Association was formed with the following stated goals:

> The progressive development of the therapeutic use of art, the advancement of research, the improvement of standards of practice, the development of criteria for training art therapists, the encouragement of the development of professional training opportunities, and the exchange of information and experience through publications, meetings, and seminars. (AATA Bylaws, cf. Rubin, 1980, p. 7)

Today, there are more than 2,000 registered art therapists (ATRs). Moreover, a national certifying exam is being instituted that will lead to the new credential ATR-BC (Registered Art Therapist-Board Certified) (AATA, 1994).

Conditions for Conducting Art Therapy

Two components crucial to the success of art therapy sessions are the media used in sessions and the environment. Rubin (1984) suggested that the media be simple and sturdy, including such items as pens, markers, pastels, crayons, pencils, paints, and chalks, with appropriate paper for each. Simple media are not intimidating to the client and can be used without instruction. In addition, art therapy sessions are generally conducted with time constraints, and simple materials allow the client to complete a work in a limited time period. The art therapy room should be equipped with proper lighting and a work area including comfortable seating and work tables.

Limitations of Art Therapy
Contraindications

Art therapy is based on the assumption that everyone has a creative potential that can be elicited by the opportunity to express that creativity through art. As suggested by the range of applicability described earlier, art therapy is seen as an appropriate treatment for every population, with problems ranging from functional to organic disorders. In addition, art therapy is used with normal populations for enhancement purposes.

Hazards

The greatest hazard of art therapy is found when the inexperienced novice proceeds with therapy. Rubin (1980) stated that "few would now support the notion that a natural fondness for humans and art materials is sufficient preparation for the sophisticated diagnostic and therapeutic work to be done" (p. 7). Prior to the establishment of the American Art Therapy Association, art therapy was sometimes conducted by professionals and paraprofessionals who saw the possibilities inherent in self-expression through art, but who lacked the proper training. Practitioners of art therapy today concur that art therapists must have adequate training in both art and a relevant discipline, such as counseling, psychology, or social work, along with supervised clinical training.

The Effectiveness of Art Therapy

Art therapy is a rapidly growing field; for that reason, the method's effectiveness needs to be assessed. As is the case with most other therapies, the literature on art therapy contains numerous case studies of successful treatment outcomes with a wide variety of populations. According to Judith Rubin (1984), a respected and widely read practitioner, "much of the research being done in art therapy is of mediocre quality, and generally inadequate in both quantity and scope" (p. 181). She attributed the paucity and mediocrity of research in art therapy to the scarcity of individuals who possess training in both art therapy and research methods. In addition, her experience in conducting descriptive research has been that difficulties arise in attempting to assess both the outcome of art therapy and the process of creativity.

Presently the preferred methodology of the behavioral sciences involves quantitative rather than qualitative methods. As a result, the researcher must deal with the business of turning observations into numbers for purposes of statistical analyses. This process of quantifying data is problematic for researchers who attempt to perform empirical studies of art therapy. Since the creative experience of producing art is by its very nature subjective, one must ask whether quantitative research, which generally ignores the individual's experience in favor of uncovering general laws, is an adequate and appropriate method to understand and evaluate the process of art therapy.

References

American Art Therapy Association. (1994). American Art Therapy Association Newsletter, 27(2), 8.

Hall, C., & Lindzey, G. (1978). *Theories of personality*. New York: Wiley.

Jung, C. (1964). *Man and his symbols*. New York: Doubleday.

Kramer, E. (1987). Sublimation and art therapy. In J. Rubin (Ed.), *Approaches to art therapy: Theory and practice* (pp. 26–43). New York: Brunner/Mazel.

Naumburg, M. (1966). *Dynamically oriented art therapy: Its principles and practices*. New York: Grune & Stratton.

Rubin, J. (1980). Art therapy today. *Art Education, 33*(4), 6–8.

Rubin, J. (1984). *The art of therapy*. New York: Brunner/Mazel.

Rubin, J. (1987). *Approaches to art therapy: Theory and practice*. New York: Brunner/Mazel.

··

CHAPTER 20

Music
Therapy

··

■

Music therapy is the structured use of music or musical activities to restore, maintain, or enhance an individual's psychological well-being. The general purposes of this approach are to improve self-esteem, encourage self-expression, provide the opportunity for mastery and independence, and foster a sense of community in a group situation. Boxill stated that the broad goals of treatment are "(a) to effect personal change, (b) to facilitate interpersonal relations, (c) to nourish growth and development, (d) to contribute to the attainment of self-actualization, and (e) to assist the individual's entry into society" (1985, p. 6). Music therapists attest to the value of music as an avenue for eliciting an immediate psychological and physiological response from the client. Because of the experiential nature of this type of therapy, participants are grounded in the present and are enabled to experience fully their immediate reaction to the musical stimulus.

History of Music Therapy

Music has been used to treat both psychological and physiological problems since antiquity (Maranto, 1993). The use of music as an adjunct therapy in institutional settings dates back to the early 1920s and the pioneering work of Willem van de Wall and E. Thayer Gaston. Working with the Russell Sage Foundation, van de Wall studied the therapeutic aspects of music in such diverse settings as prisons, hospitals, and asylums. He firmly believed that music stimulates one's natural healing tendencies and plays a key role in emotionally disturbed individuals' recovery. Observing the behavior of institutionalized individuals, van de Wall noted that their inappropriate social behavior was replaced by socially appropriate behavior while they were participating in music-centered activities. He claimed that music stimulates memory and its accompanying emotions, and thus enables patients to uncover and express those emotions. Moreover, he believed that in order to recover from an illness, patients must be active participants in treatment, and he saw music as providing an excellent opportunity for such active participation. In essence, van de Wall believed that inmates in prisons and patients in hospitals alike possess positive characteristics that can be elicited through music. Thus, van de Wall saw music as a catalyst for eliciting the best of human nature (Tyson, 1981).

Both van de Wall and Gaston began their work in the arts, van de Wall as the choral director of the Washington Opera Company and Gaston as a conductor and later as a music educator. Gaston saw the role of the arts in general as benefiting individuals' mental well-being. Like van de Wall, Gaston was convinced that music has the potential to draw out the best in people. Because of the nonthreatening and nonverbal nature of music, Gaston felt music is a vehicle for individuals to experience a closeness in groups that might otherwise be repressed. The shared experience of music enables the patient and therapist, or a group of patients and their therapist, to form a connection and foster a feeling of belonging. He felt that when one participates in creating music, the participation fosters feelings of accomplishment, independence, and self-worth.

Gaston insisted that music be held in as high esteem as mathematics and science. He wrote extensively on the need for scholarly papers and research in the area of music education and music therapy. He argued that the arts are a basic necessity for everyone's mental and physical well-being (Gaston, 1960). Gaston believed that music provides a sensory stimulus necessary for the development of a healthy brain. He thought of music as having an important function in human development, both in the biological sphere and in fostering emotional experiences of a "positive and tender" nature (Gaston, 1958, p. 301).

Music therapy was developed in psychiatric hospitals both as an adjunct to psychiatric treatment and as a psychological stimulus in the hospital milieu. Prior to the introduction of psychotropic drugs in the 1950s, music was used on open wards to calm patients' moods and lessen anxiety and destructive behavior. As patients became less violent and confused through the use of tranquilizing drugs, music therapists expanded the goals of music therapy to include improving interpersonal relationships and raising self-esteem through self-actualization (Tyson, 1981). Music as a tool in group therapy provided a safe experience for those seriously disturbed patients who found other activities too threatening. After a successful experience with music, many patients were willing to involve themselves in other forms of therapy.

Although music had an obvious therapeutic effect, it was generally regarded as a strictly recreational pursuit until the period after World War II. At that point, hospitals began to use music therapy in the daily schedule of activities as a vital force in rehabilitation and recovery. The National Association for Music Therapy was established in 1950. The association's purpose is to support the use of music therapy in diverse settings, to oversee the education and training of music therapists, and to encourage research in music therapy.

Range of Applicability

Music therapy is commonly used as an adjunct therapy in institutional settings and outpatient group situations to facilitate social participation and self-expression. Michel (1985) discussed the use of music therapy with children, adolescents, and adults who may be mentally challenged, physically challenged, sight- or hearing-impaired, or learning-disabled. In addition, Michel recommended music therapy in treating individuals with behavioral or psychological disorders (of either a neurotic or a psychotic nature), drug addictions, and delinquent or criminal histories. Music therapy is also recommended for working with elderly populations at senior citizens' centers or in nursing homes, and as a primary therapy for treating stress disorders (Maranto, 1993).

Theoretical Foundations
Assumptions About Human Nature

The use of music as a therapeutic technique rests on particular assumptions made concerning music's influence on the emotions, and the changes that result in both the psyche and the body. Music is seen as presenting "pervasive sensory stimuli [that can give] us immediate sensations of reward and pleasure" (Thaut, 1990, p. 4). The theoretical foundations of music therapy center on assumptions about music's physiological and psychological effects.

Thaut (1990) offered a clear albeit rather technical discussion of the role of neuropsychological processes in music perception that offers scientific evidence for music's therapeutic value in eliciting change in individuals' moods. He stated that "there is considerable evidence that emotional reactions to music involve strong arousal of the autonomic nervous system" (p. 5). The central assumption of music therapy is that music is a stimulus that engages the individual in "an active thinking and feeling process" (Thaut, 1990, p. 19) that can be used to achieve desired therapeutic goals.

Gfeller stated that "music can reflect, influence, and alter emotional response" (1990, p. 59). Music is thus an effective tool to stimulate awareness and expression of feelings. Music not only stimulates communication, but is considered to constitute communication in itself. A therapeutic strength of music as a form of communication is that, unlike language, music does not require a rational or intellectual response. Whereas words may pose an intellectual obstacle for some individuals, music is free of that pressure. The use of music in a therapeutic setting provides the therapist with an avenue for tapping an immediate, vital experience in the client without the self-consciousness or misunderstandings that can arise during verbal exchanges.

An individual who suffers from some type of emotional disturbance or from circumstances that result in dysfunction generally feels isolated from others to some extent. Music is assumed to have the potential to heal this sense of isolation by facilitating contact between individuals as they share their experience of listening, whether that sharing is with the therapist or with other clients in a group setting. Patients are often sent to music therapy for the purpose of facilitating social interaction. Gaston (1968) stated that "music aids in the establishment or reestablishment of desirable interpersonal relationships" (p. v). Music therapists assume that music "provides a means by which self-expression is socially acceptable" (Sears, 1968, p. 33). Music, then, is a universally understood common denominator that can serve as a focal point for group interaction. When one is able to participate in a positive way in interpersonal situations, one experiences a rise in self-esteem, which is a desired component of a healthy self-concept.

Besides being a catalyst for self-expression and consequent satisfying social interactions, music can be used to bring about a number of other therapeutic goals. Thaut listed a number of changes that may occur in an individual as a result of the music therapy experience. Those changes include "altering of feeling states; rewarding self experiences; reduction of anxiety and tension; distraction from pathological concerns; heightened attention and concentration; stimulation and expression of feeling experiences; and insight into one's own thinking/feeling/behavior" (1990, p. 25). It is assumed that the client will perceive these positive feeling states as a benefit, so that these feelings will serve as a motivating force in producing behavioral change and a more permanent positive mood change.

Assumptions About Conducting Music Therapy

Because music therapy is not associated with one particular psychotherapeutic model or theory of personality, it may be adapted for use with any psychotherapeutic approach. Scovel (1990) identified the six major models to which music therapy may be adapted as the biomedical, behavioral, psychodynamic, cognitive, humanistic, and holistic-wellness models. Although individual music therapists may favor a particular philosophical orientation, they are not restricted to one and can be eclectic in their approach to treatment. For example, using a biomedical or holistic-wellness model, the music therapist may use music therapy in conjunction with relaxation exercises as a method of stress reduction. In the context of the behavioral model, music may be used as a contingency for the presence of desired behavioral goals. Using a humanistic model, the music therapist would take a nondirective stance in facilitating in clients the development of an internal frame of reference for exploring and expressing their experience of music therapy.

Key Concepts

Sears identified three concepts that provide the foundation for the process of music therapy: (1) experience with structure, (2) experience in self-organization, and (3) experience in relating to others (1968, p. 31). Sears pointed out that providing a particular experience for the client is the key to successful music therapy. Although therapists cannot change their clients' past experiences, they can provide their clients with a "present situation so that the effect of the past is altered for a more adequate future" (1968, p. 32).

Experience with structure.   When music is used as a therapeutic tool, particular demands are made on the client that require behaviors inherent to the structure of the musical experience. For example, the general mood of the individual (or group members) can be influenced by the type of musical selection. Slow music with simple melody lines tends to relax individuals, whereas a faster tempo with complex melodies and abrupt changes tends to energize people. In addition, music is a stimulus for ideas and associations. Music is a sensory experience that brings about responses on various levels, from neuromuscular reactions to intellectualization. In this way, music elicits increased sensory and cognitive activity.

Experience in self-organization.   One's experience in self-organization, according to Sears, "concerns inner responses that may only be inferred from behavior, and has to do with a person's attitudes, interests, values, and appreciations, with his meaning to himself" (1968, p. 39). This experience is highly idiosyncratic and is crucial in individuals' exploration of who they are. Music provides an opportunity for self-expression. Music therapists aim to provide a context in which clients' expressive responses will add to their self-knowledge and bring about an appreciation of self. Music can also lead to a cathartic experience in the Freudian sense of completing a previously interrupted sequence of self-expression. This component of the musical experience, then, brings about change through insight and revelation.

Experience in relating to others.   In the musical experience, self-expression is encouraged and socially acceptable behavior is rewarded. In this way, the individual gains valuable experience in relating to others. In addition, the individual is privy to others' experiences and comes to appreciate individual differences. Group experiences provide the individual with the opportunity to make comparisons between self and other. Consequently, the individual comes to appreciate both the similarities and differences that are always present in group situations. When the musical experience involves performance, the individual must learn to cooperate with the group for the purpose of presenting a cohesive performance. While this cooperation requires a certain degree of subordination of self, the group performance is possible only through the dedication of all members. As such, both individuality and a sense of belonging are fostered in the group experience.

Implementing Music Therapy

Broadly stated, a goal of music therapy is to facilitate clients' experience, identification, and expression of emotion. In addition, clients are helped to understand others' emotional communications and to control their own emotional behavior (Thaut, 1990). Although discussions of music therapy do not generally prescribe step-by-step procedures, four general steps are involved in planning a music therapy intervention, according to Peters:

> (1) defining the client's problem or area of need (assessment); (2) setting a goal for the client that will help ameliorate the problem or need; (3) planning appropriate music activities to help the client reach the goal; and (4) implementing the procedures and activities and evaluating the client's responses. (1987, p. 52)

The genre of music selected should be appealing to the client's taste. Music therapy can include a number of aspects of the musical experience, including listening, singing, learning to play an instrument, keeping a rhythm, dancing, composing, and performing.

The following example of music therapy involves listening and dancing to music. The setting is group therapy, and the psychotherapeutic approach is humanistic. The material is taken from a group session conducted by one of the authors in a residential treatment center for emotionally disturbed adolescents. The group consisted of six females whose diagnoses ranged from schizophrenia to delinquency. The therapist and two other group members played the guitar. During this particular group session, members were responding to a popular contemporary piece entitled *Home* by Karla Bonoff.

Therapist: How does that song make you feel, Laura?

Laura: Sad . . . just kind of sad.

Therapist: It makes me sad too. Why does it make *you* feel sad?

Laura: Thinking about being away from home . . . about the way it could be at home.

Dawn: Yeah. Especially that part that goes (*she sings*) "home sings me of sweet things" . . . "sweet things . . . good things."

Laura: Right. I wish things at home could be good.

Dawn: If they were you wouldn't be here!

Mary: (*To therapist*) Play that one about the dad who's never home! (*Referring to Harry Chapin's song* Cat's in the Cradle. *The song was played and everyone sang along on the chorus.*)

Therapist: (*To Mary*) What is it about that song that gets to you?

Mary: When the dad says "we'll have a good time then" but "then" never comes. I like to sing it *real* loud 'cause I feel angry. That's how parents can be . . . don't bother me now . . . later.

Therapist: Like they don't have time for you now.

Susan: Right. I'm not gonna be like that with my kids.

Therapist: You'll have time for your kids.

Susan: Right.

Therapist: How about you, Tanya? What do you feel when we sing that song?

Tanya: Tired! I'm tired of it! I wanna' hear *Proud Mary* 'cause I wanna leave group feeling happy. I'm tired of talking about home 'cause we're all stuck here and I don't wanna be here and I don't wanna be home either.

Laura: Yeah! Let's do *Proud Mary* and we can dance 'til we drop! Come on, Cara! (*Cara is the sixth member of the group, who joined recently. She has been silent thus far in the session.*) You need to dance too! Dance with us! (*Everyone agrees. The therapist plays* Proud Mary *and everyone sings; ultimately, the girls are up on their feet dancing to the intense rhythm of the rock-and-roll song.*)

Therapist: How do you feel now, Tanya?

Tanya: Like no one can bring me down! Like I'm bad!
Susan: (*Laughing*) Yeah! Look out!

In this example, music was used to facilitate the expression of feelings among group members and to encourage the participation of all group members. Cara was a 14-year-old girl from an abusive family, who was extremely withdrawn. This was the first group session in which she identified herself as a full member of the group through her involvement in dancing. The therapist had tried several times to draw her into the conversation, but these attempts failed. When Laura insisted that Cara take part in the dancing, Cara responded and danced with obvious pleasure and abandon. In subsequent sessions, Cara shared more of herself with the group.

Means and Conditions for Implementing Music Therapy
The Therapist's Qualifications

Music therapists are both therapists and musicians. As such, they must be skilled as musicians and as therapists, and they must know how to use music as a medium to foster positive development in the individual. Both the National Association for Music Therapy (NAMT) and the American Association for Music Therapy (AAMT) specify that an individual may apply for certification upon completing 4 years or more of coursework at an approved undergraduate college or university. In addition to an approved undergraduate degree, the individual must complete a pre-internship experience and an internship at an approved clinical site. Presently, a doctorate in music therapy does not exist, but one may pursue a master's degree. Peters (1987) provided the interested reader with specific details about the curricula involved in undergraduate degrees in music therapy and the content covered in the examination to become a board-certified music therapist.

Conditions for Conducting Music Therapy

The equipment needed to conduct music therapy will vary according to the type of musical experience involved in therapy. For example, if the focus of therapy were listening to relaxing music, in addition to cassette recordings and a cassette player, one would place comfortable chairs (or padded floor mats) in a darkened room. The type of activity, then, dictates the type of equipment needed. Maranto stated that it is also essential that visual and auditory distractions be minimized, "since auditory distractions in particular will interfere with the music procedures" (1993, p. 428).

Limitations of Music Therapy
Contraindications and Hazards

When one reads the literature on the application of music therapy to various disorders, it becomes apparent that music therapy is never contraindicated. Everyone can benefit from some type of musical experience. As with any other therapy, music therapy certainly has the potential to do harm rather than good when administered by an incompetent therapist. Maranto (1993) suggested that arbitrary selection of musical compositions by an untrained therapist may result in accessing undesired emotions such as frustration and irritation. As such, the therapist is advised to select music for therapeutic use on the basis of an individualized client assessment.

The Effectiveness of Music Therapy

Considerable research demonstrates the effectiveness of music therapy with a wide variety of clinical populations in promoting self-esteem, prosocial behavior, and a feeling of being in control of one's life (Peters, 1987; Michel, 1985). These clinical populations include the learning-disabled, the hearing-impaired, adults and children hospitalized for both physical illnesses and psychiatric conditions, mentally and physically challenged individuals, and prison populations. Smeltekop and Houghton reported research that suggests that "music therapy contributes, with other psychosocial therapies, to the rehabilitation component of treatment that is potentiated by administering psychotropic medication to the psychiatric patient" (1990, p. 124). In other words, it was found that patients' responses to medications were enhanced when medications were coupled with participation in music therapy. Maranto (1993) offered a comprehensive summary of research findings on physiological responses to music. In addition to her exhaustive summary, she offered a sound discussion of some methodological problems that may account for contradictory findings in the area of physiological responses to music. Researchers often assume that one can expect general or shared responses to musical stimuli from individuals. Maranto stated that "there are response patterns unique to each individual [and these responses vary with] age, health, life style, fitness, and situational variables" (1993, p. 410).

The considerable literature exploring the role of music therapy in treating a variety of disorders consists of case studies, experimental designs, and quasi-experimental designs. Although the results are impressive, two questions remain. First, how long-lasting are the results? The majority of studies include a pre- and post-treatment assessment of the beneficial effects of music therapy but fail to test the lasting effects of the intervention. Second, in quasi-experimental research, the trustworthiness of the results may suffer when subjects are not randomly assigned to experimental and control groups. Thus, we must ask if clients who received no adjunct therapy or a different adjunct therapy would exhibit a comparable improvement in functioning. Although these questions are important to address, we must applaud the growing number of practitioners of music therapy who are engaged in the ongoing process of researching the method's effects.

References

Boxill, E. H. (1985). *Music therapy for the developmentally disabled*. Rockville, MD: Aspen System.

Gaston, E. T. (1958). Music in therapy. In J. H. Masserman & J. L. Moreno (Eds.), *Progress in psychotherapy* (pp. 142–148). New York: Grune & Stratton.

Gaston, E. T. (1960). The place of music in the age of science. *Kansas Music Review, 22*, 13.

Gaston, E. T. (1968). *Music in therapy*. New York: Macmillan.

Gfeller, K. E. (1990). Music as communication. In R. F. Unkefer (Ed.), *Music therapy in the treatment of adults with mental disorders: Theoretical bases and clinical interventions* (pp. 50–62). New York: Macmillan.

Maranto, C. D. (1993). Music therapy and stress management. In P. M. Lehrer & R. L. Woolfolk (Eds.), *Principles and practice of stress management* (2nd ed., pp. 407–442). New York: Guilford Press.

Michel, D. (1985). *Music therapy: An introduction* (2nd ed.). Springfield, IL: Charles C Thomas.

Peters, J. (1987). *Music therapy: An introduction*. Springfield, IL: Charles C Thomas.

Sears, R. (1968). *Music therapy*. New York: Basic Books.

Scovel, M. A. (1990). Music therapy within the context of psychotherapeutic models. In R. F. Unkefer (Ed.), *Music therapy in the treatment of adults with mental disorders: Theoretical bases and clinical interventions* (pp. 96–108). New York: Macmillan.

Smeltekop, R. A., & Houghton, B. A. (1990). Music therapy and psychopharmacology. In R. F. Unkefer (Eds.), *Music therapy in the treatment of adults with mental disorders: Theoretical bases and clinical interventions* (pp. 109–125). New York: Macmillan.

Thaut, M. H. (1990). Neuropsychological processes in music perception and their relevance in music therapy. In R. F. Unkefer (Ed.), *Music therapy in the treatment of adults with mental disorders: Theoretical bases and clinical interventions* (pp. 3–32). New York: Macmillan.

Tyson, F. (1981). *Psychiatric music therapy: Origins and development.* New York: Creative Arts Rehabilitation Center.

CHAPTER 21

....

Dance
Therapy

....

■

Dance was first used in the United States as a form of psychotherapy in the early 1940s. The underlying philosophy of dance therapy was then, and is now, that body and mind are inseparable. The notion of the unity of body and mind is a leading topic of investigation in the fields of mental health and medicine today, although it met with resistance as late as a decade ago. With this increased acceptance of the inseparability of body and mind, dance therapists have found unexpected support for their position that a reciprocal influence exists between one's emotions and body movement, and that changes in body movement can bring about positive changes in one's psychic life and vice versa. Although dance has been recognized as a therapeutic tool in healing mind and body since civilization began, Western thought, until quite recently, conceived of body and mind as separate entities. As a result of such thinking, dance in the Western world had been thought of as only a performing art, with emphasis on technique—an attitude that has been changing, thanks to increased acceptance of dance therapy.

General Purpose of Dance Therapy

The goal of dance therapy is to enable the individual to experience a sense of wholeness as body, mind, and spirit are united through the use of body movement in dance (Levy, 1988). Liljan Espenak wrote that "in the movements, gestures, and stance of the body all emotions can be experienced, expressed, and perceived" (1981, p. xi). Dance therapy is a nonverbal technique and, as such, might be considered rather primitive. But Espenak believed that it is this primitive quality that allows dance to reach and release trauma that resists verbal expression. Dance, then, provides an opportunity for catharsis, a deep release of tension, through the releasing of emotions in movement.

History of Dance Therapy

Most of the founders of dance therapy began their careers in modern dance, a movement that emerged in the early 1900s as a reaction against the highly technical performances of the only form of dance considered to be art—namely, classical ballet. For the pioneers of modern dance, ballet had become a form of expression that required dancers to adhere to a structure they felt was unnatural and stultifying. Dancers such as Isadora Duncan (1878–1927) saw dance as an avenue for expressing one's inner emotions and for providing a cathartic experience for one's audience.

As the modern dance movement took hold in the United States in the early 1900s, Europe was home to a number of influential figures in improvisational and expressive movement. Students of modern dance were encouraged to build on the basic elements of dance by uncovering their own individual interpretations of emotional expression. In essence, these modern dance teachers were dance therapists for their students. Teachers and students of modern dance were revolutionaries and visionaries; as such, they were open to radical elements of the intellectual climate of the period. It should come as no surprise that modern dance was influenced by the work of Sigmund Freud. Freud's work held great appeal for these free spirits, as he advocated the open expression of feelings and emphasized the power of the subconscious mind on the outward behavior of everyday life. Through modern dance, the body gave expression to the inner workings of the mind, and the power of that experience was not lost on the practitioners of dance. Dance teachers such as Mary Whitehouse and Marian Chase turned their attention to the psychotherapeutic value of modern dance, and in the 1940s dance therapy began (Levy, 1988). Levy (1988) offered a comprehensive review of the clinical styles of six major American pioneers who developed the foundations of theory and practice for dance therapy as it exists today. According to Levy, those six pioneers are Marian Chase, Blanche Evan, Liljan Espenak, Mary Whitehouse, Trudi Shoop, and Alma Hawkins.

Dance therapy was first practiced in psychiatric hospitals, but in the 1950s, a small number of dance therapists began to include private clients in their practices. They saw themselves as primary therapists and immersed themselves in the study of theories of personality in order to pin their intuitive knowledge on an existing framework. By the end of the 1950s, the work of outlining the basic teachings of dance therapy theory had begun.

Range of Applicability

During its infancy, the practice of dance therapy was limited to use with deeply disturbed hospitalized populations. In the 1950s, the scope of dance therapy expanded to include work with neurotic individuals and others without any particular diagnosis, but whose goals included achieving an expanded awareness of self. During the last two decades, dance therapy has been made available to a variety of populations, including physically and mentally challenged individuals; the elderly; and autistic, learning-disabled, and school-phobic children. More recently, Levy reported that dance therapy has been used "with families, with traumatic brain injury patients, with sexually abused children, and with individuals suffering from eating disorders" (1988, p. 249). Dance therapy may be used with these various populations either as a primary therapy or as an adjunct therapy.

Theoretical Foundations
Assumptions About Human Nature

In their search for a theoretical framework, dance therapists found that the disciplines of psychology, sociology, and anthropology did, in fact, address the nonverbal aspects of emotional expression. Beginning in the 1930s, various scholars carried out extensive research aimed at exploring the connection between emotional expression and body postures. Bernstein cited numerous studies conducted by such luminaries as William James and Gordon Allport, in which evidence was found to indicate that, indeed, "every emotion has its expression in the postural model of the body" (Bernstein, 1975, p. 1) and "complex dynamic dispositions exert a dynamic determination upon specific movements" (p. 2). Once the relationship had been established between bodily motion and emotion, Wilhelm Reich, a physician and psychotherapist, began to use body movement in psychotherapy. Nonverbal communication was especially valuable with patients who had either regressed to the point where they had ceased to verbalize, or had not yet progressed to the verbal level.

The basic view underlying dance therapy is that an individual's bodily postures are the physical manifestations of that individual's psychic life. In addition, somatic processes produce a certain degree of change in one's psychic life, just as changes in one's psychic life can produce change in one's somatic processes. Espenak stated that "in posture, in pose, in mannerism, in attitude, in gesture, in movement, and in breathing, the individual communicates with an eloquence that transcends his verbalizations and that surpasses his own perceptions of his inner state" (1981, p. 4). In other words, an individual's body expresses far more about the individual than the individual's words or even awareness. Dance therapists attend to the language of the body, based on the thinking involved in psychokinetic theory.

Psychokinetic theory, according to Paul Schilder (1950), stated that outward movement has a reciprocal relationship to inner movement. In other words, a muscular sequence can evoke an emotional state, and an emotional state can evoke a muscular sequence. For example, many of us are aware of the high that results from running, or the exhilaration we feel during dancing. Also, therapists often ask patients to breathe deeply in order to encourage relaxation. These are examples of emotional states induced by muscular sequences. On the other hand, we can perceive the emotional state of depressed or bereaved individuals from their bodily stance, which might include arms wrapped around their chest, slumped shoulders, or sagging face muscles. These are examples of emotions' causing particular muscular sequences.

The psychoanalytic technique has included work with particular muscular sequences to induce emotional states. For example, Espenak (1981) described Ferenczi's work with easing muscular rigidity by encouraging the patient's conscious control of muscular tension. Ferenczi felt that his work in this area brought him into contact with the "unconscious mechanism of repression itself" (Espenak, 1981, p. 6). Wilhelm Reich (1949) developed the notion of character armor, a term used to describe those patients who had difficulty verbalizing thoughts and feelings and who developed a somatic defense in the form of muscular tension. Reich felt that the way to get past these patients' defenses was to use muscular manipulation, which he believed released repressed psychological material.

Humanistic theory's major contribution to dance therapy is found in its emphasis on a nonjudgmental, nonanalytical, and antidiagnostic approach to emotional disturbance. Dance therapy also draws from the work of Carl Rogers (1961) and Abraham Maslow (1970), in that its aim is to uncover processes that are involved in fulfilling one's potential and moving toward health rather than concentrating on pathology. Dance therapy shares the humanists' notion that human beings possess an innate tendency to excel and create. The aim of dance therapy is to uncover those blockages that keep us from moving in a positive direction.

Harry Stack Sullivan's (1953) contribution to the field of psychology, and dance therapy in particular, was his notion that the individual can be understood only in the context of culture and interpersonal relations. Sullivan's work with schizophrenic patients focused on engaging in an interpersonal relationship with them, which began at the patient's developmental level. Dance therapists followed Sullivan's lead in engaging severely withdrawn patients in nonverbal interactions. Dance therapists agreed with Sullivan's notion that since one's self-concept is formed out of one's experience in interpersonal relationships, the self-concept can be healed through contact with others in interpersonal relationships.

Assumptions About Conducting Dance Therapy

Liljan Espenak, considered a leading pioneer of dance therapy, developed her own particular approach involving the use of movement as therapy. In *Dance Therapy: Theory and Application* (1981), Espenak listed what she considered to be the most influential factors leading to effective dance therapy. Although Espenak's approach to dance therapy is distinct from others, the following factors as elaborated by Espenak can be considered universal assumptions about the conduct of dance therapy.

1. Emotions are stimulated and released through body movements and gestures. The dance therapist, in her or his awareness of all body movement, is able to recognize where emotion is either being released or inhibited. The aim of the dance therapist is to release feelings that have been blocked both verbally and physically.

2. Nonverbal activity is a form of contact and communication. Dance therapy provides the patient with the opportunity to be in a nonverbal conversation with others. For patients who are reluctant or unable to engage in verbal communication, dance offers a nonthreatening alternative. In addition, movement permits the expression of feelings that have been heretofore unavailable to the patient's consciousness.

3. The dance therapist maintains a nonthreatening stance with patients. In this way, the dance setting decreases, rather than increases, anxiety in patients. In dance, patients are able to achieve a similar experience to that of the dream state, in which the controlling functions of the ego are suspended.

4. While patients experience the freedom of movement present in dance therapy and the impact of the rhythm on the senses, they are enabled to

experience sheer joy, both physical and emotional. Espenak stated that "dance therapy is in fact one, if not the only one, of the psychotherapeutic approaches that can counterbalance some of the pain of dealing with unconscious conflict with the experience of physically oriented release and joy" (1981, p. 10).

5. Rhythm is perhaps the most crucial component in dance therapy. When patients become engaged in dance, a surrender to the rhythm takes place that allows them to express deep emotional and psychic needs as they move in time to the music. In addition, rhythm is the catalyst for involving oneself with others in a participatory way, as experience is shared simultaneously. The rhythm is the thread that connects the unique experience of each individual with the common experience of the group.

Implementing Dance Therapy

According to Espenak (1981), evaluation precedes therapy as the dance therapist assesses clients with regard to their physiological condition. Evaluation includes determining "which physiological resources are inherent and which are limited by psychological stress" (Espenak, 1981, p. 42). In other words, each individual possesses physical characteristics such as height, strength, joint flexibility, and stamina that are due to genetic inheritance or developmental circumstances. Certain of the client's physical characteristics, however, result from psychological stress, and those characteristics will be targeted for change. The results of the evaluation provide the basis for planning a treatment program that accounts for both the psychological needs and the physiological condition of the client.

Dance therapy, in its broadest sense, emphasizes the use of dance and movement as the primary expressive modality in treatment. Presently, the practice of dance therapy incorporates a wide range of clinical styles and theoretical perspectives; there is no uniform approach to treatment. Today's dance therapists practice as primary therapists or as ancillary therapists. Whereas some dance therapists practice with a psychoanalytic perspective, others approach their work from a humanistic perspective. Diversity, then, is apparent in the broad spectrum of theoretical frameworks represented in the field of dance therapy.

Whatever a particular therapist chooses as a theoretical base, dance therapists share a common goal—to encourage the emotional expression and communication of a whole person. The underlying philosophy present at the beginning remains the same—namely, that the body and the mind are inseparable.

Means and Conditions for Implementing Dance Therapy
The Therapist's Qualifications

In the 1950s, the individual who wished to become a dance therapist received training through a private apprenticeship with an established dance therapist. In the late 1960s, undergraduate-level courses in dance therapy were being offered at some colleges and universities. By 1970, one could earn a master's degree in dance therapy, with the first being offered at Hunter College in 1971 (Levy, 1988). Presently, the American Dance Therapy Association is devoted to establishing guidelines for the curriculum for graduate degree programs and for levels of professional competence.

Limitations of Dance Therapy
Contraindications and Hazards

Since dance therapy requires that clients possess a degree of control of movement, the very seriously physically handicapped individual would not be a candidate for dance therapy. Espenak (1981) felt that dance therapy would be hazardous for hyperactive children, as a result of the stimulating rhythms and movements involved. According to Espenak, other populations for whom dance therapy would be inappropriate include mentally retarded individuals in custodial care, exhibitionistic individuals, and adults who have a history of violent acting-out. For exhibitionistic and violent individuals, the physical aspect of dance therapy might serve to reinforce those problematic behaviors.

The Effectiveness of Dance Therapy

Studies attempting to ascertain the effectiveness of dance therapy have generally been case histories of successful therapy. Dance therapy has been reported to be effective with a wide variety of populations, including patients diagnosed with schizophrenia (Siegel, 1984), autism (Siegel, 1984), neurosis (Espenak, 1981), character disorder (Espenak, 1981), depression (Bernstein, 1975), and families in therapy (Dulicai, 1976). In general, these case studies describe the condition of the patients at the onset of treatment, the specific techniques employed to treat the problems, and the specific changes that occurred immediately after treatment. This type of methodology is plagued by the usual questions that arise when research is carried out without control groups, assessment of the long-term effects of therapy, or objective measures of change. As is the case with other therapies that attempt to wed the arts to psychotherapy, it is rare that practitioners are skilled in both the methodology of empirical inquiry and dance therapy. Presently, dance therapists are aware of the need to encourage, facilitate, and disseminate research (Levy, 1988). Both the American Alliance for Health, Physical Education, Recreation, and Dance, and the American Dance Therapy Association are professional organizations that offer support for professionals interested in conducting and disseminating research on dance therapy.

References

Bernstein, P. (1975). *Theory and methods in dance-movement therapy.* Dubuque, IA: Kendall/Hunt Publishing.

Dulicai, D. (1976). Movement therapy with families. *APA Monograph, Special Education*, 1104.

Espenak, L. (1981). *Dance therapy theory and application.* Springfield, IL: Charles C Thomas.

Levy, F. (1988). *Dance/movement therapy: A healing art.* Reston, VA: American Alliance for Health, Physical Education, Recreation, and Dance.

Maslow, A. (1970). *Motivation and personality.* New York: Harper & Row.

Reich, W. (1949). *Character analysis.* New York: Noonday Press.

Rogers, C. R. (1961). *On becoming a person.* Boston, MA: Houghton Mifflin.

Schilder, P. (1950). *The image and appearance of the human body.* New York: International Universities Press.

Siegel, E. V. (1984). *Dance-movement therapy, the mirror of ourselves: The psychoanalytic approach.* New York: Human Sciences Press.

Sullivan, H. S. (1953). *The interpersonal theory of psychiatry.* New York: Norton.

PART VII

....

Relaxation-Based
Approaches

....

CHAPTER 22

....

Biofeedback

....

■

M any factors have contributed to the increasing use of biofeedback as a treatment modality in the broad field of behavior change methods. Moreover, the biofeedback field is multidisciplinary, and a large variety of different professionals make use of biofeedback. Consequently, the term *biofeedback* cannot fully convey the complexity and diversity of this field, which is continuing its rapid evolution. Because biofeedback applications have been made in many different areas, using a great variety of instruments, it is difficult to arrive at a satisfactory definition for *biofeedback* that conveys the full contemporary meaning of the term. The following, however, is a good start:

> Biofeedback may be defined as the technique of using equipment (usually electronic) to reveal to human beings some of their internal physiological events, normal and abnormal, in the form of visual and auditory signals in order to teach them to manipulate these otherwise involuntary or unfelt events by manipulating the displayed signal. This technique inserts a person's volition into the gap of an open feedback loop—hence the artificial name *biofeedback*, a name that some scientists and clinicians abhor for linguistic and other reasons. (Basmagian, 1983, p. 1)

History of Biofeedback

Some reviewers have claimed that the term *biofeedback* became accepted at a research symposium on clinical biofeedback held in Santa Monica, California in October 1969. Reportedly, some scientists argued for simply calling the phenomenon *operant conditioning*, and others preferred the term *self-regulation*; but those who eventually prevailed favored use of the term *biofeedback* (Orne, 1982, p. 422). The term has retained its appeal and continues to be used today, even though some researchers (for example, Tursky, 1982) have questioned its appropriateness. One reason for the term's persistence may be its institutionalization in the name of the Biofeedback Research Society, founded in 1968; the name was changed in 1976 to the Biofeedback Society of America. The objectives of the society are "to advance biofeedback as a means of human welfare," to encourage scientific research, clinical use, and diffusion of knowledge about biofeedback (Butler, 1978, p. 295). Judging by the number of publications about biofeedback and its varied applications, the Biofeedback Society of America has succeeded in accomplishing its major objectives.

It has been reported that biofeedback research in the former Soviet Union began in the late 1950s, with pioneer studies being carried out at a number of research institutes. Much of this research was carried out in the fields of experimental medicine, neurophysiology, and related areas (Sokhadze & Shtack, 1991). These same authors reported that biofeedback continues to be a widely used method in both experimental and clinical institutes. This report suggests that biofeedback, despite initially being viewed with considerable suspicion and suspected of being a fad, has found broad acceptance as a viable field of research and clinical application in the United States as well as abroad.

Range of Applicability

Clinical use of biofeedback methods involves a diverse and ever-expanding range of applications. "Every month seems to bring about new applications of biofeedback" (Budzynski, Stoyva, & Peffer, 1980, p. 193). For example, a highly regarded volume on clinical biofeedback (White & Tursky, 1982a) contains chapters on biofeedback use in the treatment of hypertension, cardiac arrhythmias, migraine, Raynaud's disease, chronic neurological disorders, epilepsy, tension headaches, and anxiety. Biofeedback has also been used with patients who suffer from fecal incontinence, bruxism, vascular and mixed headaches, nocturnal enuresis, spasmodic torticollis, hemiplegia and paraplegia, cerebral palsy, and disorders involving peripheral nerve damage, incomplete spinal cord lesions, and lower motor neuron lesions. In addition, biofeedback has been used in treating hyperactivity and learning disabilities, phobias, insomnia, chemical addictions, and various sexual disorders (Schwartz & associates, 1987). This list of clinical applications is certainly not exhaustive. It also does not include one of the more popular early applications—namely, the use of biofeedback to increase alpha density, which was originally thought to help individuals to reach the higher level of relaxation often associated with such methods as transcendental meditation or yoga. The excitement concerning alpha and EEG biofeedback in general has dissipated in view of recent, more sophisticated theoretical and conceptual analyses.

Theoretical Foundations
Assumptions About Human Nature

Although writers on clinical applications of biofeedback have not addressed the issue of normal human development extensively, their conceptualizations appear to be based on the notion that biological homeostasis is essential to an organism's proper development. This insight is certainly not a new one, since the notion of biological homeostasis goes back to the important work of Claude Bernard. When disorder occurs, it is assumed that it involves some form of disequilibrium. Aberrant physiological responses associated with disorders typically treated using biofeedback techniques are assumed to have started out as predictable adaptive reactions of the organism that somehow exceeded the acceptable range. As stated by Gaarder and Montgomery, "disease conditions can be defined by the fact that some homeostatic mechanism is deranged. Most often, this will mean that the values of physiological measures are outside of their normal limits" (1981, p. 22). Gaarder and Montgomery have also made the important point that, although there are salient variables that may be controlled with biofeedback, in other instances of deranged homeostasis, a quantitative variable may be outside its normal limits but, for a variety of reasons, cannot be used as a feedback parameter. Examples of such variables include white blood counts in infections or elevated blood sugars in diabetes.

Homeostasis may be disturbed by a variety of factors, including stress. In the healthy person, homeostasis is maintained by homeostatic adaptive control systems (HACS), which are feedback-mediated and thereby control the value of the salient psychophysiological variables, keeping them within acceptable limits (Gaarder & Montgomery, 1981). Precisely how HACS function is an important issue, but beyond the scope of this chapter. Suffice it to note that the flow of information between the environment and various components of the organism is of central importance. This flow of information occurs from the environment to the organism, as well as from the organism to the environment. Homeostasis thus is maintained on the basis of the organism's internal feedback mechanisms. This conceptualization opens up the possibility of considering biofeedback "as a way of imposing an additional external feedback loop upon the already existing feedback loops of the homeostatic adaptive control system (HACS)" (Gaarder & Montgomery, 1981, pp. 23–24).

Another conceptualization occasionally invoked by proponents of biofeedback is that both normal and disordered behavior is at least partly learned. This assumption justifies the use of biofeedback (viewed as a specialized learning technique) to alter the maladaptive (and partly learned) responses that constitute the disorder to be treated (Budzynski, Stoyva, & Peffer, 1980).

Assumptions About Conducting Biofeedback Therapy

At the outset, a distinction should be drawn between, on the one hand, *biofeedback* as a term used in research to refer to external psychophysiological feedback, and, on the other hand, biofeedback therapy or biofeedback training, which is likely to be used in clinical settings. For example, White and Tursky (1982b) distinguished between narrow and broad conceptualizations of biofeedback. They pointed out that the former reflects the paradigm of operant conditioning of autonomic responses, which was first reported by Miller (1969) and DiCara (1970), and which involves the presentation of feedback following the occurrence of a desired response. Assuming that this response enhances the functioning of the organism, its probability of occurrence will increase. White and Tursky pointed out that this conceptualization requires neither a biological nor a cognitive explanation, since the only determining factor is the contiguity between stimulus and response. White and Tursky (1982b, p. 445) further observed that "when operant procedures were initially applied to uninformed human subjects, the results proved to be statistically significant but clinically unimportant, and subsequent studies actively instructed the subjects in the process of altering their responses." Thus, they noted that conceptualizations of clinical biofeedback increasingly relied on something the operant conditioning proponents shied away from— namely, intraorganismic biological and cognitive processes.

As biofeedback became accepted in an increasing number of applied settings, many definitions of feedback referred not just to biological and cognitive processes, but also to objectives. Olson (1987) reviewed a host of definitions of biofeedback and suggested that the various definitions can be classified into process definitions, which describe the processes involved in biofeedback; teleological definitions, which emphasize the goals of bio- feedback; and combined definitions, which contain features of both. He pro- posed a synthesis of various extant definitions, which included seven procedural elements (1 to 7) and three goals (8 to 10):

> As a process, applied biofeedback is (1) a group of therapeutic procedures that (2) utilizes electronic or electromechanical instruments (3) to accurately measure, process, and "feed back" to persons (4) information with rein- forcing properties (5) about their neuromuscular and autonomic activity, both normal and abnormal, (6) in the form of analog or binary, auditory and/or visual feedback signals. (7) Best achieved with a competent bio- feedback professional, (8) the objectives are to help persons develop greater awareness and voluntary control, (9) by first controlling the external signal, (10) and then by the use of internal psychophysiological cues. (p. 35)

Although this definition is quite comprehensive and useful, particularly for the practitioner, the assumptions underlying the conduct of biofeedback as so defined are by no means universally agreed upon. White and Tursky (1982b, pp. 445–447) list ten unique (though somewhat overlapping) para- digms that have been used to conceptualize, define, and explain clinical bio- feedback. Their list includes operant conditioning, response learning, bioengineering, response discrimination and control, motor learning and rehabilitation, systems disregulation, multimodal therapy and lifestyle change, relaxation therapy, instructional effects, and finally various types of placebo effects. The order of these paradigms moves from noncognitive or biologically determined modes of information processing toward increasing inclusion of cognitive processes.

The complexity of the clinical biofeedback field assures that some dis- agreements will persist about what makes biofeedback effective and what spe- cific physiological and psychological processes are involved. In an effort to clarify some of these issues, Budzynski and colleagues (1980) have made a useful distinction between direct and indirect methods of biofeedback. Direct biofeedback involves the measurement (monitoring) of a particular response, followed by modification of its frequency or magnitude through reinforce- ment. For example, patients suffering from tension (muscle contraction) headache may be taught to relax the pertinent muscles. In indirect bio- feedback, one response is measured and altered, and the change is assumed to affect other, related physiological responses that may not be as readily accessed and measured. For example, a patient may be taught muscle relaxation on the assumption that it affects other physiological activity that will serve to decrease anxiety.

Implementing Biofeedback
Preliminary Considerations

In applying biofeedback in clinical settings, serious consideration must be given to whether biofeedback is appropriate for a particular patient. Clearly, biofeedback should be used only in the treatment of conditions for which its efficacy has been demonstrated. In addition, it is important to implement a method of stepped care or successive hurdles—based on what has occasionally been called the principle of least intervention. This kind of approach is gradual, using less intrusive, expensive, and time-consuming treatment first before moving on to more complex, expensive, and time-consuming approaches (Schwartz & associates, 1987). For example, in the treatment of some conditions, simple relaxation procedures are appropriate instead of biofeedback, when there is reason to expect that such relaxation procedures may adequately remedy the problem. Such a conservative approach is generally considered good practice and enhances the practitioner's credibility with both patients and the insurance companies who may pay for services.

Because the patient's motivation is critical in biofeedback procedures, patients must be well informed about their choices concerning alternative treatments, the cost of therapy, and the probability of achieving the desired outcome. In addition, the therapist contemplating the use of biofeedback may need to make decisions about the impact of instrumentation on the patient's motivation and compliance. Schwartz and associates (1987) suggested that in some cases the availability of data produced by instruments used in biofeedback may help to increase patients' confidence in themselves and in the therapist, so that instrumentation acts as a valuable motivational tool. Consequently, in some cases instrumentation may be used quite early in the initial evaluative process in order to lay the groundwork for the eventual full-fledged use of biofeedback.

Initial Evaluation and Initial Biofeedback Session

Budzynski and colleagues (1980) have stressed that biofeedback is a multidimensional approach to modifying disordered behavior. Initial analysis of the patient should include a review of the history of the patient's difficulties, the perceived antecedents and consequences of the disordered behavior, and the precise nature of these behaviors themselves. As this information is assembled and evaluated, the therapist can engage in some initial discussions with the patient about biofeedback's potential suitability. Once a preliminary decision to proceed with biofeedback is made, an initial physiological evaluation needs to be conducted. At this time the therapist has an opportunity to explain the operation of the instrumentation to the patient and to reassure the patient that properly functioning instrumentation cannot harm or hurt the patient in any way. One thing that must be examined initially is whether the physiologic response that represents the potential target behavior shows variability outside of the normal range. If the target response does not vary outside the range of normal functioning, then the use of biofeedback would be inappropriate. Of course, such variability may conceivably occur outside the clinician's office, but not during the physiological evaluation. In those cases, it may be useful to proceed with an alternative approach to dealing with the problem behavior that is not based on instruments, provided that other evidence is available to support the diagnosis (Schwartz & associates, 1987).

Once the patient and therapist agree that biofeedback is appropriate, they should also agree on the specific problem to be treated and the objectives to be accomplished through biofeedback training. This agreement should be followed by an explanation of what biofeedback is, how instruments are used in biofeedback, what biofeedback has been shown to accomplish in relation to the patient's problem, and what its limitations are. Budzynski and colleagues (1980) pointed out that patients frequently are unaware that thoughts are capable of producing physiological changes. Moreover, Budzynski and colleagues suggested that patients should clearly understand the nature of maladaptive responses in the cognitive, physiological, and overt behavioral response systems. Particularly important to explain are such practical matters as the length and frequency of sessions, as well as the expected duration of the overall treatment (Brown, 1977). Patients should be told that the length of treatment depends on several different factors, including the nature of the problem, the age of the patient, and ongoing environmental problems. In order to avoid creating unrealistic expectations, a wide range may be given—for example, from 10 to 30 sessions (Budzynski, Stoyva, & Peffer, 1980).

Some writers have noted that cognitive preparation of patients for biofeedback does not always receive the time and attention it deserves. For example, Shaw and Blanchard (1983) pointed out that well-prepared, highly motivated patients are best able to generate the active participation required for successful biofeedback treatment. Moreover, various researchers have noted that placebo effects, as well as specific effects associated with biofeedback, play a role in modifying the target behaviors (Furedy, 1987; Orne, 1982).

Implementing Biofeedback Training Sessions

Assuming that the patient is cognitively prepared for biofeedback training, the stage is set for the actual implementation. At the first session, the patient is shown the instrumentation, and the therapist explains how it will be used to provide biofeedback. The patient should be given an opportunity to ask questions and to obtain reassurance about the instrumentation's safety and effectiveness. The patient is then attached to the instrument. The therapist explains precisely how the feedback signals will change depending on variations in the patient's physiological activity. The instrument is then tested and adjusted so as to be maximally sensitive to small differences in the patient's physiological functioning. Baseline segments are recorded so as to evaluate the patient's unique physiological activity and to lay the groundwork for determining the stability of such activity across sessions.

An example (adapted from Brown, 1977, pp. 194–196) may be useful in illustrating how biofeedback training sessions are conducted from beginning through end. Let's assume that a patient has agreed to participate in biofeedback training sessions to achieve complete deep muscle relaxation. The most likely instrument to be used in such an approach would be an electromyography (EMG) instrument, which monitors the relative contraction or relaxation of a given muscle. At the beginning of each training period, the instrument is adjusted to reflect the slightest possible changes in muscle tension. The patient is then instructed about muscle relaxation and the various strategies that have been shown effective in producing muscle relaxation. These techniques could include progressive muscle relaxation, autogenic training, imagery exercises, or other techniques. The patient is then instructed to monitor the changes in EMG activity produced by his or her efforts to relax. The patient may do so during several 10- to 20-minute periods, which are always followed by brief rest periods. The therapist may offer encouragement or discuss the patient's initial response to the biofeedback experience in between training periods, particularly during the first several sessions. At the end of each session, the therapist may help the patient assess the patient's subjective experience of progress or lack thereof. The patient is then instructed in the use of homework assignments, such as muscle relaxation procedures based on the Jacobson method.

Each subsequent session may be used to review progress and ways that the patient has found useful to relax outside the actual biofeedback training sessions. Objective as well as subjective changes in the target behavior should be discussed; if necessary, adjustments may be made in the overall training program. The actual feedback training periods may be set up so as to make the task more difficult and to permit the patient to learn not only to decrease muscle tension, but also to increase it. The latter task would be designed to increase the patient's control and confidence. Assuming that the patient has made satisfactory progress, the final series of biofeedback training sessions would be designed to ensure that the patient has learned to control the target behavior and can exercise this control in real-life situations, away from biofeedback instrumentation and the therapist's support. These ends may be accomplished by having the patient control his or her tension without the aid of the feedback instrument, but with the therapist monitoring the patient's effectiveness. Before the biofeedback training is terminated, final recordings should be made of the physiological as well as psychological changes that have occurred from the first session through the last. Finally, patients should be encouraged to return for booster sessions as needed.

Means and Conditions for Implementing Biofeedback
The Therapist's Qualifications

Because many different professions use biofeedback technology, arriving at a single job description for biofeedback therapists and technicians that is acceptable to those involved is a difficult undertaking. Schwartz (1987) noted that such titles as biofeedback therapist, biofeedback technician, clinical psychophysiologist, biofeedback clinician, and biofeedback practitioner have been in common usage, as have others. This variety of titles exists even though the Biofeedback Certification Institute of America (BCIA) and the American Association of Biofeedback Clinicians (AABC) have both offered certification in the field of biofeedback. Certification may also be obtained at different levels. Although those who obtain such certification may wish to refer to the certification part of their professional identity, most professionals who have other identities—such as psychologist, psychiatrist, dentist, or clinical social worker—may be reluctant to give up their traditional discipline titles in favor of a new title reflecting their biofeedback expertise. As a consequence, many different titles continue to be used in the area of biofeedback.

However an individual may wish to refer to his or her professional identity, those who practice biofeedback techniques should possess the following capabilities and qualities, according to Schwartz and associates (1987, pp. 467–468):

1. Training, knowledge, experience, and skill with a variety of non-instrumentation-based physiological self-regulatory procedures.
2. Training, knowledge, experience, and skill with at least a few biofeedback modalities, including electromyography (EMG), temperature biofeedback, and electrodermal biofeedback.

3. At least a fundamental knowledge of behavioral analysis and behavior therapy principles and procedures.

4. At least a fundamental knowledge of several disorders typically treated in clinical settings (such as headache, hypertension, anxiety, Raynaud's disease, sleep-onset insomnia, bruxism and myofacial pain, and tension myalgias).

5. At least a fundamental knowledge of the research literature concerning efficacy, procedures, theoretical issues, and practical issues.

6. Training, knowledge, experience, and skills for providing other stress management therapies, including cognitive therapies, relaxed breathing, assertiveness, and systematic desensitization, among others.

7. Good interviewing skills.

8. Ability to write clear, well-organized, and complete reports with appropriate use of terminology.

9. Good verbal communication skills, in order to provide appropriate cognitive preparation of patients, to create realistic but positive expectations, and to communicate with other professionals.

10. A mature attitude, and the ability to establish rapidly and to maintain positive therapeutic relationships with patients and to relate to them easily in a sensitive and empathetic manner.

11. Ability to be responsible, reliable, well-organized, flexible, and relaxed (at least with patients).

12. Ability to work relatively independently, at least for some sessions or short series of sessions.

13. Willingness and ability to demonstrate fundamental knowledge and fundamental instrumentation skills in written and practical examinations through the BCIA or the AABC.

Schwartz also identified the specific duties of biofeedback therapists, noting, however, that some individuals who may have less extensive responsibilities might consider a title such as biofeedback technician. Those individuals who wish to become biofeedback therapists or technicians should consult with the BCIA or the AABC, which is a part of the American Board of Clinical Biofeedback (ABCB). They should also consult the professional association most closely identified with their primary professional practice.

Conditions for Conducting Biofeedback

The most important requirement for the conduct of biofeedback, as opposed to other therapeutic techniques, is the instrumentation. Tursky (1982) described the development of biofeedback instrumentation as the con-

sequence of a symbiotic relationship between psychophysiology and engineering. He described the early development of relatively simple instruments
and how they progressed to the kind of sophisticated instruments used today.
He concluded that most instruments developed for clinical biofeedback "are
well engineered and, for the most part, accomplish the primary purpose of
providing binary, proportional, or continuous visual or auditory information
related to criterion changes in the physiological measure of interest to the
practitioner" (p. 113).

Peek (1987), in presenting what he called "A Primer of Biofeedback
Instrumentation," noted that the three physiological processes most commonly associated with overarousal are targeted by biofeedback instrumentation. Biofeedback instruments are designed to (1) monitor the physiological
process of interest, (2) measure (objectify) what is monitored, and (3) present
what is monitored or measured as meaningful and useful information (Peek,
1987, p. 75). Moreover, Peek noted that since direct monitoring of the physiological processes of interest to biofeedback therapists is typically not possible, biofeedback instrumentation is commonly used to monitor aspects or
correlates of these processes. These correlates generally have been shown to
correspond quite closely to the associated physiological processes, although
they should not be confused with them.

The most commonly used instruments are designed to measure the following (Peek, 1987):

1. Electrical activity associated with muscle contraction; this measurement process is called electromyography (EMG).
2. Peripheral temperature, which is a correlate of peripheral vasocon-
   striction.
3. Finger photo transmission, which is also a correlate of peripheral va-
   soconstriction.
4. Skin conductance activity (SCA), which is a correlate of sweat gland
   activity.

Many other instruments are in common use today, which measure, in
some cases, highly specialized physiological functions. These include electro-
encephalographic (EEG) instrumentation used to monitor alpha frequency
activity. In addition, heart rate and heart rhythms may be monitored by
applying electrodes to the chest and connecting them to an auditory or visual
signal. In some cases, electrocardiographic (EKG) feedback may be shown
directly to the patient on an oscilloscope (Gaarder & Montgomery, 1981).
Still other biofeedback instrumentation has been designed around microcomputers, which have greatly simplified the recording, storage, and evaluation of
massive amounts of information.

Limitations of Biofeedback

Great caution must be exercised in the application of any method or technique that intervenes in a person's physiological or psychological status, even when the intent is totally laudable. For biofeedback, limitations thus include clear contraindications—situations in which biofeedback may be considered potentially harmful and should not be attempted under any circumstances. In certain additional circumstances, biofeedback should be used only when specific criteria are met concerning the condition of the patient, the competence of the therapist, and the state of knowledge about the specific responses to be modified.

Contraindications

Schwartz and associates (1987) suggested that "logic and good professional judgment" should preclude the use of biofeedback with patients who are suffering from severe depression, acute agitation, situational crisis, acute or fragile schizophrenia, strong potential for psychotic decompensation, mania, some paranoid disorders (for example, delusions of influence), severe obsessive-compulsive disorders, delirium, acute medical decompensation, and strong potential for dissociative reaction, fugue states, or depersonalization (p. 170). What is implied, of course, is that patients are properly evaluated and diagnosed prior to the use of biofeedback. Although a thorough diagnostic evaluation should be standard procedure prior to any professional intervention, biofeedback requires perhaps even more care than some other techniques do. This care is particularly necessary because both physiological and psychological functioning are affected in a more immediate way by biofeedback than by methods that are less intrusive, such as a variety of verbal interventions.

Hazards

When examining potential hazards of biofeedback, the patient's condition must again be one of the first considerations. For example, Schwartz pointed out that in a small number of patients with seizure disorders, some signals used in EEG biofeedback might actually trigger seizure activity. In addition—as is the case with many therapeutic approaches—when patients are seen as obtaining significant secondary benefits from their symptoms, symptom removal alone is unlikely to produce significant improvement and may even make the condition worse. Moreover, the usefulness of biofeedback is clearly limited by patients' compliance with the treatment regimen. Also, as Cox and Hobbs (1982) suggested, a necessarily time-limited biofeedback experience may be overwhelmed by patients' life stresses and their general difficulties in coping.

Shapiro (1982) has noted that few, if any, cases have been documented in which biofeedback treatment caused harm or serious side effects. He suggested that the most serious complication might arise from inappropriately diverting a patient who had a serious disorder from other appropriate treatment. Another potential hazard, however, has to do with the nature of the biofeedback instrumentation. Since virtually all biofeedback equipment is electrically operated, the possibility of electric shock is very real. When the biofeedback equipment consists of small battery-operated devices, the risk is probably minimal. In cases, however, when more sophisticated instruments (such as the EEG, EKG, and EMG) are used, great care must be taken to ensure that the instrument and any ancillary equipment are maintained in top condition and that there are absolutely no electrical current leaks. Peek has suggested that precautions should include periodically evaluating each power-line–operated piece of equipment, keeping patients away from all metal building parts, grounding all equipment, and in some cases installing a ground fault interrupter, which senses very small leakages of current.

Ascertaining the Success of Biofeedback

Whether and how biofeedback works are questions that have occupied researchers and clinicians from the time biofeedback was first used. Even now, considerable controversy exists regarding these questions. This controversy may come as something of a surprise, since it has been suggested that the concrete nature of biofeedback should make research on its outcomes fairly straightforward. Shapiro (1982, pp. 50–59) suggested that biofeedback outcome research should not be problematic, because the physiological measurements are objective and because biofeedback is typically applied to disorders with well-defined and objectified symptoms. Yet, after reviewing the problems involved in conducting well-controlled studies on biofeedback, he was moved to conclude that biofeedback was being pressed into service before being demonstrated effective. Among the reasons for the paucity of well-controlled outcome studies, he noted that the targeted physiological response often does not have a clear relationship to the disorder being treated. Moreover, he pointed out that it is extremely difficult to control for the effects of intervening factors, such as changes in patients' habit patterns, life stresses, and risk factors. Finally, he suggested that adequate joint consideration must be given to both behavioral and biological concepts in determining the effects of biofeedback.

Considerable discussion has focused on the gap between biofeedback clinicians and researchers (for example, Furedy, 1987; Schwartz & associates, 1987). One key complaint is that clinicians and researchers have taken adversary roles in discussions about biofeedback's effectiveness. Nevertheless, many of the problems involved in determining the proper methods and criteria for evaluating biofeedback research are clearly the same problems encountered by those examining the effectiveness of other forms of psychotherapy and other behavior change methods. As Schwartz noted, variability in specific therapists' qualifications, attitudes, and behaviors need to be accounted for, as do patient variables such as patient selection, preparation, and attitudes. In addition, Schwartz identified numerous variables related to the treatment and measurement of behavioral and physiological data that may influence conclusions about the outcome of biofeedback interventions.

Ultimately, thoughtful observers like Schwartz have acknowledged that although well-controlled research studies are very difficult to conduct, clinicians have a responsibility to consumers to continue their efforts to evaluate biofeedback using the best possible methodology and the most stringent criteria. Furedy (1987) went one step further by suggesting that laboratory studies of biofeedback are only of "illustrative" significance for laymen and clinicians and that technical arguments among experts are basically irrelevant. He stressed that what really matters is answering the question whether biofeedback really works. He suggested that well-controlled clinical studies with appropriate control groups, rather than laboratory studies, are needed to determine whether biofeedback has beneficial effects that other treatments do not have.

The Effectiveness of Biofeedback

Researchers who have conducted controlled studies on the effectiveness of biofeedback often have reported findings at odds with practitioners' frequent reports of success with biofeedback training (Tursky, 1982). Indeed, the differences between laboratory studies of biofeedback and application of biofeedback techniques in clinical settings are sufficiently important that findings from one setting cannot be assumed to apply automatically to the other setting. In addition, the effectiveness of clinical biofeedback cannot be assessed unless the specific problem being addressed is specified, along with the specific biofeedback modality being used to address that problem. Because biofeedback is being applied to an ever-increasing array of symptoms and disorders, and because new instrumentation and the use of microcomputers has expanded the range of biofeedback modalities, the task of assessing its effectiveness has taken on daunting proportions. To further complicate matters, the efficacy of biofeedback treatment clearly must be evaluated over time, and not just in terms of short-term or even transient effects.

As the foregoing makes apparent, a thorough review of the empirical evidence is far too complex an undertaking to be accomplished in this chapter. Fortunately, however, others have summarized the clinical efficacy of biofeedback in a number of different areas. In the following section we will rely extensively on the compendium *Biofeedback: Studies in Clinical Efficacy*, edited by Hatch, Fisher, and Rugh (1987), and sponsored by the Biofeedback Society of America. In this volume, experts in eight different applications of biofeedback treatment summarize the evidence regarding the clinical efficacy of treatment in their area.

Vascular Headache

Vascular headache has been treated fairly frequently using biofeedback, and a sizable number of control group outcome studies of biofeedback treatment of migraine headache in particular are summarized by Blanchard and Andrasik (1987). The main conclusions they reach are that the use of thermal biofeedback for hand warming combined with autogenic training is generally superior to no treatment and to thermal biofeedback for hand warming alone. The combination of thermal biofeedback and autogenic training may also be superior to psychological placebo treatments, some forms of drug therapy, and relaxation training alone. There is evidence that the headache relief effects of this combined method persist for at least several months. The evidence regarding other forms of headache appears inconclusive (Blanchard & Andrasik, 1987).

Hypertension

Although Glasgow and Engel reach the overall conclusion that blood pressure can be reduced through biofeedback, many complications currently preclude recommending using biofeedback as a substitute for pharmacotherapy to reduce blood pressure. Some complications have arisen because researchers have commonly combined biofeedback procedures and relaxation procedures to treat hypertension. Although the results of such a combined procedure have been reported to be generally positive, it has been most difficult to ascertain the efficacy of biofeedback alone. Moreover, in some cases hypertension has been treated by means of direct feedback of blood pressure, and in other cases through electromyographic (EMG) feedback, galvanic skin resistance (GSR) feedback, or skin temperature feedback. All of these modalities have shown some promise, but many questions remain regarding the complex relationships between these types of responses and hypertension. Thus, it is concluded that as long as biofeedback methods cannot be shown to be consistently superior to medical treatment of hypertension on several important criteria, treatment using biofeedback will continue to be viewed as basically experimental (Glasgow & Engel, 1987).

Temporomandibular Disorders and Bruxism

Both temporomandibular disorders (also called TMJ syndrome—severe pain associated with chewing) and bruxism (teeth grinding) are not well understood in terms of their etiology. Nevertheless, relationships have been established between increased muscle activity and the occurrence of these specific disorders. Consequently, electromyographic (EMG) biofeedback has been used in their treatment. Methodologically sound clinical studies of the efficacy of EMG biofeedback in the treatment of TMJ disorders and bruxism are few and far between. Moreover, evidence for the effectiveness of biofeedback in such treatment is modest, but comparable to a number of other commonly used treatments (Mealiea & McGlynn, 1987).

Disorders of Motor Function

Because of the large variety of neuromuscular and musculoskeletal disorders that may potentially be treated using biofeedback, this area is difficult to evaluate. Most studies reviewed by Wolf and Fischer-Williams (1987) deal with using EMG biofeedback to rehabilitate stroke patients. The authors concluded that there is preliminary evidence of the growing utility of EMG biofeedback in such treatments, but that the complexity of the clinical circumstances surrounding most patients, especially in the area of rehabilitation, have made controlled clinical studies a rarity (Wolf & Fischer-Williams, 1987).

Gastrointestinal Disorders

Manometric biofeedback (also called balloon biofeedback) has been used in the treatment of fecal incontinence. It consists of inserting a tube into the anal canal and rectum. Three balloons are attached to the tube, and pressure inside the balloons can be manipulated by the therapist. The pressure inside the balloons is recorded on a polygraph, which is used as the biofeedback device. Essentially, patients with fecal incontinence are trained to sense changes of pressure and to contract the external anal sphincter in response to rectal distension. This ingenious procedure was first reported by Engel, Nikoomanesh, and Schuster (1974). Current evidence indicates that it is effective and thus considered the treatment of choice for most common manifestations of fecal incontinence. In addition, EMG biofeedback for patients with fecal incontinence due to sphincter weakness has also been found effective. EMG biofeedback combined with psychotherapy has shown promise in the treatment of irritable bowel syndrome. Biofeedback treatments for peptic ulcer disease and a variety of other gastrointestinal disorders are still in the experimental stages and their effectiveness has not yet been demonstrated (Whitehead & Schuster, 1987).

Chronic Pain Syndromes

Biofeedback in the treatment of chronic pain syndromes has become increasingly popular, undoubtedly because EMG biofeedback has been shown effective in treating the most common chronic pain condition—namely, muscular low back pain. Preliminary evidence also suggests that biofeedback may be effective in treating other chronic pain conditions, such as central pain, rheumatoid arthritis, and dysmenorrhea. Finally, biofeedback may be helpful as part of a multidisciplinary treatment program for so-called intractable (heterogeneous) pain (Keefe & Hoelscher, 1987).

Raynaud's Syndrome

Skin temperature biofeedback has been the typical modality used in the biofeedback treatment of Raynaud's syndrome (a peripheral vascular disorder that abnormally limits blood supply to the extremities in patients exposed to cold and to emotional stress). In most cases, however, skin temperature biofeedback has been combined with autogenic training, muscle relaxation methods, or both. Such hybrid studies have reported symptom reductions comparable to the most successful surgical and pharmacologic interventions. Reports appear to be conflicting regarding the relative advantage of using skin temperature biofeedback as opposed to other behavioral methods (Surwit & Jordan, 1987).

Tension Headache

EMG biofeedback (recorded on the forehead) is reported to be an effective treatment for tension headache. Although relaxation training appears to have a similar success rate, evidence suggests that biofeedback alone may offer unique benefits to some patients (Andrasik & Blanchard, 1987).

Because biofeedback is a relatively new field of behavioral treatment, virtually all researchers and clinicians in the field are acutely aware of the need for more well-designed, well-controlled research. Findings to date, however, suggest that biofeedback will continue to be a promising field with expanding applications in the foreseeable future.

References

Andrasik, F., & Blanchard, E. B. (1987). The biofeedback treatment of tension headache. In J. P. Hatch, J. G. Fisher, & J. D. Rugh (Eds.), *Biofeedback: Studies in clinical efficacy* (pp. 281–321). New York: Plenum.

Basmagian, J. V. (1983). Introduction: Principles and background. In J. V. Basmagian (Ed.), *Biofeedback: Principles and practice for clinicians* (2nd ed., pp. 1–4). Baltimore, MD: Williams & Wilkins.

Blanchard, E. B., & Andrasik, F. (1987). Biofeedback treatment of vascular headache. In J. P. Hatch, J. G. Fisher, & J. D. Rugh (Eds.), *Biofeedback: Studies in clinical efficacy* (pp. 1–79). New York: Plenum.

Brown, B. B. (1977). *Stress and the art of biofeedback.* New York: Harper & Row.

Budzynski, T. H., Stoyva, J. M., & Peffer, K. E. (1980). Biofeedback techniques in psychosomatic disorders. In A. Goldstein & E. B. Foa (Eds.), *Handbook of behavioral interventions: A clinical guide* (pp. 186–265). New York: Wiley.

Butler, F. (1978). *Biofeedback: A survey of the literature.* New York: Plenum.

Cox, D. J., & Hobbs, W. (1982). Biofeedback as a treatment for tension headaches. In L. White & B. Tursky (Eds.), *Clinical biofeedback: Efficacy and mechanisms* (pp. 338–357). New York: Guilford Press.

DiCara, L. V. (1970). Learning in the autonomic nervous system. *Scientific American, 222,* 30–39.

Engel, B. T., Nikoomanesh, P., & Schuster, M. M. (1974). Operant conditioning of rectosphincteric responses in the treatment of fecal incontinence. *New England Journal of Medicine, 290,* 646–649.

Furedy, J. J. (1987). Specific versus placebo effects in biofeedback training: A critical lay perspective. *Biofeedback and Self-Regulation, 12,* 169–184.

Gaarder, K. R., & Montgomery, P. S. (1981). *Clinical biofeedback: A procedural manual for behavioral medicine* (2nd ed.). Baltimore, MD: Williams & Wilkins.

Glasgow, M. S., & Engel, B. T. (1987). Clinical issues in biofeedback and relaxation therapy for hypertension: Review and recommendations. In J. P. Hatch, J. G. Fisher, & J. D. Rugh (Eds.), *Biofeedback: Studies in clinical efficacy* (pp. 81–121). New York: Plenum.

Hatch, J. P., Fisher, J. G., & Rugh, J. D. (Eds.). (1987). *Biofeedback: Studies in clinical efficacy*. New York: Plenum.

Keefe, F. J., & Hoelscher, T. J. (1987). Biofeedback in the management of chronic pain syndromes. In J. P. Hatch, J. G. Fisher, & J. D. Rugh (Eds.), *Biofeedback: Studies in clinical efficacy* (pp. 211–253). New York: Plenum.

Mealiea, W. L., & McGlynn, F. D. (1987). Temporomandibular disorders and bruxism. In J. P. Hatch, J. G. Fisher, & J. D. Rugh (Eds.), *Biofeedback: Studies in clinical efficacy* (pp. 123–151). New York: Plenum.

Miller, N. E. (1969). Learning of visceral and glandular responses. *Science, 163,* 434–445.

Olson, R. P. (1987). Definitions of biofeedback. In M. S. Schwartz (Ed.), *Biofeedback: A practitioner's guide* (pp. 33–38). New York: Guilford Press.

Orne, M. T. (1982). Perspectives in biofeedback: Ten years ago, today, and . . . In L. White & B. Tursky (Eds.), *Clinical biofeedback: Efficacy and mechanisms* (pp. 422–437). New York: Guilford Press.

Peek, C. J. (1987). A primer of biofeedback instrumentation. In M. S. Schwartz (Ed.), *Biofeedback: A practitioner's guide* (pp. 73–127). New York: Guilford Press.

Schwartz, M. S., & associates. (1987). *Biofeedback: A practitioner's guide*. New York: Guilford Press.

Shapiro, D. (1982). Research design and assessment in clinical biofeedback. In L. White & B. Tursky (Eds.), *Clinical biofeedback: Efficacy and mechanisms* (pp. 48–60). New York: Guilford Press.

Shaw, E. R., & Blanchard, E. B. (1983). The effects of instructional set on the outcome of a stress management program. *Biofeedback and Self-Regulation, 8,* 555–565.

Sokhadze, E. M., & Shtack, M. B. (1991). Scientific and clinical biofeedback in the USSR. *Biofeedback and Self-Regulation, 16,* 253–260.

Surwit, R. S., & Jordan, J. S. (1987). Behavioral treatment of Raynaud's syndrome. In J. P. Hatch, J. G. Fisher, & J. D. Rugh (Eds.), *Biofeedback: Studies in clinical efficacy* (pp. 255–279). New York: Plenum.

Tursky, B. (1982). An engineering approach to biofeedback. In L. White & B. Tursky (Eds.), *Clinical biofeedback: Efficacy and mechanisms* (pp. 108–126). New York: Guilford Press.

White, L., & Tursky, B. (1982a). (Eds.). *Clinical biofeedback: Efficacy and mechanisms.* New York: Guilford Press.

White, L., & Tursky, B. (1982b). Where are we . . . Where are we going? In L. White & B. Tursky, (Eds.), *Clinical biofeedback: Efficacy and mechanisms* (pp. 438–448). New York: Guilford Press.

Whitehead, W. E., & Schuster, M. M. (1987). Biofeedback in the treatment of gastrointestinal disorders. In J. P. Hatch, J. G. Fisher, & J. D. Rugh (Eds.), *Biofeedback: Studies in clinical efficacy* (pp. 179–209). New York: Plenum.

Wolf, S. L., & Fischer-Williams, M. (1987). The use of biofeedback in disorders of motor function. In J. P. Hatch, J. G. Fisher, & J. D. Rugh (Eds.), *Biofeedback: Studies in clinical efficacy* (pp. 153–177). New York: Plenum.

··

CHAPTER 23

Clinical Applications
of Hypnosis

··

■

A lthough many of the ancient societies knew of hypnotic phenomena or
other phenomena related to suggestibility, their practice was focused on
tribal rites and the practice of native medicine. Hypnotism as it is known
today was not understood in ancient times (Pattie, 1967). Today, hypnosis is
used in many different applications, usually as an adjunct to other methods.

General Purpose of Hypnosis

In most cases, the purpose of including hypnosis in a given intervention
is to utilize the special state of consciousness that is thought to be associated
with it in order to facilitate the conduct of the intervention itself. Some disagreements remain, however, about the proper domain of hypnosis in
therapy. For example, Ambrose and Newbold (1980) suggested that any medical application of hypnotism represents hypnotherapy. On the other hand,
Brown and Fromm (1986) contended that hypnosis can be used with any
type of therapy; they called it dynamic hypnotherapy or hypnoanalysis when
combined with psychoanalytic methods, and hypnotherapy when combined
with other methods (p. 3). In the present chapter the term *hypnotic interventions* will be used to refer collectively to all clinical applications of hypnosis.
Other terms, such as *clinical hypnosis, hypnotherapy*, and *hypnoanalysis* will be
used when appropriate.

History of Hypnosis

Although ancient cultures practiced rituals that used hypnotic suggestion, the modern history of hypnotism and hypnotic interventions is usually traced back to Franz Anton Mesmer (1734–1815). Mesmer was an Austrian physician who gained fame in Paris by promoting a form of hypnosis that he called animal magnetism, and which eventually came to be called mesmerism. Mesmer's flamboyant healing sessions gained him fame and notoriety until he was discredited by a committee of inquiry set up by the king of France. The committee was composed of leading scientists, including Benjamin Franklin, then U.S. ambassador to France. The committee demonstrated that hypnotic (magnetic) influence did not depend on any of the instruments and props Mesmer used—such as a tub filled with water and iron filings—and that whatever success he achieved was the result of the patient's imagination. Although some of Mesmer's contemporaries concluded that he was a charlatan, it is now clear that, although mistaken in attributing the effects of hypnotism to animal magnetism, he did produce the results he claimed and he attempted to explain his results scientifically (Hilgard & Hilgard, 1975).

Scientific objections to mesmerism were unable to halt the use of hypnotism by an ever-increasing number of physicians. Among other things, hypnotism was used as an anesthetic in major surgery, especially prior to the introduction of ether in 1846. After ether and chloroform were routinely used in surgery, hypnotism as a method of anesthesia was generally discontinued, although today it is again widely used for this purpose, especially by dentists. Following Mesmer's death in 1815, the British physician John Elliotson revived the practice of hypnotism in the conduct of his medical practice. Although also discredited because it could not be shown that any form of magnetism played a role in the effects he produced, Elliotson is credited, among other things, with rescuing medical hypnotism from oblivion. What Elliotson did for the medical application of hypnotism, the Scottish surgeon James Braid accomplished with regard to its scientific status. The use of the term *hypnotism* is attributed to Braid, and he is largely credited with pioneering true scientific study of this phenomenon. Among other accomplishments, he was the first to realize that hypnotism depends on suggestion (Ambrose & Newbold, 1980).

In spite of Braid's pioneering work in separating hypnotism from the discredited mesmerism, the use of hypnosis declined until revived in France largely due to the influence of the famous neurologist Charcot. Charcot erroneously viewed hypnosis as a pathological state. The so-called Nancy school, whose leaders were Liebeault and Bernheim, eventually brought the use of hypnosis within the bounds of legitimate medical practice, and accurately recognized hypnosis as a natural phenomenon primarily based on the power of suggestion (Hilgard & Hilgard, 1975). Interestingly, both Charcot and Bernheim—who held opposing views about the nature of hypnosis—stimulated Freud's interest in it. Freud eventually chose hypnosis as his major treatment method until he was persuaded that the central role of suggestibility was a serious drawback. At that point, he largely abandoned hypnosis and started to use free association instead. Although Freud's abandonment of hypnosis was a setback, the British Medical Association issued a report in 1892 declaring that "hypnotic phenomena were genuine and hypnotism was valuable as a therapeutic agent" (Ambrose & Newbold, 1980, p. 9).

The use of hypnotism has experienced many ups and downs since the days of Mesmer. Several prominent psychologists, including William James, Wilhelm Wundt, and Clark Hull, published books on hypnosis and elevated the phenomenon to scientific respectability. Both World War I and World War II produced increased interest in the use of hypnosis in medical treatment. Today, the use of hypnosis is well established in medical and psychological practice, as indicated by, among other things, the establishment of the Division of Hypnosis of the American Psychological Association and the founding of the American Society of Clinical Hypnosis in 1957 and the International Society for Medical and Psychological Hypnosis in 1985.

Range of Applicability

The most important point to understand about hypnosis is that it is not itself a clinical procedure or a treatment method. Most clinicians view hypnosis as an adjunct to clinical practice. In hypnotherapy, hypnosis is used in conjunction with psychotherapy. In dentistry and medicine, it may be used as an anesthetic. The recently published *Handbook of Hypnotic Suggestions and Metaphors*, edited by Hammond (1990), describes numerous applications of hypnosis and hypnotic suggestion in a great variety of medical and psychological settings. For example, numerous specific techniques are described for using hypnosis in managing and treating various forms of pain. Other sections of the handbook deal with hypnoanesthesia and the use of hypnosis in ego-strengthening therapies. Still other sections describe the use of hypnosis in treating anxiety, phobias, dental disorders, a variety of medical disorders, psychiatric disorders, sexual dysfunction, relationship problems, eating disorders, and addictions. Moreover, the use of hypnosis is discussed in obstetrics and gynecology, in dealing with cancer patients, and in working with children. Finally, its use in enhancing academic and athletic performance and in producing time reorientation are discussed in detail.

A review of all these applications of hypnosis is clearly beyond the scope of this chapter. In fact, it has been claimed that clinical hypnosis may be useful in treating any physical complaint that has an emotional basis (Kohn, 1984). So as to both inform readers about the range of clinical applications of hypnosis, and also impart some specific information about the procedures commonly used in hypnosis, we will focus on two types of applications in this chapter: (1) hypnotherapy—that is, the use of hypnosis in conjunction with psychotherapy; and (2) the treatment of pain using hypnosis.

Theoretical Foundations
Assumptions About Human Nature

The assumptions underlying the use of hypnosis are particularly difficult to discuss because researchers and practitioners in this field have come from such a wide variety of disciplinary and theoretical backgrounds. It is probably fair to state that those engaged in the clinical application of hypnosis do not hold any one position about the course of human development in general or the development of maladaptive behaviors in particular. Because hypnosis is basically an adjunct to other methods of intervention, the perspective of those other interventions occupies the central role in any given case. Views about the specific contribution of hypnosis tend to be superimposed on those notions, in ways that differ, to some extent, depending on the core theory. For example, in the case of psychoanalysis the phenomenon of hypnosis has been well integrated into the larger theory. Thus, Gill and Brenman (1967) interpreted hypnosis as "regression in the service of the ego," which makes it an adaptive regression. When used in conjunction with other theories, hypnosis may be viewed as relatively neutral with regard to how human development unfolds and how change is produced.

Theoretical Assumptions About Hypnosis

Views have diverged more widely regarding the nature of hypnosis than of perhaps any other method of intervention. One reason for this diversity is likely to be the early use of hypnosis in magic, witchcraft, and primitive rituals. Hypnosis has been a source of fascination and wonder, and it has been exploited by magicians and charlatans. Misconceptions about the nature of hypnosis continue to be widely held among the general population. One reason such various views and misconceptions persist may be that researchers and experts on hypnosis do not agree among themselves about the nature of the phenomenon. Most do agree that it is a natural phenomenon and not a pathological condition, as Charcot proposed only a century ago. Beyond that, however, little agreement is evident.

One school of thought has contended that hypnosis represents an altered physiological state. For example, Pavlov considered hypnosis to be akin to normal sleep, a position that could not be maintained after it was found that the physiological and neurological functions of hypnotized subjects are much more like those of fully conscious subjects than of sleeping subjects (cf., Ambrose & Newbold, 1980). Volgyesi's (1966) modification of Pavlov's theory—namely, that hypnosis represents a special state between wakefulness and sleep—has also been shown to have serious flaws.

Hilgard and Hilgard (1975), who have been pioneers in both scientific investigation and application of hypnosis in the relief of pain, have raised issues about whether hypnosis represents a state or not. They pointed out that nonstate theorists object to conceptualizing hypnosis as a special state of consciousness because the state concept would mean that hypnosis represents a change from normal—much as sleep is different from waking. At the same time, however, it is clear that individual differences in hypnotizability represent a trait of hypnotic responsiveness. Hilgard and Hilgard stated that one can thus hold a strictly trait theory that denies that hypnosis is a state, or one can hold an extreme state theory that assumes everyone can enter a state of hypnosis under proper circumstances. They concluded that most workers in this field accept a conceptualization that mixes the trait and state theories—on the one hand recognizing differences in hypnotizability, and on the other acknowledging that even a "highly hypnotized person is not in the hypnotic state all of the time" (p. 14). More recently, Coe (1992) suggested that the state and nonstate views on hypnosis are roughly equivalent to special process and social-psychological conceptualizations of hypnosis.

Current psychological theories of hypnosis generally focus on the central role of suggestion and suggestibility in explaining hypnotic phenomena. Somewhat surprisingly, however, there is not even agreement about whether a hypnotized subject or patient is actually in a trance, even though some subjectively report experiencing something like a trance and others do not. The key difficulty in dealing with this seemingly basic question is that investigations into the nature of hypnosis must ultimately rely on the hypnotized subject's later recall of subjectively experienced states. As Rowley (1986) pointed out, theorists differ in the weight they give to subjective reports, and they may even argue that subjects are simply mistaken in interpreting their experiences as a trance state.

Modern practitioners of hypnotherapy (for example, Wright & Wright, 1987) have attempted to demystify the hypnotic experience by pointing out that experiences resembling hypnosis occur frequently in everyday life. Thus, they pointed out that everyone has had experiences of drifting away with open eyes. Among examples they cite are becoming immersed in one's thoughts while driving along a familiar route, or becoming involved in a book to the extent of not noticing another person entering the room. In other words, most people have had experiences of tuning out sensory experiences from the environment and tuning in to their internal experience. The inevitable conclusion is that almost all phenomena that may be experienced during hypnosis can also occur in the waking state. The use of hypnosis thus represents a way of assisting clients to tune in to inner experiences, to reexperience past events, and to envision new possibilities more efficiently and more intensely than is generally possible without the use of hypnosis.

Hypnosis in Hypnotherapy and Pain Treatment
Hypnotic Induction

There are many different ways to induce hypnosis, but in the professional application of hypnosis, either as part of therapy or in the service of pain reduction, some general conditions assist in promoting an atmosphere favorable for the successful induction of hypnosis. These conditions include having a reasonable measure of trust in the therapist, or at least a good rapport. In addition, a reduction of sensory input is desirable, as are a fixation of attention and heightened awareness of one's inner life (Wright & Wright, 1987, pp. 21–23). Most practitioners also believe that a general state of relaxation, which is actually implied by the previous conditions, is also particularly helpful in promoting induction.

Different practitioners may use different styles of producing hypnotic suggestion. The original style, practiced by Mesmer and Bernheim, was directive and authoritarian. It has been observed, however, that this style works well only with intellectually unsophisticated persons and individuals who have an external locus of control. In a second style, described as permissive, the hypnotist is portrayed as playing a facilitative role rather than an authoritarian one. This appears to be the most popular style, and it has been claimed to be applicable to a wider range of patients. The third style, called the Ericksonian style and developed by Milton Erickson (1964), induces hypnosis through nonspecific, indirect, ambiguous, and often disguised suggestions that may be embedded in ordinary conversation. Moreover, Ericksonian practitioners used confusion and surprise in their suggestions. Ultimately, the therapist hits upon a method of suggestion best suited to the individual patient. Interestingly, using this approach makes it possible to hypnotize a person without that person's knowledge (Brown & Fromm, 1986).

It is commonly suggested that the use of hypnosis requires at least four phases—the first one devoted to the induction of the hypnotic state; the second one devoted to its deepening; the third one its exploitation or utilization, either in therapy or pain reduction or any other means; and the final one involving its termination. Different practitioners prefer different methods to accomplish these objectives. Several methods of induction should be available so that if one method is unsuccessful, the practitioner can try another one that may have a greater chance of success. Most methods can be used by practitioners who are either permissive or authoritarian. What changes with those styles is the specific wording and overall presentation of the hypnosis experience.

Many specific methods of hypnotic induction are available, and most practitioners have preferences for using one method as opposed to another. A large variety of induction techniques are extensively discussed in a number of books, such as Rowley (1986), Wright and Wright (1987), and Brown and Fromm (1986). Some of the most widely used methods of hypnotic induction and enhancement may be described as follows:

1. *Progressive relaxation*: This technique was pioneered by Jacobson (1938) although he did not relate it to hypnosis. Essentially, the technique involves instructing individuals in the progressive relaxation of one muscle group after another until a state of complete physical and mental relaxation exists.

2. *Chevreul pendulum*: In this induction technique, the patient rests his or her elbows on a table while holding a shiny object (the pendulum) on a string so that it hangs just above the surface of the table. The patient is then told to fixate on this shiny object while the hypnotist suggests where the pendulum will go next. Eventually, it is suggested that the pendulum will drop to the table and the subject will sink, from that point on, into an ever-deeper state of hypnosis.

3. *Counting technique*: This fairly straightforward method for induction and deepening involves asking the patient to count backward from 50 to 1. In addition, it may be suggested that the patient will go into a deeper and deeper trance with each breath that is taken (Brown & Fromm, 1986). The counting technique is sometimes combined with imagery, as in the so-called staircase technique. In that technique the patient is asked to imagine standing at the top of a staircase and that, as he or she goes down the stairs, a deeper and deeper trance will be achieved with every step.

4. *Arm levitation*: In effect, the therapist suggests first a state of relaxation that is then followed by one arm becoming lighter and lighter, eventually beginning to drift upward as if pulled by a magnet. The patient becomes totally absorbed in attending to the sensations that are suggested to be occur-

ring in relation to his or her arm. As the therapist perceives evidence that the patient is following the suggestions, it is finally suggested that the patient enter an ever-deepening trance.

5. *Coin drop*: This technique may be used while the patient's eyes are either open or closed. The patient is asked to put a coin into his or her hand, to make a fist around it, and to concentrate attention on sensations in the hand. Moreover, the patient is instructed to imagine that the coin is in a little balloon that will expand so that it will force the fist open. Eventually, the fingers will open so far that the coin will drop, and the patient will enter a deep trance.

6. *Confusion technique*: This technique is commonly used with individuals who are unable to accept suggestions of a more straightforward type because they have a critical mental attitude and are resistant. Essentially, the practitioner will speak rapidly and present confusing and even contradictory ideas, leaving the client confused and more likely to accept straightforward hypnotic induction.

Whether the induction is successful depends on the subject's hypnotizability (suggestibility) and the hypnotist's skill and experience. The number of attempts needed to induce hypnosis may vary from case to case and from situation to situation. Generally, if a subject has been hypnotized previously, the induction is thought to be easier. In some cases, three or four induction attempts may be made, sometimes using different induction techniques, before it is concluded that the subject cannot be successfully hypnotized on that occasion. In any case, subjects should never be told that they are not hypnotizable. What should be conveyed to them, however, is that being in a state of hypnosis is almost always a pleasurable experience. This idea may ultimately enhance a subject's receptivity to hypnosis.

Procedures Used in Pain Control

Whether hypnosis is used as an adjunct to psychotherapy or in an effort to control pain, the induction procedures are essentially the same. When pain reduction is the primary focus of the hypnotic procedure, however, at least three classes of procedures may be employed (Hilgard & Hilgard, 1975). The first of these is a direct suggestion of pain reduction. For example, a direct suggestion (under hypnosis) may be that a section of gum and a tooth are getting numb and that it is no longer possible to feel pain or other sensations in that area. This suggestion is often adequate for highly suggestible patients, but for others it may be necessary to draw upon their prior experience with local anesthetics by suggesting to them to imagine that a local anesthetic has been injected. Thus, patients may be told to imagine that they have just received an injection of novocaine.

A second procedure used in reducing pain essentially aims to alter the experience of pain even though the pain itself may persist. For example, when a disturbing pain is not well localized, it may be localized in a small compact area through hypnotic suggestion, and then transferred, again through hypnotic suggestion, to a place on the body that may be tolerant to the experience of pain. A related procedure may be not only to move the pain, but also to suggest that it is converted from, for example, an intense stabbing pain to a tingling sensation. The third method of controlling pain through hypnosis is to direct attention away from the pain. For example, the suggestion may be made that the patient temporarily does not possess a right arm or left knee, depending on where the pain had been localized. Alternatively, patients could be told that they could regress to an earlier age when they did not have the affliction causing their current pain, or they could be told to fantasize themselves absorbed in an activity they enjoyed when they had no pain. In either case, the hypnotic suggestion would result in the patient's being distracted or removed from the present experience of pain (Hilgard & Hilgard, 1975, pp. 64–67).

Hypnosis may be used to produce analgesia (a state in which pain is prevented or decreased), or to produce anesthesia (the inability to feel anything in the anesthetized part of the body). It is generally accepted that analgesia can be produced more readily than anesthesia and that hypnotic induction of analgesia is a less complicated undertaking that also requires a lower level of suggestibility than is needed for the production of hypnoanesthesia. Although hypnoanesthesia for major surgery was reported by Esdaile as early as 1846, it has never found wide acceptance, in part because it has been shown that suggestive anesthesia may be possible in only about 10% of cases. Moreover, when complete anesthesia is desired, it is incumbent upon the practitioner to ensure that it has been achieved prior to giving a green light for commencement of major surgery. Kroger (1963) suggested a rehearsal phase in addition to a preparatory period, a maintenance phase, and a post-operative phase. During this rehearsal procedure, the patient is led, step by step, through the entire surgical procedure (by a surgeon). Typically, this process will involve going through the actual motions of surgery and actually producing some of the superficial tactile sensations that may be experienced as part of the surgery.

The preparatory phase generally requires that the hypnotist discuss with the patient the exact procedures to be used, being completely open and honest about the process and reassuring patients about any anxieties and fears they may have with regard to the impending procedure. The active maintenance of hypnoanesthesia during surgery may be optional with highly suggestible patients. With others, however, it may be necessary for the hypnotist to be present and to reiterate pertinent suggestions throughout the procedure. For obvious reasons, the use of hypnoanesthesia in major surgery requires great care and should certainly not be attempted by an inexperienced hypnotist. Moreover, because surgery usually involves the combined efforts of a team of experts, it is very important to ensure that all professionals involved are fully apprised of, and agreeable to, the use of hypnosis to produce anesthesia (Weitzenhoffer, 1989).

Procedures Used in Hypnotherapy

The specific procedures used in hypnotherapy depend very much on the therapist's theoretical framework. It is generally agreed that hypnoanalysis—the use of hypnosis in conjunction with psychoanalysis—utilizes a series of techniques designed to capitalize on the basic premises of psychoanalysis. Thus, in hypnoanalysis, concerns with transference and countertransference, uncovering unconscious sources of conflict, and dealing with defenses and resistances tend to be of central importance. Moreover, a variety of diagnostic techniques based on psychoanalytic theory, such as various projective techniques, may be used in hypnoanalysis. Hypnotism may also be used in conjunction with behavior therapy, in supportive therapies, and in eclectic therapy (Weitzenhoffer, 1989). Because no set of specific hypnotherapy procedures is generally agreed upon, a representative sample of procedures often used in hypnotherapy will be presented in the following sections.

Posthypnotic suggestions.   Posthypnotic suggestions are made by the therapist while the patient is under hypnosis and are designed to take effect after termination of the hypnotic trance. It has been suggested that the posthypnotic suggestion made in hypnotherapy constitutes an implicit contractual agreement between patient and therapist, and that it generally addresses something the patient has been asking for, such as to stop overeating, to stop smoking, or to stop experiencing headaches. Generally, posthypnotic suggestions made in the course of hypnotherapy are intended to be long-lasting, and are usually given with the added remark that the patient may forget that the suggestion was actually made by the therapist. Because posthypnotic suggestions can have a powerful impact on the patient's behavior, the therapist must choose the specific words and expressions used as part of the posthypnotic suggestion carefully, in order to reduce the danger that mistakes in wording inadvertently produce undesired effects (Brown & Fromm, 1986).

Affect enhancement.   When patients are emotionally constricted for one reason or another, and have little conscious awareness of their affective experiences, hypnosis may be used "to bring the patient's current emotional experience into full awareness" (Brown & Fromm, 1986, p. 172). Specific statements made by the therapist may be designed to help the patient recognize feelings, suggesting that those feelings are clearly recognized and that the patient can describe them. Generally, the hypnotherapist's instructions will be straightforward and direct, such as "a specific feeling will become clear to you. . . . It will become clearer . . . and clearer. . . . You will be able to recognize exactly what this particular feeling is . . . and you will be able to describe it to me. . . . Now, what is it that you are feeling?" (Brown & Fromm, 1986, p. 173).

Time reorientation.   The subjective experience of the passage of time may significantly differ from objective time. Moreover, humans typically think in terms of past, present, and future time. During hypnosis these perceptions of the passage of time and of the overall time framework may be altered, resulting in important therapeutic possibilities for various systems of psychotherapy (Wright & Wright, 1987). For example, much has been written about age regression, in which the patient is taken back during the hypnotic trance to an earlier time in his or her life in order to gain new insight and understanding about important early events that may not be remembered clearly or at all, for a variety of reasons. Various specific techniques may be used to accomplish age regression. One technique is to suggest that patients count back from their present age, one year at a time, until they reach the age to which they like to be regressed. An alternate method is to suggest to patients that they are imagining, for example, their 6th birthday and to further imagine that they are really the age they were at this remembered event (Rowley, 1986).

Another form of time reorientation under hypnosis is time distortion. This technique may be used, for example, to assist the patient in developing coping strategies. The patient is told to imagine a rapid series of scenes in which he or she discovers new and better ways of coping. After a very brief time, the patient may be able to report having discovered several new coping strategies that may work for him or her.

Symptom substitution.   In some cases it is found that substituting a less debilitating symptom for one that is more debilitating makes therapeutic sense, especially when patients are resistant to giving up the crutch of the original symptom. It has been proposed that the best strategy to pursue in using symptom substitution is to remove the most handicapping symptom (by substituting another symptom that is less serious), and to find out how the symptom is acting as a crutch so that it may then be possible to remove the need for the symptom altogether. A closely related technique is symptom transformation, in which the symptom's nature is not changed but its negative effects are reduced. For example, a patient who is engaging in serious self-mutilation by cutting her arms with a knife may be told, under hypnosis, to simply scratch her arms with her fingernails. Such a transformation may buy time for the therapist to develop a way to address the underlying problem as part of the overall therapeutic strategy (Rowley, 1986).

Means and Conditions for Implementing Clinical Hypnosis
The Therapist's Qualifications

The American Society of Clinical Hypnosis, founded in 1957, was established as an association of professionals in medicine, psychology, and dentistry who use hypnosis in their clinical practice. Among the objectives of the association, which currently has more than 4,000 members, is to provide the public with accurate information about hypnosis and its clinical applications. Moreover, the society conducts beginning, intermediate, and advanced training workshops throughout the United States and Canada. The training is available to licensed dentists, marriage and family therapists, physicians, psychologists, and master's degree–level registered nurses with advanced subspeciality training and certification (Hammond, 1990). The proper qualification for a clinical hypnotist is first and foremost to be a properly trained and licensed professional in one of the areas just listed. In addition to the requisite professional training, the American Society of Clinical Hypnosis requires a minimum of 40 hours of appropriate professional training and experience in clinical or experimental hypnosis for full society membership. Other professional associations, both national and international, have also concerned themselves with formulating ethical guidelines and standards of training for clinicians and researchers in the field of hypnosis.

Above and beyond the formal educational requirements for legitimate practitioners of clinical hypnosis, practitioners should also have some other characteristics. For example, Ambrose and Newbold (1980) point out that a dogmatic commitment to the scientific method may represent a handicap to the practitioner attempting to use the principles of suggestion. Such individuals may have ambivalent attitudes about the power of suggestion that they may subtly communicate to the patient, interfering with the effectiveness of hypnosis. Others have observed that the relationship between the hypnotist and patient is of critical importance in determining the effectiveness of hypnosis. Although in the early days of hypnosis the hypnotist was more likely to assume an authoritarian role, modern clinical applications of hypnosis have emphasized a more permissive approach, with most subjects favoring the hypnotist as guide (Hilgard & Hilgard, 1975). Moreover, hypnotherapy has, for the most part, replaced the original focus on the unique characteristics and skills of the hypnotherapist with a central focus on the experience and adaptive capacities of the individual client (Baker, 1987).

Conditions for Conducting Hypnosis

As in any medical or psychological intervention, the patient must have a reasonable amount of trust and confidence in the practitioner. After that, it is probably essential in most cases to initially address the many misconceptions about hypnosis commonly held by naive subjects. Patients also need to be reassured about the potential for harm, either as a consequence of the procedure that is immediately contemplated or as a consequence of having been hypnotized in general.

No special facilities are required for the practice of hypnotherapy or for the clinical application of hypnosis beyond the facilities required for conducting the clinical procedure necessitating the use of hypnosis in the first place. Moreover, although the devices used to facilitate hypnotic induction are sometimes described as hypnotists' tools, they are of only tangential importance and certainly not essential to the conduct of any type of clinical hypnosis.

Limitations of Clinical Hypnosis

Most practitioners of clinical hypnosis take the position that hypnosis has no inherent dangers; what is dangerous is the incompetent or fraudulent use of hypnosis. Because of the many commonly held misconceptions about the nature of hypnosis that tend to be promulgated and exploited by stage hypnotists and others who do not have the requisite professional training to be clinical hypnotists, a great deal of damage can be done to unsuspecting individuals who are not well-informed about the true nature of hypnotic phenomena. Still, Kohn (1984) observed that serious or permanent damage as a result of the improper use of hypnosis occurs very rarely if at all, and that most damage is frequently done through the creation of unrealistic expectations in unsophisticated individuals. Nevertheless, a number of specific potential hazards and contraindications should be noted.

Contraindications

Olness and Gardner (1988) discussed specific contraindications for child hypnotherapy. These contraindications are, however, broadly applicable to virtually any population and any legitimate application of clinical hypnosis. Generally, Olness and Gardner take the position that hypnosis should not be used in the following circumstances:

1. When it is likely to place the patient in physical danger (for example, in athletics).
2. When it is likely to aggravate an existing problem or create new ones.
3. When it is done for entertainment.
4. When a problem can be treated more effectively without the use of hypnosis.
5. When a patient is referred for hypnotherapy or some other clinical application of hypnosis based on a misdiagnosis.

Moreover, hypnosis is generally not considered to be a treatment in itself. Thus, if a practitioner of clinical hypnosis is asked to use hypnosis in an area for which he or she is not otherwise qualified, a referral should be made to a practitioner who has the proper professional qualification and is also qualified as a clinical hypnotist (Hammond, 1990).

It has also been suggested that lack of susceptibility or responsiveness to hypnosis should be considered a contraindication (Brown & Fromm, 1986), although others have claimed that almost anyone can be hypnotized (for example, Erickson, 1981) or that it is not hypnotic susceptibility but simply suggestibility that counts when working with most patients (for example, Weitzenhoffer, 1989). Indeed, it is likely that estimates of the percentage of patients who cannot be effectively hypnotized have been far too high because these estimates have generally been based on fairly rigorous tests of susceptibility (for example, Hilgard, 1965). It is clear, nevertheless, that individuals differ greatly in susceptibility to hypnosis; some may be so refractory to such treatment that the clinician might as well try a different treatment approach.

Hazards

Whether subjects can be persuaded under hypnosis to engage in immoral or antisocial behaviors has been extensively discussed. The general conclusion regarding this potential problem appears to be that most subjects will not engage in behaviors that are contrary to their own wishes and that they nor-mally consider unacceptable (Orne, 1961). This conclusion is warranted even though, in some well-known experiments, some highly susceptible subjects have been persuaded to divulge state secrets or physically attack their friends. Rowley (1986) suggested, however, that subjects always perceive these behav-iors, conducted in the context of a contrived experimental situation, as dif-ferent from real-life situations.

Some practitioners have argued that ethical questions can be raised about the use of posthypnotic suggestions, because they may be construed as the hypnotist's exercise of undue influence over patients' future behavior, even when the posthypnotic suggestion is entirely in the patient's interest and does not involve antisocial or otherwise undesirable behaviors (London, 1967). Whether such influence is ultimately different from the influence exerted on patients who are in a conscious state, especially when strong transference is taking place, is open to interpretation.

A number of procedural errors can also be considered potential hazards. Most notably, improperly worded suggestions and instructions may be a source of later difficulties. For example, Weitzenhoffer (1989) reported that an obstetrician suggested to a patient under hypnosis that upon experiencing the very first labor contractions, she would become totally unaware of sensa-tions in her abdominal and pelvic areas. The woman apparently followed the suggestion to such an extent that she did not become aware of entering labor until she felt amniotic fluid streaming down her legs. Obviously, the sugges-tion was improperly worded. Another potential danger Weitzenhoffer pointed out is that through hypnosis, a patient's psychological defenses may be reduced or eliminated prematurely—before the patient is ready to deal with repressed material. Clearly, the best safeguard against this situation is to ensure that the practitioner is properly trained to deal with such circum-stances, which can in some cases lead to significant problems.

Some patients have reported anxiety, panic, depression, and even unpleasant physical sensations as a consequence of their hypnotic experience. Udolf (1981) discussed these reports in some detail and suggested that in virtually every case it could be shown that hypnosis itself was unlikely to be the precipitating factor. As a matter of fact, some of these undesirable side effects may have taken place in spite of psychotherapy or hypnosis rather than because of them (Kohn, 1984). In other cases, repeated hypnosis has been reported to lead to an excessive liking for the hypnotic trance and a possible reluctance to terminate the condition. This situation, however, is again not viewed as a serious danger when an experienced clinical hypnotist is involved; in fact, such a circumstance might even be exploited for the patient's benefit (Ambrose & Newbold, 1980).

Ascertaining the Success of Clinical Hypnosis

Determining the success of clinical hypnosis is exceedingly complex. Because clinical hypnosis is generally used in conjunction with other methods, it is often necessary to ascertain the overall success of the intervention (a difficult task in most cases) and then to determine separately the relative contribution of the hypnotic experience to this overall success. The resulting complexity becomes even more apparent when one considers that some practitioners believe the induction of a relatively deep hypnotic trance to be necessary for successful intervention, whereas others maintain that whether a patient actually achieves a hypnotic trance is immaterial. The result of these complexities is that in the clinical literature case studies and anecdotal case histories represent the great majority of evidence pertaining to the efficacy of clinical hypnosis.

The problem of obtaining scientifically acceptable evidence to support the clinical application of hypnosis is further compounded by the likelihood of a natural inclination to report successes and to keep quiet about failures. For example, commenting on the successes of the legendary hypnotherapist Milton H. Erickson, Weitzenhoffer (1989, p. 24) complained:

> Listening to or reading Erickson's accounts of brief hypnotherapy cases, one receives the impression that his approach never failed him. Indeed, it may be true that he never knew failure; however, it is more likely that he never reported his failures. This is unfortunate, because there is much to be learned from failures. I think, too, that Erickson had a way of presenting what may have been unique, one-time successes in such a way that one cannot help but think that they were reflective of all his cases.

Although case studies describing the application of hypnosis in clinical settings will continue to be valuable and colorful components of any effort to describe and evaluate clinical hypnosis, they are also becoming ever less compelling in the current emphasis on documenting efficacy (Frankel, 1987). Indeed, Wadden and Anderton (1982), after reviewing a fair number of clinical and experimental studies on the effectiveness of hypnotic treatment, felt compelled to recommend that future research should be more attentive to the nature of disorders and patient populations; the context, adequacy, and implementation of therapeutic techniques; and the influence of hypnotic susceptibility and other factors on outcome. Unfortunately, 10 years later, Coe (1992) reported that practitioners still relied primarily on case reports to advance their views of hypnosis.

The Effectiveness of Clinical Hypnosis

In spite of the relative paucity of well-controlled clinical research on the effectiveness of clinical hypnosis, thoughtful reviewers (for example, Wadden & Anderton, 1982) have concluded that "hypnosis appears to be of unique value in the treatment of clinical pain, warts, and asthma" (p. 215). At the same time, these authors concluded that although hypnosis may be effective in the treatment of other problems, such as addictive behavior, limitations of the research design did not permit the determination of whether treatment success was attributable to hypnosis or to other nonhypnotic factors. In fact, this issue has been of concern to other investigators, who have noted the similarity between the application of hypnosis and various self-management and cognitive-behavioral procedures (Cautela, 1975; Spinhoven, 1987). Thus, when hypnosis is used in conjunction with other procedures—as it usually is—separating out the confounded effects of hypnosis and of associated therapeutic procedures is a particularly daunting methodological challenge.

In reviewing significant developments in clinical hypnosis over the past 25 years, Fromm (1987) noted that significant progress has been made in a number of areas. In particular, she reviewed applications of clinical hypnosis in smoking cessation, weight control, phobias, and sexual dysfunction, noting that claims of success varied from one study to another and that in some areas almost all studies were flawed by a lack of experimental rigor. Nevertheless, she concluded that "the field of clinical hypnosis has become more scientifically oriented as it has moved from publishing anecdotal case reports to testing hypotheses on larger patient populations" (p. 226). Moreover, she noted that the application of hypnosis had recently been expanded to deal with psychotic, borderline, and narcissistic patients, as well as with those suffering from posttraumatic stress disorders. In conclusion, sufficient evidence, both anecdotal and experimental, exists to support the conclusion that hypnosis can benefit individuals suffering from a great variety of behavioral and physical dysfunction. Many questions, however, remain to be answered about the specific role of hypnosis and hypnotizability in producing the positive clinical outcomes reported by clinicians over the years (Frankel, 1987).

References

Ambrose, G., & Newbold, G. (1980). *A handbook of medical hypnosis* (4th ed.). London: Bailliere Tindall.

Baker, E. L. (1987). The state of the art of clinical hypnosis. *The International Journal of Clinical and Experimental Hypnosis, 35,* 203–214.

Brown, D. P., & Fromm, E. (1986). *Hypnotherapy and hypnoanalysis.* Hillsdale, NJ: Erlbaum.

Cautela, J. R. (1975). The use of covert conditioning in hypnotherapy. *International Journal of Clinical and Experimental Hypnosis, 23,* 15–27.

Coe, W. C. (1992). Hypnosis: Wherefore art thou? *The International Journal of Clinical and Experimental Hypnosis, 40,* 219–237.

Erickson, M. H. (1964). An hypnotic technique for resistant patients: The patient, the technique and its rationale and field experiments. *American Journal of Clinical Hypnosis, 1,* 8–32.

Erickson, M. H. (1981). *Experiencing hypnosis: Therapeutic approaches to altered states.* New York: Irvington.

Frankel, F. H. (1987). Significant developments in medical hypnosis during the past 25 years. *The International Journal of Clinical and Experimental Hypnosis, 35,* 231–245.

Fromm, E. (1987). Significant developments in clinical hypnosis during the past 25 years. *The International Journal of Clinical and Experimental Hypnosis, 35,* 215–230.

Gill, M. M., & Brenman, M. (1967). The metapsychology of regression and hypnosis. In J. E. Gordon (Ed.), *Handbook of clinical and experimental hypnosis* (pp. 281–318). New York: Macmillan.

Hammond, D. C. (Ed.). (1990). *Handbook of hypnotic suggestions and metaphors.* New York: Norton.

Hilgard, E. R. (1965). *Hypnotic susceptibility.* New York: Harcourt Brace Jovanovich.

Hilgard, E. R., & Hilgard, J. R. (1975). *Hypnosis in the relief of pain.* Los Altos, CA: William Kaufmann.

Jacobson, E. (1938). *Progressive relaxation.* Chicago, IL: University of Chicago Press.

Kohn, H. B. (1984). *Clinical applications of hypnosis: A manual for the health professional.* Springfield, IL: Charles C Thomas.

Kroger, W. S. (1963). *Clinical and experimental hypnosis in medicine, dentistry, and psychology.* Philadelphia, PA: Lippincott.

London, P. (1967). Ethics in hypnosis. In J. E. Gordon (Ed.), *Handbook of clinical and experimental hypnosis* (pp. 591–612). New York: Macmillan.

Olness, K., & Gardner, G. G. (1988). *Hypnosis and hypnotherapy with children* (2nd ed.). Philadelphia, PA: Grune & Stratton.

Orne, M. T. (1961). The potential uses of hypnosis in interrogation. In A. D. Biderman & H. Zimmer (Eds.), *The manipulation of human behavior* (pp. 169–215). New York: Wiley.

Pattie, F. A. (1967). A brief history of hypnotism. In J. E. Gordon (Ed.), *Handbook of clinical and experimental hypnosis* (pp. 10–43). New York: Macmillan.

Rowley, D. T. (1986). *Hypnosis and hypnotherapy*. Beckenham, England: Croom Helm.

Spinhoven, P. (1987). Hypnosis and behavior therapy: A review. *The International Journal of Clinical and Experimental Hypnosis, 35*, 8–31.

Udolf, R. (1981). *Handbook of hypnosis for professionals*. New York: Van Nostrand Reinhold.

Volgyesi, F. A. (1966). *Hypnosis in man and animals*. London: Bailliere, Tindall & Cassell.

Wadden, T. A., & Anderton, C. H. (1982). The clinical use of hypnosis. *Psychological Bulletin, 91*, 215–243.

Wright, M. E., & Wright, B. A. (1987). *Clinical practice of hypnotherapy*. New York: Guilford Press.

Weitzenhoffer, A. M. (1989). *The practice of hypnotism*, Vol. II: *Applications of traditional and semitraditional hypnotism—Nontraditional hypnotism*. New York: Wiley.

PART VIII

Psychopharmacologic Approaches

CHAPTER 24

Antipsychotic Drug Therapy

■

A number of different terms have been used to refer to antipsychotic medication. Caldwell (1978) reported that the term *neuroleptics* was introduced by the French psychiatrist Delay in 1955. Roughly translated, the term means "affecting nerve," although it has also been translated as "reduced neurologic tension" (Mason & Granacher, 1981). Another term used is *ataractics*, which means "equanimity" (Caldwell, 1978). More recently, the term *major tranquilizers* has been used, because Levenson (1981), for example, argued that several different classes of psychotropic drugs are effective in treating some psychotic conditions, so that reserving the term *antipsychotic* for the phenothiazines and related drugs would be inaccurate. Nevertheless, the term *tranquilizer* has been considered inappropriate and misleading in reference to these drugs. More recent publications appear to have settled on the term *antipsychotics*, which will be used in this chapter.

General Purpose of Antipsychotic Drug Therapy

The primary purpose of antipsychotic drugs is to reduce or eliminate psychotic symptoms in patients suffering from schizophrenia and a variety of other psychotic disorders. Indeed, antipsychotics are administered to reduce the patient's interest in, and reactivity to, the environment. Moreover, they are used to reduce agitation and restlessness, as well as aggressive and impulsive behaviors. Ultimately, antipsychotics are designed to eliminate hallucinations, delusions, and disorganized thought processes, and to allow patients to resume relatively normal lives.

History of Antipsychotic Drug Therapy

The history of psychopharmacology is, surprisingly, both ancient and modern. Drugs affecting the mind were known in ancient history, and their effects described by Homer. Caldwell (1978), in her splendid chapter on the history of psychopharmacology, traced the use of psychotropic substances from prehistory and antiquity to the beginnings of modern medicine and the revolution in psychopharmacology that was produced by the creation of chlorpromazine. Chlorpromazine, which later became known as Thorazine in the United States, did indeed revolutionize the field of psychopharmacology, and by 1955 its worldwide acceptance was demonstrated by the scientific meetings, held in Barcelona, Philadelphia, Milano, and Paris, devoted entirely to the drug (Caldwell, 1978).

The creation of chlorpromazine (CPZ) grew out of French surgeon Henri Laborit's desire to find a means of preventing surgical shock. In a series of clinical studies using antihistamines, he discovered a combination of drugs that were successful in shock prevention because they inhibited or abolished conditioned reflexes and thereby stabilized the autonomic nervous system. Apparently, however, Laborit was still dissatisfied with the cumbersome combination of drugs used in his efforts to prevent shock, and he continued to seek a single drug that would more effectively and efficiently accomplish the prevention of surgical shock. Encouraged by Laborit's success, Charpentier was charged with directing research for the French pharmaceutical company Specia to develop just such a drug. Charpentier succeeded in late 1950 with the creation of what he called chlorpromazine (Caldwell, 1978, pp. 23–27). "CPZ did exactly what Laborit wanted: it abolished preoperative anxiety, reduced surgical stress and eliminated its postoperative consequences" (Caldwell, 1978, p. 28). It was certainly not lost on Laborit that a drug capable of these accomplishments could be of great utility in psychiatry. He persuaded some of his colleagues to try CPZ in treating psychotic patients, and the first report of successful treatment was published by Sigwald and Bouttier in 1953 (as reported by Caldwell, 1978). From that point on, CPZ transformed psychiatry around the world. In France, and several other countries, CPZ was sold as Largactil, while in the United States it was introduced in 1953 as Thorazine by Smith, Kline & French.

The impact of CPZ was such that it spawned numerous investigations of related phenothiazines and other compounds in the hope of finding drugs even more effective than CPZ. Nevertheless, as recently as 1981, Iversen and Iversen concluded that CPZ remained the most important drug in clinical use as of that time. Moreover, they estimated that more than 50 million patients around the world had been treated with CPZ. The effect on psychiatric hospital populations was immediately apparent and has continued to grow. In the early 1950s, projections of California's state hospital population suggested that the number of hospitalized psychiatric patients was likely to increase tenfold within 20 years, from 30,000 to 300,000. Instead, that time period saw the patient population reduced to just 7,000 (Aden, 1978). Similar results were obtained throughout the rest of the United States and the rest of the world where CPZ was used (Julien, 1988). It is appropriate, therefore, to speak of a revolution in the field of psychopharmacology and to mark its beginning with the introduction of CPZ.

Range of Applicability

Antipsychotic medication—which today includes not only CPZ and a number of other phenothiazines, but also several nonphenothiazines—is most commonly used in the treatment of schizophrenia. Most frequently, schizophrenia is seen as involving hallucinations, delusions, incoherence, loosening of associations, catatonic behavior, blunted or grossly inappropriate emotion, and a deterioration of functioning in such areas as work, social relations, and self-care. Numerous other psychotic conditions, however, may also be appropriately treated with antipsychotic medications. Most notable among these are depressions that have psychotic features or are involutional in type, including delusional, morbid ruminations (Mason & Granacher, 1981). Bender (1990) has emphasized, however, that "no medication can serve as sole antipsychotic therapy. Pharmacotherapy will continue to be integrated with strategies that convey, rebuild, and enhance interpersonal and vocational life skills" (p. 60).

The utility of antipsychotic medication has even been extended beyond the major psychotic disorders. For example, haloperidol (Haldol) has been found effective in the treatment of Tourette's syndrome (Shapiro, Shapiro, & Wayne, 1973). Haldol has also been used successfully in treating various pain syndromes (Cavenar & Maltbie, 1976) and severe stuttering (Rosenberger, Wheelden, & Kaltokin, 1976). Antipsychotic drugs have also been used to control severe nausea and vomiting such as may be associated with surgery, and they have been used successfully in the treatment of acute intermittent porphyria (a metabolic disturbance), intractable hiccups, and tetanus (Mason & Granacher, 1981). Additional applications for antipsychotic medications may well be discovered in the future. In the meantime, however, the significant undesirable (side) effects of antipsychotic drugs require caution in extending their range of applicability.

Theoretical Foundations
Assumptions About Human Nature

The essential features of psychotic disorders are usually thought to include disordered thought processes, sensory perceptions that seem to depart from reality, disturbances in affective functioning, and impairment in social and interpersonal relationships and functioning. Although various psychotic conditions are likely to have different etiologies, these conditions are currently thought to reflect some as yet elusive biochemical or biophysiological defect. For example, Levenson (1981) noted the existence of a number of biological theories to explain the etiology of schizophrenia. Among other things, he noted that some researchers have suspected that problems occurring at the subcortical level of the brain may be responsible for schizophrenia. Others have implicated elevated levels of dopamine in the brain, and still others have blamed a hyperactive cerebral subcortical neuronal state. The discovery that lysergic acid diethylamide (LSD) had a chemical structure similar to that of the neurotransmitter serotonin also reinforced speculation about a chemical basis for schizophrenia (Dykstra, 1992). Psychoses other than schizophrenia may also be caused, at least in part, by altered levels of central nervous system biogenic amines (such as dopamine).

Although a great deal has been learned about psychotic conditions, definitive conclusions have been elusive. Evidence appears to be converging about the importance of the dopamine system in psychotic functioning. Thus, the so-called dopamine hypothesis of schizophrenia suggests that schizophrenic patients have an overactive dopamine system, for reasons not yet understood. Evidence to support this hypothesis has been accumulating for many years, but much still needs to be learned. It is no surprise, however, that antipsychotic drugs such as CPZ appear to affect the dopamine system by blocking dopamine receptors. The nature of psychoses may well be illuminated as understanding of how antipsychotic medications work increases.

Assumptions About the Action of Antipsychotic Drugs

Mode of action.   As early as 1963, animal studies suggested that antipsychotics increased the turnover of dopamine (Carlsson & Lindqvist, 1963). It was hypothesized that this increase was accomplished through the blocking of dopamine receptors. It has since been confirmed that antipsychotics act as dopamine antagonists. The specific action, however, is still not fully understood; it may include alterations in long-term receptor sensitivity, number, or both (Dykstra, 1992). All antipsychotic drugs are known to inhibit dopamine transmission in the brain in some way. It is not clear, however, whether this characteristic alone is responsible for the antipsychotic effects. At present, research is continuing to clarify the specific nature of the antipsychotics' inhibition of dopamine transmission (for example, Carlsson, 1988).

Pharmacokinetics.   Pharmacokinetics is concerned with the absorption, distribution, metabolism, and excretion of a drug in the organism (Mason & Granacher, 1981). All these factors are important in determining the therapeutic response to particular antipsychotic drugs. Pharmacokinetics is particularly important because there is still no accurate method for establishing the appropriate dose or dosage schedule in using these drugs. Kinetic information on antipsychotic drugs is thus important in guiding their clinical use. Although the risk of acute toxicity is low with all of the commonly used antipsychotic drugs, their considerable side effects make prolonged overdosage particularly troublesome.

The therapeutic effect resulting from the administration of antipsychotic drugs clearly is related not only to its action on dopamine transmission in the brain, but also to the human body's effects on the drug. At this point, it is known that intramuscular forms of antipsychotic drugs provide the fastest absorption and bioavailability (Mason & Granacher, 1981). It is also known that monitoring the plasma levels of antipsychotic agents is difficult and does not provide clear guidance to the prescribing physician. Finally, it should be noted that antipsychotic drugs are metabolized almost exclusively through the liver and eliminated primarily through the kidneys.

Chemical structure.   The specific chemical structure of the antipsychotic drugs is not directly relevant to the focus of the present chapter. Nevertheless, it is useful to understand that the majority of antipsychotic drugs in use today belong to the same chemical class as the original antipsychotic drug, CPZ, which is marketed as Thorazine. This class is the phenothiazines. Other drugs in this class are known by the trade names Prolixin, Trilafon, Mellaril, and Stelazine. There are others, and new ones are introduced almost every year. Among the nonphenothiazines, haloperidol—known by its trade name, Haldol—has received the most attention. Others, however, include drugs known by the trade names of Clozaril, Loxitane, Moban, and Navane.

Implementing Antipsychotic Drug Therapy
Assessment Before Psychopharmacological Disposition

The decision to prescribe antipsychotic medication has potentially far-reaching consequences. Although antipsychotic drugs are relatively safe, their side effects may be serious. Moreover, if antipsychotic drugs are prescribed inappropriately, the effects of the medication may mask the condition that should be treated instead, thereby causing potentially significant harm to the patient. Consequently, proper evaluation of the patient should be thorough, focusing on understanding the whole person and his or her life circumstances. Although some emergency circumstances may mandate a "rapid psychiatric assessment" (Levenson, 1981), decisions about whether or not to use antipsychotic drugs should ideally be based on a thorough assessment prior to their initial administration.

History.   Several features of the patient's history should be evaluated prior to prescribing antipsychotic medication. Obviously, the patient's prior psychiatric history is of paramount interest. Particularly important is determining whether the patient has ever been diagnosed as previously having a psychotic disorder that resulted in the prescription of antipsychotic medications. Obviously, the patient's drug history should be obtained because it is particularly relevant in making a rational psychopharmacological disposition. The drug history should include not only drugs prescribed for psychiatric disorder, but any drugs that have been prescribed in the past, as well as the patient's reactions to those drugs. If the patient has previously taken antipsychotic medication, the patient's subjective assessment of such past experience may be particularly important and predictive of how the patient will deal with antipsychotic medication in the future. Family drug history should also be obtained, if possible, because response to psychoactive drugs may be similar among blood relatives.

In addition to examining the patient's prescription drug history, the patient's illicit drug history and past and current patterns of alcohol use must also be reviewed. Establishing a good history in those areas is important for several reasons. For example, diagnostic evaluations designed to determine the etiology of psychotic symptoms are particularly difficult if the patient has used, for example, hallucinogens or other psychoactive substances that are capable of producing hallucinations and other sensory aberrations. In addition, it is important to determine whether psychotic symptoms that may be experienced at the time of hospitalization are the consequence of illicit drug use, alcohol abuse, or an underlying psychotic disorder. Because antipsychotic medications may interact with various illicit psychoactive substances as well as with alcohol, the prescribing physician should assess the likelihood that such unwanted interactions will occur once the patient is no longer under the around-the-clock supervision likely to be provided in a psychiatric hospital or drug and alcohol rehabilitation center.

Other potentially important aspects of the patient's history are frequently neglected. These include the developmental history of the patient—whether developmental milestones were reached at appropriate times, and whether the patient had unusual childhood illnesses or special problems during puberty, in school, or in dealing with peers. Although family background and current family circumstances may be more extensively evaluated by a social worker, such information should be available as part of the predisposition assessment. In addition, especially when working with adolescents, determining whether a patient is actually psychotic and therefore a candidate for receiving antipsychotic medication is often very difficult. Under such circumstances, a psychological evaluation, including both objective and projective tests, may be necessary to help clarify the diagnosis. Since antipsychotic medication may significantly affect a patient's performance on such tests, they should be conducted prior to the administration of such drugs whenever possible.

Physical examination.   A physical examination is routinely administered to patients admitted to psychiatric hospitals, as well as to patients who go to hospital emergency rooms. The routine physical examination should also include a routine neurological examination (Mason & Granacher, 1981). Even when patients are treated on an outpatient basis, such examinations should be part of the overall evaluation.

Psychiatric review of symptoms.   Levenson (1981) suggested that the subjective component of this review should consist of a series of questions designed to elicit information about sleep, appetite, mood, thought processes, conflicts, fears, and hallucinations. In addition, several questions regarding short- and long-term memory, reality testing, and cognitive functioning should be included. The objective component of this mental status examination should consist of observations made during the clinical interview regarding the patient's motor activity, affect, thought processes, thought content, and level of central nervous system state of consciousness (Levenson, 1981, p. 86). "As a general rule, no medication should be prescribed until as accurate as possible diagnosis has been made and then only if the patient's symptoms are of a type known to be relieved by antipsychotics" (Mason & Granacher, 1981, p. 24).

Choice of Drug and Determination of Dosage

Chlorpromazine (CPZ), the first antipsychotic drug, belongs to the chemical class of phenothiazines. Since the introduction of CPZ, at least 20 additional antipsychotics have been developed, most of which also belong to the phenothiazine class. Four classes of antipsychotics, however, have a chemical structure different from the phenothiazines. Antipsychotics based on different chemical bases may affect individual patients differently. None of the antipsychotics developed thus far has been proven to be more or less effective in the treatment of psychosis (Mason & Granacher, 1981). It has been shown, however, that some antipsychotics produce more sedation than others—a side effect that is not always desirable. Also, some drugs can be administered intramuscularly (for quick response in a disruptive or violent patient), whereas others are not available in this form. Thus, the choice of a specific antipsychotic drug needs to be based on a number of considerations, including the patient's response to antipsychotic medication during a previous illness. In addition, the choice of antipsychotic drug will be made primarily to ensure compliance, to reduce possible complications based on preexisting conditions, to reduce the intensity of side effects, and, of course, to maximize the therapeutic benefit.

Antipsychotic drug therapy sometimes fails because too low a dosage is prescribed. Mason and Granacher (1981) pointed out that overly conservative clinicians may start out with a dosage that is far too low, which is then raised gradually over the course of several weeks. This practice sometimes results in unnecessarily delaying the elimination of acute psychotic symptoms and in prolonging the patient's hospitalization. Prescribing adequate initial dosages requires that physicians clearly understand the relationship between dose and potency in the different antipsychotic drugs they may use. Moreover, the specific dosage of the drug must be related to the patient's status and needs. With some exceptions, dosage ceilings have generally not been recommended, because in some instances therapeutic responses have occurred only at megadoses that could be administered only to hospitalized patients (Bender, 1990). An additional consideration in choosing the proper drug and dosage is that only one antipsychotic agent should be used at a time (Mason & Granacher, 1981). Although the use of multiple agents has been shown to be beneficial in treating other disorders, there is no evidence to suggest that the administration of multiple antipsychotic drugs offers any benefits. Moreover, such multiple administration is likely to increase the chances of producing side effects and to confuse the issue of which drug is producing what effect.

Target Symptoms

Once the decision is made that antipsychotic medication is appropriate, it is important to identify target symptoms being treated with the prescribed medication. It is assumed, of course, that these target symptoms are part of a potentially psychopharmacologically responsive clinical syndrome. The elimination or amelioration of the target symptoms should be a clearly enunciated and communicated therapeutic goal, which should be reflected in the patient's treatment plan. The effects of the prescribed medication on the target symptoms, and on patient behavior in general, should be carefully recorded on a regular basis (Mason & Granacher, 1981).

The Course of Therapy

Patients' responses to specific antipsychotic drugs vary considerably. After a drug has been chosen for a given patient, however, the patient should be given an optimal dosage for a sufficient length of time to determine whether the drug produces the desired effects. The length of a drug trial will always depend on the patient's status, as well as on the clinician's preferences. Usually, if a patient fails to improve after receiving a drug for approximately 6 weeks, a shift to another drug may be warranted. Lehmann (1975) suggested a timetable to predict approximately the response of particular symptoms to antipsychotic drug medication. This timetable suggests that arousal symptoms may respond within 2 to 3 weeks, affective symptoms within 2 to 5 weeks, and symptoms related to perceptual and cognitive functions within 6 to 8 weeks. Clearly, however, this timetable is only a general guide; significant deviations frequently occur.

Once the patient's psychotic symptoms have been eliminated or greatly reduced, the antipsychotic medication should be reduced to a maintenance level. Only very rarely can antipsychotic medication be discontinued as soon as the patient's condition has stabilized and acute psychotic symptoms have disappeared. Although reducing medication to the lowest level necessary to maintain therapeutic effectiveness is a desirable goal, it has been suggested that the most common error in maintenance therapy is to reduce the dosage too quickly (Mason & Granacher, 1981).

Over the years, several studies have demonstrated that complete discontinuation of antipsychotic drug therapy is likely to result in relapse (Prien & Klett, 1972). This finding suggests that most patients need continuing (prophylactic) antipsychotic drug therapy. Some patients, however, do not relapse even when antipsychotic medication is permanently withdrawn. At best, caution is recommended prior to withdrawal of antipsychotic medication; even then withdrawal of medication should be accompanied by continuous supervision.

The Problem of Compliance

"The most important single cause of the return of psychotic symptoms, relapse and readmission to a psychiatric facility is still the failure of the patient to take the antipsychotic drug or in the dosage prescribed" (Mason & Granacher, 1981, p. 88). Patients often do not take their prescribed antipsychotic medication, for many different reasons. One major reason is that some of the side effects are extremely unpleasant and result in drug discontinuation once patients are discharged from the hospital. Another reason is that a significant subset of patients has a very negative attitude toward taking medication, which is sometimes unwittingly reinforced by well-meaning individuals concerned about patients using medications as crutches and as excuses for failing to take charge of their lives.

A number of means are available to maximize compliance with a prescribed medication regimen. For example, whenever possible, the patient's family should be educated about the need for continuing medication even when overt symptoms of psychosis disappear. Ideally, the patient and his or her family should be involved in discharge and aftercare planning that should include provision for ensuring compliance, especially when a long-term maintenance drug regimen is indicated. In some cases, sustained release depot injection of high-potency antipsychotic medication, which lasts for 2 to 4 weeks, may be used when compliance cannot be otherwise ensured (Bender, 1990).

Informed Consent

Ideally, every patient who receives antipsychotic medication, or any other treatment, should have an opportunity to give fully informed consent to the treatment in question. In some instances of acute psychotic conditions, informed consent may not be possible, and the patient's family may need to be enlisted to make these decisions for the patient. In each case, however, it is the physician's responsibility to assist the patient, the patient's family, or both in deciding whether to give or withhold informed consent on the basis of a sound understanding of both the benefits and the risks or disadvantages that accompany the treatment. In the case of antipsychotic drugs, the risks are well-known. Although the specific occurrence of risk factors in a given patient cannot be predicted with certainty, patients can be informed about the relative likelihood of suffering certain side effects or discomfort from the use of such medications. At the same time, patients must be given a realistic assessment of their prospects if they choose not to participate in the recommended treatment and to take the prescribed antipsychotic medication. Ultimately, it should be the patient's decision whether to take antipsychotic drugs or to attempt alternative treatments instead.

Means and Conditions for Implementing Antipsychotic Drug Therapy
Qualifications of Personnel

Antipsychotic medication must be administered by a properly qualified physician. Special psychiatric training is generally preferred in prescribing and supervising antipsychotic medication, primarily because of the seriousness of psychotic disorders, on the one hand, and the potential for serious side effects, on the other. A psychiatrist with experience in the administration of antipsychotic drugs is highly desirable also because many psychotic patients constitute a danger to themselves or to others, in part because they may be quite out of touch with reality. Moreover, the effects of psychoactive medications are very difficult to quantify (Hughes & Pierattini, 1992), and selection of specific drugs and dosage regimens is typically guided as much by the experience of the prescribing psychiatrist as by any generalizable rules.

Frequently, the treatment of psychotic patients requires collaborative relationships between physicians and nonmedical mental health professionals, such as social workers and psychologists. In order for antipsychotic drug therapy to be maximally helpful to the patient, such nonmedical professionals must understand and appreciate both the potential and the limitations of the use of drugs in treating psychotic conditions. Moreover, a basic understanding of the therapeutic effect and the side effects of various drugs will enable nonmedical professionals to collaborate with medical personnel in ensuring the most beneficial use of medication on behalf of the patient. Equally important, the prescribing physician must understand and appreciate the interdependence of the various mental health professionals in the treatment of psychotic patients (Hughes & Pierattini, 1992), particularly once patients are discharged from the hospital and treated on an outpatient basis. Under those circumstances, nonmedical professionals are most likely to see the patient on a frequent basis and thus are best situated to identify possible adverse reactions to the antipsychotic drug regimen. Effective communication between prescribing physician and other professionals is therefore essential (see, for example, Beitman & Klerman, 1991).

Conditions for Conducting Antipsychotic Drug Therapy

The initial administration of antipsychotic medication is most likely to occur in a psychiatric ward or psychiatric hospital. Obviously, such facilities would require the usual staffing, including qualified psychiatric nurses and other personnel to ensure constant clinical observation and supervision of patients who are beginning antipsychotic drug therapy (Shearer, 1975). Moreover, such facilities would be expected to be fully staffed and supplied with medications and apparatus that may be necessary to investigate the causes of unusual side effects or other unfavorable reactions patients may display when first receiving antipsychotic drugs.

Limitations of Antipsychotic Drug Therapy
Contraindications

There are at least two absolute contraindications to the use of antipsychotic medication. The first of these is a previously observed allergic reaction. The most frequently noted allergic reaction has been referred to as CPZ-induced jaundice, although the reaction can also be produced by other phenothiazines. This jaundice generally occurs in fewer than 1% of patients and typically closely resembles the jaundice from infectious hepatitis (Davis & Casper, 1978). The second absolute contraindication is a declining level of central nervous system consciousness, which may be due to any cause, either intracerebral or extracerebral (Levenson, 1981).

Hazards

The hazards involved in the clinical use of antipsychotic drugs are typically discussed under the topic of so-called side effects. There has been some discussion about whether the term *adverse effects* is more appropriate. Mason and Granacher (1981) have argued, however, that some of the effects produced by antipsychotic drugs, such as the orthostatic hypotension produced by CPZ, may be desirable from the standpoint of a neurosurgeon managing posttraumatic hypertension. In spite of this and other potential exceptions, most side effects produced by antipsychotic drugs are unpleasant at best and quite serious at worst. Moreover, it can be difficult, at times, to distinguish some side effects from symptoms of the disease that the medication is intended to treat (Hughes & Pierattini, 1992). There are several major classes of side effects of antipsychotic drugs.

Autonomic side effects.   Perhaps the most frequent complaints of patients treated with antipsychotic drugs are related to the anticholinergic properties of these drugs. The most annoying of these is the experience of dry mouth. The more anticholinergic the antipsychotic, the more likely dry mouth is to occur. Although frequently annoying to patients, this condition is not particularly serious, except in cases when it interferes with the wearing of dentures, which in turn can lead to poor eating habits (Fann & Shannon, 1978). Patients may also experience nasal congestion and constipation. Mason and Granacher (1981) have observed that antipsychotic drugs probably decrease bowel function and that, due to their anticholinergic activity, they may mask various surgical complications. Moreover, a number of ophthalmological side effects, including blurred vision and acute glaucoma, are possible as a consequence of antipsychotic agents. Finally, it should be noted that inhibition of ejaculation can occur, thus seriously interfering with sexual functioning in men.

Cardiac side effects.   By far the most common cardiovascular side effect of antipsychotic agents is orthostatic hypotension (hypotension that is made worse upon assuming an upright posture). Apparently, however, tolerance of this side effect develops quite quickly. Obviously, this side effect can be more serious in the elderly and in cardiac patients. Antipsychotic drugs also produce electrocardiogram (EKG) changes in approximately half of all patients. It is unclear whether any of these EKG changes are implicated in the occasional reports of unexpected and sudden death in psychotic patients who receive antipsychotic drugs (Mason & Granacher, 1981).

Central nervous system (CNS) side effects.   Neurologic side effects are recognized as the most dramatic side effects of all antipsychotic drugs. Generally, they are classified into extrapyramidal (EPS) and nonextrapyramidal CNS symptoms. The extrapyramidal symptoms include three subcategories—namely, dystonic reactions, akathesia, and parkinsonian reactions. All of them are movement disorders. Dystonic reactions include dystonias, such as exaggerated posturing of the head, face, or neck, difficulty swallowing, lip and tongue movements, and fixed upward gaze; dyskinesias, or repetitive movements of the shoulders and legs and various facial tics; and tardive dyskinesia. Tardive dyskinesia is considered a potentially irreversible side effect that occurs late in the course of treatment, sometimes appearing after treatment has been discontinued. It is characterized by grimacing, sucking and smacking movements of the lips, and tongue protrusion. It may also be accompanied by unusual pelvic thrust movements; finger, ankle, or toe jerks; and neck twisting.

The second subcategory of EPS is akathesia, which consists of restlessness and inability to refrain from moving. The third component of EPS, parkinsonian reactions, include akinesias (rigidity, stiffness, unusual gait, mask-like facial expression, and slowed speech) and tremors (pill-rolling movements of fingers and rhythmic movement of hands and arms). Nonextrapyramidal CNS effects include variable degrees of sedation, depending on the specific drug used, and a raising of the seizure threshold (Bender, 1990; Davis & Casper, 1978; Mason & Granacher, 1981).

When drug-induced extrapyramidal side effects occur, standard practice has been to use antiparkinson medication in order to alleviate these symptoms. The most commonly used antiparkinson drug has been benzotropine (most commonly sold as Cogentin), although several others are also available. Some disagreements among experts have occurred about whether to use antiparkinson drugs concurrently with antipsychotics on a routine basis as a prophylactic. At this time, however, the consensus appears to be that antiparkinson drugs should be added only after EPS is observed and then should be discontinued after approximately 3 months. In most patients, extrapyramidal symptoms will not recur to any significant degree. If they do return, antiparkinson drugs should be reinstated (Bender, 1990; Mason & Granacher, 1981).

Dermatological side effects.   A variety of drug eruptions have been reported to be associated with antipsychotic drugs, most commonly allergic dermatitis, affecting primarily the face, neck, upper chest, and extremities. In addition, photosensitivity and hyperpigmentation represent rarely observed side effects. Most of these are quickly reversed when the offending drug is withdrawn (Mason & Granacher, 1981).

Inappropriate use.   When originally introduced, antipsychotic drugs were sometimes seen as wonder drugs that could turn previously chaotic psychiatric hospital wards into peaceful and quiet units populated by calm and rational patients. As a consequence, concerns were raised about overprescribing antipsychotic drugs in order simply to sedate all patients and keep them quiet and submissive. Although such abuses undoubtedly occurred, current uses of antipsychotic medications are far more sophisticated and based on many years of experience, resulting in a far more judicious use of these drugs. Legitimate concerns remain, however, about the possibility that in some patients antipsychotic medications mask symptoms that need to be observed and understood in order to effectively help the patient. For example, in some cases the symptoms of posttraumatic stress disorder may be masked through the use of antipsychotic drugs, producing a situation in which the most critical problem of the patient is not understood or treated properly.

The Effectiveness of Antipsychotic Drug Therapy

The history of antipsychotic drugs, starting with the introduction of CPZ in the early 1950s, is a history of success. CPZ and related drugs that were subsequently developed did, indeed, revolutionize the treatment of psychiatric patients in general and psychotic patients in particular. Large mental hospitals for chronic patients became a thing of the past, and even the most optimistic projections for the number of people hospitalized in psychiatric hospitals turned out to be far too conservative. In spite of this success story, Dykstra (1992, p. 91) quoted Barnes (1987) as follows:

> If you put everything that is known about schizophrenia into a pot and boiled it down you would come up with three things—it seems to run in families, . . . [antipsychotics] make it better, and there may be something structurally abnormal in the brains of schizophrenics.

Part of the reason for this uncertain verdict is that there is disagreement over whether antipsychotic drugs simply ameliorate symptoms or whether they actually change (improve or even cure) the underlying condition. At this point, it is safe to say that no serious mental health professional or researcher would take the position that the antipsychotic drugs positively cure schizophrenia or any other psychotic disorder. On the other hand, increasing evidence suggests that antipsychotic medication does more than simply remove the most serious symptoms of psychosis (while producing serious side effects). Clearly, the field is far too complex to permit simplistic generalizations about the effectiveness of antipsychotic drugs. Whether they work, how well they work, and what they accomplish is ultimately dependent upon a complex interaction between a complex biological organism, the environment within which that organism operates, and the drug that is administered to the organism. There are great difficulties in measuring psychosis (Dykstra, 1992), and animal models in experimental psychopharmacology (see, for example,

Willner, 1991) can offer only limited insight into the action of specific drugs upon a given disease. Consequently, the extensive research literature on the effectiveness of antipsychotic medication leads to the conclusion that this medication either is very effective or else does not work, depending on what frame of reference one chooses to employ. In the absence of an objective and agreed-upon means of establishing the effectiveness of antipsychotic medication, the transformation of psychiatric practice outlined in this chapter represents the strongest evidence that antipsychotic medication does something, and that something is generally good.

References

Aden, G. C. (1978). Foreword. In W. G. Clark & J. del Giudice (Eds.), *Principles of psychopharmacology* (2nd ed., pp. xix–xxii). New York: Academic Press.

Barnes, D. M. (1987). Biological issues in schizophrenia. *Science, 235,* 430–433.

Beitman, B. D., & Klerman, G. L. (1991). *Integrating pharmacotherapy and psychotherapy.* Washington, D.C.: American Psychiatric Press.

Bender, K. J. (1990). *Psychiatric medications: A guide for mental health professionals.* Newbury Park, CA: Russell Sage Foundation.

Caldwell, A. E. (1978). History of psychopharmacology. In W. G. Clark & J. del Giudice (Eds.), *Principles of psychopharmacology* (2nd ed., pp. 9–40). New York: Academic Press.

Carlsson, A. (1988). The current status of the dopamine hypothesis of schizophrenia. *Neuropsychopharmacology, 1,* 179–186.

Carlsson, A., & Lindqvist, J. (1963). Effect of chlorpromazine and haloperidol on formation of 3-methoxytyramine and normetanephrine in mouse brain. *Acta Pharmacol, 20,* 140–144.

Cavenar, J. O., Jr., & Maltbie, A. A. (1976). Another indication for haloperidol. *Psychosomatics, 17,* 128–130.

Davis, J. M., & Casper, R. C. (1978). Side effects of psychotropic drugs and their management. In W. G. Clark & J. del Giudice (Eds.), *Principles of psychopharmacology* (2nd ed., pp. 479–536). New York: Academic Press.

Dykstra, L. (1992). Drug action. In J. Grabowski & G. R. VandenBos (Eds.), *Psychopharmacology: Basic mechanisms and applied interventions* (pp. 63–96). Washington, D.C.: American Psychological Association.

Fann, W. E., & Shannon, I. L. (1978). A treatment for dry mouth in psychiatric patients. *American Journal of Psychiatry, 135,* 251–252.

Hughes, J. R., & Pierattini, R. A. (1992). An introduction to pharmacotherapy for mental disorders. In J. Grabowski & G. R. VandenBos (Eds.),

Psychopharmacology: Basic mechanisms and applied interventions (pp. 97–125). Washington, D.C.: American Psychological Association.

Iversen, S. D., & Iversen, L. L. (1981). *Behavioral pharmacology*. New York: Oxford University Press.

Julien, R. M. (1988). *A primer of drug action* (5th ed.). New York: W. H. Freeman.

Lehmann, H. E. (1975). Psychopharmacological treatment of schizophrenia. *Schizophrenia Bulletin*, Whole Issue No. 13.

Levenson, A. J. (1981). *Basic psychopharmacology*. New York: Springer.

Mason, A. S., & Granacher, R. P. (1981). *Clinical handbook of antipsychotic drug therapy*. New York: Brunner/Mazel.

Prien, R. F., & Klett, C. J. (1972). An appraisal of long-term use of tranquilizing medication with hospitalized chronic schizophrenics. *Schizophrenia Bulletin*, 5, 64–73.

Rosenberger, P. B., Wheelden, J. A., & Kaltokin, M. (1976). Effect of haloperidol on stuttering. *American Journal of Psychiatry*, 133, 331–334.

Shapiro, A. K., Shapiro, E., & Wayne, H. (1973). Treatment of Tourette's Syndrome with haloperidol, a review of 34 cases. *Archives of General Psychiatry*, 28, 92–97.

Shearer, J. C. (1975). *Introductory clinical pharmacology*. Philadelphia: Lippincott.

Willner, P. (Ed.). (1991). *Behavioural models in psychopharmacology: Theoretical, industrial, and clinical perspectives*. New York: Cambridge University Press.

CHAPTER 25

Antidepressant Drug Therapy

The term *depression* has multiple meanings, both in everyday language and in psychopathology. In clinical psychology and in psychiatry, a number of different types of depressive syndromes are recognized, which manifest themselves in a variety of ways. Depression is likely to be the most common psychiatric disturbance, with some estimates indicating that as many as 10 to 20% of the adult population in the United States may experience a depressive episode at some time in their adult life (Mandel & Klerman, 1978). Two types of antidepressant medication were introduced during the 1950s: the mono-amine oxidase inhibitor (MAOI) antidepressants and the tricyclic antidepressants. Both of these drug groups will be discussed in this chapter.

General Purpose of Antidepressant Drug Therapy

The essential feature of depression is dysphoric mood, often accompanied by loss of interest or pleasure in most aspects of daily life. Associated with this dysphoria, to varying degrees, are a variety of other symptoms, including appetite and sleep disturbance, psychomotor agitation or retardation, decreased energy, difficulty concentrating, and suicidal ideation (APA, 1989). The principal purpose of antidepressant drug therapy is to restore normal affective functioning and thereby restore more adequate regulation of appetite, sleep, motor activity, and energy. Moreover, individuals who are treated successfully will regain the capacity to experience pleasure, to feel worthwhile, and to enjoy life.

History of Antidepressant Drug Therapy

Although the history of psychiatric efforts to treat depression with drugs and by other means (such as electroconvulsive therapy) is quite lengthy, the era of modern antidepressive drug therapy dates back to the 1950s. Caldwell (1978) reported that the antidepressant action of monoamine oxidase inhibitors (MAOIs) was first discovered in tuberculosis patients who were treated with the antituberculosis drug iproniazid in 1952. Apparently, subsequent clinical trials received mixed reviews, particularly because some patients developed severe toxic reactions to iproniazid. Still, iproniazid and subsequently other MAOIs began to be routinely used in psychiatry starting in 1957.

The development of tricyclic antidepressants was actually closely related to the development of the first of the modern antipsychotic drugs, chlorpromazine (CPZ). The Swiss psychiatrist, Roland Kuhn, had been working with the pharmaceutical company Geigy on developing a less expensive drug that could produce effects similar to CPZ. By 1957 this effort led to the rediscovery of a compound that had first been synthesized in 1948. It failed to meet Kuhn's expectation of having effects similar to CPZ, but he did discover that it had significant antidepressive effects. The drug was the first tricyclic antidepressant, imipramine (Caldwell, 1978). Although tricyclic antidepressants began to be routinely used in psychiatry almost immediately and continue to be used at present, currently available non-MAOI antidepressants are more accurately described as heterocyclics, or second-generation antidepressants, because in recent years new antidepressants with one-, two-, and many-ring chemical structures have been added to the compounds with three-ring chemical structures, the original tricyclics (Bender, 1990; Hughes & Pierattini, 1992).

Range of Applicability

Both heterocyclic antidepressants and MAOIs are used first and foremost in the treatment of depression. Hughes and Pierattini (1992) have recently summarized the applicability of antidepressants and suggested that antidepressants are indicated in the treatment of organic mental disorders (specifically, dementia with depression), as well as in the treatment of organic mental disorders associated with physical disorders when depression is manifested.

Moreover, they specified that antidepressants are the treatment of choice in major depression and that they can also be used in the treatment of panic disorder or agoraphobia. They are also used in the treatment of bipolar disorder, depressed phase. It should be emphasized, however, that lithium has generally been the treatment of choice in the treatment of bipolar disorder because of its effectiveness in virtually eliminating the manic excitement that is usually associated with bipolar disorder. In some cases, lithium may be prescribed concurrently with a tricyclic, or second-generation, antidepressant (Schou, 1978).

One particular tricyclic antidepressant, clomipramine (Anafranil) has been used in recent years in the treatment of obsessive-compulsive disorder (Hughes & Pierattini, 1992). Another recently introduced antidepressant, actually a bicyclic antidepressant named fluoxetine (Prozac), has also shown promise in the treatment of obsessive-compulsive disorder (Bender, 1990). Finally, it should be noted that imipramine (Tofranil) has been used extensively in the treatment of what is now called attention deficit hyperactivity disorder, a disorder that has been referred to by a variety of names, including minimal brain dysfunction or hyperkinesis (Kornetsky, 1976). Imipramine has also been used in the treatment of enuresis.

Theoretical Foundations

Assumptions About Human Nature

The specific biochemical basis for depression is not completely understood at this time. It is known, however, that depression is associated with a deficiency of norepinephrine at synapses in the brain. There is speculation, based primarily on animal studies, that norepinephrine plays a role in mediating conscious arousal and reward and reinforcement functions, all of which may be affected in depression. Moreover, it has been shown that drugs that lower the relative concentration of norepinephrine can produce depression. Conversely, drugs that restore norepinephrine have the potential for effectively treating depression. Thus, it is not surprising that most of the major drug groups that have been used in the treatment of depression have the effect of elevating the level of norepinephrine in the brain (Levenson, 1981).

From a clinical perspective, a number of different syndromes are primarily depressive in nature. In addition, depression occurs as a symptom in a variety of psychopathological states; in some syndromes it is more central than in others. Clinically, depression is usually characterized by a low mood. Consequently, early efforts to treat depression pharmacologically focused on drugs that could elevate mood. Hence, stimulants (for the most part amphetamines) were used extensively in the treatment of depression, especially prior to the discovery of tricyclic antidepressants. Since depression usually involves a great deal more than lowered mood, however, amphetamines were found to be generally unsatisfactory, and they are no longer widely used in the treatment of clinical depression.

Some clinicians have found it useful to divide depression into endogenous and exogenous types. Endogenous depression is typically not obviously related to any environmental events, whereas exogenous or reactive depression is felt to occur as a consequence of stressful environmental events. Even so, exogenous depressions are assumed to represent depressive reactions that go beyond the reactions of grief and sadness the average person may experience following a loss or other catastrophic event. The revised third edition of the *Diagnostic and Statistical Manual of the American Psychiatric Association* (APA, 1989) no longer makes the distinction between endogenous and exogenous depression, in part because it is often difficult to establish and in part because it may not be meaningful from the standpoint of treatment.

The DSM-III-R still identifies a number of different depressive syndromes, including major depression, which may occur with or without psychotic features, and dysthymia (formerly called depressive neurosis). In addition, the DSM-III-R identifies two types of affective disorders that include both depressive and manic features. One of these is bipolar disorder, which may or may not include psychotic features; the other is cyclothymia, which is considered to be a less severe cyclic disorder.

The variety of disease entities that include depressive symptomatology precludes the identification of a single mechanism of depression and consequently the development of a single drug that is likely to be effective in treating depression. Hence, the following discussion of heterocyclic antidepressants and MAOIs will attempt to identify the conditions for which they have been found to be effective. We will not deal with conditions that may include depressive features but for which other drugs may be more appropriate (such as lithium in the treatment of bipolar disorder).

Assumptions About the Action of Antidepressant Drugs

Mode of action.   The specific mechanisms of action of the MAOIs, the tricyclic antidepressants, and the heterocyclic antidepressants (the latter also being called atypical or second-generation antidepressants) are not clear (Dykstra, 1992). Current scientific evidence suggests that they may reestablish regulation of dysfunctional neurotransmitter release and receptor responses that may form the basis of depression (Lipinski, Cohen, Zubenko, & Waternaux, 1987). The biogenic amine theory of depression, originally proposed by Schildkraut (1965), was based on the observation that reserpine, which decreased levels of the monoamines, norepinephrine, dopamine, and serotonin, also produced sedation in animals and depression in some people. The tricyclic antidepressants increased the concentration of monoamines by blocking their reuptake back into the presynaptic element, thereby increasing the level of monoamines at the synapse; the monoamine oxidase inhibitors also increased the concentration of monoamines by blocking their enzymatic destruction. (Dykstra, 1992, p. 83)

Although this view was prevalent for more than two decades, evidence accumulated in recent years has raised questions about its adequacy—partly because much of the supporting research was obtained from animal studies that used analogs of depression in humans to study the effects of these drugs. Research with humans, and particularly with depressed individuals, has not produced the same results. Moreover, various substances that are also known to increase levels of monoamines, such as cocaine and amphetamines, have not been found to be effective antidepressants. In addition, although monoamine concentrations are raised almost immediately after administration of antidepressant drugs, their clinical effects as antidepressants require as much as 2 or 3 weeks to become evident (Dykstra, 1992).

Current views on the action of antidepressant drugs suggest that their method of action may be more complicated than originally thought. Moreover, the second-generation antidepressants work still differently than the tricyclic antidepressants or the MAOIs do (Dykstra, 1992). Current research is focusing on multiple changes that may be produced in receptor sensitivity as a result of administration of antidepressants. At this point, it is probably safe to assume that successful antidepressant drug therapy restores complex neuroregulatory processes and that the functioning of the pertinent receptor systems is somehow normalized (Bender, 1990).

Pharmacokinetics.   The pharmacokinetics of tricyclic antidepressants are similar to those of antipsychotic drugs. One major difference, however, is that the time required to establish effective plasma concentrations delays the onset of therapeutic effects for approximately 10 days to 3 weeks (Levenson, 1981). Also, when tricyclic antidepressants are administered concurrently with antipsychotic drugs, a two- to threefold potentiation of the antidepressant occurs. Moreover, since both antipsychotic drugs and tricyclic antidepressants can cause anticholinergic side effects, those side effects may be exacerbated when these drugs are combined (Levenson, 1981).

Chemical structure.   Monoamine oxidase (MAO) is an enzyme that breaks down catecholamines. By inhibiting this enzyme, MAOIs act by making more catecholamines available at the synapses. The heterocyclic antidepressants, on the other hand, do not inhibit monoamine oxidase, but they are potent inhibitors of catecholamine uptake mechanisms. Consequently, both types of chemical compounds (the MAOIs and the heterocyclic antidepressants) have a similar effect.

The MAOIs consist of two classes of compounds—namely, the hydrazine and nonhydrazine derivatives. Hydrazine is highly toxic to the liver; consequently, compounds that served as potent MAO inhibitors but were not hydrazine derivatives were developed (Iversen & Iversen, 1981). The nonhydrazine MAOIs are compounds that are structurally related to amphetamine. Hydrazine derivative MAOIs include isocarboxazid (Marplan), phenelzine (Nardil), and nialamide (Niamid). The nonhydrazines include tranylcypromine (Parnate) and pargyline (Eutonyl) (Kornetsky, 1976).

The first antidepressants, originally introduced by Roland Kuhn, were the tricyclic antidepressants, so-called because of their three-ring molecular core. They include, among others, amitriptyline (Elavil), desipramine (Norpramin), doxepin (Sinequan), imipramine (Tofranil), nortriptyline (Aventyl), protriptyline (Vivactil), and trimipramine (Surmontil) (Bender, 1990, p. 32). The so-called second-generation antidepressants include compounds with a variety of ring structures, including fluoxetine (Prozac), a two-ring structure, and bupropion (Wellbutrin), which is a single-ring compound. Other second-generation compounds include amoxapine (Asendin), maprotiline (Ludiomil), and trazadone (Desyrel) (Bender, 1990).

Implementing Antidepressant Drug Therapy
Assessment Before Psychopharmacological Disposition

Depression is a potentially lethal disease. Suicide attempts are common in depressed patients, and thousands of depressed individuals succeed in taking their own lives. Because there are a number of different depressive syndromes, each with several subtypes, proper identification and accurate diagnosis of depression is essential. In addition, different kinds of depression respond to different antidepressant drugs. Thus, although the prevention of suicide may be the top priority in emergency cases, thorough and comprehensive evaluation of the patient and the patient's life circumstances should ordinarily be accomplished before antidepressant drug therapy is begun.

History.   Serious depressive conditions often have both a biological and psychological basis. Although it is now widely accepted that there is a biological basis for bipolar disorder (formerly known as manic depressive disorder), the role of environmental stress in the occurrence and timing of either manic or depressive episodes is not well understood. Moreover, even though there appears to be a genetic link in the etiology of bipolar disorder, specific mechanisms remain elusive. Nevertheless, a patient's family history of depressive disorder, especially bipolar disorder, needs to be ascertained, since it may be a key to differentiating a depressive episode occurring as part of a major depression from a depressive episode occurring within a bipolar cycle. In the former case a tricyclic antidepressant may be the most appropriate drug, whereas in the latter case lithium may be the drug of choice.

The patient's history is also a useful means to determine the role of psychosocial and other environmental stresses in the person's life. The relative centrality of stress in the development of a particular disorder can often be ascertained by establishing the coincident occurrence of a stressful life event, on the one hand, and the initial occurrence of depressive symptomatology, on the other. The particular life-stage of the individual may also offer clues to the specific nature of depression. For example, younger persons suffering from adolescent depression tend to be more environmentally reactive than older persons, who may be suffering from involutional depression. This difference is significant, in part, because some less reactive types of depression respond better to tricyclic antidepressants than more reactive types do (Mandel & Klerman, 1978).

Inquiry into the patient's prior psychiatric history is, of course, always an important and necessary part of the evaluative process—particularly because most depressive conditions are either cyclic in nature or recurrent. When antidepressant drug therapy is being contemplated, especially relevant are whether the patient has previously been treated with antidepressant medication and what the patient's previous response to such medication has been.

Physical examination.   In addition to primary clinical depressive syndromes, a number of central nervous system (CNS) diseases, such as multiple sclerosis or cerebral vascular disease, may produce secondary depressive symptoms. The same is true of cerebral vascular disease, cardiovascular disease, and endocrine disorders, including abnormal adrenal or thyroid functioning (Mandel & Klerman, 1978). Moreover, depressive symptoms may be elicited through the use of both illicit and prescription drugs. Consequently, when there is reason to suspect that depressive symptoms are occurring secondary to some other disease process, appropriate physical examination and laboratory tests should be performed.

Psychiatric review of symptoms.   A decision to prescribe antidepressant medication should be made only after the psychiatrist is satisfied that a depressive condition actually exists, that it is of the type likely to respond to the particular medication being contemplated, and that no known facts in the patient's history counsel against use of a particular drug. The psychiatric review of symptoms, also referred to as a mental status evaluation, is generally designed to generate information helpful in answering these questions. When a depressive condition is the focal concern, the psychiatrist is likely to examine dysfunctional sleep patterns, including early morning awakening, intermittent wakefulness, difficulty falling asleep, and hypersomnia—all of which have been associated with various types of depression. In addition, appetite disorders that may result in either weight loss (in the absence of dieting) or weight gain may be associated with depression. Another area that requires scrutiny is that of psychomotor functioning. Both psychomotor retardation and psychomotor agitation have been associated with depression, as has anergia (loss of energy and fatigue). Patients suffering from depression will also often complain of diminished ability to think or concentrate, as well as inability to experience pleasure (anhedonia). Typically, it is not necessary for all of these symptoms to appear in order for a psychiatrist to diagnose a clinical depression.

Choice of Drug and Determination of Dosage

Tricyclic antidepressants have been the treatment of choice for major depression virtually since their introduction. Kuhn's (1958) original suggestion—that the major indication for tricyclic antidepressants is a retarded depression without evidence of schizophrenia—is still widely followed. More recently introduced heterocyclic and noncyclic antidepressants have been reported to be equally efficacious, while sometimes producing fewer or less severe side effects (Hughes & Pierattini, 1992). Although attempts have been made to match specific antidepressants to specific manifestations of depression, these attempts have generally not been very successful, with some limited exceptions (Bender, 1990)—perhaps because the precise action of these drugs is not sufficiently well understood to account for individual patients' relatively variable responses to them.

Nevertheless, efforts to arrive at specific indications for specific drugs continue, especially with a variety of drugs that have chemical structures other than the original three-ring structure of the tricyclics. For example, amoxapine (Asendin), which resembles the antipsychotic loxapine in chemical structure, may be particularly appropriate and effective in treating depressions with psychotic features (Bender, 1990). Many clinicians, however, routinely consider adding an antipsychotic medication when the tricyclic or heterocyclic antidepressant alone does not appear to be effective.

Monoamine oxidase inhibitors (MAOIs) are the other major drugs used in the treatment of depression. They have been found particularly effective in the treatment of dysthymia—that is, depressions that appear to be based on situational factors and to have less of a biological basis than is typical with major depression. They have also been found to be more effective in the treatment of depressive disorders that are usually referred to as atypical depressions (Hughes & Pierattini, 1992; Perry & Alexander, 1987).

One important feature that is shared by MAOIs and the heterocyclic antidepressants is that response may be just beginning approximately 2 to 3 weeks after the start of treatment. Thus, if the patient does not appear to respond immediately, it certainly does not mean that his or her depression is resistant to treatment. Some antidepressant effects, such as a lessening of symptoms of anxiety and insomnia, may occur almost immediately. Observable effects on mood, however, frequently are not noted until 2 or 3 weeks have passed, assuming that the patient is receiving a therapeutic dosage. It has been noted (for example, Bockar, 1976) that many physicians tend to underdose and therefore often inappropriately conclude that the medication trial has failed. The daily dose for most tricyclic antidepressants ranges between 75 and 250 mgs. The second generation heterocyclic antidepressants have widely differing dosage recommendations ranging from 20 to 60 mgs for fluoxetine (Prozac) to 200 to 400 mgs for bupropion (Wellbutrin) (Bender, 1990). Most recommended dosage regimens call for a gradual increase in the dosage, so that the therapeutic dosage is reached within 2 to 3 weeks (Levenson, 1981).

Recommended dosages for MAOIs range from 10 to 60 mgs (Bender, 1990). MAOIs are somewhat more difficult to administer than the heterocyclic antidepressants because their use requires that patients follow a very specific diet in order to exclude tyramine, a substance found in beer, wine, and many specific foods. Ingestion of tyramine can provoke a hypertensive crisis in patients who take MAOIs (Hughes & Pierattini, 1992). The dosages noted here are merely recommendations; physicians must make specific decisions about appropriate dosages for individual patients.

Target Symptoms

The identification of target symptoms represents a very practical and useful means for determining the effectiveness of any prescribed medication for any particular patient. Identifying target symptoms is particularly important in the use of psychoactive medications, since the effects of medication may be more difficult to quantify than in most other pharmacologic applications. In the case of depression, target symptoms that should be specifically monitored may include sleep patterns, appetite (including weight gain or loss), and psychomotor behavior. Often, rating scales are useful; although subjective, they may provide the clinician with important quantifiable information regarding the patient's perception of the effects of medication. It may also be useful to have family members complete such rating scales in order to obtain independent verification of the changes that have occurred in the patient, as well as the timing of those changes. Often, clinicians also employ rating scales for the assessment of mood as an additional means of determining the effectiveness of medication. Although the identification and assessment of target symptoms may be cumbersome and time-consuming, this approach is preferable to relying exclusively on memory and one's clinical intuition.

The Course of Therapy

The effects of both heterocyclic antidepressants and MAOIs vary considerably from patient to patient. These differences may be due to differences in the rate of absorption, metabolism by the liver, and elimination by the kidneys, among other causes. Also, cigarette smoking, coffee drinking, and taking other medications such as barbiturates can increase the rate of elimination of drugs, thus making higher dosages necessary. Moreover, dose-response relationships often occur in a way that can be represented by an inverted U: at low levels, virtually no effect is observed; at medium levels the desired therapeutic effect takes place; and at high levels the side effects are so severe as to interfere with the desired therapeutic effect (Hughes & Pierattini, 1992).

As was mentioned previously, the most common error in prescribing antidepressant medication, especially the heterocyclics, is to prescribe a dosage that is simply too low. Although most recommended dosage regimens call for a gradual increase in dosage over a period of several days to 3 weeks, it is very important to make a trial at therapeutic dosage levels for at least 3 to 4 weeks before considering the patient to be a treatment failure on that particular drug. In view of the relatively slow action of most antidepressant medications, it is wise to inform the patient that significant improvement should not be expected before 3 weeks. Moreover, since depressed patients are often suicidal, it is advisable to see the patient as frequently as possible until the desired medication effects take place. In addition, a patient's supply of antidepressant medication should be limited to 1 week's supply because of the potential danger of overdose (Mandel & Klerman, 1978).

Compliance with medications such as the MAOIs and heterocyclic antidepressants, which have significant side effects, tends to be particularly poor. Moreover, since therapeutic effects frequently occur a considerable period after the appearance of therapeutic benefits, patients have additional cause to be noncompliant. Continuing frequent contact with the depressed patient and involvement of the depressed patient's family (as appropriate) tends to increase compliance, as does careful explanation of both therapeutic and side effects the patient can expect from a given drug.

Means and Conditions for Implementing Antidepressant Drug Therapy
Qualifications of Personnel

Frequently, depressed patients come to the attention of a prescribing physician after referral from ministers, psychologists, social workers, or others. In those cases, it is especially important to choose a physician who is able to treat the patient properly and is also willing to participate in developing an overall treatment plan with other professionals. In cases when the depression occurs as a consequence of an identifiable psychosocial stressor, and when the patient is involved in an ongoing treatment situation with a qualified mental health professional, referral to the patient's family physician may be most appropriate. Most general practitioners are comfortable in providing antidepressant drug therapy under such circumstances. If the patient's depression is sufficiently severe, however, to warrant concern about the possibility of suicide, a referral should be made to a fully qualified psychiatric physician, who is experienced in offering antidepressant drug therapy and in dealing with severely depressed patients. Although some mental health professionals may object to this recommendation, concern for the safety and survival of their patients and proper recognition of professional liability issues should persuade them to follow it.

When a depressed patient is acutely suicidal, 24-hour supervision may be necessary. Under such circumstances, hospitalization is usually the only viable option. Even when hospitalized, such patients require special precautions and may be placed on a special suicide watch. Such intensive suicide prevention measures require a well-trained nursing staff, which is frequently augmented with mental health technicians. In addition, such patients require the care of a qualified psychiatrist and other mental health professionals. Antidepressant drug therapy will typically represent only one aspect of an overall treatment program designed to prevent suicide, to reduce or eliminate the various symptoms associated with the patient's depressive condition, and to assist the patient in once again becoming a functioning member of his or her family, work setting, and other social settings, as may be appropriate. Such broad objectives require the collaborative efforts of a number of professionals who bring with them a variety of pertinent skills.

Limitations of Antidepressant Drug Therapy
Contraindications

As with all pharmacological interventions, antidepressant drugs should not be prescribed to patients who have a history of hypersensitivity to the drug or drugs being considered. Moreover, antidepressant drugs are generally contraindicated when the patient's level of central nervous system consciousness is declining, whether the decline is a consequence of intracerebral causes or of extracerebral causes, such as barbiturates or alcohol (Levenson, 1981). Clearly, physicians who prescribe any antidepressant medication also must be aware of the overall health status of the patient, including preexisting conditions that might be exacerbated by the action of the planned medication.

Hazards

The behavioral effects of many of the heterocyclic antidepressants are in many ways similar to those of the phenothiazine-based antipsychotics, in large part due to their chemical similarity (Iversen & Iversen, 1981). For example, when given in sufficiently high doses, most heterocyclic antidepressants produce some sedation, as well as various anticholinergic effects such as dry mouth, blurred vision, and constipation. In some cases, these anticholinergic effects can exacerbate problems such as urinary retention and various ophthalmological problems, including glaucoma (due to increased intraocular pressure) (Levenson, 1981). In most cases, the anticholinergic effects are well tolerated, however, and specific antidepressants, especially some of the second-generation heterocyclics, have been designed to reduce the occurrence and intensity of anticholinergic effects (Bender, 1990).

Weight gain often accompanies the use of antidepressants and may be a source of distress to the patient. This weight gain may be caused, in part, by a return of normal appetite and in part by the consumption of high-calorie beverages to counter dry mouth symptoms associated with the anticholinergic properties of these drugs. Some more recently introduced antidepressants, such as fluoxetine (Prozac), have been shown to not produce weight gain (Bender, 1990). The problem of weight gain may be compounded in patients who also take antipsychotic medications or lithium, both of which have also been associated with weight gain.

Some relatively infrequently occurring side effects of some of the heterocyclic antidepressants include a lowering of the seizure threshold, an increase in the pulse rate, and various cardiac irregularities (Levenson, 1981). Although these side effects are relatively infrequent, they underscore the necessity for administration of these medications to be supervised and monitored by a qualified psychiatrist. Also, the heterocyclic antidepressants have a fairly high level of toxicity; prescribing them for potentially suicidal patients on an outpatient basis thus requires special precautions.

Side effects produced by the monoamine oxidase inhibitors (MAOIs) are very similar to those produced by most of the heterocyclic antidepressants. These side effects pose an additional important hazard, however, because of the dietary restrictions mandated in patients who use MAOIs. When those dietary restrictions are not followed precisely, the patient's blood pressure could rise to levels that would constitute a hypertensive crisis (Hughes & Pierattini, 1992). The food restrictions are designed to eliminate foods with high tyramine content, which include beer and wine, cheese, smoked or pickled fish, beef and chicken liver, and various yeast supplements (McCabe & Tsuang, 1982).

The abrupt withdrawal of psychoactive medications can apparently induce withdrawal, in part because some patients may experience physical dependence, behavioral dependence, or both. Symptoms of withdrawal are often difficult to identify and may be based, in part, on factors related to the patient's premorbid adjustment (Hughes & Pierattini, 1992). These potential difficulties, as well as the relatively high probability of misuse, abuse, and noncompliance, highlight the necessity for viewing antidepressant drug therapy as only one component of the overall treatment of the depressed patient.

The Effectiveness of Antidepressant Drug Therapy

"Presently, understanding of the behavioral effects and presumed mechanism of action of the antidepressants is just beginning to unravel" (Dykstra, 1992, p. 86). Although a great deal of animal research has demonstrated the effects of certain antidepressants on animal analogs of human depression (for example, early separation from mother—Henn & McKinney, 1987), this statement still holds true. Clinical research with depressed patients, however, has consistently shown that tricyclic antidepressants, as well as the second-generation heterocyclics, result in improvement in most of the patients treated (Hollister, 1981; Morris & Beck, 1974). Comparisons of heterocyclic antidepressants and MAOIs have shown that only some patients with atypical depressions or with chronic dysthymic disorders respond better to MAOIs than to tricyclics (Mandel & Klerman, 1978).

Since antidepressants are differentiated by the degree to which they selectively affect norepinephrine or serotonin, it may be advisable under some circumstances to choose an alternative antidepressant, with a somewhat different mode of action, than the one initially prescribed. There have been relatively few successes, however, in predicting which particular tricyclic or second-generation antidepressant will be most effective with a particular type of depression in a particular patient. Finally, there have been persistent reports that electroconvulsive treatment (ECT) is at least as effective in the treatment of depression as antidepressant drugs, and more effective in the treatment of delusional and severe endogenous depression (Bender, 1990; Mandel & Klerman, 1978). ECT, however, has become increasingly controversial and currently tends to be used only in the treatment of depression that has been unresponsive to medication. Moreover, antidepressant medication has been found superior as a continuing prophylactic in preventing the recurrence of depression (Bender, 1990).

References

American Psychiatric Association. (1989). *Diagnostic and statistical manual of mental disorders* (3rd rev. ed.). Washington, D.C.: American Psychiatric Association.

Bender, K. J. (1990). *Psychiatric medications: A guide for mental health professionals*. Newbury Park, CA: Russell Sage Foundation.

Bockar, J. A. (1976). *Primer for the nonmedical psychotherapist*. New York: Spectrum.

Caldwell, A. E. (1978). History of psychopharmacology. In W. G. Clark & J. del Giudice (Eds.), *Principles of psychopharmacology* (2nd ed., pp. 9–40). New York: Academic Press.

Dykstra, L. (1992). Drug action. In J. Grabowski & G. R. VandenBos (Eds.), *Psychopharmacology: Basic mechanisms and applied interventions* (pp. 63–96). Washington, D.C.: American Psychological Association.

Henn, F. A., & McKinney, W. T. (1987). Animal models in psychiatry. In H. Y. Meltzer (Ed.), *Psychopharmacology: The third generation of progress* (pp. 513–526). New York: Raven Press.

Hollister, L. E. (1981). Current antidepressant drugs: Their clinical use. *Drugs, 22*, 129–152.

Hughes, J. R., & Pierattini, R. A. (1992). An introduction to pharmacotherapy for mental disorders. In J. Grabowski & G. R. VandenBos (Eds.), *Psychopharmacology: Basic mechanisms and applied interventions* (pp. 101–125). Washington, D.C.: American Psychological Association.

Iversen, S. D., & Iversen, L. L. (1981). *Behavioral pharmacology*. New York: Oxford University Press.

Kornetsky, C. (1976). *Pharmacology: Drugs affecting behavior*. New York: Wiley.

Kuhn, R. (1958). The treatment of depressive states with G-22355 (imipramine). *American Journal of Psychiatry, 115,* 459–464.

Levenson, A. J. (1981). *Basic psychopharmacology.* New York: Springer.

Lipinski, J. F., Cohen, B. M., Zubenko, G. S., & Waternaux, C. M. (1987). Adrenoceptors and the pharmacology of affective illness: A unifying theory. *Life Science, 40,* 1947–1963.

McCabe, B., & Tsuang, M. T. (1982). Dietary considerations in MAOI inhibitor regimens. *Journal of Clinical Psychiatry, 43,* 178–181.

Mandel, M. R., & Klerman, G. L. (1978). Clinical use of antidepressants, stimulants, tricyclics, and monoamine oxidase inhibitors. In W. G. Clark & J. del Giudice (Eds.), *Principles of psychopharmacology* (2nd ed., pp. 537–551). New York: Academic Press.

Morris, J. B., & Beck, A. T. (1974). The efficacy of antidepressant drugs: A review of research (1958–1972). *Archives of General Psychiatry, 30,* 667–674.

Perry, P. J., & Alexander, B. (1987). Rational use of antidepressants. *Primary Care, 14,* 773–783.

Schildkraut, J. J. (1965). The catecholamine hypothesis of affective disorders: A review of supporting evidence. *American Journal of Psychiatry, 122,* 509–522.

Schou, M. (1978). Clinical use of lithium. In W. G. Clark & J. del Giudice (Eds.), *Principles of psychopharmacology* (2nd ed., pp. 553–571). New York: Academic Press.

CHAPTER 26

....

Antianxiety
Drug Therapy

....

■

Through the course of their development and introduction into psychiatry, antianxiety drugs have been known by a number of different terms. Originally, they were referred to as tranquilizers; indeed, barbiturates that primarily produce sedation were used as the most promising antianxiety agents prior to the introduction of the first true antianxiety drug, which was meprobamate (for example, Miltown, Equanil). Even after the introduction of meprobamate the label of *tranquilizer* persisted, even though with experience it became apparent that meprobamate, and the drugs that followed, were more than tranquilizers. Most importantly, it was realized that they were quite different from the antipsychotics, which also were called tranquilizers. That the latter were qualified by the word *major* before *tranquilizers*, and meprobamate was qualified as a *minor tranquilizer*, continued to suggest a quantitative difference between the two classes of drugs. In fact, however, the difference is qualitative, and around 1965 the term *antianxiety drugs* became the favorite term, joined by the term *anxiolytics* around 1972 (Caldwell, 1978). Both of these terms are currently in use, but in the present chapter we will primarily use the term *antianxiety drugs* to refer to the various agents used in today's antianxiety drug therapy.

General Purpose of Antianxiety Drug Therapy

The primary purpose of antianxiety drug therapy is to reduce or eliminate symptoms of anxiety and tension,

> without producing sufficient CNS depression to cause drowsiness or hypnosis in therapeutic doses, or other bothersome side effects related to the fact that the primary drug effect may be designed for another purpose, such as with the antihistamines. (del Giudice, 1978, p. 563)

Antianxiety drug therapy should be designed to combat anxiety that has significantly exceeded levels at which it may be functional and that is interfering materially in the individual's carrying out ordinary tasks of living.

History of Antianxiety Drug Therapy

Excessive anxiety is experienced, at one time or another, by almost every person. Most anxiety, like test-taking anxiety or anxiety preceding a visit to the dentist, represents an appropriate response to a perceived stressor. The kind of anxiety that is experienced in the so-called anxiety disorders, however, far exceeds these common everyday experiences. Consequently, efforts to alleviate the distress of those suffering from anxiety disorders date back to the beginning of psychiatry and before. Prior to the introduction of the modern antianxiety drugs (which are the focus of this chapter), barbiturates, such as phenobarbital, were used to produce sedation and drowsiness in order to decrease the patient's apprehension, distress, and other symptoms of anxiety. Unfortunately, the sedation produced by the barbiturates frequently failed to significantly reduce the level of distress experienced by the patient. Moreover, efforts to then increase the dosage were likely to increase sedation to dangerous levels. In response to this unsatisfactory state of affairs, the search for better antianxiety agents was carried out (Bender, 1990).

The first modern anxiolytic, or antianxiety agent, was meprobamate, which was synthesized in 1950 and introduced to psychiatric practice in 1955 (Caldwell, 1978). The anxiolytic effect of meprobamate was originally observed when it was found that it could tame monkeys. Further studies indicated that its anxiety-reducing effects were correlated with its ability to induce muscle relaxation. Unlike the barbiturates, however, meprobamate was found to have an antianxiety effect at doses that did not significantly impair motor or intellectual performance (Iversen & Iversen, 1981).

In spite of the early popularity of meprobamate, newer antianxiety agents belonging to the benzodiazepines have effectively replaced it and become the most widely prescribed drugs in the world. The most popular of these include chlordiazepoxide (Librium), introduced in 1961, and diazepam (Valium), also introduced in the same year (Dykstra, 1992). Several other drugs from the benzodiazepine class of drugs have been introduced since then. The most recent development in antianxiety drugs has been the introduction of buspirone, a member of the azaspirodecanedione class of drugs marketed as Buspar (Bender, 1990; Hughes & Pierattini, 1992).

Range of Applicability

The primary application of the benzodiazepines is in the treatment of anxiety or anxious depression without accompanying delusions or hallucinations. Some authors have suggested that they are used primarily in the treatment of a variety of neurotic disorders that have a strong anxiety component. They have been found to be particularly effective in treating generalized anxiety disorder, which is characterized by persistent anxiety manifested by motor tension (shakiness, jitteriness, trembling, tension); autonomic hyperactivity (sweating, pounding or racing heart, upset stomach, lightheadedness); and hypervigilance (feeling on edge, difficulty in concentrating, various sleep disturbances) (APA, 1989).

The benzodiazepine compounds have also been used quite extensively in the treatment of alcoholism, particularly in an effort to relieve the symptoms of alcohol withdrawal. In addition, they have been used as therapy in certain types of convulsive disorders (Levenson, 1981). Because they have significant muscle-relaxing properties, they are also frequently used to treat muscle spasms and low back muscle pain (Kornetsky, 1976). It is noteworthy that some of the anxiety disorders, such as panic disorder, agoraphobia, and obsessive-compulsive disorder, have been shown to be more responsive to treatment via the tricyclic antidepressants than to treatment with the benzodiazepines or other antianxiety drugs.

Theoretical Foundations
Assumptions About Human Nature

Anxiety is part of everyday life, a normal human emotion. It should therefore not be considered a symptom without reference to the circumstances under which it is experienced. Anxiety per se is not a disorder. It may be treated as a disorder when it is out of proportion to the person's circumstances, and when it interferes with the person's behavior to such an extent that it becomes debilitating. Anxiety plays an important role in emergencies or other stressful situations by mobilizing the person, by means of the autonomic nervous system, to cope more effectively and in effect rise to the occasion. Thus, anxiety is a positive force; it becomes "pathological when it no longer serves to sustain life and only hinders the functioning of the individual" (Kornetsky, 1976, p. 110).

In clinical practice the term *anxiety* has been ubiquitous. It refers to a subjectively experienced emotion, but it may also refer to a complex clinical syndrome, as in generalized anxiety disorder. Although anxiety appears to be related to phobic behavior, obsessive-compulsive behavior, and some forms of depression, it is often difficult to identify clear boundaries among these concepts. One way to avoid some of these difficulties in defining anxiety has been suggested by del Giudice (1978). He proposed that anxiety should be considered a problem when it interferes with "moderately optimal functioning." He also suggested that it be conceptualized as consisting of two major areas of symptoms and signs:

1. A pervasive subjective feeling of apprehension, including a feeling of foreboding, unrelated to any definable external threat.
2. A variety of somatic signs and subjective symptoms of anxiety, including palpitations, hyperventilation, and other autonomic phenomena. (1978, p. 562)

Assumptions About the Action of Antianxiety Drugs

Mode of action. The first of the antianxiety drugs, meprobamate, acted in much the same way as barbiturates, which had been previously used in the treatment of anxiety, except that meprobamate was safer and more effective. Meprobamate still produced dependence, however, and more sedation than anxiolytic effect (Kornetsky, 1976).

The benzodiazepine compounds have now replaced the barbiturates, as well as meprobamate, in most applications designed to treat anxiety. The effects produced by the benzodiazepines result primarily from their actions on the central nervous system. Moreover, "it is generally agreed that most, if not all, of the actions of the benzodiazepines are mediated by the inhibitory neurotransmitter gamma-aminobutyric acid (GABA)" (Dyskstra, 1992, p. 75). Specifically, the benzodiazepines appear to potentiate the effects of GABA. Ultimately, this enhancement of the effects of GABA produces a decrease in the firing rate of critical neurons throughout the central nervous system and thus serves to moderate excitatory states. It is currently hypothesized that the GABA system plays a critical role in the expression of anxiety. This hypothesis lends further support to the notion that the GABA system represents the primary mechanism through which the benzodiazepines have their antianxiety effect (Dykstra, 1992).

The evidence for the GABA/anxiety theory is far from conclusive at this time. Questions have been raised, in part, by the recent introduction of a new type of antianxiety drug, namely buspirone, which appears to produce its anxiolytic effect without any accompanying sedation (Bender, 1990). Moreover, buspirone does not act on the GABA receptor, thereby providing further evidence for the complex relationships between psychoactive drugs and behavior (Dykstra, 1992).

Pharmacokinetics.   The benzodiazepines have somewhat different absorption rates, and peak blood levels are typically reached in one to four hours. They are excreted primarily through the kidneys and the gastrointestinal tract, and they possess varying patterns of tissue accumulation. In addition, the relative potency of a given benzodiazepine compound is related to its relative affinity for its receptor. Even when dosages are adjusted for different potency, these compounds are not interchangeable because of the differences in their absorption, fate, and excretion. When they are discontinued, blood levels decrease rapidly, but virtually all benzodiazepines persist to some extent within the body to cause some accumulation, especially if they are taken daily (Kornetsky, 1976). The benzodiazepines are usually administered orally, but chlordiazepoxide (Librium) and diazepam (Valium) may be administered intramuscularly (Levenson, 1981).

Chemical structure.   Virtually all of the antianxiety drugs commonly used today belong to the chemical class called benzodiazepine. The benzodiazepines include many compounds varying in their pharmacokinetic properties, as we have seen, and they may also differ in terms of their potency. It is very important to note that the benzodiazepines do act as central nervous system depressants and may act synergistically with other CNS depressants, such as alcohol. The number of different benzodiazepine compounds currently in use precludes a complete listing. Nevertheless, the most commonly used benzodiazepines include alprazolam (Xanax), chlordiazepoxide (for example, Librium), clorazepate (for instance, Tranxene), diazepam (for example, Valium), and lorazepam (for instance, Ativan) (Bender, 1990). A new addition to the antianxiety drugs that does not belong to the benzodiazepine class is buspirone (Buspar), which belongs to the azapirodecanedione class of compounds. Because it represents a different chemical class, its mode of action, as well as its side effects, are quite different from those of the benzodiazepines.

Implementing Antianxiety Drug Therapy
Assessment Before Psychopharmacological Disposition

Soon after their introduction, the benzodiazepines rapidly became the most widely prescribed drugs in the world. Some of this popularity has been due, undoubtedly, to the common practice of prescribing these drugs inappropriately in order to assist people with anxieties of everyday life. Bender (1990) has observed that excessive benzodiazepine usage is still common and may be ascribed to expedient prescribing, as well as to abuse. He suggested that appropriate use of benzodiazepine anxiolytics can be determined, in part, by assessing the level of discomfort that the client experiences without medication and in spite of other therapies (Bender, 1990, p. 40). It is necessary, however, not only to determine the patient's level of discomfort, but also to establish pertinent features of the patient's life circumstances and overall health status before proceeding with antianxiety (benzodiazepine) drug therapy.

History.   Assuming that generalized anxiety disorder is the principal (though not only) indication for use of benzodiazepines, it is necessary to establish the duration of the person's anxiety symptoms. Specifically, unrealistic or excessive anxiety and worry about two, or more life circumstances must have occurred for 6 months or longer to warrant this diagnosis (APA, 1989). Also important to ascertain is whether the symptoms of anxiety are part of a mood disorder or a psychotic disorder. When there is a prior history of such disorders, it is important to take special care to rule out their co-occurrence with the anxiety symptoms, since in those cases benzodiazepine therapy may be inappropriate. As is always the case when considering the use of psychoactive medications, specific organic factors must also be ruled out as the likely cause of the anxiety symptoms. Finally, examining the patient's past pattern of coping with stressful life events may also offer clues about the nature and significance of any excessive anxiety or worry. In sum, a careful examination of the patient's history often represents an important first step in evaluating the appropriateness of antianxiety drug therapy.

Physical examination.   The conduct of a physical examination, including any laboratory tests deemed appropriate, is particularly important when dealing with symptoms of excessive anxiety because these symptoms, in various combinations, are often associated with a variety of physical disorders. For example, hyperthyroidism, organic mental disorders, and caffeine intoxication can cause a clinical picture identical to that of generalized anxiety disorder. Excessive anxiety and worry are also prominent in psychotic disorders, eating disorders, and depressive disorders (APA, 1989, p. 252). It is also well known that the symptoms of motor tension and autonomic hyperactivity commonly associated with generalized anxiety disorder may be indicative of neurological problems (such as concussions), as well as cardiac problems (for example, tachycardia, nausea, and so on). Treating such symptoms with benzodiazepines would represent serious maltreatment if, in fact, they represented neurological or cardiac disease. Clearly, a thorough physical should precede any antianxiety drug therapy.

Psychiatric review of symptoms.   Antianxiety drugs are not appropriate for every patient who complains of being anxious and distressed. There have been repeated concerns about the inappropriate application of antianxiety drugs (see, for example, Bender, 1990; del Giudice, 1978). Physicians who are considering prescribing drugs to treat anxiety should carefully assess the patient's symptoms in order to maximize the chances of success. For example, del Giudice (1978) suggested that clinicians could use "clinical global psychometric tests available to determine the extent of anxiety present in a patient" (p. 563). He also suggested the application of several minimum criteria for determining when drug therapy for anxiety is appropriate (1978, pp. 564–565). Specifically, del Giudice suggested that patients considered for antianxiety drug therapy should clearly express subjective complaints of anxiety that can be differentiated from the anxious agitation found in schizophrenia and some forms of depression. In addition, he suggested that patients should exhibit various somatic signs and symptoms, which would frequently be autonomic in nature and occur episodically (such as headaches, dizziness, hyperventilation, excessive perspiration, hyperactive bowel, and so on). Finally, del Giudice suggested that special care must be taken in assessing anxiety states that are chronic and that may accompany personality disorders. Ultimately, he suggested, patients with a history of adequate adjustment who suddenly experience acute anxiety attacks may respond best to antianxiety drug therapy.

Target Symptoms

When barbiturates were used to treat anxiety, they were used for their sedating effects. Meprobamate still produced significant sedation, but also had the effect of reducing the subjective experience of anxiety, as well as the somatic manifestations of anxiety. The benzodiazepines still produce some sedation, although much less than the barbiturates, and they produce muscle relaxation, albeit more effectively and with less danger than the barbiturates. The anxiolytic effect of the benzodiazepines, however, is what differentiates them from their predecessors, the barbiturates and, to a lesser extent, meprobamate. Anxiety symptoms that are specifically targeted by the benzodiazepines are feelings of nervousness, agitation, and apprehension, difficulty in concentrating, difficulty in falling asleep, and difficulty in staying asleep. In addition, benzodiazepines may be used to reduce the discomfort of alcohol withdrawal (Bender, 1990).

Choice of Drug and Determination of Dosage

From a clinical standpoint, specifying which antianxiety drug is most appropriately prescribed for which anxiety condition or symptoms is a desirable goal. Although such specificity is generally not possible, it is known that the onset of effects and duration of action of the benzodiazepines differ depending on the specific compound used. Some are known to have relatively quick-acting sedative effects; others may be chosen on the basis of whether they are quickly discharged from the body, or gradually built up within the tissue. Generally, absorption and metabolic patterns are unique to each drug. In addition, each individual will respond uniquely to each drug. Consequently, standard dosage regimens cannot be designed for use with different patients. Generally, however, the amount of antianxiety medication initially needed may be higher than that needed after a short period of antianxiety drug therapy. Also, although some tolerance may develop with regard to sedation, no tolerance appears to develop to the antianxiety or muscle relaxant effects of the benzodiazepines for periods of several months (Bender, 1990). Thus, it is unlikely that dosage has to be increased during the course of treatment, and in many cases the dosage can be gradually reduced.

The benzodiazepines have the potential to produce dependency, which can result in withdrawal symptoms if the medication is discontinued abruptly. Interestingly, the effects of withdrawal from the benzodiazepines are opposite from their therapeutic effects. Thus, withdrawal may disrupt sleep and cause muscle tremors and even convulsions; agitation, restlessness, and irritability may be experienced (Bender, 1990). Apparently, withdrawal symptoms are more severe when benzodiazepines are used daily for long periods of time, or when they are used in relatively high dosages. In order to forestall withdrawal effects, termination of benzodiazepine therapy may be facilitated by a process of gradual supervised tapering (Bender, 1990).

The Course of Therapy

Since the introduction of the benzodiazepines there have been a variety of opinions regarding the proper course of antianxiety drug therapy. Many years after their introduction, del Giudice (1978) noted that no guidelines existed as to how long a period of time antianxiety drugs should be used, although he noted that they are sometimes routinely given for long periods, even years. He warned that such practices should be seriously questioned. Shortly after the publication of his warning, the Food and Drug Administration recommended a 4-month maximum limitation for maintenance prescription of benzodiazepines (as reported by Bender, 1990).

Still, some clinicians believe firmly in the benefit of long-term treatment with antianxiety drugs. They have noted, for example, that although generalized anxiety states are not cured by anxiolytics, the symptoms associated with such states are greatly alleviated by these drugs. This conclusion, however, clearly suggests that antianxiety drug therapy should almost always occur in conjunction with psychological treatment designed to assist the patient in acquiring more effective coping skills that could then forestall the recurrence of excessive anxiety. Even developing those skills would, of course, not preclude the possibility of a relapse in which case renewed use of antianxiety drugs would be warranted. Rickels (1987) noted that with some patients a case can be made for continuous or intermittent long-term treatment with antianxiety drugs, especially when the patient is not experiencing significant side effects and is using the medication in prescribed amounts. Some clinicians (such as del Giudice) have suggested that since anxiety is usually episodic, antianxiety drugs, when effective, should be discontinued after short-term treatment and resumed when another episode of excessive anxiety occurs.

Treatment of acute anxiety and panic usually requires a somewhat different regimen. For example, most clinicians would limit acute treatment with benzodiazepines to approximately 2 weeks. When such acute treatment is indicated, diazepine and chlordiazepoxide can be given intravenously in order to accelerate the sedative and hypnotic effects. This form of administration will typically quiet the patient fairly rapidly. After the patient is calmer and more rested, crisis intervention techniques may be combined with antianxiety drug therapy.

As noted previously, benzodiazepines have the potential to produce physiological dependence and withdrawal symptoms. Consequently, in addition to proper medication management and supervision, it is necessary to educate the patient about these possible drawbacks of using benzodiazepines. In addition, patients may need special psychological support during the period of benzodiazepine termination, especially since the symptoms of anxiety may rebound during the gradual withdrawal and termination of the drug. If such rebound symptoms persist beyond 1 month, it may be necessary to consider reinstating antianxiety drug therapy (Bender, 1990). Whenever antianxiety drugs are used, however, clinicians must be aware of the potential for abuse based on the pleasant and calming effects produced by the benzodiazepines.

Thus, when patients appear to request increased dosages not warranted by their condition and apparently designed to produce effects other than the anxiolytic effects, such as a high, steps must be taken to wean the patient from the drug altogether. Moreover, great concern must be expressed (and acted upon if necessary) about the potentially dangerous potentiation of anti-anxiety drugs through their combination with alcohol.

Means and Conditions for Implementing Antianxiety Drug Therapy
Qualifications of Personnel

As with all other psychopharmacological interventions, a qualified physician must be in charge of antianxiety drug therapy. The prescribing physician must be cognizant that of all the psychoactive medications, the anxiolytics have the highest potential for abuse. In addition, even in the absence of patient abuse of such medication, it is probably often prescribed inappropriately and unnecessarily. That antianxiety drugs have been the most prescribed drugs in the world is powerful evidence in support of this conclusion. It is necessary, therefore, constantly to monitor the use of these drugs to ensure that they are not being misused or abused. Such monitoring is mandated by law, since the antianxiety drugs have been declared controlled substances by the U.S. Food and Drug Administration. Clearly, however, a responsible physician would in any case engage in the requisite monitoring for the protection and welfare of the patient whose treatment includes antianxiety drugs.

As noted previously, there continues to be some disagreement over precise specification of the kind and intensity of anxiety that warrants treatment with antianxiety drugs. There is little disagreement, however, that in most instances antianxiety drug therapy alone is inadequate, and that psychological interventions such as behavior therapy or other forms of psychotherapy should be provided along with the drug therapy. In the long run, it is very likely that those interventions could alter the patient's capabilities for coping with high levels of anxiety and thereby prevent the future occurrence of circumstances that might necessitate antianxiety drug therapy. Obviously, the provision of psychological interventions also requires a fully qualified professional. In some cases, the prescribing physician may have appropriate training, but in many cases a licensed psychologist is the most likely provider of such services.

Generalized anxiety disorders are ordinarily unlikely to necessitate hospitalization of the patient. In some cases, nevertheless, especially when acute anxiety or panic is observed, short-term hospitalization may be necessary, which may occur in the psychiatric unit of a general hospital or in a psychiatric hospital.

Limitations of Antianxiety Drug Therapy
Contraindications

As with all drugs, any kind of previously observed hypersensitivity, or allergic reaction, should be treated as an absolute contraindication. A second contraindication is glaucoma. If the glaucoma has been properly evaluated and treated, however, and if an ophthalmologist is consulted, some physicians may feel that, with proper monitoring, antianxiety drugs may be used (Levenson, 1981). Two additional contraindications are declining central nervous system level of consciousness from either intracerebral causes (such as tumor or trauma), or from extracerebral causes (such as alcohol) (Levenson, 1981). In all cases, the mild sedation and mildly impaired motor control commonly observed in patients who take benzodiazepines can be dangerously exacerbated by alcohol. Consequently, some physicians require extraordinary precautions when using antianxiety drugs with alcoholics, even if they are recovered alcoholics. Finally, benzodiazepines should not be administered during pregnancy (Kantes, 1982).

Hazards

Hazards in the use of antianxiety drugs may consist, on the one hand, of undesired (side) effects produced by these drugs, and, on the other hand, of patients' abuse and dependence on these medications. Some of the most commonly observed side effects of benzodiazepines include drowsiness and sedation. This effect is usually fairly small, but may be dose-related, and can also be exacerbated by alcohol, as well as by other drugs, such as the phenothiazines. Phenothiazines have the potential to cause some disinhibition, which may have the effect of exacerbating states of agitation and mania. This effect has been called a paradoxical agitation reaction (Levenson, 1981). Antianxiety drugs also have the potential for exacerbating depression when administered too aggressively for anxiety associated with depression (Bender, 1990).

Benzodiazepines have also been demonstrated to have an amnestic effect, which is an impairment of memory. Specifically, although benzodiazepines do not appear to impair the retrieval of long-term memory, they do appear to disrupt the transfer of information from short-term to long-term memory. Some benzodiazepine compounds appear to have a stronger amnestic effect than others; if this effect is of concern in a particular patient, the clinician can select a drug so as to minimize this side effect (Bender, 1990).

Of the major psychoactive drugs that are currently widely used, the benzodiazepines have by far the highest potential for abuse. Abuse generally refers to overuse of the medication to the point where such overuse has undesirable social, psychological, or physiological consequences. Typically, abuse will occur in individuals who use benzodiazepines as a crutch and who refuse to put forth the psychological effort involved in acquiring better coping skills through psychological intervention. Such individuals are likely to use the benzodiazepines not so much for their anxiolytic effects, but rather in order to obtain a high. Careful monitoring and, as appropriate, insistence on participation in psychological intervention are likely to curtail and prevent most such abuse.

Dependence is a potential problem in the use of antianxiety drugs, particularly with patients who have a past history of alcohol or drug abuse. Hughes and Pierattini (1992) suggested two kinds of dependence: behavioral dependence, which occurs when the patient loses control of drug use (by using it more than intended or by being unable to stop using it); and physical dependence, which is defined by the onset of withdrawal symptoms upon cessation of the medication. The latter can be particularly troublesome with antianxiety drugs, especially when the cessation is abrupt. In such cases, it is particularly difficult to distinguish withdrawal symptoms from rebound symptoms or from a simple relapse in the condition that was being treated in the first place. In many cases, these distinctions can be made only after the patient is forced to abstain from benzodiazepines for a period of 4 to 6 weeks (Hughes & Pierattini, 1992).

In 1978, del Giudice noted that the ideal drug would decrease or eliminate anxiety without impairing alertness and performance in any way. Clearly, the benzodiazepines fall short of this ideal. There is some reason to believe that the most recent addition to the antianxiety drugs, buspirone, represents a noticeable improvement because it does not share the side effects of the benzodiazepines. However, Bender (1990) noted that it will not replace the benzodiazepines because it has a much longer lag time for clinical effects, as well as some mild side effects, including dizziness, headache, nervousness, and diarrhea.

The Effectiveness of Antianxiety Drug Therapy

The approval of any prescription drug for use in the United States requires an extensive and lengthy review of its effectiveness, side effects, and potential danger. All of the drugs referred to in the present chapter, including

meprobamate and the benzodiazepines as well as some of the newer heterocyclic compounds, are prescription drugs that have undergone such extensive
review. It is outside the scope of this chapter to review the specific experimental findings related to these drugs. One measure of their effectiveness,
however, is their popularity. For example, Julien (1981) reported that more
than 45 million prescriptions are filled for diazepam alone each year, and that
prescriptions for chlordiazepoxide are probably not far behind. Although
such numbers reflect, in part, abuse of these drugs, the overwhelming
majority of these prescriptions are undoubtedly appropriate and reflect these
drugs' effectiveness in alleviating the conditions for which they are being prescribed.

Many mental health professionals regard progressive relaxation as an
alternative, or adjunct to, drug treatment of anxiety. A good deal of clinical
outcome research supports the effectiveness of relaxation procedures in the
treatment of some patients; however, drugs may be more effective in the treatment of others (for a review see Lichtstein, 1988). Each individual patient's
specific needs must be taken into account before the preferred treatment
approach can be determined. In order to make an appropriate determination,
individual practitioners need to become more aware of alternative strategies.
Raising practitioners' level of awareness is one of the purposes of the present
volume.

References

American Psychiatric Association. (1989). *Diagnostic and statistical manual of mental disorders* (3rd ed., rev.). Washington, D.C.: American Psychiatric Association.

Bender, K. J. (1990). *Psychiatric medications: A guide for mental health professionals.* Newbury Park, CA: Russell Sage Foundation.

Caldwell, A. E. (1978). History of psychopharmacology. In W. G. Clark & J. del Giudice (Eds.), *Principles of psychopharmacology* (2nd ed., pp. 9–40). New York: Academic Press.

del Giudice, J. (1978). Clinical use of anxiolytic drugs in psychiatry. In W. G. Clark & J. del Giudice (Eds.), *Principles of psychopharmacology* (2nd ed., pp. 561–571). New York: Academic Press.

Dykstra, L. (1992). Drug action. In J. Grabowski & G. R. VandenBos (Eds.), *Psychopharmacology: Basic mechanisms and applied interventions* (pp. 63–96). Washington, D.C.: American Psychological Association.

Hughes, J. R., & Pierattini, R. A. (1992). An introduction to pharmaco-therapy for mental disorders. In J. Grabowski & G. R. VandenBos (Eds.),

Psychopharmacology: Basic mechanisms and applied interventions (pp. 97–125). Washington, D.C.: American Psychological Association.

Iversen, S. D., & Iversen, L. L. (1981). *Behavioral pharmacology*. New York: Oxford University Press.

Julien, R. M. (1981). *A primer of drug action* (3rd ed.). San Francisco: W. H. Freeman.

Kantes, J. H. (1982). Use of benzodiazepines during pregnancy, labour, and lactation with particular reference to pharmacokinetic considerations. *Drugs, 23,* 351.

Kornetsky, C. (1976). *Pharmacology: Drugs affecting behavior*. New York: Wiley.

Levenson, A. J. (1981). *Basic psychopharmacology*. New York: Springer.

Lichtstein, K. L. (1988). *Clinical relaxation strategies*. New York: Wiley.

Rickels, K. (1987). Antianxiety therapy: Potential value of long-term treatment. *Journal of Clinical Psychiatry, 48* (Suppl.), 7–10.

PART IX

Career
Counseling

CHAPTER 27

Counseling for
Effective Career Choices

■

Writing this chapter presents a special challenge because it attempts to address a topic that is somewhat different from the topics of the previous chapters. Rather than focusing on a specific method of intervention, the aim is to describe a whole array of methods designed to facilitate individuals' career development. Almost all the specific behavior change methods discussed in the present volume may be (and have been) used in career counseling, either in their traditional or in some modified form. In addition, however, career counseling includes a number of specific methodologies that are unique to it; these represent the substance of the present chapter.

General Purpose of Career Counseling

The mission of career counseling is to assist individuals to successfully engage in the activities and processes that lead to and sustain a productive and rewarding work life. Thus, career counseling includes counseling designed to facilitate career exploration, decision-making, and commitment. Moreover, it includes counseling designed to guide individuals through the intricacies of the workplace (organizational and otherwise) and through the inevitable transitions that occur in the course of one's career. Note that

Chapter 28 will focus more explicitly on counseling for career transitions, including retirement.

History of Career Counseling

Career counseling as it is known today developed after World War II. Concern with many of the issues of career development goes back much further, however. The person usually credited with originating vocational guidance in the United States is Frank Parsons, who established the Vocations Bureau in Boston, which constituted the first facility dedicated to what we might today call career counseling. His posthumously published book, *Choosing a Vocation* (Parsons, 1909), specified a methodology for helping adolescents to choose suitable vocations. His procedure involved what he called true reasoning; he suggested that career aspirants should have a clear understanding of their own resources and limitations, an understanding of what is required to succeed, and knowledge of the advantages and disadvantages afforded by different lines of work. Armed with this background, true reasoning would enable them to ascertain the relationship between self-knowledge and knowledge of occupations (Herr & Cramer, 1979).

The movement toward vocational guidance in the schools that Parsons initiated joined with a related emphasis on vocational education that actually began even before Parsons's groundbreaking work. Whereas the emphasis in vocational guidance tended to be on the dissemination of vocational information, vocational education emphasized practical training of students in occupations and industries that needed workers. Unfortunately, vocational guidance and vocational education, which had been quite complementary, lost this relationship in the period following World War I, apparently in part due to the refusal of the National Education Association (NEA) to view vocational education and vocational guidance as parts of one unit (Herr & Cramer, 1979, p. 4). More recent efforts, some of them legislative, have attempted to repair this schism and restore the complementarity of vocational guidance and vocational education.

Modern career counseling is firmly rooted in the efforts of pioneers like Frank Parsons and others. The emphasis on individual differences originally fostered by the work on intelligence assessment by Binet also made a significant impact in this area. For example, Strong first published the Vocational Interest Blank in 1927. The Vocational Interest Blank became one of the most widely used assessment instruments in the history of psychology, in part due to periodic revisions that have kept it relatively current. In its current form it is called the Strong-Campbell Interest Inventory (Hansen & Campbell, 1985). Other interest inventories and psychometric instruments designed to measure a variety of career-related attributes have been developed over the years and have become part of the methodology of today's career counseling. Perhaps more important, however, these assessment tools have been instrumental in the historical development of career counseling by helping to establish its scientific legitimacy and practical utility.

Contemporary career counseling is more indebted, however, to the emergence of several major theories of career functioning and development. The first of these modern theories, purported to be a general theory of occupational choice, was proposed by Ginzberg and associates (Ginzberg, Ginsburg, Axelrad, & Herma, 1951). Partly in response to that work, Super (1953, 1957) proposed his self-concept theory of vocational behavior. This theory was followed by important and influential formulations of a career typology by Holland (1959, 1966), and a social learning approach to career development by Krumboltz (1979) and by Krumboltz and associates (Krumboltz, Mitchell, & Jones, 1976). These and other scholars developed a rich theoretical heritage, which today represents the foundation upon which contemporary career counseling is based.

Range of Applicability

Career counseling, as defined in this chapter, includes what has traditionally been called vocational guidance. Typically, vocational guidance is practiced by guidance counselors in the school system and is designed to assist students in the processes necessary to successfully select an occupation. The age range of individuals involved in vocational guidance activities is typically between 16 and 18, although some efforts have been made to provide vocational guidance to younger students as well. Because most contemporary views of career development recognize that the initial selection of an occupation represents only the first of a series of career decisions to be made by the typical person over the course of the adult life span, career counseling is also important for adults who have already been members of the work force.

The setting within which adult career counseling takes place may, at least in part, determine the focus of the intervention. In organizational settings, the primary focus may be on matching individual characteristics with the needs of the organization. Career counseling in the private practice or consulting setting is typically more concerned with helping individuals to optimize their career development, to negotiate career transitions (whether self-initiated or externally imposed), or to repeat the processes of career search, selection, and entry that were completed at an earlier time in the individual's work life. Midlife career changers are candidates for the repetition of these processes, as is anyone who desires to change careers for any reason.

Another potential application of career counseling is to deal with specific problems in career development. Individuals may seek career counseling because they are unhappy in their work and wish to identify the reasons for their dissatisfaction and possible alternatives to their current careers. In other cases, individuals may be experiencing personal problems as a result of interpersonal conflict, harassment, or discrimination, and they may seek career counseling to find ways to address those issues. Within organizations, career counseling may be subsumed under Human Resources Planning and Development (HRPD). There, it may be prescribed for plateaued managers or for individuals who are unhappy with lateral transfers. Moreover, in many organizations there is a growing recognition of the need for multiple career paths, the identification and development of which also require the involvement of career counselors (Shullman & Carder, 1983). Finally, issues of obsolescence and preparation for retirement are likely to be addressed by career counselors both in private and organizational settings.

Theoretical Foundations
Assumptions About Human Nature

The underlying assumptions about human nature vary considerably from one theorist to another. One central underlying assumption, however, is that work represents a basic human activity that is in important ways related to most other areas of human functioning. Freud was once reported to have said that to be able to work and to be able to love were the two most important things in a person's life. Erikson proposed that the development of industry— that is, the ability to do things—and the subsequent development of identity, including vocational identity, were important ingredients in mature adult functioning (Erikson, 1959). Adler believed that love, social relations, and work were essential tasks that confronted individuals as they moved through life (cf. Watkins & Savickas, 1990).

Writers who are more directly identified with career theories have also, sometimes explicitly and sometimes implicitly, made assumptions about human nature. For example, Holland (1966, 1985), known for his typology of vocational personalities and work environments, proposed that individuals project their views of themselves and the world of work onto occupational titles. Consequently, personality and vocational interests are one and the same. Thus, individuals with certain types of personalities are likely to end up in certain types of occupations. Krumboltz (1979; Krumboltz, Mitchell, & Jones, 1976), who originated the social learning theory of career decision-making, suggested that people acquire beliefs about themselves and the world

through learning experiences that eventually cause them to prefer one occupation or another. Super (1953, 1957) is closely identified with developmental approaches of career counseling. He proposed that people try to
implement their self-concepts through their choice of occupation. Moreover,
he suggested that individuals negotiate developmental stages as they mature
and that vocational decisions are influenced by the particular stage of an individual.

Although vocational psychology has been dominated by updated versions
of theories initially proposed by Super and by Holland, some more recent
formulations have received increasing attention. One of these is the recent
attempt by Krumboltz and Nichols (1990) to use the living systems framework of Ford (1987) to reconceptualize the social learning theory of career
decision-making by incorporating it into a comprehensive theory of human
development, in which career development is viewed as occurring within the
context of overall human development. In a related vein, Vondracek, Lerner,
and Schulenberg (1986) proposed that career development must be understood from the perspective of a life span view of human development, in
which individual development is seen as having important bidirectional links
to an ever-changing social context. Individuals are seen as having the capability of creating their own development through the choices they make in all
spheres of their lives, including their occupations.

Assumptions About Conducting Career Counseling

Because of the diversity of career counseling approaches that may be
derived from the various career theories, it is impossible to describe them and
their underlying assumptions in detail. Instead, attention will be focused on
the two most frequently used approaches—namely, person-environment fit
counseling and developmental career counseling. Person-environment fit
counseling is represented most prominently by Holland's theory of vocational
personalities and work environments (Holland, 1985), but also by the work
adjustment theory of Dawis and Lofquist (1984; Lofquist & Dawis, 1969).
Developmental career counseling is represented most prominently by the
work of Super (1957, 1980). The goodness-of-fit model of Vondracek, Lerner,
and Schulenberg (1986) incorporates features of both the person-environment
fit approach and the developmental approach.

The basic theoretical assumptions that guide the conduct of person-
environment fit counseling were described recently by Rounds and Tracey
(1990, p. 21). Specifically, they proposed that person-environment fit counseling, which may also be referred to as trait-and-factor counseling, assumes
the following:

1. The reciprocal and ongoing nature of person-environment fit is a central feature of career planning.
2. Acquiring an understanding of the person-environment fit model represents important client learning, which is the basis for both present and future problem-solving and decision-making.
3. The main theoretical constructs used to describe individual functioning and those used to describe the environment must be assessed and taken account of in the counseling process.
4. The quality of the assessment is related to the dependability and accuracy of the information obtained and not to the form or method of obtaining it.

Developmental career counseling is guided basically by two fundamental assumptions. The first is that descriptions and interpretations of clients' careers can help clients to construct fresh meanings and prepare them to take action. The second is that various techniques and methods of counseling are more effective when specifically geared to clients' level of development (Jepsen, 1990, p. 136).

Implementing Career Counseling

The field of career counseling is a complex and growing enterprise, as reflected in the active pace of publication in this area. For example, recent books by Morrison and Adams (1991), McDaniels and Gysbers (1992), Sharf (1992), Spokane (1991), and Walsh and Osipow (1990) are all devoted to career counseling and career interventions. The variety of these interventions is impressive, and the vitality of the field is readily apparent. Thus, any explication of the procedures involved in career counseling must be quite selective, if not actually arbitrary. Consequently, in keeping with the earlier discussion of person-environment fit approaches to career counseling on the one hand, and developmental approaches on the other, we will continue to focus on those two classes of interventions in the following section.

Person-Environment Fit Career Counseling

Although trait-and-factor or person-environment fit models have dominated a great deal of thinking on vocational interventions for quite some time, Rounds and Tracey (1990) lamented that this interest in theoretical formulations has not been matched by innovations in counseling practice. They noted that an implicit assumption in this approach is that offering information about the client and the world of work will somehow result in behavior change, which presumably is the objective of the counseling enterprise. Moreover, they noted that "the historically pragmatic focus of the trait-and-factor counseling approach leaves its operating assumptions (i.e., what accounts for the behavioral change process) open to analysis" (p. 22).

In spite of these concerns, most trait-and-factor–oriented career counseling focuses on assisting individuals in (1) gaining self-understanding, (2) gaining understanding of the world of work and occupations, and (3) using this knowledge to make effective career decisions.

Gaining self-understanding.   This task usually involves various assessment activities that may be carried out with varying degrees of counselor assistance. The specific types of information collected vary depending on the client's circumstances. Numerous psychometric instruments have been developed for the most commonly measured self-attributes thought to be relevant to the career counseling situation. Aptitudes, achievements, interests, values, and personality are most frequently assessed (Sharf, 1992). Some examples of the most prominent instruments may illustrate this process: the College Board Scholastic Aptitude Test (SAT) measures verbal, mathematical, and standard written English aptitudes; the Strong-Campbell Interest Inventory (SVIB-SCII) assesses 6 general occupational themes, 23 basic interests, and more than 100 specific occupational interests (Hansen, 1990); the Work Aspect Preference Scale (Pryor, 1984) assesses the relative importance of values such as altruism, self-development, creativity, life-style, money, and security; personality dimensions, such as dominance, empathy, tolerance, and flexibility, may be assessed with the California Psychological Inventory (Gough, 1987).

Mere assessment of these personal attributes is usually inadequate; most of the assessment instruments are designed so as to require the interpretation of results by a counselor with special training in this area. Some notable exceptions, however, include the so-called Self-Directed Search (Holland, 1987), a self-contained procedure that guides individuals through a process that helps them to assess, organize, and interpret information about themselves and about occupations. Moreover, the rapidly increasing use of computers in assessment continues to offer new opportunities for making the process of self-assessment more accessible and less labor-intensive (Sampson, 1990).

Gaining understanding of occupations.   Most people are quite surprised to learn that more than 20,000 occupations are practiced in the United States and in most industrialized countries. Although gathering information about all these occupations may seem a daunting task, the fact is that, thanks to the U.S. Department of Labor, a great deal of current information about all of these occupations is readily available in government publications. Perhaps the best known, and easily the most detailed, is the *Dictionary of Occupational Titles* (U.S. Department of Labor, 1977), which lists, describes, and classifies more than 20,000 occupations. It is periodically revised, and supplements are issued from time to time in order to keep it as current as possible. Another government publication that may be even more helpful to laypersons is the *Occupational Outlook Handbook* (U.S. Department of Labor, 1992), which is issued every 2 years. It projects employment prospects for the near- and intermediate-term future by geographic region, salary information, and qualifications for the most common and popular occupations and occupational groups.

Using self- and occupational information to make career decisions.   The underlying assumption in person-environment fit or trait-and-factor approaches to career counseling is that specific personal characteristics can be matched with the requirements of various occupations. This matching process is assumed to produce a fit between person and environment that is ultimately pleasing to employees (because the chosen occupation permits them to pursue something that interests them, allows them to implement their value preferences, and so on) and to employers (because satisfied employees are better performers than unhappy ones). The counselor's role consists, essentially, of helping clients to obtain the requisite information, and then in assisting them by interpreting the information and demonstrating how it can be employed in effective decision-making.

Conceptually, trait-and-factor counseling is relatively straightforward. In practice, however, it is not always as easy as one might assume. For example, a person may have vocational interests that are consistent with choosing medicine as a profession. The same person may not, however, have the intellectual capabilities for that occupation. When conflicts of this sort occur, it is often necessary to consider compromise solutions. For example, the person just described may be encouraged to pursue a health-related occupation that is less demanding in terms of educational requirements than the study of medicine. Often, counselors will proceed by helping clients in reviewing the relative advantages and disadvantages of various possible occupational choices that have been arrived at on the basis of newly acquired self-knowledge and knowledge about the world of work.

In spite of ample information and assistance from the counselor, some individual clients may still experience difficulties in making decisions. In such cases the counselor may also be able to assist in resolving problems in or barriers to career decision-making. There is, in fact, an extensive literature in this area (for example, Phillips, 1992; Slaney, 1988). Moreover, Rounds and Tracey (1990) suggested that trait-and-factor counseling can easily be reconceptualized as problem-solving and thereby benefit from the advances made in modern theories of problem-solving. They also proposed that some of the advances of information-processing models may be usefully adapted to the area of trait-and-factor oriented counseling.

Developmental Career Counseling

Developmental career counselors view career development as occurring within the framework of the overall development of the person over the entire life span. The adolescent's initial career decisions are seen as consequences of earlier developments in the acquisition of skills, aptitudes, values, interests, and self-conceptions, including an emerging vocational identity (Vondracek, 1992). Vocational choices are made throughout life and may include those necessitated by environmental or organizational changes, as well as those deemed desirable or necessary by virtue of personal changes that occur with increasing age. Obviously, this framework is exceedingly broad, as confirmed by Super's (1951, p. 88) definition of vocational guidance:

> The process of helping a person to develop and accept an integrated and adequate picture of him/herself and of his/her role in the world of work, to test this concept against reality, and to convert it into a reality, with satisfaction to him/herself and benefit to society.

Because the objectives of developmental career counseling are so broad and complex, career counselors have used the whole array of counseling methods to facilitate the development of people's careers within the context of their overall development. Jepsen (1990, p. 137) identified some shared features in the overall strategy employed by developmental career counselors:

1. the counselor collaborates with the client;
2. a thorough appraisal of the client's situation is conducted using multiple methods and sources;
3. dynamic descriptions of the client's career development processes are constructed using the appraisal data; and
4. interpretations of the descriptions lead the client to discover new meanings and possibilities for actions.

All these steps may be repeated, as necessary, as the client or the client's circumstances change to make new career decisions desirable or necessary.

One defining feature of the developmental career counseling approach is that the counselor selects specific intervention methods appropriate for the client's developmental level or stage. Obviously, an adolescent trying to formulate a first, tentative career choice will require an approach different from that needed for a middle-aged executive who is contemplating a career change or early retirement. Consequently, career counselors who follow a developmental methodology must adapt their specific methodology to the (career) developmental stage of their client.

Means and Conditions for Implementing Career Counseling

The Counselor's Qualifications

Career counselors represent a relatively heterogeneous group of professionals who work in many different settings. Moreover, although vocational guidance counselors and career counselors of various types have been around for quite a number of years, career counseling has not been used in as systematic a manner as would seem to be necessary according to a 1990 Gallup poll, a National Survey of Working America. That poll, commissioned by the National Career Development Association, indicated that many working adults were unsure of their job future and that most would get more information about jobs and careers if they could plan their work lives again. In spite of that, the majority of individuals do not consult professional career counselors and know little about the work of such counselors or do not know where to find them (Sywak, 1992). As a consequence, career counseling must be considered a still-emerging discipline in the human services or human resources area.

Part of the reason that career counseling is still not established and a well-known profession is that the licensing or certification of counselors has been controversial, and not all states have laws to make licensing or certification possible. For example, Sywak (1992) reported that, nationally, fewer than 1,000 individuals have met the requirements to be national certified career counselors. Moreover, she observed that most career counselors in private practice start out in other professions because "no one professional degree qualifies people to work in the field" (p. 302). The academic preparation of career counselors most often involves obtaining either a master's degree or doctorate in counseling or clinical psychology. Many of those programs have course work in career development theory, but they have no specific degrees in career counseling. Generally it may be assumed, therefore, that the personal and educational characteristics of counselors or psychologists in general also apply to career counselors.

Another important subset of individuals work as career counselors, but may call themselves business consultants, human resources specialists, outplacement consultants, retirement counselors, and so on. Most of those individuals work within the organizational structures of business and industry. Their backgrounds may be similar to those of more traditional career counselors, but often they have more of a background in business than in human services (Sywak, 1992). What is emerging at this time is the realization that work, which occupies such a central role in almost every adult's life, needs to be planned more carefully. In addition, the world of work is becoming increasingly complex and is likely to be much more dynamic and changing in the future than it has been in the past. Those developments bode well for the profession of career counseling, but they also underscore the necessity for the field to become better organized, to establish standards for its practitioners, and to develop greater visibility and credibility with the public.

Conditions for Conducting Career Counseling

The facilities and equipment required for the efficacious conduct of career counseling vary considerably depending on the specific purpose of the career counseling and the setting within which it is carried out. For example, the high school guidance counselor needs little more than a consulting room, access to the student's school record, and a variety of test instruments to assess aptitudes, interests, and other characteristics that may be helpful in guiding the student toward a suitable occupation. Similar requirements may be experienced by most other types of career counselors, although the specific nature of the information they collect from clients will depend on the specific needs that clients bring to the consulting room.

Limitations of Career Counseling
Contraindications and Hazards

There are no absolute contraindications to career counseling, but some cautions must be exercised in special cases. Specifically, it should be apparent that career counseling assumes the existence of significant options and opportunities in the socioeconomic environment; it also assumes the presence of some basic capabilities on the part of the client (the ability to learn and the motivation to work). If these conditions do not exist, the enterprise of career counseling should proceed with considerable caution, if at all. In some cases the counselor may be able to work toward producing the requisite conditions for career counseling to take place, but in other cases this may not be possible.

Caution must be exercised to help clients to dream about and work toward what is possible—not to encourage them to have dreams that simply cannot be fulfilled because of limitations imposed from the outside or from within. Clients must also exercise caution in the selection of career counselors. Because of the lack of widely accepted standards for the practice of career counseling, inadequately trained individuals have, on occasion, held themselves out as qualified counselors. Potential clients may also be persuaded that using some form of self-help materials (sometimes published in newspapers or magazines) can take the place of competent counseling.

Organizations have increasingly recognized that employees' career development is a necessary and desirable feature of the overall process of human resources management. Unfortunately, however, organizational and individual objectives are not always identical, opening the door to the possibility of serious conflict. No set of matching processes can ensure that individual and organizational objectives are synchronized and that career counseling can equally benefit the individual and the organization (Adams, 1991). Consequently, both individual and organizational clients of career counselors must be explicitly apprised of the specific objectives of any intervention.

The Effectiveness of Career Counseling

Vocational interventions have been the subject of considerable outcome research. Yet the task of evaluating the effectiveness of career counseling is quite difficult for a number of reasons. First, although many individuals seek career counseling because they are unhappy with their jobs or careers, they typically do not carefully exclude personal problems, even psychiatric problems, from discussion during career counseling. Consequently, many clients may obtain at least some symptom relief in addition to addressing their vocational problems. Second, as has been noted throughout this chapter, the variety of career counseling interventions is substantial, the goals of particular interventions are quite varied, and the targets (individuals or groups) of specific interventions are extremely diverse. All these considerations represent methodological complications for researchers attempting to determine the efficacy of a particular type of intervention.

One means of overcoming some of the difficulties involved in reviewing outcome studies that reflect the tremendous diversity noted above is to use a procedure called a meta-analysis (Cook & Leviton, 1980). Meta-analysis usually involves using a single, standard procedure for calculating or recalculating the effect sizes reported in published outcome studies, which produces a common measure of the observed differences between treatment group and no-treatment controls, and allows for the comparison of treatment effects from one study to another.

Using a meta-analysis procedure, Spokane and Oliver (1983) reviewed 90 vocational intervention studies covering a three-decade period (1950–1980). They concluded that in 80% of all studies, the outcome of any kind of vocational intervention was positive when compared to a no-treatment control group. Moreover, they found that in more than 80% of all cases, the outcome status of individual clients who received any kind of vocational intervention was superior to the outcome status of untreated controls. When they attempted to compare the relative effectiveness of different kinds of vocational interventions, however, they typically found much smaller differences between groups, as well as almost insurmountable methodological problems. They concluded that encouraging evidence supported the effectiveness of vocational interventions, but they also urged the conduct of more well-designed outcome studies.

An extension and refinement of Spokane and Oliver's (1983) work (Oliver & Spokane, 1988) produced findings consistent with their original meta-analysis. In addition, however, Spokane and Oliver found that individual interventions were most effective and that relative effectiveness of different intervention modes varied considerably. Numerous additional outcome studies led Phillips (1992, p. 513) to conclude:

> Regardless of the difficulty in defining what career counseling is, there is considerable evidence that it works. The evidence accumulated over many decades, with many different intervention strategies, and for many different populations, is reassuring; what career counselors do, helps.

References

Adams, J. (1991). Issues in the management of careers. In R. F. Morrison & J. Adams (Eds.), *Contemporary career development issues* (pp. 1–24). Hillsdale, NJ: Erlbaum.

Cook, T. D., & Leviton, L. C. (1980). Reviewing the literature: A comparison of traditional methods with meta-analysis. *Journal of Personality, 48,* 449–472.

Dawis, R. V., & Lofquist, L. H. (1984). *A psychological theory of work adjustment: An individual differences model and its applications.* Minneapolis: University of Minnesota Press.

Erikson, E. H. (1959). Identity and the life cycle. *Psychological Issues, 1,* 18–164.

Ford, D. H. (1987). *Humans as self constructing living systems: A developmental perspective on personality and behavior*. Hillsdale, NJ: Erlbaum.

Ginzberg, E., Ginsburg, S. W., Axelrad, S., & Herma, J. L. (1951). *Occupational choice: An approach to a general theory*. New York: Columbia University.

Gough, H. G. (1987). *The California Psychological Inventory administrator's guide*. Palo Alto, CA: Consulting Psychologists Press.

Hansen, J. C. (1990). Interpretation of the Strong Interest Inventory. In C. E. Watkins, Jr., & V. L. Campbell (Eds.), *Testing in counseling practice* (pp. 177–209). Hillsdale, NJ: Erlbaum.

Hansen, J. C., & Campbell, D. P. (1985). *Manual for the SVIB-SCII* (4th ed.). Stanford, CA: Stanford University Press.

Herr, E. L., & Cramer, S. H. (1979). *Career guidance through the life span: Systematic approaches*. Boston: Little, Brown.

Holland, J. L. (1959). A theory of vocational choice. *Journal of Counseling Psychology, 6*, 35–45.

Holland, J. L. (1966). *The psychology of vocational choice*. Waltham, MA: Blaisdell.

Holland, J. L. (1985). *Making vocational choices: A theory of vocational personalities and work environments*. Englewood Cliffs, NJ: Prentice-Hall.

Holland, J. L. (1987). *The Self-directed Search professional manual*. Odessa, FL: Psychological Assessment Resources.

Jepsen, D. A. (1990). Developmental career counseling. In W. B. Walsh & S. H. Osipow (Eds.), *Career counseling: Contemporary topics in vocational psychology* (pp. 117–157). Hillsdale, NJ: Erlbaum.

Krumboltz, J. D. (1979). A social learning theory of career decision making. In A. M. Mitchell, G. B. Jones, & J. D. Krumboltz (Eds.), *Social learning and career decision making* (pp. 19–49). Cranston, RI: Carroll Press.

Krumboltz, J. D., Mitchell, A. M., & Jones, G. B. (1976). A social learning theory of career selection. *The Counseling Psychologist, 6*, 71–81.

Krumboltz, J. D., & Nichols, C. W. (1990). Integrating the social learning theory of career decision making. In W. B. Walsh & S. H. Osipow (Eds.), *Career counseling: Contemporary topics in vocational psychology* (pp. 159–192). Hillsdale, NJ: Erlbaum.

Lofquist, L. H., & Dawis, R. V. (1969). *Adjustment to work*. New York: Appleton-Century-Crofts.

McDaniels, C., & Gysbers, N. C. (1992). *Counseling for career development: Theories, resources, and practice*. San Francisco: Jossey-Bass.

Morrison, R. F., & Adams, J. (1991). *Contemporary career development issues*. Hillsdale, NJ: Erlbaum.

Oliver, L. W., & Spokane, A. R. (1988). Career-intervention outcome: What contributes to client gain? *Journal of Counseling Psychology, 35*, 447–462.

Parsons, F. (1909). *Choosing a vocation.* Boston: Houghton Mifflin.

Phillips, S. D. (1992). Career counseling: Choice and implementation. In S. D. Brown & R. W. Lent (Eds.), *Handbook of counseling psychology* (2nd ed., pp. 513–547). New York: Wiley.

Pryor, R. G. L. (1984). *Work Aspect Preference Scale.* Darlinghurst, New South Wales: Australian Council for Educational Research.

Rounds, J. B., & Tracey, T. J. (1990). From trait-and-factor to person-environment fit counseling: Theory and process. In W. B. Walsh & S. H. Osipow (Eds.), *Career counseling: Contemporary topics in vocational psychology* (pp. 1–44). Hillsdale, NJ: Erlbaum.

Sampson, J. P., Jr. (1990). Computer applications and issues in using tests in counseling. In C. E. Watkins, Jr., & V. L. Campbell (Eds.), *Testing in counseling practice* (pp. 451–474). Hillsdale, NJ: Erlbaum.

Sharf, R. S. (1992). *Applying career development theory to counseling.* Pacific Grove, CA: Brooks/Cole.

Shullman, S. L., & Carder, C. E. (1983). Vocational psychology in industrial settings. In W. B. Walsh & S. H. Osipow (Eds.), *Handbook of vocational psychology,* Vol. 2, *Applications* (pp. 141–179). Hillsdale, NJ: Erlbaum.

Slaney, R. B. (1988). The assessment of career decision making. In W. B. Walsh & S. H. Osipow (Eds.), *Career decision making* (pp. 33–76). Hillsdale, NJ: Erlbaum.

Spokane, A. R. (1991). *Career intervention.* Englewood Cliffs, NJ: Prentice-Hall.

Spokane, A. R., & Oliver, L. W. (1983). The outcomes of vocational interventions. In W. B. Walsh & S. H. Osipow (Eds.), *Handbook of vocational psychology,* Vol. 2, *Applications* (pp. 99–136). Hillsdale, NJ: Erlbaum.

Strong, E. K., Jr. (1927). *Vocational Interest Blank.* Stanford, CA: Stanford University Press.

Super, D. E. (1951). Vocational adjustment: Implementing a self-concept. *Occupations, 30,* 88–92.

Super, D. E. (1953). A theory of vocational development. *American Psychologist, 8,* 185–190.

Super, D. E. (1957). *The psychology of careers.* New York: Harper & Row.

Super, D. E. (1980). A life-span, life-space approach to career development. *Journal of Vocational Behavior, 16,* 282–298.

Sywak, M. (1992). The career development professional. In D. H. Montross & C. J. Shinkman (Eds.), *Career development: Theory and practice* (pp. 294–305). Springfield, IL: Charles C Thomas.

U.S. Department of Labor. (1977). *Dictionary of occupational titles* (4th ed.). Washington, D.C.: U.S. Government Printing Office.

U.S. Department of Labor. (1992). *Occupational outlook handbook.* Washington, D.C.: U.S. Government Printing Office.

Vondracek, F. W. (1992). The construct of identity and its use in career theory and research. *Career Development Quarterly*, *41*, 130–144.

Vondracek, F. W., Lerner, R. M., & Schulenberg, J. E. (1986). *Career development: A life-span developmental approach*. Hillsdale, NJ: Erlbaum.

Walsh, W. B., & Osipow, S. H. (1990). *Career counseling: Contemporary topics in vocational psychology*. Hillsdale, NJ: Erlbaum.

Watkins, C. E., Jr., & Savickas, M. L. (1990). Psychodynamic career counseling. In W. B. Walsh & S. H. Osipow (Eds.), *Career counseling: Contemporary topics in vocational psychology* (pp. 79–116). Hillsdale, NJ: Erlbaum.

....

Counseling Adults to Cope with Life and Career Transitions

....

■

In recent years, a great deal has been written about how much more complicated life has become and how rapidly the pace of change in our society has
accelerated. These trends have led some to complain that the traditional
American family is a thing of the past; they have also been felt by workers
who have lost jobs that they thought were secure. The mobility of individuals
and families has resulted in fundamental changes in the structure of interpersonal relationships: lifelong relationships of any kind have become the exception rather than the norm. It appears that stability is rapidly becoming an
endangered state of being, and change has become a way of life. As a consequence, adults in our society are forced to cope with many more transitions
than their parents and grandparents did. Unfortunately, many are not prepared to cope with the relative lack of stability and the seemingly unending
chain of transitions imposed upon them by their rapidly changing environment. This chapter will explore some of these issues, as well as some methods
that are being developed to address them.

General Purpose of Transition Counseling

The general purpose of counseling for transitions is to help people to
understand that transitions represent a normal and expected aspect of life in
general and careers in particular. Moreover, transition counseling is designed

to apply for the client's benefit what has been learned about role ambiguities, risks, and opportunities that frequently accompany life transitions. Ultimately, the purpose of transition counseling is to ease and facilitate the transition process and help clients not only to accept the reality of transition situations, but to behave so as to maximize the benefits and minimize the losses inherent in most transitions.

History of Transition Counseling

Adult life transitions are, of course, as old as humankind. At the same time, however, changes in life expectancy have resulted in demographic changes that have dramatically increased the expected life span of most individuals. For example, whereas a person born in the United States in 1900 could expect to live about 47 years, in 1988 the corresponding life expectancy had increased to almost 75 years (Smolak, 1993). It stands to reason that as people live longer lives, they face more transitions in the course of their lives, independent of the rapid changes in the sociocultural and economic environment that are also contributing to the number of transitions people face during their life spans. These concerns have begun to be addressed in the field of adult development and aging. It is instructive to note that in the United States, the National Institute on Aging was not founded until 1974.

A widely quoted landmark in the study of adulthood that preceded the National Institute on Aging by more than 50 years was G. Stanley Hall's (1922) *Senescence: The Second Half of Life*. More recent landmark publications that have called attention to important adult life transitions have been Erikson's writings regarding the psychosocial crises of the life span (Erikson, 1959, 1982), Gould's study of the phases of adult life (Gould, 1972), and Levinson's study of *The Seasons of a Man's Life* (1978). Major theoretical formulations presented in some of these publications will be summarized in the next section. Interventions specifically designed to cope with transitions, however, have been emerging only recently and thus cannot be said to have much history. Their origins will be discussed as they are presented.

Range of Applicability

Counseling to cope more effectively with life and career transitions is, in principle, applicable to any and all adults who are in the process of negotiating an important transition. Because transitions represent a necessary part of every individual's experience, every person is a potential client for specialists in this area. Of course, some individuals develop a history of effective coping starting in childhood, and require little or no assistance in making successful transitions. Some transitions, however, such as the changes necessitated by the death of a long-time partner, test the coping and adaptive resources of even the most well-adjusted and adaptive individual.

Specific areas that have received particular attention from professionals have included various types of life transitions, which have been defined as "turning points, bridges, or passages" (Gibson & Brown, 1992, p. 286). Often, transitions are associated with different kinds of life events (Brim & Ryff, 1980; Danish, 1981) or with crises (Parry, 1990). Gibson and Brown (1992, p. 287) suggested that life transitions be defined by the following four criteria:

1. The changes constituting the life transition are occurring in response to an external event.
2. They may be related to the course of adult development, but are not necessarily a developmental phenomena.
3. Life transitions are not necessarily crises, but many crises may result in changes that may represent life transitions.
4. Life transitions should be defined as such only when they are perceived as times of significant change by the individual.

Clearly, most career transitions (involving any significant change in one's work life) fall within this definitional framework, although some authors (such as Erikson, 1968) would argue that most transitions are part of the normal course of development and may be generated by internal, rather than external changes.

Theoretical Foundations
Assumptions About Human Nature

A number of important assumptions, mainly in theories of development, bear on the conceptualization of humans and how they negotiate important life transitions. One common notion is that the very idea of transitions means that people can change and that their capacity to adapt to changes is evident into old age. Thus, the plasticity (modifiability) of individuals continues into old age, but may represent a declining phenomenon as age advances (Lerner, 1984). Clearly, however, when adult transitions are the focus of study, it is not appropriate to speak of growth alone, because there are ample indications that developmental changes are both multidimensional and multidirectional (Baltes, 1987).

In the study of adult development, focus has often been on intraindividual changes. Moreover, much research has focused on the nature of decline in various functions with age. Fortunately, some in the research community have started to question the almost universal assumption that decline is necessarily associated with advancing age. Consequently, more recent conceptualizations of the aging person have focused on continuity (Atchley, 1989) and stability (McCrae & Costa, 1982), as well as the continuing ability of individuals to adapt, to modify their behaviors, and to grow (Hetherington & Baltes, 1988).

Key Concepts

Erik Erikson (1959, 1963) is often credited with advancing the field of adult development through his explicit focus on the lifelong task of identity formation. Contrary to the popular notion that one's identity is established during adolescence, Erikson explicitly stated that "identity formation neither begins nor ends with adolescence: It is a lifelong development" (Erikson, 1968, p. 204). Indeed, Erikson incorporated the central theme of continuity and change into his eight psychosocial stages, which are often referred to as psychosocial crises because Erikson believed that successfully resolving various life crises enabled individuals to live their lives successfully.

The first four of Erikson's psychosocial crises occur during childhood. If successfully resolved, they advance the person to the point at which a sense of self must be established that links the person's past, present, and future and gives the person a feeling of "progressive continuity," a feeling of identity. Hence, the final stage of adolescence that prepares the person for adult crises is the stage of identity versus role confusion. In the next stage, individuals must develop the capacity to develop a love relationship in which work, play, and daily living are shared in an atmosphere of trust and mutuality. Erikson called that stage the stage of intimacy versus isolation. During middle adulthood, individuals who develop successfully focus on transmitting to the next generation their values, knowledge, and skills. Erikson called that stage generativity versus stagnation. Finally, in the stage of ego integrity versus despair, the mature adult acquires a sense of fulfillment, accepting the shortcomings in one's life and enjoying the accomplishments. Interventions, according to Erikson's framework, would consequently involve assisting individuals in successfully resolving their psychosocial crises.

The work of Daniel Levenson (1978) has been particularly influential in shaping our understanding of adult transitions. Although his study used a small sample of exclusively male subjects, and may thus not be applicable to women (Gilligan, 1982), his focus on making explicit various normative transitions during the adult life course has stimulated a great deal of work in this area. Although many writers have focused on what Levenson called the midlife transition, he actually identified five specific transitions: (1) the early adult transition, (2) the age 30 transition, (3) the midlife transition, (4) the age 50 transition, and (5) the late adult transition. Moreover, he specified tasks to be accomplished in between transition periods, such as exploring various options related to entering adult life, establishing a niche in society through attaining goals and contributing to society, and modifying earlier perspectives and life structures in accordance with advancing age. Again, interventions could be designed to focus on facilitating the component tasks that must be accomplished in making the various transitions of adult life as smooth and successful as possible.

Super (1990) is another theorist who has addressed adult development, primarily by focusing on individuals' life-careers, which can be best understood by examining the various life roles individuals assume in the course of their development. He combined a developmental stage theory, which proposed that the growth and exploration stages occur during childhood and adolescence, followed by the establishment stage in early adulthood, the maintenance stage in middle adulthood, and a disengagement stage in old age. During these various stages, individuals are portrayed as fulfilling, to various extents, the six major life-career roles including child, student, worker, homemaker, leisurite, and citizen. He proposed that the importance of all of these roles (with the exception of the child role) varies in the course of an individual's life. This, in turn, may require transitions such as that from worker to leisurite, which is viewed as part of the disengagement stage. Other notable transitions are those from student to worker, or student to homemaker. Super (1984) has addressed, in general terms, the issue of role transitions, noting that transitions generally take place within the person rather than in events external to the person. He has proposed that at various periods during the life span any given individual may recycle through the developmental stages, starting with the exploration stage.

Another way to conceptualize life transitions is to view them in relation to marker events, or milestones that occur in every individual's life and are usually associated with the occurrence of an important transition. One popular conceptualization of life events is that proposed by Baltes, Cornelius, and Nesselroade (1978), which represents a tripartite division of major influences on behavioral development: (1) ontogenetic or age-graded influences that co-vary with chronological age, (2) evolutionary or history-graded influences that co-vary with biocultural change, and (3) nonnormative influences that do not occur in any general, systematic, or universal fashion (in terms of frequency, patterning, and timing). The distinction between normative and nonnormative events has been called into question, however, because it is based, in part, on social desirability and prevalence in any given reference group (Reese & Smyer, 1983). In addition, it has been noted that life events that are expected to occur, but do not occur, also represent a distinctive influence on development and may precipitate transitions (Schlossberg, 1984).

Implementing Transition Counseling

The variety of theoretical formulations that pertain to life and career transitions corresponds to the variety of intervention methods that have been used to facilitate transition processes ranging from the transition to school to the ultimate life transition (preparing people for death). Consequently, it may be useful to review briefly a general model for dealing with transitions outlined by Schlossberg (1989). Essentially, she proposed that individuals must master three tasks in order to successfully deal with transitions. The first of these is to approach change by identifying the nature of the transition in terms of "what it is," "how it has changed . . . roles, routines, assumptions, relationships," and where one is in relation to the transition process. Second, she suggested that individuals need to take stock by assessing their resources which she defines by the "four S's—your *Situation, Self, Supports,* and *Strategies.*" Third, Schlossberg counseled that individuals must take charge through strengthening their coping resources, developing an action plan, and ensuring that they can profit from change (1989, p. xviii).

Although most individuals cope with transitions without direct professional assistance, education about transition processes and self-help devices, such as Schlossberg's (1989) informative book, are important resources. Those individuals who do need professional assistance are likely to receive help from counselors who follow the basic steps presented by Schlossberg (1989). Thus, counselors are likely to begin transition counseling by carefully assessing the individual's perception of the impending transition and the individual's resources for coping with the transition. At the same time, however, the huge variety of life transitions and the uniqueness of every individual who is trying to cope with a particular transition preclude the development of any one specific intervention or sequence of interventions that is best suited to assist adults in successfully completing important transitions (Gibson & Brown, 1992). Nevertheless, some methods may be applicable in most cases.

Strengthening Coping Responses

Gibson and Brown (1992) suggested that the process of adapting to various transitions represents an opportunity for individuals to mobilize their coping resources. Coping resources, in turn, are generally conceptualized as learned behaviors that focus on problem-solving. Although not all transitions are inherently stressful, a process such as that recommended by Meichenbaum (1985) for stress management would certainly be appropriate in helping people to strengthen their coping resources. His approach included education about the nature of stress reactions, followed by the teaching of a variety of coping behaviors designed to enable individuals to deal more effectively with stressful life events. As part of this overall intervention, which relies heavily on cognitive-behavioral methods, Meichenbaum advised that individuals should be given supervised practice in using newly learned coping skills by applying them to actual stressful situations. This practice, Meichenbaum suggested, could prepare people to cope with stressful events (and transitions) they might encounter in the future (Meichenbaum & Cameron, 1983).

Another approach has focused on enhancing individuals' coping abilities by teaching them a more optimistic outlook on life in general and on their particular transition circumstances in particular (Seligman, 1990). Seligman has noted that individuals who tend to view life through a lens of pessimism tend to have much greater difficulty adapting to life transitions. As a consequence, he has developed a cognitive therapy approach to helping people to adopt a more optimistic explanatory framework as a means to energize, mobilize, and prepare them to approach life transitions more effectively.

Self-Efficacy Counseling

This approach is associated with the work of Carl Thoresen (1976, 1978; Thoreson & Coates, 1978; Thoresen & Ewart, 1976; Thoresen & Mahoney, 1974). Fundamental to Thoresen and his colleagues' position is the notion that, while people are influenced by external conditions, they can be both products and producers of their own environments. Moreover, individuals are seen as having the potential to alter the course of their development through the exercise of personal responsibility, capability, and efficacy. Accordingly, self-efficacy counseling assumes that if individuals' efficacy expectations are raised, they are more likely to feel confident and positive about their abilities to make successful transitions and to produce desirable and positive outcomes in the process of completing a transition process.

Training for self-efficacy skills is conceptualized as providing individuals with the skills to manage life's challenges in various situational contexts. Thoresen and his colleagues used a broad variety of learning theory–based behavioral techniques in their counseling approach. They included techniques based on operant and classical conditioning paradigms, as well as modeling techniques that represent what has been called vicarious learning. Tosi, Leclair, Peters, and Murphy (1987, p. 185) reported that Thoresen's (1976) framework for teaching self-efficacy skills incorporates four broad strategies for enhancing self-control: (1) commitment, (2) awareness, (3) restructuring environments, and (4) consequences and standards. Commitment skills are focused primarily on the capacity for developing and sustaining motivation. Awareness skills represent the individuals' ability to engage in effective self-monitoring. Specific techniques for restructuring environments include rearranging the external physical environment, altering undesirable internal stimuli, including thoughts, feelings, and images, and teaching family, friends, and significant others to be supportive and facilitative of changes deemed necessary and desirable (Tosi et al., 1987, pp. 186–187).

The means to accomplish these various objectives are focused around cognitive restructuring methods and various reinforcement techniques. The restructuring of cognitive processes revolves (as in Ellis's rational-emotive therapy) around the identification and modification of internalized sentences, particularly the substitution of positive self-statements for negative ones and rational beliefs for irrational ones. As a consequence, individuals gradually come to believe that they are able to cope with the changes that are occurring in their lives (that is, they have positive self-efficacy expectations). In turn, positive self-efficacy expectations result in more effective behaviors (Bandura, 1977), particularly when dealing with important life transitions.

Means and Conditions for Implementing Transition Counseling
The Counselor's Qualifications

Transition counseling represents an emerging specialty in the field of counseling. Its emerging nature is underscored by the fact that many business organizations, as well as governmental and educational institutions, have developed special programs to assist individuals in making successful midlife career transitions and to prepare them for the important transition to retirement (Abrego & Brammer, 1992; Horton & Engels, 1992). In addition, almost every community has special programs, both professional ones and others of the self-help or support-group type, that deal with grief or loss (assisting people in the transition to a life without a loved one), divorce, or trauma. All these transition circumstances require special sensitivities and skills on the part of the counselor. Ordinarily, counselors who have the requisite educational preparation for their counselor roles, as well as the proper professional certification or licensure, can acquire the specialized skills for various kinds of transition counseling by attending professional seminars or special workshops.

Perhaps most important in dealing with mature adults is the recognition of ageism, which is defined as implicit and explicit discrimination against individuals on the basis of age (Horton & Engels, 1992). Any counselor whose professional work involves dealing with mature (older) adults must be aware of the subtle personal and cultural biases that represent ageism and that stand in the way of effective transition counseling with adults. Being aware of and knowledgeable about legislation that specifically prohibits age discrimination represents an important prerequisite for counseling adults about transitions.

Equally important in transition counseling with adults is the counselor's sensitivity to various other forms of discrimination that may have played an important role in the individual client's life, or even in precipitating the particular transition that the client may be facing. Although it is undoubtedly true that such sensitivity is needed in any kind of professional intervention, it is also clear that it is in the nature of transitions to make people feel especially vulnerable to bias and discrimination. Sex discrimination and racial discrimination in the workplace represent two of the most visible examples of this problem (Betz & Fitzgerald, 1987; Smith, 1983). Any counselor wishing to help adults in workplace-related transitions must certainly be knowledgeable about, and able to deal with, the many forms of discrimination that may have necessitated or produced the transition in the first place.

Conditions for Conducting Transition Counseling

No special facilities or equipment are needed for counseling adults to cope with transitions. A consulting room or office that offers privacy and quiet is all that is needed. In institutional settings (such as a business organization or home for the aged), it is particularly important also to ensure confidentiality and to reassure the adults being counseled about the possibility of negative consequences arising from the act of their seeking help with a transition. Although no special equipment is ordinarily needed for these kinds of services, it is particularly important when working with mature adults to make certain that proper access is provided for physically handicapped individuals. While this is a legal requirement for public institutions and for large service providers, it is incumbent upon all service providers to ensure that those who need their services can in fact receive them.

Finally, certain assessment instruments may be needed in order to ascertain the degree of impairment suffered by a client who seeks transition counseling. In some instances it may be determined, for example, that more intensive services, such as psychiatric hospitalization, may be needed in order to treat the acute consequences of the trauma or loss that necessitated a major life or career transition. Following such intensive treatment, transition counseling may well be an integral part of the after-care treatment plan.

Limitations of Transition Counseling
Contraindications and Hazards

How individuals cope with important transitions appears to depend on factors that are, in part at least, within the person. In short, some persons may be better able to handle life's difficult times because they are hardier than others, are disposed toward an optimistic outlook, and have better coping responses available to them. The social resources of the person, however, may also play a large role in determining their ability to negotiate transitions successfully. Although transition counseling may affect the intrapersonal resources that are available, it clearly is limited in the extent to which it can affect the individual's social support system. Even so, the generation and perception of social support may be intricately linked to personality variables that, although relatively stable, may nevertheless be susceptible to modification through counseling (Gibson & Brown, 1992). The key warning to the counselor is a modified golden rule: assist individual clients in their efforts to change and modify what is modifiable, but do not raise false hopes and precipitate disappointments and setbacks by trying to get clients to change the things that they cannot change.

The Effectiveness of Transition Counseling

Research on the effectiveness of transition counseling is scarce, primarily because this emerging field has not received a great deal of attention from applied researchers. Thus, when examining the literature pertaining directly to the outcomes of transition counseling, one is likely to come up empty. There is research, however, on various strategies to enhance coping skills and to promote self-efficacy. Unfortunately, the research is typically reported on subjects and in populations other than mature adults. The overall conclusion that emerges is that transition counseling works about as well as the specific change procedures that are used. Thus, if transition counseling uses a cognitive-behavioral approach, it is likely to produce favorable outcomes in line with expectations based on cognitive-behavioral outcome research. If one uses modeling procedures to enhance self-efficacy, the expected outcome would be in line with research that has focused on evaluating the effectiveness of modeling techniques. In short, the target of the intervention—transition-related behaviors—may be modified through the application of a number of different techniques. The selection of the specific technique used should depend primarily on the client's circumstances and on the counselor's assessment of what will work best in a particular situation.

References

Abrego, P., & Brammer, L. (1992). Counseling adults in midlife career transitions. In H. D. Lea & Z. B. Leibowitz (Eds.), *Adult career development: Concepts, issues, and practices* (pp. 234–254). Alexandria, VA: The National Career Development Association.

Atchley, R. (1989). A continuity theory of normal aging. *The Gerontologist, 29,* 183–190.

Baltes, P. B. (1987). Theoretical propositions of life-span developmental psychology: On the dynamics between growth and decline. *Developmental Psychology, 23,* 611–626.

Baltes, P. B., Cornelius, S. W., & Nesselroade, J. R. (1979). Cohort effects in developmental psychology. In J. R. Nesselroade & P. B. Baltes (Eds.), *Longitudinal research in the study of behavior and development* (pp. 61–88). New York: Academic Press.

Bandura, A. (1977). *Social learning theory.* Englewood Cliffs, NJ: Prentice-Hall.

Betz, N. E., & Fitzgerald, L. F. (1987). *The career psychology of women.* New York: Academic Press.

Brim, O. G., & Ryff, C. D. (1980). On the properties of life events. In P. B. Baltes & O. G. Brim, Jr. (Eds.), *Life-span development and behavior,* Vol. 3 (pp. 368–388). New York: Academic Press.

Danish, S. J. (1981). Life-span human development and intervention: A necessary link. *The Counseling Psychologist, 9,* 40–43.

Erikson, E. H. (1959). Identity and the life cycle. *Psychological Issues, 1,* 18–164.

Erikson, E. H. (1963). *Childhood and society.* New York: Norton.

Erikson, E. H. (1968). *Identity: Youth and crisis.* New York: Norton.

Erikson, E. H. (1982). *The life cycle completed.* New York: Norton.

Gibson, J., & Brown, S. D. (1992). Counseling adults for life transitions. In S. D. Brown & R. W. Lent (Eds.), *Handbook of counseling psychology* (2nd ed., pp. 285–313). New York: Wiley.

Gilligan, C. (1982). *In a different voice.* Cambridge, MA: Harvard University Press.

Gould, R. (1972). The phases of adult life: A study in developmental psychology. *American Journal of Psychiatry, 129,* 521–531.

Hall, G. S. (1922). *Senescence, the second half of life.* New York: Appleton-Century-Crofts.

Hetherington, E. M., & Baltes, P. B. (1988). Child psychology and life-span development. In E. M. Hetherington, R. M. Lerner, & M. Perlmutter (Eds.), *Child development in life-span perspective* (pp. 1–20). Hillsdale, NJ: Erlbaum.

Horton, G. M., & Engels, D. W. (1992). Career counseling for the mature worker. In H. D. Lea & Z. B. Leibowitz (Eds.), *Adult career development: Concepts, issues, and practices* (pp. 255–268). Alexandria, VA: The National Career Development Association.

Lerner, R. M. (1984). *On the nature of human plasticity.* Cambridge: Cambridge University Press.

Levinson, D. (1978). *The seasons of a man's life.* New York: Knopf.

McCrae, R., & Costa, P. (1986). Personality, coping, and coping effectiveness in an adult sample. *Journal of Personality, 54,* 385–405.

Meichenbaum, D. (1985). *Stress inoculation training.* New York: Pergamon Press.

Meichenbaum, D., & Cameron, R. (1983). Stress inoculation training: Toward a general paradigm for training coping skills. In D. Meichenbaum & M. E. Jeremko (Eds.), *Stress reduction and prevention* (pp. 115–154). New York: Plenum.

Parry, G. (1990). *Coping with crises.* London: Routledge & Kegan Paul.

Reese, H. W., & Smyer, M. A. (1983). The dimensionalization of life events. In E. J. Callahan & K. A. McCluskey (Eds.), *Life-span developmental psychology: Nonnormative life events* (pp. 1–33). New York: Academic Press.

Schlossberg, N. (1984). *Counseling adults in transition.* New York: Springer.

Schlossberg, N. (1989). *Overwhelmed: Coping with life's ups and downs.* Lexington, MA: D. C. Heath.

Seligman, M. E. P. (1990). *Learned optimism.* New York: Knopf.

Smith, E. J. (1983). Issues in racial minorities' career behavior. In W. B. Walsh & S. H. Osipow (Eds.), *Handbook of vocational psychology* (pp. 161–222). Hillsdale, NJ: Erlbaum.

Smolak, L. (1993). *Adult development.* Englewood Cliffs, NJ: Prentice-Hall.

Super, D. E. (1984). Career and life development. In D. Brown, L. Brooks, & Associates (Eds.), *Career choice and development* (pp. 27–53). San Francisco: Jossey-Bass.

Super, D. E. (1990). A life-span, life-space approach to career development. In D. Brown, L. Brooks, & associates (Eds.), *Career choice and development: Applying contemporary theories to practice* (2nd ed., pp. 197–261). San Francisco: Jossey-Bass.

Thoresen, C. (1976). *Self-control: Learning how to C.A.R.E. for yourself.* Madison, WI: Counseling Films, Box 1047 (film).

Thoresen, C. (1978). Making better science, intensively. *Personnel and Guidance Journal, 56,* 279–282.

Thoresen, C., & Coates, T. (1978). What does it mean to be a behavior therapist? *The Counseling Psychologist, 1,* 3–20.

Thoresen, C., & Ewart, C. (1976). Behavioral self-control and career development. *The Counseling Psychologist, 6,* 29–42.

Thoresen, C., & Mahoney, M. (1974). *Self-control: Power to the person.* Pacific Grove, CA: Brooks/Cole.

Tosi, D. J., Leclair, S. W., Peters, H. J., & Murphy, M. A. (1987). *Theories and applications of counseling: Systems and techniques of counseling and psychotherapy.* Springfield, IL: Charles C Thomas.

NAME INDEX

SUBJECT INDEX

CREDITS

TO THE OWNER OF THIS BOOK:

We hope that you have found *Strategies for Resolving Individual and Family Problems* useful. So that this book can be improved in a future edition, would you take the time to complete this sheet and return it? Thank you.

School and address: ————————————————————————

Department: ————————————————————————————

Instructor's name: ———————————————————————————

1. What I like most about this book is: —————————————————

———————————————————————————————————

———————————————————————————————————

2. What I like least about this book is: ————————————————

———————————————————————————————————

———————————————————————————————————

3. My general reaction to this book is: ————————————————

———————————————————————————————————

4. The name of the course in which I used this book is: ———————————

———————————————————————————————————

5. Were all of the chapters of the book assigned for you to read? ——————

   If not, which ones weren't? ————————————————————

6. In the space below, or on a separate sheet of paper, please write specific suggestions for improving this book and anything else you'd care to share about your experience in using the book.

———————————————————————————————————

———————————————————————————————————

———————————————————————————————————

———————————————————————————————————

———————————————————————————————————

Optional:

Your name: _____ Date: _____

May Brooks/Cole quote you, either in promotion for *Strategies for Resolving Individual and Family Problems,* or in future publishing ventures?

Yes: _____ No: _____

Sincerely,

Fred W. Vondracek
Sherry Corneal

Brooks/Cole is dedicated to publishing quality publications for education in the human services fields. If you are interested in learning more about our publications, please fill in your name and address and request our latest catalogue, using ths prepaid mailer.

Name: _____

Street Address: _____

City, State, and Zip: _____

FOLD HERE

BUSINESS REPLY MAIL

FIRST CLASS   PERMIT NO. 358   PACIFIC GROVE, CA

POSTAGE WILL BE PAID BY ADDRESSEE

ATT: *Human Services Catalogue*

**Brooks/Cole Publishing Company
511 Forest Lodge Road
Pacific Grove, California 93950-9968**

FOLD HERE